THE POWER OF
100

100 International Women Share Powerful Stories of How to Stay Focused on Your Dreams

JANET BECKERS

The Power of 100: 100 International Women Share Powerful Stories on How to Stay Focused on Your Dreams

Copyright © 2011 Janet Beckers

www.ThePowerof100Book.com

First published in Australia 2011 by Wonderful Web Press, a division of Niche Partners Pty Ltd and Wonderful Web Women

www.WonderfulWebWomen.com

All rights reserved. No part of this publication may be reproduced or transmitted by any means, electronic, photocopying or otherwise without prior written permission of the author.

ISBN-13: 978-0-9870944-0-7

All the information, ideas, techniques, skills and concepts contained within this publication are of the nature of general comment only and are not in any way recommended as individual advice. The intent is to offer a variety of information to provide a wider range of choice now and in the future, recognizing that we all have widely diverse circumstances and viewpoints. Should any reader choose to make use f the information contained herein, that is their decision, and the contributors (and their companies), authors and publishers do not assume any responsibility whatsoever under any circumstances. It is recommended that the reader obtain their own professional advice.

DEDICATION

This book is dedicated to my beautiful mother Beverley Wood (a.k.a. Groover Gran). Mum is my most inspiring role model and I aspire to be as loving and accepting of people as she is. Thanks for always encouraging me to follow my dreams and always making me feel I can be anything I want.

CONTENTS

Acknowledgements

Welcome to the Power of 100 15

One Hundred Years of International Women's Day 16

Janet Beckers 19
Life Cycle of a Dream with Wings

Aishah Macgill 24
The New Age Bookshop - The Electronic Bookstore

Aldwyn Altuney 28
The world is your oyster

Alison Filihia 32
Life is a journey, not a destination

Alisse Bradley 37
How To Easily Realize Your Infinite Potential In Business.

Angie O'Shannessy 42
How I Stay Focused On My Dreams

Beatrice Burg 46
Persevering with Passion.

Belinda Jackson 51
Combining Mindset & Marketing for Massive results!

Beverley Charles 55
What Your Mind Can Conceive You Can Achieve

Buzz McCarthy, PhDC 59
Love stops time and starts eternity. But how do we get it right?

Candice Hazeltine 64
Until I Left High School I Thought My Name Was "Dont Be Stupid"

Carol Campbell 68
Awaken the possibility of freedom , and empowerment for the mind ….

Carolyn Dufton 71
How Franchising motivated me to create a dream lifestyle

Cassie Grant 75
Focusing on the love in my life

Cath Resnick 80
Giving Birth to a Dream

Charly Leetham 85
My $1 Million Dollar Debt Initiated The Realisation Of My Dream...

Cherry-Ann Carew 91
Follow Your North Star

Chris Georgopoulos 94
Keeping the vision alive.

Christine Hepburn 98
Leap Of Faith

Cinaea Dallinger 103
How to Keep Your Entrepreneurial Dreams Alive with Diamonds and Disco!

Claire McFee 109
Connect, connect; Give, give; Rewards, Rewards'

Clare Kyle 114
Work To Your Skills To Achieve True Motivation

Colleen Lording 118
When the "why" is big enough, the "how" takes care of itself when Selling...

Cydney O'Sullivan 122
Design A Life of Rich Rewards!

Dana Dunn 126
Big Dreams ... Big Life ... Living with Passion and Purpose

Dana Hughs 130
Career Creation 101

Daryl Grant 133
What are you doing to make a difference?

Dawn Z Bournand 137
Yes, you can!

Debbie Allen 142
Your Personal Mission Statement to Stay Focused

Debbie LaChusa 146
Illuminate The Path of Your Dreams With Clarity, Focus, and Inspired Ideas

Dee Britton 150
The Chicken or The Pig?   It's time to get committed!

Diana Vogel 154
Resistance, Confront and Staying Focused Through it All.

Eve Grace-Kelly 158
Discover Your Hedgehog

Fabe Keily 165
Keeping Your Sanity while Pursuing your Dream

Gabriela Rosa 168
How to Ignite Your Vision and Keep it Alive In 3 Easy Steps2

Helen Brougham 173
Women with Empowering Secrets

Jandra Faranda 178
Abundance Comes In A Rainbow Of Colors

Jane Hinchey 183
Passionate Pet People

Janelle Manton 187
Awakening the Goddess Within

Jedha Dening 191
'Fake it 'till you make it Life is a game'

Jenni Proctor 195
Changing My Mind: A journey from employee to entrepreneur

Jennie Harland-Khan 201
A fish, a tantrum and a choice

Johanna Baker-Dowdell	206
My Time to Shine	
J P Miller	209
Your Money Personality	
Judeth Wilson	213
How to Achieve Your Dreams with Ease and Speed	
Judi Mason	217
Single Minded Focus	
Judith Sherven, PhD	220
Extreme Life Extension - At Ageless Zoom My Vision Of Living To 120 ...	
Julie McDonald	224
How could I keep my dream alive, when I became an emotional ...	
Kandee G	231
Success can be Yours	
Karen Thomson	235
Are You Serious?	
Kathleen Gage	239
Dream often and dream big	
Katie McDonald	242
You Can Control Your Financial Future!	
Kerrie Jeffreys	247
A Travelling Destiny	
Kerry Weymouth	251
3 Easy Steps To achieve MILESTONES	
Kim Lambert	255
YOU Can DO Anything ...	
Kim Morris	262
Escape Of The Corporate Zombie	
Kim Townsend	267
Awakening Awareness	

Kirsty Greenshields 271
The Secrets to Creating Your 'Magical Sparkle'

Kris Lafferty 276
Sweet T.E.A.

Kristi Sayles 279
Dream BIG!

Kylee Legge 283
Just Start and Don't Stop!

Lee Martin 286
I am not a cockroach.

Lenore Miller 290
Death, Resilience and Success – a Vision for Living!

Linda Philip 294
Move Beyond Resistance to Your Path of Creation

Linky Muller 297
Fridge Magnets, Melodies and Mum

Lisa Robbins 302
Gorilla Glue Dreams

Lisa Taliga 307
How To Keep Your Freelance Dream Alive

Liz Raad 312
Letting Joy Be Your Guide

Lorrah Berg 318
Ask Quality Questions to Get Quality Results to Keep Your Dreams Alive

Louise Brogan 322
Every Milli-second Makes a Difference.

Malissa Thorpe 327
Breakable Bones - Unbreakable Spirit

Maree Lipschitz 331
Keep your Dream Alive by Feeling Fabulous, Frisky and Focused ...

Margaret Ann Beth Saunders 336
Keeping your day simple and staying motivated and focussed

Margaret Sims 340
Give Up. Give In. No Way!

Marguerita Vorobioff 344
Unleash The Power Within

Marney Perna 348
Storm Survival Skills

Meg Ringrose 352
The Authentic You

Melinda Boyer 356
The Woman Entrepreneur

Melissa Groom 361
Leap of Faith

Michele DeKinder-Smith 365
The Sweetness of Giving Dangerously

Michele PW (Pariza Wacek) 369
3 Simple Secrets to Stay Focused on Your Business So You Start ...

Michelle Marie McGrath 373
Self-love - would that change anything? Or everything ...

Nerida Osborne 379
Art of Adventure/ Adventure of Art

Pam Brossman 383
Millionaire Attitude

Pat Lynch 387
"When All Else Fails..."

Pat Marcello 391
Success Comes from Listening to Your Heart

Paula Tarrant 395
4 Essential Principles For Turning Your Divine Dreams Into Everyday Reality

Janet Beckers

ACKNOWLEDGMENTS

The pages of this book are filled with references to the power of gratitude, and for good reason. If we give others the opportunity to help, not only can you create something of greater value, the people who help you often gain just as much as you! There are many people to acknowledge and thank for their part in creating this book. I do hope that I haven't left anyone out but if I have, please know that I am genuinely grateful for your help. So here goes ...

Our wonderful authors: There are some "big names" here who are experienced authors and mentors and others who faced the challenge and have authored their first book chapter. Thank you for your wisdom and pushing yourselves out of your comfort zone. The quality of your work is amazing. Congratulations.

Thank you to Michael Petter, the incredibly talented artist who gifted us his unique fractal image for the cover of the book. The story behind Michael's artwork is intriguing. Who would have thought you could create something so beautiful using mathematical equations! Thanks also to Tabitha King, Graphic Designer and Ambassador for Opportunity International who adapted Michael's artwork to create a unique and creative cover for the book.

Thank you to Jedha Dening who came up with the title of the book. It really captured what I wanted to create. Thank you to Monika Newman, Virtual Assistant Extraordinaire and e-book editing specialist. Monika volunteered hours of her time and expertise to format the layout, look, images etc of the book. Monika is amazingly patient. Thank you for your calmness and meeting very tight deadlines – you're a star!

Thank you to the Wonderful Web Team of Charly Leetham, Laura Trenerry and Lisa Taliga for helping to coordinate such a big project.

To all the wonderful women (and enlightened men) who make up the Wonderful Web Women community. I am continually inspired by the wonderful women I am privileged to interview and the amazing women and men who make up our community. Your stories inspired this book. I consider myself very lucky to have the opportunity to share my knowledge with you and also to learn so much from each of you.

Now on a more personal note …

Thank you to my gorgeous children Phoebe and Clancy. There is something extra special about kids who will cook a meal for you and bring you cups of tea because you are focused on a tight deadline.

My biggest thanks go to the Wonderful Web Man himself Douglas Beckers. I love this man so much and I wish every woman could have someone in their life who supports their dreams the way Douglas supports mine. Douglas edited nearly every chapter in this book and encouraged me every step of the way. Douglas has that wonderful mix which is perfect in a business (and life) partner. A great lateral thinker and a man of action. After 25 years he still makes me a bit weak at the knees!

Janet Beckers

Welcome to The Power of 100

Do you have a dream? It could be a burning desire that consumes your thoughts or it could be a vague fantasy you think may be way beyond your capabilities. But still, it is a dream. The thing with dreams is they can tend to get swamped by the reality of life. With so many things competing for our attention, such as work, partners, children, friends, family, and health and so on it is so easy for dreams to stay just that; a dream that never becomes reality. My wish for you is to keep that dream in focus so that bit by bit (or huge leap at a time) it becomes a reality for you.

You are not alone. In this book you will find women, many just like you, who have a dream and are determined to see it become a reality. Some of the authors are self-made millionaires while others are surviving below the poverty line. They all share incredible gifts of stories, advice and practical tips that are down to earth and shared from the heart. It's like having 100 girlfriends to turn to for support when you get frustrated and think you will never get the clarity and focus to reach your goal.

This book is the result of team work – but not your typical team!

The team who created this publication are spread throughout the globe. Contributors come from all parts of the world ... from Australia to the USA, from Canada to France, from New Zealand to The Maldives.

Every part of this book, from concept to title, every article, artwork, formatting, distribution and marketing – everything – has been the result of the collaboration of women (and enlightened men). Each contributor is a GOLD or VIP member of the Wonderful Web Women community who not only saw an opportunity, BUT TOOK ACTION.

Action is what has set the authors and contributors of this book apart from every one else and that is why action is an important part of this book. Each author shares 3 action steps you can take today to stay focused on your dreams.

100 Years of International Women's Day

The year of publication of this book celebrates 100 years of International Women's Day. I am incredibly grateful for the women who have fought hard for the freedoms many women take for granted today. Believe it or not, women have still not achieved equality of pay in developed countries and in many developing countries, women and their children are greatly disadvantaged simply because of their gender.

I look back at the last 100 years and I see incredible determination and focus on a dream. The type of focus needed over the last 100 years is the same focus we need to nurture our personal dreams. It is my hope this book will give you the inspiration and skills to really focus on your dreams.

Opportunity International and the 1 Million Women Project

I am very proud to introduce you to our partner Opportunity International Australia. I believe strongly that every woman you help achieve her own dreams, especially through entrepreneurial endeavour, will go on to help many other women and men achieve theirs. So simply by helping one woman you become a catalyst for change. One of the most powerful ways to do this is by helping women who live below the poverty line, to create their own businesses through small loans. This is what our charity partner does.

Opportunity International Australia exists to provide opportunities for people living in poverty to transform their lives. With over 35 years' experience in microfinance and support services, they enable the empowerment of individuals by using a business approach to solve poverty. Rather than a hand-out, they provide their clients with a loan as small as $100 to help grow their small business. This allows them to earn an income and afford food, water, shelter and an education for their children.

Here's how it works ...

By helping a mother buy a sewing machine to start a tailoring business or a father to buy seeds to plant a vegetable garden, small loans enable people in poverty to earn an income and provide for their families. As each business grows, loans are paid back and lent out again. And with 97% of loans repaid, the cycle continues, year after year. Each successful business feeds a family, employs more people and eventually helps to empower a whole community.

Part of a global network, Opportunity's aim is to see people lifted out of poverty permanently.

In 2007, Opportunity International Australia established a team based in Delhi to manage and implement a significant poverty alleviation program for the women of India. In December 2009, the program passed the milestone of one million clients and the 1 Million Women Project was born.

The 1 Million Women Project is about taking the India program to the next one million women. It's people and businesses saying 'I believe in that' and joining together to make a difference. India accounts for the largest share of the world's poor, with more than 900 million people living on less than US$2 a day. Hundreds of millions of Indian people are trapped in an intergenerational cycle of poverty.

Women in particular are disenfranchised and are too often unable to access education and fair employment. Yet women remain the brightest hope for change in India. When women and girls earn an income, they reinvest 90% of it into their families, compared to only 30-40% for men. Investing in women is the most effective way to bring about change in poor communities.

A portion of all memberships of Wonderful Web Women and sales of the hard copy of this book go to support Opportunity International Australia. I also encourage you to join others in our community and donate directly. Even a small donation will make a difference.

You can do that here:

https://www.WonderfulWebWomen.com/recommends/opportunity

Thousands of Dollars of Gifts

Every one of the contributors to this book has gifted you further help. Many of the gifts offered here are only available because you have taken the time to read this book. Gifts range from free courses, books, generous discounts to complimentary coaching and memberships. I urge you to take action and make the most of the gifts offered to you. After all, the path those gifts take you on might very well be the reason this book has come into your life. You can find links to all of these gifts at the end of each chapter and also on our web site http://www.ThePowerof100Book.com Please contact the author directly to talk to them about their gifts.

Share Your Stories With Us

I'm sure you have wonderful stories and tips you can share to help others stay focused on their dreams. We'd love to hear from you too. When you visit the website for this book please take the time to share your tips with us. You can leave your comments for each author or share your story with us on our "Share Your Dream" page of the site. Your ideas may be just the catalyst another woman needs to stay focused and achieve the dream she may have held for years.

Cheers

Janet Beckers

Founder and host
Wonderful Web Women

P.S: You can join our dynamic community of entrepreneurial women (and enlightened men) and also receive the resell rights to the digital version of this book (so you can gift it to your customers and use it to grow your list of prospective customers). Simply visit http://www.WonderfulWebWomen.com – it's free to join us

Janet Beckers

The Life Cycle Of A Dream With Wings

Janet Beckers

When I look back at whom I used to be and what my dreams were, even three years ago, I can hardly recognize myself. Of course, I'm still Janet with the same core values but at the same time, I am completely different.

I think the big thing that has changed is my dreams. Over the last 3 years I have learned to dream BIG and more importantly, my belief in my ability to achieve bigger and bigger dreams has grown. I don't believe this change can happen overnight.

Sure, you can have a life-changing "ah ha" or have a wonderful experience (or exposure to someone else's thoughts) that makes you suddenly think so much bigger. More often than not there is an occasion that acts as a catalyst to a bigger dream but what WON'T happen overnight is your true belief, deep down, that you are capable of achieving those bigger dreams.

This takes time . The good news is, there is a process to follow and the speed at which you go from dream to your true belief that you are capable of achieving it, gets faster every time you repeat the process.

To explain the process, I first have to talk about the life cycle of a butterfly. You my friend and your expanding dreams, have a similar cycle. So this is also the life cycle of a dream with wings.

It All Starts With an Egg

The life cycle of a butterfly starts with an egg and the same thing happens with our dreams. Our dreams start out small and very often have been fertilized by our experiences or ideas triggered by someone else. There is incredible potential within that tiny little egg.

The Caterpillar

The next step in the cycle of our "dream with wings" is the caterpillar. In nature, the sole purpose of the caterpillar is to eat and grow and store up amazing energy. The same happens with our dreams.

For our dreams to ever stand the chance of developing wings we need to feed them. We need to feed them with research, sharing, imagination and the very real and practical steps of brainstorming, business planning and taking action.

Unfortunately, too many dreams never get past the caterpillar stage. They wither away without action and without ever sharing them with others who can help to make the dream come true. Often they are starved because the dreamer gets distracted by another idea because they can't believe caterpillars need so much feeding!

If the caterpillar is nurtured and the dream is ready to be launched with the beautiful wings of a butterfly there is another stage that is essential.

Cocooning

From the outside, when you look at a cocoon it looks as if nothing is happening. It could almost appear dead! But inside an incredible process of transformation is happening. It is, in fact, the time in the lifecycle of a butterfly when there is the most energy used. The same is for the process of cocooning in the life cycle of achieving a dream.

Cocooning is a time for connecting with your subconscious and allowing yourself to "go within". If your dreams are bigger than you have dreamt before it is important to prepare yourself emotionally for the challenge. This is a time to use your imagination and visualize yourself actually achieving what you truly dream of.

For me, this is a time when I allow myself to day dream. I meditate often during this time, connect with nature and create opportunities to just "be". I consciously use my imagination to see what I am truly capable of and continually repeat to myself a mantra that reinforces what I intend to create. For example, I often repeat in the shower "I am a catalyst for change. I help women world-wide to create passionate and profitable businesses. Opportunities flow to me and will always flow to me, because I help people achieve their dreams". This is one mantra I have chanted to myself many times during the times I cocoon.

In the past I used to fight this process. I would get frustrated with myself and ignore the internal conflict that came from claiming a dream I did not deep down feel capable of. I tried to fly without cocooning and would inevitably self-sabotage.

Now I allow myself the time and space to seek quietness and use my imagination to prepare myself for what I am about to become. This does not mean I stop taking action and moving towards my goal. I just give equal priority to the process of being centred and confident.

As an example, when I set myself the goal of motivating more than 100 women world-wide to create this book with me I knew I had set a big dream. Getting hundreds of people interested is one thing but mobilizing more than 100 women to take action in a short time frame is a completely different achievement. My dream is very big and this book is only one small part of it so I knew I had to be completely confident and in tune with my big vision to make this happen smoothly and without struggle.

So I consciously cocooned. I visualized the impact this book would have on so many people (readers, authors and the women of the 1 Million Women Out Of Poverty Project) and I visualized myself calmly and confidently leading the way. Within 1 week we went from less than 20 authors to over my goal of 100. The energy flowed and what had previously been a struggle happened easily. This is what it feels like to emerge as the butterfly.

The Butterfly Emerges

When the butterfly emerges, your dreams have wings and you know you are the right person to make it fly. It feels like someone in the traffic control centre of life is making sure you only get green traffic lights on the way to your destination.

The Life Cycle Repeats

Our dreams are never complete. As we feel the confidence of the wind under our wings, we start to dream bigger and bigger. We see we are capable of even more. And so the idea is born and the next eggs start to hatch. The life cycle repeats itself. One thing I have noticed over the last 3 years since I have truly focused on the importance of giving my subconscious the time and attention it needs. The lifecycle of the dreams you can achieve gets shorter and shorter. What used to take months or years to nurture can now take weeks and in some cases days or even hours. As long as you respect the importance of each stage in the cycle.

My wish for you is you enjoy the process of the full life-cycle of your dreams and you emerge from the cocoon magically metamorphosed into a dreamer with wings.

3 Tips To Stay Focused On Your Dreams

Dare to dream bigger than you have before. Your dreams should scare you.

Have the persistence to feed your dream with the attention, research, action and sharing that is essential for it to grow. Your dreams need fuel to grow. They won't manifest without you taking massive action.

Respect the importance of connecting with your subconscious. Allow yourself time to cocoon so your faith that you are as big as your dreams can grow.

that dream to be a writer, but now I am assisting other authors to self publish and fulfil their dreams of being a published author.

I am now helping others help themselves to get their message, knowledge or real life story out into the world. This is now easier and quicker than ever. No longer do we have to wait for the printer to finish the job for us and for a distributor to get our books out there. We are at present in the midst of an information revolution. We have well and truly entered the brave new electronic age of the internet. This startling new paradigm of communication, the internet, has in turn propigated an amazing opportunity for authors to have their work available for reading in record time. There is an electronic tsunami happening in the world of publishing. We are all familiar with our local bookshop. There is nothing like the look and feel of a paper book and the smell of the ink. However, today there is a new medium overtaking traditional book sales. The electronic bookstore. I am talking Amazons Kindle, iPad, iPhone, Blackberry, Sony E reader, Nook and a plethora of others in the development stage. You can even purchase a book from the Kindle bookstore and download it to your PC. Mac or iPhone.

When you go on holidays, you can literally take thousands of books with you on the one small book size reader. Also, on Amazon.com, Kindle books are now outselling print books! It is possible for self published authors to get their content 'out there' in the universe very quickly now. The only hurdle is getting your book content formatted to suit the specific electronic formats so it can be read easily on all different electronic reading devices. At present Amazons Kindle have the lions share of this industry.

Write, publish and prosper!

Once you have written your book, it's quicker, simpler and cheaper to publish your work on an electronic bookstore. There are several different formats used and they are quite different to a 'traditional' ebook that is downloaded directly onto a computer, usually as a PDF file. With an electronic book that is sold on Kindle and suchlike you can still have 'live' links back to your own website. This is a remarkable marketing opportunity for all online authors and entrepreneurs. The possiblities are endless ….

3 Tips To Stay Focused On Your Dreams

1. Never stop dreaming. It took me 25 years, but the dream lived on. Writing and publishing is my destiny. No matter what path life takes you on, you are never too old to embark on a new venture. I embarked on this brilliant new career at age 50! You can do anything you put your mind to. Just decide to do it! Believe it and don't listen to the nay-sayers!

2. Do a little bit each day. Rome wasn't built in a day. Chip away and at the end of the year, when you look back, it will all add up to more than you ever expected to achieve.

3. When times get tough I have a simple remedy. Take some time out! Reflect on how life just gets better and better. Setbacks are only learning curves. Remember each new day is just that, a new beginning!

About The Author

I am a writer, publisher and lover of life, an online entrepreneur and internet marketer. A mother of three grown up children and a fantastic cook, Indian curries being my specialty. I spent 25 years meditating and pursuing the ideal of enlightenment, which so far, I have not achieved! I love to travel and especially love Asia and Europe. I have now found a special place in my life and love to help others get their message out there via their books. I love to read about other peoples' life stories. That's what makes up our world. The people and their experiences.

Janet Beckers

Special Gift

If you would like to have your book formatted and published on any of the new electronic publishing formats, I have a service that will do it all for you. Send me your book file and I will convert it to electronic book format. If you require any assistance at all in self publishing, I also offer services in how to self publish. Let me know you found me through "The Power of 100" book or website and I will give you a free one hour consultation on how to self publish your book!

Visit my website http://finitepublishing.com http://aishahmacgill.com

skype: Aishah Macgill Facebook: http://facebook.com/aishahmacgill

Send me a message at info@finitepublishing.com

The World Is Your Oyster

Aldwyn Altuney

I am pleased and honoured to contribute to this book about my ideas on things people can do this year to create change and keep their dreams alive. I have always believed that if you really want to achieve something, you will find a way to do it. I have had many high points in my life where I have achieved my dreams from a very young age. Some of these include being Dux of North Balgowlah Primary School in Sydney, Australian Junior Table Tennis Champion in the under 17 age group when I was only 13, defeating the 32nd world ranked table tennis player when I was only 16 and the top Australian senior female player was ranked 200. I have contributed work for books and magazines worldwide, been a TV and radio host, had artwork in exhibitions and MC'd for people like George Negus, Kerry O'Brien, Ernie Dingo, Brian Ritchie (Violent Femmes) and James Morrison before thousands of people at the Woodford Folk Festival.

When I was at the University of Canberra, I applied to be Editor of the University newspaper CUrio three times before I was accepted to the position. I then went on to become the longest serving editor of the publication at the time.

I also followed my heart to make a difference for animals and the environment by starting Animal Action Day on the Gold Coast in 2007. My goal is for the event to be a worldwide annual event to raise awareness, appreciation and respect for animals

Janet Beckers

and the environment worldwide. Celebrating its fifth year in 2011, this vision is fast becoming a reality, with growing support worldwide through social networks such as Facebook, Twitter and LinkedIn plus amazing support locally.

I have also had my low times

I left home at 16 years of age, suffered from bullying, drug and alcohol abuse in my teens; have been the victim of crime and theft many times and bouts of financial hardship. I believe life is like the share market – we all have our ups and downs. The trick to success however, I believe, is to appreciate the downs as learning experiences and celebrate and recognize the highs as achievements. My lessons in these ups and downs have brought home the importance of being resilient, determined and focused on your goals. As in the movie, The Secret, the more you are grateful for the things that 'are working' in your life, the more you will have to be grateful for and the more blessings will come your way. Every morning and night, I ponder on the things I'm grateful for. A gratitude journal is fantastic. I also have gratitude rocks around the house so whenever I look at them, it reminds me to be thankful for my life. There are always people out there less fortunate than us. However, if you compare yourself to others, you may become vain and bitter. The thing to realise is that we are all unique, special, miracles of life and we all have different journeys.

My mission is clear – to inspire people to live life to the full and encourage awareness, appreciation and respect for all animals and the environment. Long term, I would like to host inspiring TV shows and donate $1 million per year to animal charities. The wheels are in motion now for me to achieve these goals. I'm not sure how I will make that money yet, however I trust, visualise and have faith that it will happen. So there are plenty of tips I could give you to create change and keep your dreams alive.

Firstly, you need to be aware of what you want and why (the bigger reason beyond yourself of how you can contribute to the world).

Secondly, you need to have a plan of attack to achieve your goals. Some tips include clearly defined goal cards (read every day covering the seven key areas of life - Health, Family, Financial, Business/Career, Social/Community, Intellectual and Spiritual); meditation, visualization and keeping faith and gratitude at all times – even when things don't seem to be working out. An example of a challenge that turned into a blessing in my life was when I went to rent a beachfront unit in Main

Beach in 2002 and was ripped off about $1000 in rent and bond money by a young surfer and his pregnant girlfriend who said they owned the place. They were renting and ran off with the money. The case has now been closed by the police, even though I had a receipt and his mobile number with text messages from him, it meant nothing! I never recovered the money and was so ashamed that I fell for the trick, I never told anyone for years. Since then, however, I decided I would never rent again and bought my first house on the Gold Coast within a few months of this incident. Now, I am so grateful for that experience, as I have since made more than $100,000 in my property. I didn't see the lesson at the time but now I do and now I share this to inspire people to look for the lessons in everything.

Lastly, you need education, determination, an unshakable will power and vision to see your goals through to success. If you really want something, it's yours. Life is full of abundance and only 5% of people tap into that. So I suggest, play life above the line, take full responsibility for your actions, hang out with like-minded go-getters (pushers, not pullers) – often found at inspiring seminars - and go for it! The world is your oyster, so I trust and pray that you will enjoy the journey in this sea of wonder and fellowship! And I have faith that when you lie on your death bed, you can look back on your life and say, "I am proud of what I achieved and how I contributed to the world". If we all just do our little bit to live fulfilled lives, the ripple effect will radiate to create a better world. And we will all be blessed for it.

3 Tips To Stay Focused On Your Dreams

Be aware of what you want and why (the bigger reason beyond yourself of how you can contribute to the world).

Have a plan of attack to achieve your goals. Some tips include clearly defined goal cards, meditation, visualization and keeping faith and gratitude at all times – even when things don't seem to be working out.

You need education, determination, an unshakable will power and vision to see your goals through to success.

Janet Beckers

About The Author

Aldwyn Altuney is an outgoing Photojournalist who has worked in traditional media (newspapers, magazines, TV and radio) across Australia for about 20 years.

She has been a Radio Host for radio stations along Australia's (add apostrophe) east coast, worked as an MC, TV reporter and Actress in Australian film and stage productions.

Born in Sydney and with a BA in Communications (MEDIA) from the University of Canberra, she has interviewed stars including Hugh Jackman, Russell Crowe, Cyndi Lauper, Debbie Harry (Blondie), Alby Mangels, Jimmy Barnes, Jimeoin and Mikey Robins. Based on the Gold Coast since 2000, she is a Corporate Communications Consultant, Freelance Photojournalist and Director of AA Xpos, (CHANGE this word to Xposé) Media.

She was named National College of Business 2005 Climber of the Year and has represented Australia in Europe and Asia as Junior and Youth Table Tennis Champion from 1987 to 1993. After a five-year break from the sport, she won the Gold Coast Table Tennis Championships Women's (add apostrophe) Open Singles in 2006.
She founded Animal Action Day, an annual charity fun day of awareness, appreciation and respect for animals and the environment, in 2007.

She is passionate about inspiring people to live life to the full and make a difference through positive media.

Special Gift

Receive '15 Tips to Market Yourself to the Media' to help build your profile, credibility and cashflow, valued at $150. Go to http://www.aaxpose.com

http://www.aaxpose.com   www.WhatisQuestTravelNetwork.com
http://www.Freedom.QuestTravelNetwork.com/Overview.php
http://www.WhatisOurMissionCoffee.com
http://www.Freedom.OurMissionCoffee.com

Life Is A Journey, Not A Destination

Alison Filihia

What drives me to follow my dreams is my 100% determination to prove to myself and my two daughters that I can make my dreams come true and set a shining example for them.

Find your passion, spend time growing it and ask the universe and your angels for help.

Don't live your life in fear and regret. I see and hear so many women out there who need help to restore their health and happiness naturally and I want to share my knowledge and experience with them. Life is a journey, not a destination! What do I do when things go wrong or have feelings of doubt? Lately this has been an important question for me. Often I find myself excited and passionate about something or about to take on a new challenge, when something will sabotage my path. Something will break down (eg: the car or computer), a big money expense will pop up or someone gets sick and needs my attention. This is something that can cause lots of frustration and self defeating thoughts. So I have started to ask the question – why does this happen?

What I have found is that the universe truly does mirror our deep down subconscious thoughts and beliefs and another classic example happened recently. I had just finished listening on my computer about the wonderful opportunity to publish a chapter in Janet's new book for 2011 when another unexpected problem appeared from nowhere! I spilt water on my laptop! I was all pumped and excited about this new opportunity to grow my business. How could I have done this! What am I going to do now! Why do I keep being challenged like this! Everything happens for a reason – right? But again??? In the end I was without a computer for nearly a month, but it forced me to look harder at why these blocks kept appearing.

What is in my inner world that keeps mirroring in my outer world this way? What subconscious limiting beliefs do I have that are causing my obstacles? For me it is usually two things – "I am not as good as others" or "I don't love and accept myself completely". And after a little soul searching I found my old friends hiding not too far from the surface. I decided I needed to do some work on clearing them for good! Like the layers of an onion you can peel away one layer of limiting belief to find a similar one attached to a different theme. Affirmations, visualisations and a technique called EFT (emotional freedom technique) are my favourite tools I can do myself. I also see a kinesiologist regularly to stay balanced and clear any blocks.

Without my computer I had heaps of time to spend on doing these things. Our negative subconscious beliefs are like weeds in a garden. If the garden is neglected and the ugly weeds are left to grow, they can take over. Flowers and plants have to fight harder to stay alive. Negative thoughts and limiting beliefs are like weeds. If they stay around, soon they will take over and make you feel negative and defeated. Regular mental and emotional weeding helps keep you blooming! In conclusion, while my computer was away being assessed for damages, I spent time affirming my belief that "I am good enough" and clearing out my limiting beliefs. My computer was returned to me being too expensive to fix but when I turned it on to try to recover any data I needed, it was working completely fine ...UNBELIEVABLE!! ..... A MIRACLE! I was so amazed. Guess weeding does work - and it will help you BLOOM.

Three things I do DAILY to stay focused?

Assess my body, mind and spirit connection!

Step 1 – BODY

Every day I ask myself, "how am I feeling?" Usually I do this over my morning meditation or if I don't have time – while I drink my coffee (my morning treat). Do I have any physical pain anywhere? Illness or disease? Bringing my attention to this helps me link any emotions, thoughts or feelings I have that could be contributing to it. Knowing what emotions affect different muscles, organs, glands and meridians (energy flows) in the body is an important tool. I do a quick scan of my whole body then think about what is going on in my life at the moment. You cannot think a single thought without it affecting your physical body and its physiology, so this is a very useful technique I use. Assessing all these pieces of my body's holistic puzzle, helps me stay balanced and focused so I can achieve my goals. (See a kinesiologist for help learning about which emotions affect different parts of the body.)

Step 2 – MIND

I ask myself a few direct questions:

1. "What would courage have me do today?" – and DO IT! This is a sure fire way to stop beating around the bush and look at what I have been avoiding or putting off. This is often the very thing you need to do the most!

2. "What is stopping me?" Often you will find it is because you feel scared, worried, fear or you don't know how.

3. "Why do I feel like this?" Your answers may be "I am not good enough", "I might fail" or "I don't want to make a mistake and look silly" It may even be because you feel you should do it, or someone else wants you to do it. It may not be aligned with your true self. These are instant red flags to acknowledge and let go of. These underlying core beliefs are what is stopping you from achieving success and staying focused. THE WEEDS! They are only thoughts and they CAN be changed and pulled out.

Janet Beckers

4. Start turning these beliefs around - affirm and create new beliefs! "I am good enough; I love and accept myself unconditionally, in ALL areas of my life" Even start by saying you are willing to change or I am beginning to feel more ... NOW DO THE THING YOU WERE PUTTING OFF IN STEP 1 ... TAKE ACTION!

Step 3 – SPIRIT

Ask for help. I call on my angels to help me with everything I am struggling with! Especially with the task I identified in Step 2. I spend a few minutes every day in quiet meditation and use my angel cards to receive the messages. I also look out for signs and any help they send me. This could be simply by having great ideas pop into my head out of the blue, receiving the exact info I needed in an email, TV show or book I see or meeting the right person who can help me. It's amazing!

3 Tips To Stay Focused On Your Dreams

My 3 action steps involve me Assessing my body, mind and spirit connection!

BODY Everyday ask yourself, "how am I feeling?" Do I have any physical pain anywhere? Illness or dis-ease? Link any emotions, feelings or thoughts that may be lingering around. What is going on in your life at the moment. All this is probably manifesting in your body as pain or illness. Repeat "I am willing to release any pain or dis-ease from my body".

MIND Ask yourself "What would courage have me do today?" "Why aren't I doing it?" - Clear that fear or limiting belief. Affirm new positive feelings and beliefs. Then take ACTION!

SPIRIT Ask your angels for help with anything I you are struggling with (eg from step 2). Have faith that you are not alone. The angels and universal energy have an amazing way to help you, even beyond your wildest imagination.

About The Author

Today I am so grateful to even HAVE a dream and vision, this alone fuels my drive. Up until I was 35 years old, I had no passion and no real vision for the future. I got married at 23 yrs to a wonderful man, but he took me on the rollercoaster ride of my life for 10 years with his alcohol addiction. I had the first of my two daughters at 24 yrs, had no qualifications, worked an unfulfilling job in a restaurant and had no idea how to change things. My health had been going downhill steadily for 5 years and no doctor new why? I struggled to find solutions to my declining health when I finally figured out what was wrong with me – chronic fatigue, fibromyalgia AND – a 15 year chronic case of SELF SACRIFICE, BLOCKED EMOTIONS AND PEOPLE PLEASING! Since then I have been on an amazing journey back to health and happiness. Kinesiology and energy healing balanced out my chronically blocked and out of balanced body, which has brought about incredible changes to my body, mind and spirit. This inspired me to obtain my own Diploma in Holistic Kinesiology and start my own practice called Bloom Kinesiology. I have also started an online business called www.LiveLifeBloom. This is my way of connecting to women and mothers all over the world who are struggling to get help for their own health and unhappiness. The website offers great, easy to follow information and programs on how they too can restore their health and happiness naturally and BLOOM! For me there is no turning back! Nothing to turn back too! I now can see a light at the end of my tunnel. I choose to move forward toward love, joy and health not go backward to a dark place with chronic illness, anxiety, feeling stuck and unfulfilled.

Special Gift

Alison has gifted to you her 7 great energy restoring tips you can do for FREE!

Go to http://livelifebloom.com to receive a free audio interview, where Alison reveals these 7 great energy restoring tips PLUS a fascinating talk about "what IS kinesiology and the mind/body connection".

Or visit http://www.bloomkinesiology.com.au for information on kinesiology and how to make a client booking.

Janet Beckers

How To Easily Realize Your Infinite Potential In Business.

Alisse Bradley

Living Your Infinite Potential ...

Within each and every one of us there is a burning desire to do something great, to pursue our dreams and live through that infinite part of ourselves. We want to make a difference in our world, find the hero within ourselves, and fully express who we are. And the truth is - this is possible!

Finding Your Burning Desire

In my opinion finding your burning desire is the most significant part of living a life of fulfillment and succeeding in business, however it was not immediately obvious to me what mine was. Early in my career I set monstrous goals of material possessions and world travel, and with a great deal of focus and hard work I achieved them. Unfortunately this was at the expense of something I valued more. It was a surreal experience to reach the pinnacle of my business goals only to realize that I had missed a great big chunk of my children's lives (four years to be exact) and although my efforts were paved with good intentions, at that point all I wanted was the time over to relive what I had missed. I was entrenched in the belief that the only road to success, was to master my positive focus and administer my ambitious drive (trade time for $).

This was a major turning point for me, what had seemed to be the answer to all my dreams and desires was instead the catalyst to my physical exhaustion, poor health, excessive weight problem and badly strained relationships. My absolute heart break and frustration had me challenge everything I knew and I decided there had to be some way out there to have it all. I wanted an incredible relationship with my husband and children, a prosperous business that I was madly passionate about, as well as the freedom to do with my time what I wanted. Because I had been down the road of numerous passive income models already and not found anything that 'rang my bell', I looked for other solutions, and this is how I found myself on what I call my 'spiritual journey'.

Ironically I discovered that the complex effects of the 'universal flow of energy' has a lot to do with the health, wealth and success of your business and here are some of the basics which really set the scene for my abundant energy and ultimate success.

Find Your Soul's Purpose

There is so much health, wealth and happiness tied up in that deep yearning you have within your soul. The question is how do you connect with it, and then create it into a tangible plan to benefit from in your business and life. Tuning in to your own energy and using modalities that can give you great insight, can quickly and easily assist you to identify this information, like who am I, what are my greatest strengths and where does my greatest fulfillment lie?

The information I learned from these modalities made it easy for me to peel off what wasn't true for me and accept and honor what was. I gained clear direction which naturally improved my energy levels, my poor health and my weight issues. From this I designed my own formula to learn from my physical body when I was and wasn't on my Soul Path and my business responds every time.

Janet Beckers

Express Your Strengths and Talent

Once I identified my strengths and talents using the 'energy based modalities' I made a point of simply working from them. Everything else I either molded out of my business model or found someone else whose strength it was. I only pay myself to do what I am best at because when I do it creates easy flow and I feel happy and energized.

I do still stretch myself to improve my talents; however I don't waste money, time and energy on what I don't love to do, at all. Initially I felt uncomfortable only doing what I loved because I had been brought up to believe that 'life wasn't made to be easy' however when I studied the lives of extraordinary people who did extraordinary things, I found they had dedicated their life to expressing their talent and as a result transformed our world.

Be of Service to Humanity

A wise business mentor once told me 'if I could shift my focus from myself to my audience when I spoke, I would go from good to great'. It took me a while to completely understand what she meant. Now I relate this to all facets of my life and most certainly my business. I realized that once you take your focus away from 'what if I am not good enough yet, what if I make a mistake and what will people think of me' to 'how can I be of service' then you have universal energy working on your side. Deepak Chopra says it like this, "Everyone has a purpose in life ... a unique gift or special talent to give to others. And when we blend this unique talent with service to others, we experience the ecstasy and exultation of our own spirit, which is the ultimate goal of all goals."

The Secret Sauce

Once on the road to mastering these steps it is time to add the secret sauce of success. And that is where Feng Shui comes into play. Your environment is influencing your unconscious mind each and every second of the day, and it is speaking health, wealth and success or it is not. You cannot stop this process so it is vital that you become aware of it, understand it and work with it. It was when I added the secret sauce to my business and life the magic began instantly.

Everything in my life transformed. My annual income was over 5 times what it was the year before, my relationship with my husband improved immediately, I regained my health and happiness and this was only the beginning. I now have this incredible tool of empowerment I use every day. It assists me to stay focused, maintain balanced, stay motivated and live my inspired life to say the least.

I have been so excited about my discovery and all of the other amazing things that have come about in my life, including working with Bob Proctor and Marie Diamond from 'The Secret' fame as well as time being coached by Dr Wayne Dyer, that I decided to write a book which contained all of the tools that I use in my day to day business and life and share it with as many people as were interested to know.

This was the birth of my 'Feng Shui Secrets Series'. So far there are 3 books in the series; Feng Shui Secrets To Achieve Business Prosperity, Feng Shui Secrets To Create A Million Dollar Mindset, Feng Shui Secrets To Realize Your Infinite Potential

3 Tips To Stay Focused On Your Dreams

Find Your Souls Purpose

Express Your Strengths And Talents

Be Of Service To Humanity

About The Author

Alisse Bradley is Australia's own Prosperity Whisperer. An International Speaker, Author of the "Feng Shui Secrets" series and Enlightened Business Coach, she is a revolutionary of our time. She empowers female entrepreneurs to thrive in these unusual times, teaching them simple step by step processes to overcome the fears and limitations that their inner voice screams and work with the 'universal energy' to birth their dreams and passions. Alisse's coaching method is unique, combining her extensive studies in Feng Shui, Astrology, Neuro Linguistic Programming and Spiritual Mastery. She has worked personally with some of the world's leaders in these fields, including Bob Proctor and Marie Diamond, both of 'The Secret' fame and the 'Father of Motivation' himself Dr Wayne Dyer.

Janet Beckers

Special Gift

As my very special gift to you ... I am giving you a free downloadable copy of my favorite chapter from my 3rd book 'Feng Shui Secrets To Realize Your Infinite Potential' http://fengshui-thesecrets.com/free-book-chapter/ so that you too can live your infinite potential in this lifetime. Love, Light and Laughter, Alisse

www.fengshui-thesecrets.com

How I Stay Focused On My Dreams

Angie O'Shannessy

It's very interesting to me to look back at my life and see where I have come from and it amazes me how I achieved so much. I certainly didn't know then, what I know now.

What I have learnt in the past 15 years being a student of personal development has reinforced in me that knowing is not the answer to achieving successes. All the information on gaining success (whatever that is to you) is there for the taking. Someone on the planet has already achieved your burning desires, so there aren't any reasons why you to can't achieve the same or even greater. In saying that, I would like to tell you a short story about my life.

I was an extremely outgoing child, very extraverted, would love to chat to anyone and everyone telling them all about my family (which didn't impress my family at times) and sharing the things I loved. When I started school I was always in trouble for talking too much and often sent to the corner. As I grew older, I felt that talking would get me into trouble so I became very conscious of what I said and by the time I was in 6th class, couldn't stand up in front of the class and read, I would stutter and the words just wouldn't come out, so the children laughed at me and called me dumb. Looking back I can't believe this happened to that bright outgoing child but it did. The thing is anything is possible in your life ... It's what you do with what happens to you that counts.

By the time I went to high school not a lot had changed. In year ten I had decided to become a hairdresser, so off I went to get myself a great salon for work experience. Which I did! Going to school the next day I was so proud of what I had achieved in getting this placement, only to be told by my careers adviser that this placement was much too good for someone like me. She was going to give it to someone that would make the most of this opportunity. Once again I was squashed. Looking back now this was a major turning point in my life. To cut a long story short I did the work experience and not only did I get the best report in our year, they offered me an apprentice in the salon, which I took. You see, at that moment in the darkest hour of my school life, I took it and said to myself. "I will do whatever it takes to prove her wrong" and now looking at what I have learnt, this is a major learning in having success in my life. It's not what happens to you, it's what you do after that that really matters.

I have had lots of ups and downs in my life but having the attitude "whatever it takes" has made me the person that I am today. 'Whatever it takes' has made the stuttering little girl into a world class trainer and speaker and successful business owner. I now work all over the country teaching people how to grow their businesses and increase profits. Staying focused is a major component to achieving success in your life and here are the daily things I do to stay focused.

- Plug into personal development CD's / books daily

- Work out what it is you want and believe you will have it (daily visualisation)

- Write down your goals and take daily action to achieving them (the action is the most important step)

- Test and measure your results

- Get a mentor or two

- Have a coach help you, someone who you feel comfortable with that will be honest and really push you when you need it, but also give you the praise when you deserve it!

- Be Grateful for what you have now

- Give lots of love for everything and everyone in your life. Celebrate the life you have now and give thanks for the life that you want and will be receiving shortly.

The biggest message I can give to you would be don't give up ... You can Be, Do and Have anything you want. You just have to want it bad enough and be willing to do "whatever it takes to make it happen" it's also getting the right information in the right order to achieve the success that others have achieved. I wish you all the success in the world and hope that my little story has helped you in your life journey.

3 Tips To Stay Focused On Your Dreams

Plug into personal development CD's / books daily and action what resonates for you

Write down your goals and take daily actions toward achieving them (the action is the most important step). Test and measure your results

Have a coach help you, someone who you feel comfortable with that will be honest and really push you when you need it, but also give you the praise when you deserve it!

About The Author

Co-founder of The Small Business Gurus, Angie is a National Business Coach, trainer and marketing guru. She has just completed her first book, The Relationship Age. She co-authored the book with social media expert Marie Smith and with contributions from other marketing experts from around the world. An accomplished author, Angie also writes articles for many business magazines. Angie's mission is to get the best information on the planet to business owners – to show them there are many simple but effective ways to approach things. Angie is passionate about helping business owners and managers achieve their goals and grow their businesses to the next level. She has worked with hundreds of businesses nationally to build their bottom line profit, increase productivity and achieve a better work-life balance.

Janet Beckers

Special Gift

To Receive your BONUS GIFT – Tips to Grow your Business, CD Series Valued @ $497 Go to: www.thesmallbusinessgurus.com and follow the link

http://www.thesmallbusinessgurus.com

Persevering with Passion.

Beatrice Burg

What motivates me to keep going when I feel like I want to give up?

"Let me tell you a little story ...

SETTING: a year four class in a small island school about 10 years ago

MAIN CHARACTER: a boy who is smaller than the others in his class. He can't read, spell or write very well but has not repeated any year levels because that is not 'education policy'. If he forgets his medication, he tries very hard to behave well, but is not very successful at that either. He has average intelligence and is enthralled by a series of horror stories called 'Goosebumps'. His one wish at school is that he will one day be able to read them for himself.

SECOND MAIN CHARACTER: this boy's teacher. No-one at the school can tell her why the boy is not learning. Her training has only taught her to work with 'middle-of-the-road' children, and she often doesn't have the time to modify the lessons so that the boy is able to finish them successfully. She tries to help him and works closely with the literacy teacher, but he doesn't learn very much in her class. She gets her daughter to put the 'Goosebumps' stories on tape so that he can listen to them, and he does – over and over again! She is grateful he is not as disruptive in her class as he was the year before."

That teacher was me - and the child was real. And he - and children like him - are what keep me going.

When I saw that face and how much he really wanted to make sense of those words on the page, I truly understood that if kids were able do something they would do it. Sure, sometimes they don't put all their effort into the task, take longer to do the work or are untidy because they have rushed to finish, but if they were able to do the work, they would, because kids don't want to fail, anymore than adults do.

So when I saw the struggle going on in that boy's face, the effort in his eyes and the tense anxiety in his hands and body, I knew ... If he could read, he would. There was something else going on that was stopping him from learning to read.

Many times in the last ten years of tutoring children, I have seen that look, that anxiety and frustration, even anger.

When a parent brought her 9 year old boy to me for tuition, I knew I had to find a way to help them. What kept me motivated and on track?

Seeing that boy struggle with almost every word on the page and not give up. Was it worth it?

"Results are out and Mitchell has achieved what he set out to do - complete and graduate from year 12 and now he also has achieved his TEE with an ATAR of 84.20. We are so proud of him as you can imagine.

You have been a part of Mitchell's journey as we all battled "the system" and overcame the hurdles big and small, careful never to lose "Mitchell" in our efforts but to cherish and nurture him along the way ever mindful of his struggle with all that lay ahead for him.

Thank you for all your help and encouragement over the years, kind words to an often stressed mother ! and your faith in Mitchell and his ability.

As Beatrice and Shirley will remember that little boy with such a low opinion of himself and his ability, now the young man who quietly said to me on his way home after his last exam "Mum, I did it". He certainly did but not without your friendship, guidance, support, kindness and caring. Thank you from the bottom of our hearts. Karen and Ric"

When I am writing pages of reports after assessments or travelling thousands of kilometres twice a year to visit clients and wonder: "what am I doing here?", that is what keeps me going - knowing I make a difference!

It's what has inspired me to search for ways of helping parents with kids struggling at school.

It's what has inspired me to educate myself in teaching dyslexic kids.

It's what has inspired me to find ways to help these kids learn.

It's my motivation to keep going.

The extra buzz comes from helping adults - who always thought they were dumb because they struggled at school.

"Jay has started wearing her filtered glasses at school. The results are FANTASTIC and her teachers are being a lot more positive as the day progresses. I think that she has seen the results with her confidence, with her reading and that speaks for itself. Sometimes I think that the teaching staff could do with some education on Dyslexia which would make things a little easier for us.

Beatrice, I just want to again thank you for everything you have done for myself and Jay. The university has converted my readings onto blue paper and organised my exam papers to be green and I get an additional 10 minutes for exams with a break after the first hour for a 10 minute break for stretching too!! So in all that is an excellent result. I still just can't believe that I have struggled for so long without help but now there is an improvement with the use of the filters already. You have helped me out so much and things are now much easier with this additional help thanks to your diagnosis. Thanks so much and I look forward in seeing you next time. Mackenzie"

That is what makes it all worth while and that is what keeps my passion strong.

Janet Beckers

3 Tips To Stay Focused On Your Dreams

Find someone, or a group, who understands your situation, and has the expert knowledge to help you make informed decisions.

Be clear on what you want as the result; write down your goal/s so you can refresh your thoughts when life gets in the way.

Be prepared to be flexible but persevere and don't let anyone denigrate what you are trying to achieve.

About The Author

Beatrice Burg is a wife, mother of two and grandmother of three. She is a teacher, who, after 25 years in the system, decided that to have children coming out of her classroom struggling to read was unacceptable. She left the education system and began tutoring students to try to help them succeed. Most made good progress, but a few still struggled - even though their knowledge and skills were now at an appropriate age level, they still confused letters and words and were not fluent at all. To her, this was 'dyslexia' - otherwise perfectly capable people having extreme difficulty with the written word.

To understand and help children with specific learning difficulties she has undertaken specialised training including: Teaching Students with Dyslexia (level 3), Certification as an Irlen Diagnostician, started an Online Classroom for remote students, registered as a Tutor with Dyslexia SPELD in Perth, Western Australia.

Her passion is to help kids learn, whatever learning difficulties they have, so that they become happy, confident adults, not limited in choice of employment, but able to choose to be and do whatever they want.

Special Gift

Subscribe to the World Wide Learning Academy. Newsletter (www.worldwidelearningacademy.com) and you will receive my eBook "Read, Spell, Write... Right?" for free when you join.

www.worldwidelearningacademy.com

Janet Beckers

Combining Mindset & Marketing for Massive results!

Belinda Jackson

As CEO of Web Chameleon, an Online Marketing services company, I've written many articles over the years on business growth and marketing topics.

However for this year's Wonderful Web Women gold book I'm writing about something more personal. I've learnt over my years in business, and now wholeheartedly believe that massive success is a result of mindset leaps AND excellent marketing. Yes, a combination of mindset leaps AND excellent marketing are necessary to achieve truly outstanding results. If you're an entrepreneur like me, then your success will be dependent on how you think as well as what you do. The marketing is important and great marketing can boost any business. In fact without great marketing, attracting and converting clients is damn hard work.

Being in the business of providing online marketing services I've seen firsthand what a difference great marketing can make to any business. But upgrading your mindset will allow you to take your business to a whole new level and will generally make your life a whole lot easier too. If you relate to any of the following thoughts, then it's time to focus some attention on your mindset.

- I have no idea how others do it, business is such a struggle for me
- I'm confused by the many options to grow my business
- I have trouble staying focused
- I tend to play small so as not to be noticed
- I constantly compare myself to others
- I'm working hard but the financial returns seem limited
- It's cheaper and easier to do things myself

I could expand significantly on this list but it will give you an indication of common mindset issues that hold entrepreneurs back from making more money and achieving greater results. If any of these statements resonate with you, what can you do?

A good friend once told me that the greatest investment I can make in my business is to invest in myself. And over the years I have invested many $$$ and countless hours in self improvement as well as investing in my business and marketing skills. How I think today and how I operate my business bears almost no comparison to how things looked several years back when I was just getting started. Below I share just 3 personal shifts that have made a difference in my life and ultimately have resulted in a more successful and profitable business. Stop comparing. Comparing only highlights your faults and holds you back, because you are focusing on other's strengths, and not your own. If you try to emulate or copy someone else you will only ever be a shadow of that person. When you are yourself, you have no competition. No one else can be the exact same person that you are. When you stop comparing, it becomes easier to step up and allow your brilliance to shine. So stop being invisible, step up and shine!

Get absolutely clear on what you want! Not what others want or expect from you, do the hard work to uncover what YOU truly want. This often takes some intense soul searching and with the help of a great coach or mentor can be a lot easier to uncover. What YOU want is important! And it will be unique to you because this is truly about you and what makes you tick. Once you are clear on what you truly want – know it, feel it, believe it and go after it! Don't do it all yourself. This is a big lesson for so many entrepreneurs. So many of us try to do it all and once our business becomes successful we believe that we must continue to do it all. The end result of this will often be working long hours for a limited financial return, and a feeling of being overburdened and 'stuck'.

Janet Beckers

Make the mindset leap and know that what is most important is that you do what you do best and what you enjoy most! Build a support team and network that allows you to do more of these things and let go of the tasks you do not enjoy or that in truth you are not the best at. This can mean bringing in help around the house, help with the book keeping or general admin assistance. It may also mean investing in self development, or a coach or mentor to work with you in achieving greater results. You will not look back. On top of the above three shifts, you will of course need to take consistent action that is focused on achieving YOUR goals and what you want. And remember great marketing makes a massive difference in attracting clients easily.

For me as CEO of Web Chameleon, what I want to achieve this year is to streamline our growing business, creating personal freedom and flexibility, including more time off, whilst still ramping up client results and our business profits.

What do you really want to achieve?

3 Tips To Stay Focused On Your Dreams

Stop Comparing - When you are yourself, you have no competition.

Get absolutely clear on what you want! - Once you are clear on what you truly want – know it, feel it, believe it and go after it!

Don't do it all yourself - Build a support team and network to help you achieve greater results!

About The Author

As CEO of Web Chameleon, Belinda Jackson is an Australian entrepreneur, who is very passionate about online marketing and business! Belinda is also a wife and mother, living and working on the beautiful east coast of Australia.

Http://wonderfulwebwomen.com

Belinda launched Web Chameleon back in 2005 and has had great success in growing the business over the years as a reputable provider of online marketing services. Web Chameleon services include everything Online Marketing ~ websites, blogs, social media, email marketing, search engine optimisation (SEO) and more.

Her vision for Web Chameleon is to support entrepreneurs, small business owners and service professionals to effectively market their business and brand online.

Contact Belinda Jackson @ Web Chameleon on 1300 697 884 in Australia or visit www.webchameleon.com to learn more.

Special Gift

http://www.webchameleon.com

Janet Beckers

What Your Mind Can Conceive You Can Achieve

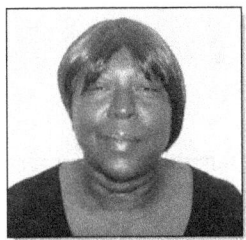

Beverley Charles

"What Your Mind Can Conceive You Can Achieve"

"What Your Mind Can Conceive You Can Achieve," is not only my favourite quote, but it is also one of my maxims for life. It is my belief that when one has a passion to accomplish a dream, it is God, Creator, or the Universe, knocking on one's door, to go forward and maximize one's potentials.

My dream is to serve humanity through teaching and counseling, and to motivate everyone who is interested in self development, and I have been keeping this dream alive from my childhood days. During my early childhood, I had the dream of being a teacher, and every day after I went home from school, I rearranged the chairs in our sitting room, pretended that there were students sitting on them, and I taught them everything I learnt in school that day. This was done throughout my elementary and middle school years. When I went to high school, the teachers saw my leadership potential, and made me peer tutor without any initial training, because they felt that I had the special gift to teach. Immediately after I graduated from high school, I was offered a teaching position at an elementary school.

My teaching vocation had officially begun; my dream became reality, and I enjoyed teaching for many, many years. I was not satisfied at just teaching at the elementary level so I entered the University of Guyana, and obtained a Bachelor's Degree in Education, majoring in the teaching of the English Language. I then began teaching English Language, in the high school.

I kept my dream of teaching and transforming lives alive, by leaving my native land, and venturing out to other Caribbean lands. I taught in Jamaica, St Lucia, and The Bahamas. As I performed my teaching duties, I spent much time helping to transform the lives of children at risk, and also being a confidant to my fellow teachers. I read many personal development books, and practised the techniques; I kept my dream of counseling alive. I earned a Master's Degree in Counseling and Psychology. I took my dream to another level.

I counseled students, teachers, parents, and other community members. I also gave voluntary service to my church community, using my teaching and counseling skills. I also dreamed of touching lives through writing a book, but I never got started. I just kept telling my family that I would write a book. In 1999, I started writing the 1st chapter, and then I parked it. I was having a fabulous life, until the global recession came and knocked me off my feet. I lost my job, and the demons of doubt, fear, anger, guilt, and self adjustment possessed me.

The self critical voice kept sending me all the negative messages you can think of - what are you going to do know? How are you going to keep your dream alive? You're done. After I recovered from the shock, I remembered that I had started writing a book, and the irony is that the title of that book is: 'How to Triumph in Life Through Change'. I immediately decided to continue writing that book, although I was going through a change that I did not welcome. As I lived one day at a time, and began accepting the change, I experienced inner peace. I decided that I would keep my dream alive, by using my experience, to motivate and teach people, how to triumph in life, through change. In the book I wrote, I demonstrated that change is inevitable; it brings out the best in us, and that it propels us to maximize our potentials. At the end of every chapter, I listed suggestions to help the readers, triumph in life through change. I have completed writing this book, but it is not published as yet.

As I reflect on what I did during my childhood days, I realize that I was applying one of the techniques in the law of attraction without knowing what the law of attraction was. What my mind conceived, I achieved. I fed my subconscious with what I wanted to create, and that energy brought my dream into manifestation. It is no coincidence that this opportunity has presented itself for me to be a co author in

Janet Beckers

this book. 'What your mind can conceive, you can achieve.' Here I am, keeping my dream alive, being an inspiration to others, while having my own dream of being a published author, becomes a reality.

3 Tips To Stay Focused On Your Dreams

Write down your dream in a place where you can see it daily.

Create a mind movie of your dream; see it being realized. Keep focused, and be prepared to encounter challenges.

Every day take at least one action to keep your dream alive, and believe with all your heart, that what your mind can conceive, you can achieve.

About The Author

Beverley Charles, co-author of this, her first prestigious publication, is small in stature, but large in heart, spirit, mind and substance. She is admired for her courage, integrity, tenacity of purpose, determination, and passion for those activities in which she shares her time, talent, and treasure. She has a flair for writing articles on personal development, and some of those articles have been published in 'Ezine Articles'.

Beverley Charles is a teacher and guidance counselor, with a Bachelor's Degree in Education, and a Master's Degree in Counseling and Psychology. The wisdom, counsel, and knowledge disseminated in her chapter, bare testimony to her personal experience and paths she traveled as she kept her dream alive.

Through Wonderful Web Women, she has now emerged as co-author of an inspiring text in which she motivates the readers to keep their dreams alive, despite the odds which they encounter.

She is also a member of the Messenger Book Collective, and will be releasing her first 32 page mini e-book, in which she continues to motivate, and give hope to her readers, so that they can triumph in life through change.

http://www.bevsmind.blogspot.com

A Special Gift For You

If you're like me (it's Janet speaking here), when you set your goals and plan how to achieve your dreams you can feel exhausted before you even start taking action on what you have planned!

Over the years I have developed a 3 step process I use at the beginning of every year and then repeat whenever I feel my focus getting blury. Let's face it, even the most motivated and organised of us feels overwhelmed at times.

The 3 Step, Get Focused Kick Start Strategy

In this free training delivered to your inbox step-by-step, you will Discover:

- The missing step very few people do when setting goals that turn overwhelm into confidence and self-belief.

- A fun process you can involve your family, staff and partners in that guarantees their ongoing support of your dreams.

- A simple step to keep your key dreams in focus at all times

- The Power of a "Celebration Box" and how to use it to keep you focused on your dreams

To claim your free gift, **valued at $147,** plus the bonus digital version of The Power of 100 Book to download to your computer and digital book reading gadgets, simply visit:

www.ThePowerof100Book.com and register now.

Cheers

Janet Beckers

Love Stops Time And Starts Eternity But How Do We Get It Right?

Buzz McCarthy, PhDC

Love stops time ... and starts eternity

Relationships are the places of the greatest joy and also the greatest pain. Joy because there is nothing to equal a deeply intimate relationship; pain because too many people are in a relationship by default and have little idea how to design their ultimate relationship or how to stay in their relationship vision and live in a state of love and acceptance. There are strategies for all this; just as there are strategies to be wealthy and healthy. To create a relationship by design there are some basic things you must do. Firstly you need to clear any beliefs that hold you back - and there will be some powerful ones in there such as "There's no-one out there for me" or "I'm not pretty/intelligent/rich/good enough etc to attract the mate I want". Secondly it is vital that you are absolutely clear on your values and your boundaries.

I'm a firm believer in boundaries: your absolute must's and absolute must never's - and if you have them in place you can toss rules out the window. Rules are only there to make someone else wrong so they don't add a lot to a relationship! It's like "do you want to be right or do you want to be in the relationship??" And the third thing is the need to be able to access a state of love - whether your beloved is in your life or not!

State is the single most important skill in the world. It is the way you greet the day each morning, the way you navigate yourself through your day and the way you go to bed each night. It is the habits you form and it is vital because it is your habits that become your personality. To be in a loving state you must focus on joy, on how you would feel to be in a loving relationship, of how good it feels to give, to share, to support and nurture a friend or relationship, and to be in a state of gratitude as much as you possibly can. I believe joy is our natural state and that everyone deserves to love and be loved. It doesn't take much but because most of us are dabblers we don't necessarily get enough of it or some of the other things that make life a masterpiece. Your radiance is what attracts your mate. If you are not yet in the relationship of your dreams you must learn to be in a state of love on a regular basis, especially in the midst of a busy life. You don't want to miss out on the relationship of your dreams, do you??

Learning how to love, enjoying the dating game and deciding what you want, creating a vision and being committed to it will give you a totally different outcome and hopefully the love of your life. And if you are in your ultimate relationship, staying loving and giving and not needing to be right will pave the way for long term relationship success. For both groups of people, mastering state is key to not just their relationship success but to their life success. So here's the deal. Mastery depends on your state - your physical, emotional and mental state, and the state you have settled to living in. Are you committed to "outstanding", or is "good" good enough? The strange thing is that they are so close. It's like the guy climbing the mountain ... the last 2 yards are the hardest, but they are nothing after all the preparation and the amount of mountain already scaled.

I believe there is only a couple of millimetres between good or even excellent, and outstanding, and the thing that will get you there, to the top, to the outstanding, to the things you decide to have, to want, to accept, the feelings you want, the whatever it is you desire is your state. So mastering your state is the key to the kingdom. And in the dating and romance game, it's the key to your heart and the heart and soul of your beloved. In what some people term the Good Old Days, people stayed with each other for a lifetime. Now we have several lifetimes in the one. We not only have several different jobs, statistically we have at least three different careers in a job life. So we don't stay with each other for a lifetime unless it's what we want or are too scared to leave. And if we do stay together then we need strategies for many things - communication, finances, conflict resolution, managing children, managing careers, managing the work-life balance and especially love. They say love conquers all, and it certainly does go a long long way.

To stay in a state of love and nurture a long term relationship or a dream to be in one there are some things you can do and focus on on a regular basis:

1. What is great is always available to us. So is what is wrong. Choosing to focus first on what is great will give you a completely different experience of life. Catch yourself when you are focussed on the bad bits and decide to focus on creating more joy for you or both of you.

2. Having someone's attention is a rare commodity these days. When your partner wants to speak to you about something important there are two things you must do. The first is to open your heart and listen, even if you are angry or hurt. The second is to allow them the space and freedom to communicate without interruption. When they are finished, ask them if there is something they want you to do or if they just wanted you to listen.

3. You will never solve a problem when you are in the energy of a problem. It increases in magnitude and emotion the more you focus on it. When you simply can't see a way ahead, you must shift gear to find a solution if you want a positive result. Focus instead on what you really want and create a strategy to make it happen. Remember there is no rainbow without a storm so learn to deal with the storms so you can really enjoy the rainbows.

When you have challenges, staying in the energy of love will ultimately mean a quicker resolution. You fell in love with this person when you had your heart open, so open it again, focus on what's good, what's working and what you love about them. A great way to do this is to create a list of Magic Moments you have had together to re-engage your feelings of love. To conclude, if you're not in a relationship, get ready for one by being focused on what you want, not what you don't want. Examine your past roadblocks and if necessary see someone to help you clear them. Create a clear vision of what you want, not just for yourself, but a vision of the relationship. And do your very best to stay in the energy of what you want. Have a big enough "why" - the emotional pull and the universe will help you out with the "how". If you are in the relationship you want for the long haul, treasure your partner, choose to be in the relationship rather than be right, give more than you thought was possible, and be full of gratitude for having someone to love and be loved by.

3 Tips To Stay Focused On Your Dreams

Decide to love. Decide to radiate beautiful energy. That is the attractor factor so enjoy the consequences! Your focus is vital, your state is vital, and so is a smile.

Decide to live in the present moment. It is the now that we can be joyful in, and it is the now that is important if we are to create a tomorrow that is filled with all the things we deeply desire.

Never give up on a dream! Whatever it is, make it happen ... or relax and enjoy life waiting for it to happen ... it will, so long as you never give up on that dream.

About The Author

Buzz McCarthy, PhDc is a Relationship Specialist offering personal consulting to singles and couples, especially those looking to either find or leave an intimate relationship. Her company Ultimate Relationships Pty Ltd runs relationship workshops and Buzz offers several lively topics to clients wanting a speaker at their functions. Buzz also hosts a 10 day annual event for women at her beautiful villa in the Tuscan hills. For 30 years she has been passionate about personal growth and choices that empower others to make more compelling decisions in their lives.

Buzz has a background in politics, ASIO, adventure travel and running her own businesses. Over the past three decades she has studied with the world's leading teachers and has a large tool-box of change skills including NLP, Hypnotherapy and Counselling.

Janet Beckers

In 2011 she will be awarded her PhD in Psychoneurology, a cutting edge qualification which, in practical terms, takes her clients away from the energy of a problem to the energy of a solution. This is a unique approach to change. Buzz has travelled the world for 15 years with Anthony Robbins, for whom she is an elite Trainer. She is masterful with her teaching and coaching around intimate relationships.

Special Gift

If you contact Ultimate Relationships via this publication you will be offered a 40% discount on our Ultimate Relationships Discovery Workshop on 9-10 April 2011 in Melbourne. If you would like a personal consultation, the first one will be complimentary.

www.UltimateRelationships.com

Until I Left High School I Thought My Name Was "Dont Be Stupid"

Candice Hazeltine

I remember looking for a new car when I was 18 and the salesman saw me looking at a new Honda S2000 and actually asked if I'd like to test drive it, I was wearing my Kmart uniform and the car was a lovely $80,000. My first response was, "no I can't afford that", which clearly was not what he asked, so he asked again "would you like to drive it?". I stared at him shocked and he said, "come on, I'm bored let's go".

We got out on an open, quiet road and he said "well give it some" I got that Honda up to 180kmh in 3rd gear, the roof was down it was amazing! What a thrill, when I returned to work I was useless, and spent a whole 4hr shift plotting how I could afford this car. I remember clearly calculating if I put $150 away a week it would take me 10yrs to afford it! Being 18 and working 4 jobs, I wasn't really interested in much more than the fun of the coming weekend.

Janet Beckers

There are some very important points in this story. The Honda, my dream is what encouraged me to start developing some goals of saving to buy it. My vision however was not strong enough to carry me to my end goal of owning it. The biggest reason being 10 years was unrealistic it didn't seem possible. Today I realize had I had support via a network, motivation via a goal timeline, I would have found it easier. If my desire burned strong enough for my goal I would have discovered along the way different tools to speed up those 10yrs. It can be incredibly easy to get off track, loose motivation and be distracted. Why? We are human. We are influenced by our surroundings and our environment. As humans 90% of our conditioning is developed by the age of 7. Our values, beliefs and self image impact our mindset. This then impacts our behaviors and inevitably our results. Have you ever noticed when things are going really good sometimes shit hits the fan? It's a test. When this happens the question I ask myself is why? Why do you want it, Why is it important to you? Why do you believe in it? Why will you stand up and fight for it? If you know this and feel it at the very core of your being you will have the strength to move forward and the power to overcome road blocks. Every setback has its lesson and it's your job to get the lesson and move forward..

I can still hear my teachers' voices from high school, "don't be stupid"! I've had many people tell me, "it can't be done" or "that's a stupid idea" or my favourite "that will never work". Lucky I was always too busy doing it to listen. Be your biggest fan. What would you be saying to that person you really want to date, to that client you really want to score or at that job interview you've been dying to get? Is what you're saying to others about you congruent to what you say to yourself in your mind? Happiness comes when what you think, say and do are in alignment. Personally I have just spent the last 4 years operating a business I started from scratch, achieving what I should have achieved in 18 months and it has been an extremely valuable lesson costing me time and money. I hope you can take some of my personal experience and use it to achieve your goals faster. After all, deep down at the core of what we really want as humans is to have it all. Have everything we want and for that to be possible we need to leverage ourselves as best and fast as possible to have endless resources of time and money.

3 Tips To Stay Focused On Your Dreams

Inspirational Quotes are a huge part of my life. Find some that really resonate with you and keep them close by. I also find a lot of inspiration in my mentors whether it is in person or via a video or DVD, music and movies.

Exercise - Is essential for the mind, body and soul. Do something daily that gets your blood moving to deliver much needed oxygen and endorphins throughout your body. Particularly important if your work is not physical. I cannot stress how important exercise has been in my life. It makes me feel fit and amazing. It removes guilt around anything I want to eat or wear. It builds self esteem which builds character and resilience.

My reason why – What is your reason for doing what you are doing? What is the essence of your goals and dreams? Know it, see it in your mind and understand it. Give your reason why power by visualizing it. Your reason why should be felt in your gut, in your heart at the very core of your being. If you don't feel it there it's not yet perfected. It hasn't yet the power and emotion behind it to be strong enough to make you a raging success. It has taken me 5 years to discover my reason why. So if you don't know it perfectly just yet keep going you will find each other.

About The Author

Candice was born October 1981. Leaving high school at 17 to earn money resulted in a string of low paying jobs across many industries. Her serious interests in business started to develop at 18 where she begun educating herself on how to operate one. She embarked on her first solo business venture at 25. Starting a cleaning agency from scratch then selling it four years later to start an international social media consulting company. Having invested more than $100,000 in her education to date, Candice does not hold a degree or any training Certificate over a Certificate III. Candice invests her profits into property and businesses, as a result has profited

Janet Beckers

more than $230,000 in the last 2 years from following her own strategies. Her new Social Media Consultancy provides a very unique service to businesses. Incorporating extensive planning and strategy into a dynamic online presence. Tipped to be Australia's next biggest Social Media Guru her love and passion for business is the driving force behind this fast growing company. If you're interested in following Candice or receiving Free Regular Social Media Tips for business or personal use you're invited to join us through facebook via Sizzling Social Media

Special Gift

7 Big Social Media Mistakes You Must Know and a Private Selection of Candice's Favourtie. Quotes, Movies and Songs. Please visit
http://www.facebook.com/pages/Sizzling-Social-Media

http://www.facebook.com/pages/Sizzling-Social-Media

Awaken the possibility of freedom , and empowerment for the mind and body .

Carol Campbell

It wasn't a sudden earth shattering moment. More a gradual dawning that maybe, just maybe I could have another career I could do something else.

You see I was born into a very academic family and I wasn't. They all ran around living in their heads and I was from my heart. I thought something was wrong with me and I struggled to find where I belonged. Because I didn't make university, my parents, who were both doctors sent me to nursing. It took me 20 years to realise I didn't have to do this, I was capable of something different. That's when my journey to freedom and empowerment began. I attended college and studied complimentary therapies, a wonderful decision. As in this course I started meeting like minded people and I started achieving really good results. My confidence started to grow, and I found a place where I felt I belonged. Spurred on by this new found direction I further developed my intuitive and spiritual side. I was now starting to think for myself.On completion of my course, I thought I am going to use these skills and serve the community. It was then I decided that I would start my own business. The college had given me a start on business knowledge but I needed more so I enrolled in a TAFE business course. Another wonderful decision because it was through this course I met a wonderful lady who introduced me to business networking. I discovered I was good at networking and built a very successful massage practise. I am also very passionate about women's health issues especially post menopausal women. This is a time many women feel they have hit the end of their productive life and physical and emotional decline is inevitable. This perception couldn't be more wrong. This can be a time of wonderful rejuvenation where women are just hitting their stride. So to help women discover how magical this journey to seniors years can be, I run seminars focusing on the benefits and wisdom of the menopausal years.

The 3 things that I have gleamed from this journey are: Never ever give up … be persistent, you never know how close you may be to having a breakthrough to a challenge you may be facing. Capitalise on your strengths and manage your weaknesses. You are not going to be able to do it all. Seek support and assistance for the areas in your business you don't enjoy or lack ability.

Have some form of a plan, with realistic goals. This will help and guide you when you have to make major decisions. If you loose your direction it will help you refocus and find your way.

Take good care of your physical and emotional health. Without wellness you will not be able to do any of the above. This may mean you seek the assistance of a health and wellness coach.

3 Tips To Stay Focused On Your Dreams

Write daily in a journal, it gives an outlet to express all your feelings . And some times we don't always see how we have changed over time . By reading back on our entries we may find a feeling or challenge that was painful or hard to manage is no longer a problem . But without going back over how we were feeling we would never have realised the subtle change that has occurred.

Put together a vision board, it will keep you on track and show you what you have achieved over time.

Join a business networking group, that will give you a team of people around you who can support, encourage and celebrate with you.

About The Author

Registered Nurse, Massage Therapist, Counsellor, inspirational motivational speaker and educator ... Carol started off her career in the wonderful world of nursing where she worked all over Sydney and then travelled the world with her nursing. All up Carol enjoyed 30 years in this job.

Seven years ago Carol decided to leave the nursing profession and studied massage as she wanted to still work with people and in a health related industry .Carol quickly established a very successful massage practice.

Women's health is also a passion for carol, especially women going through the menopause, a time of tremendous potential for women to do what they always wanted or to discover for the first time who they really are. Carol runs seminars to assist women to find and tap into this wonderful period of expansion and change.

Today Carol has her massage practice and runs her seminars from a wellness centre on the central coast .

Special Gift

For any further information on my massage or women's health seminars please don't hesitate to contact me on 0418433152. And, as a very special gift to all who read my chapter I am offering a 1/2hr complimentary massage, and/or 1/2hr complimentary health and wellness interview.

Contact me at lovelife@tpg.com.au. Happy Journeys My Friends.

Janet Beckers

How Franchising motivated me to create a dream lifestyle

Carolyn Dufton

Now let me be the first person to say that franchising is just not for everyone. It is not the "be all and the end all" of business; it is not a get rich quick scheme; and if executed professionally it is not a "walk away" business. However what franchising can offer is; Income, Flexibility, Control over a proven system. Distribution of product.

Why I chose franchising

I arrived in Australia in 1987 from The UK with a husband, toddler a trunk containing our worldly goods and a strong desire to live in "the lucky country". Some 24 years on, I have two grown up daughters who are both launching successful careers, the same wonderful husband, and two multi million homes, one a beach house on the water and the other a large beautiful home on acres. I can honestly say that franchising helped me create our current wonderful lifestyle. In 1988 I started a business called Hire for Baby. The concept of hiring baby equipment was new in those days and I was marketing not just a business but a concept in itself. To add to the challenge, as we women love to do, I had our second child in April 1989. I liked to keep the theme of "baby" close to the heart. The business grew and my client base expanded dramatically to the point where it was impossible to manage the business singlehandedly. Hubby was delivering baby equipment enroute to work and on his way home, but we couldn't keep up with the high level of service we insisted on providing our clients. We decided to try agents working in different areas, but none were truly committed to the business as I was.

The frustration of not being able to find a solution to a seamless business expansion motivated me to pursue every possible angle for delivering the high level of customer service we were renowned for.

One night in 1991 I woke up with a start with the realisation that the only way to expand the business successfully was to franchise. In those days, franchise advice was not easily available but I found a friendly lawyer and he and I worked into the night … literally, to build the agreement, whilst my husband and I thrashed the business model out. A process I would not recommend to anyone! In 1992 I sold my first Sydney franchise and continued to grow in NSW. I wanted to expand into Victoria but found myself procrastinating. The impetus came when my husband quit his Sydney position and decided to go out on business for himself. We had just built a house and had a substantial mortgage so this was a scary proposition. I realised that the expansion interstate now had to happen … and quickly.

Within the month I had four new Melbourne franchisees arrive for training. (brilliant girls too!) Isn't it amazing what you can achieve when there's a "real need" as a motivation? With self motivated franchisees who were as crazy about the business as I was, the company thrived and the franchise network grew through word of mouth referrals. We had thousands of satisfied clients many who became franchisees themselves. As a franchisor I needed to stay constantly motivated and positive in order to motivate my franchisees. I found the most useful strategy was to read motivational material over breakfast. The kids had gone off on the school bus and hubby was off at work so I had quiet time. I used to get so motivated by the reading material that I would end up abandoning my breakfast and dashing off to implement the new idea I had just had. I was then fired up for the day and ready to support my franchisees in every way. Then in 1998 with 25 franchisees on board; I was approached by a large company with nursery equipment interests, who offered to buy Hire for Baby for a large sum of money. I felt that the company culture we had painstakingly developed would not be continued under their direction and so I declined. I decided to approach a Franchisee who had always shown leadership skills and a love for the business and The Franchisees, and they bought it in June

Janet Beckers

1998. The day after the sale, I walked into the bank and said "I'd like to pay my mortgage off please." What an amazing feeling that was. Now that's a process which I can highly recommend!

The week after this we visited our favourite holiday town and bought a small cottage as a weekender. I found that with my new found freedom I really missed helping others in business. Supporting franchisees had been something I had chosen to do every day in my Franchisor life. So I offered my services as a local business mentor and did and still enjoy doing voluntary work in this area. In the mentoring arena I was always known as 'The Franchising Lady' and was constantly teamed with businesses that had franchising aspirations. This continued for years.

Realising that there was a real need in my geographic area for a franchising advisor, I embarked upon a formal qualification in franchising to cement my practical knowledge and experience. Franchisingplus began in 2007 as a 'holistic' franchising consultancy. My belief is that franchising should provide a win-win situation for Franchisee and Franchisor. Consulting work has given me flexibility with work hours and location. I now often work from our beautiful waterside home. www.hawksnestboathouse.com

Our little cottage was sold to fund the purchase of a piece of waterfront land which we built our dream holiday house on. I cannot imagine having had the capital injection to do this without having franchised and then selling the network. I have found enormous satisfaction in providing responsible caring advice to all participants in the franchising sector helping to create responsible new franchise systems and assisting Franchisors with the daily challenges they face. You owe it to yourself to explore franchising. For some business owners, franchising a business may seem like a terrifying idea. It is something that should not be done lightly BUT for those business owners who have a great business, particularly those who have a product, NOT franchising the business could be the biggest mistake you ever made. With an honest appraisal and support from someone like myself, you owe it to yourself to at least explore the franchise potential in your business. No excuses not to now …

To get you started, I'm offering my 3 part CD set called "discover your franchising potential", normally sold for $97; for only $20 AUD to cover postage within Australia. Remember the "thinking" about something is usually harder than the "doing". Don't procrastinate. Procrastination costs money and achieves nothing.

The Power of 100

3 Tips To Stay Focused On Your Dreams

Creating a clear goal with a strong "why I need to do this" will motivate you big time.

By motivating others you will motivate yourself.

Use adversity as a motivational tool. It is extremely powerful and effective.

About The Author

In 1988 Carolyn Dufton started a business from conception and grew it to 25 franchises in 6 years before selling to one of her franchisees. That franchise network is still going strong after 20 years with a total of 60+ franchises around Australia. Carolyn is now a highly respected franchising consultant. She understands all aspects of franchising and has broad based small business knowledge.

The team at franchisingplus provide advice on all aspects of franchising. www.franchisingplus.com.au Carolyn's passion is helping business owners to identify and nurture their franchising potential.

Special Gift

To get you started, I'm offering my 3 part CD set called "discover your franchising potential", normally sold for $97; for only $20 AUD to cover postage within Australia.

http://www.franchisingplus.com.au   www.hawksnestboathouse.com

Janet Beckers

Focusing On The Love In My Life

Cassie Grant

FOCUSING ON THE LOVE IN MY LIFE ... From the age of 5 years, the constant love in my life has always been my horses - they have been true companions. A significant changing point in my life was when I was told that I would never "make it ... after all you're a woman and (as such) people will never take you seriously." I 'felt' those words for a long time. Horses have always been there for me whilst many friends and clients have come and gone. The strongest desire I have is creating the most amazing relationship with my horses and helping others to experience the same. The amazing part of the horse/rider relationship is that the horse expects and wants you to act as the leader. The results I see include the expansion of confidence and a most amazing rekindling of the rider's relationship with their horse, a relationship that dreams are made of.

Seeing these results and hearing how this experience makes them feel, is what keeps my focus. A dream I share with Mr Pat Parelli, is that all horse owners worldwide reach at least level 1 in his program. Parelli's Natural Horsemanship Method is presented at the World Horsemanship Summits.

The Power of 100

I have worn many hats and some of them I still wear at different times: mental health practitioner, health professional, fitness leader, remedial therapist, NLP coach and at the time of writing, a Parelli (level 3) graduate and soon to be certified level 4. The results I have experienced as an 'ongoing student of the horse' keeps me believing in the reality of becoming an Artisan within My Horse world. The results I have experienced, and the success I have witnessed in others is the proof – it works! Those fearful riders who had completely lost all confidence in their abilities, now proudly and joyfully ride again.

This has given me a platform from which to launch my personal/professional ambitions of creating a better horse/rider world. My life has been filled with personal development and business and wealth development courses. I also work at maintaining both physical and mental good health via meditation, exercise, healthy foods and good company.

Meditation makes me feel special. I feel they are pertinent to me and my goals. Feedback is invaluable to me and it is constantly helping me to see myself and where I want to be.

When I work as a nurse my dream becomes intensified. This encourages me to keep right on heading toward my goals. One of the first personal development courses I attended was called "Your Mind and You". It focused me and proved that I could 'program' myself to get the results I desire. The more personal development courses I attend, the more I find myself developing into a strong and independent person with clear solid boundaries and ethics.

This is integral in developing real and lasting human relationships. My Horses always come first as a 'conscious choice' with which I have no complaints. I am also developing myself through Spiritual Coaching – a process which has given me immeasurable tools for keeping myself balanced and focused.

The learnt techniques help me cope in a vast range of situations. For example; surrendering to the universal consciousness/higher self. I am certain that emotions are an indicator of how close or far away one is from one's real/true self and amazed at the magnetism of spiritual coaching. Every step I take feels like a lesson that has been especially designed for me. "We are what we think we are". If you aren't aware of what you're thinking you can never really be in control of your emotions, decisions and goals. Instead, fear and anxiety could be in control, halting progress and dissolving dreams. As I work at becoming more and more aware of my thoughts and how much they are a part of me, I realise how ingrained these thought patterns/behaviours are and that they require regular attention to facilitate change.

Tips for Horse Lovers

That dream you have, can be reality It is possible to discover 'Secrets to Horses' and learn a most satisfying way of communication with them.

It's a journey you will never forget and it will certainly change the way you react to issues in your life. Believe in yourself. If at first you don't feel it, fake it and the rest will follow on ... Learn to follow your gut-feeling. Learn to 'go with the flow' and focus on outcomes. Always be the Student, be open to the new, be patient. Keep your focus even when everything seems unsure. Cultivate supportive, like-minded friends to encourage you to make your dreams a reality. It's ok to not know what you are doing - neither did most people when they started. It is possible to learn the skills and tools to develop a great horse/rider relationship. Results can be immediate but it's not the fast path. Be open to change – enjoy the tension of waiting. The horse is truly the most remarkable and magnificent animal on this earth, so let's learn how to communicate with them in the most effective and dignified/kind way, and have the most rewarding relationship/bond with your significant other, your horse.

3 Tips To Stay Focused On Your Dreams

1. Believe in yourself, we need to feel great about being ourselves. Just start impressing you and letting you become the person you admire most.

2. Learn to follow gut feel. It's there for a reason, it can help you if you let it. Once you trust it it becomes your indicator.

3. Learn to go with the flow.

About The Author

Sort of funny because those who know me know I don't talk about myself, my dreams and my relationship with the horses much and if I do it is the short version. Except for my close friends. They know ... I had worked in the horse industry in my early working life, been self-employed in the horse industry for the past 13 years, being into horses for the past 35 years. Qualified and experienced as a Horse Stud Manager. I went to the UK to study with the best doing some British horse society qualifications. I am a Horse Safe Australia Senior Instructor. I trained to become a nurse as a backup to my horse career. I competed in the eventing scene until a guy I knew showed me a basic Parelli technique. The reaction from my horse in that moment set me on my journey to become a student of the horse. I immersed myself in Parellis' levels program attaining level 3 in early 2000 and now finishing my level 4. It is my plan to develop Unity and True Unity teaching internationally and eventually develop myself as an artisan. My horsemanship teaching has evolved as has my commitment to promoting Barefoot for soundness. Helping people maintain their horses in a way that promotes optimum performance and health. I am teaching people a skill for life, I ride and play as much as I can on my 3 horses. My focus is dressage-high level animal training and my passion is ranch roping the softest style of horsemanship with purpose I know. The aim is producing all-rounder horses with a velvety soft mouth and manoeuvrability. I have worked as a health professional for almost 20 years. Health and fitness for mind body and soul have always been high on my priority list. I am developing a new program with my team mates to help people on their journey with their horses. Using the horse as a tool to pull you through the Vortex. The personal development that has shaped my life. My life has been full of opportunity that has shaped my life. My horse was the first major purchase as an adult.

Special Gift

The Offer to readers of this book ...

- If you are a true horse lover and want to discover the secrets to horses How to communicate with them in a way that creates a life changing bond.

- If you have ever imagined riding a real horse Barefoot Bareback and Bridleless.

- If you want to experience the Natural Equine Advantage If you need more from your learning experience.

- If you need understanding and help form a communication specialist.

- If you want horsemanship from the perspective of a health professional and true horse Lover.

Janet Beckers

- If you dream of the ultimate horse/human relationship.

The first 100 people to respond to my chapter can attend my clinics either in Australia or the USA (and who knows where I will get to). Just tell me in email why you think it would be great for you to attend a clinic with me. How much you value your life with or without horses. What health and happiness mean to you. And what your dreams are. Non-horsey people have the opportunity to experience my service as a health practitioner. I offer a full makeover to help you keep your focus. And get the most out of your life to help keep your Focus. If you are a horse lover with diagnosed Mental Health issues you have the opportunity to work with open minded health practitioners who may be the change you have been searching for. Make contact to be involved in our new programs. Please note the programs we offer are interactive and require commitment to a process. We will need your values and your dreams to be part of your story.

http://www.cassigrant.com   http://www.remedialtherapies.com

Giving Birth To A Dream

Cath Resnick

I have always been a passionate dreamer

Like many entrepreneurs, I love playing with possibilities, contemplating "what ifs" and seeing opportunities where none existed before.

Visioning the world as it might be, rather than as it is.

There never seems to be a day when I don't come up with some great new idea. As a child, I used to drive my mum and teachers crazy with questions – why are things this way, and not that way? Seemingly impossible questions to answer if you think 'inside the box', and impossible questions to ignore, if you live outside of it! And I certainly dwelled outside the box.

I didn't see the world as others did. I didn't understand many of the cultural assumptions that were embedded in the psyche of the isolated capital city of Perth where I grew up. The white Australia policy was still legally in force when I was a young child, and culturally still very present as I grew up. On the one hand teachers and family members were praising the bravery of those who saved the Jews from the horrors of the Nazi gas chambers, and in the same breath they would be telling the "boat people" refugees from Vietnam and Cambodia to "go back where you came from!"

It never made any sense to me then as a child, and it still doesn't today! I dreamt of a much different world ... as so many entrepreneurs do.

So what happens? Why don't more of our dreams get realised?

In part, it seems that cultural influences are very powerful forces ... and the need to belong is more powerful still. This can lead us to act in ways that are not always congruent with who we know ourselves to be.

So, perhaps not unusually, I tried to follow a 'traditional' career path, but ended up having 15 jobs by the time I was 23. Later I became involved in numerous community organisations and a few small business start ups.

Over the course of subsequent years, however, I began noticing distinct patterns. I would fully engage in things I felt passionately about, and that were congruent with my beliefs and ethics, I was always learning something new, and chose areas where I had a high level of autonomy. Then, once a project, community group or business was established, or once I had learned all there was to know I became bored ... my mind started to wander ... I wanted out, psychologically speaking, I would be looking for an escape.

How many entrepreneurs do you know, also exhibit this tendency?

As a therapist and coach I can say it represents many of them.

For entrepreneurs, thinking outside the box is necessary. Having vision, passion and drive are critical. Being autonomous is fundamental. But, alongside these strengths, come a few challenges as well.

Being able to have and to hold the 'big vision' often means a reluctance to deal with the fine detail.

Passion and drive are great, in so far as you are replenished physically and emotionally, and you haven't had too many set-backs that left you depleted.

Autonomy is fine whilst your business is in its early stages, but how willing are you to empower others to carry on your own vision as your business grows? Do you become a micromanaging tyrant, believing no one can do the job as well as you?

Then there is the "Bright Shiny Object Syndrome". Entrepreneurs see opportunity everywhere. Remaining focussed is probably the biggest challenge for those with an entrepreneurial character.

So how can an entrepreneur stay motivated AND stay focussed at the same time?

Well, it is a bit like a romance. Sometimes, as entrepreneurs, we are 'checking the business out' to see if it is 'the one'. We may find ourselves unsatisfied, looking around, unfocussed. And then one day, we (hopefully) meet our 'soul mate' - the business that is most congruent with who we are, and what we want to achieve.

We realise that if we want to keep our soul mate for the long term, there are some details that need attention – like doing the things they most want (even if we don't), meeting the parents, and honouring anniversaries. These are the foundations of our future – the structure that supports the ongoing relationship – the systems, processes, quality management and compliance required to take our relationship to the next level.

Perhaps we lose some autonomy, but we gain so much more.

Above all, we understand that we must respect our relationship – and not flirt with every opportunity that comes along. Nothing damages the heart of a relationship so completely as being unfaithful. Nothing will damage your business more either. With each opportunity or choice that arises, ask yourself the question: "Will this take me closer too, or further away from my goal?"

Whilst love and passion keep us going in the beginning – the 'in love' feeling wanes in time. What then? How do we then stay focussed, especially when things get tough?

What it takes then is a commitment to the relationship and to the future ... and it is the same in business.

In business, commitment is focus, and focus is simply a combination of vision and Discipline! Yes, that dirty little 'D' word that makes most entrepreneurs I know run away and scream.

It seems many of us associate discipline with a military regime, the prison of living 'inside the box', or perhaps worse yet – like a domineering non-negotiable parent. It can be hard to break the culturally embedded association. But break it we must, if we are to ever fully give birth to and realise our dreams.

There is no escaping it. At some point, succeeding in business simply requires discipline – self discipline. It is the commitment we make in our relationship with our business. It provides a safe, nurturing, consistent environment – a structure, a form and a process.

Discipline is the womb that offers the possibility of giving birth to a healthy dream. It is, in fact, what creates true value in our business.

And being disciplined and staying disciplined requires self knowledge. Knowing who you are, what you are about, what motivates you, what scares you, what you are, and are not prepared to do. If your personal and business values are not aligned, there will be an ongoing internal conflict ... and focus will be inevitably be the casualty.

It is only with self knowledge and the discipline to do what is necessary, that entrepreneurs can realise the full potential of, and give birth to their dreams.

3 Tips To Stay Focused On Your Dreams

1. Be honest with yourself and choose only business enterprises or business goals that are congruent with you, or who you wish to become.

2. Reconnect with your vision and purpose on a daily basis. Keep asking yourself the question "Is this (opportunity/activity/task) taking me closer to, or further away from my goal?"

3. Commit to your business, as you would your soul mate. You may not always feel 'in love', but working through the difficult times together, provides the foundation of a deeper and more

sustainable future. times together, provides the foundation of a deeper and more sustainable future.

About The Author

Founder and host of 'The Feminine Entrepreneur', Cath Resnick, is a woman on a mission to prove it is possible to create social benefit & change as an entrepreneur whilst enjoying family, good health, fun & financial security.

She is a passionate entrepreneur, psychotherapist and coach, with a background of over 20 years owning or running businesses and community organisations. With a talent for identifying emerging trends and opportunities, Cath is adept at keeping organisations at the forefront of industry best practice through innovative ideas and programs.

Her psychological expertise and unique understanding of the strengths and transformations that women undertake throughout their lives, creates a rare and insightful environment for the support and development of women entrepreneurs. She continues to use entrepreneurial skills to drive social causes and engage corporations to support social ventures.

Her professional qualifications include a Graduate Diploma in Analytic Psychotherapy, a Certificate IV in Assessment and Workplace Training, and a Certificate in Small Business Management. She is a member of the Psychotherapists & Counsellors Association of WA, Psychotherapists & Counsellors Federation of Australia Register No: 21049, The Australian Women's Mentoring Network, The Rotary Club of Crawley, and has numerous other associations and affiliations.

Special Gift

To access additional resources and the latest information for women entrepreneurs, please visit http://www.thefeminineentrepreneur.com.

Become a member of our free community, and you can also receive a $100 gift voucher redeemable for any live workshop or coaching session. Simply email info@thefeminineentrepreneur.com , place "The Power of 100" in the subject line, mention this offer, and we will email the voucher/discount code to you.

Janet Beckers

My $1 Million Dollar Debt Initiated The Realisation Of My Dream ...

Charly Leetham

A very quick history lesson before I start ...

It's 2003 and I'm at that point in my career where I've had enough! Enough of working long hours, admittedly for GOOD pay, but not honouring myself or being able to spend quality time with my family. It's definitely time for change! Having just returned from a three week holiday, where all we did was travel and enjoy ourselves as a family ... I KNEW I was doing it wrong and that I needed to change my life ... the question was how? Funny how "The Universe Provides" when you start asking for help ... within 6 months of making the decision that it was time to change, we (my husband and I) had bought into a franchise retail business and were having a really great time.

It was our first real expedition into small business ownership and retail at the same time (yep, neither of us had worked in retail, ever). Things were looking good - our stores were performing in the Top 5 Stores for the Franchise nationally, and the turnover was excellent. Within 18 months, we owned 3 stores and were managing a 4th on behalf of the franchisor however, the numbers just weren't stacking up. Each month we posted a loss, despite being some of the top performing stores in Australia, and no amount of discourse with the franchisor regarding this disparity was reaping any reward. The reality of providing a niche product which quickly became a commodity item had far reaching effects on our bottom line which, when coupled with the high rents in major centres meant that the business model was not sustainable. We made plans to exit the franchise - but we weren't quick enough. By the time we 'walked away' from the business (in June 2007), we were in debt to the tune of $1 million. By selling our investment property and other assets, we reduced this to around $600,000 and had no idea what we would do next ... We did know that bankruptcy was not an option for us. It is exactly these types of experiences that teach us what we're made of. To round out the history, my husband and my father had started an electrical contracting business, literally the day after we walked away from our franchise, and my husband decided he liked working with his hands so much that he became an apprentice electrician. The rest is a story for another time.

For me, I'm now doing EXACTLY what I wanted to do 16 years ago - I run a successful business that is based from home. I have clients, colleagues and friends all around the world - and I haven't been happier. This article shares how I recreated myself, overcame the challenges and kept motivated to succeed.

Never Give Up!

The first lesson I learnt was to NEVER GIVE UP. Winston Churchill (I believe) had it right - Never Give Up ... It is the drive to succeed that keeps us going. Yes, I had my dark days where all I did was cry and hide away in my bedroom, but ultimately that didn't put food on the table and I had more than just myself to think about. Being stubborn and just putting one foot in front of the other, was enough to keep me going. I also learnt that it's o.k to lock myself away in my bedroom and cry - just not for too long! Eventually, you have to take action and just move forward.

Mindset

Without a doubt, I felt like a failure. How could it have gone so wrong? Surely there was something I should have done? These were the thoughts that were flowing through my mind at the time ... The reality was that it did go wrong, and in hindsight there wasn't a lot more we could have done. However, it took a long time for me to realise this. This is where my mindset really needed readjustment. The thoughts of failure and blaming myself were only holding me back and in some cases I was self-sabotaging. I had to change my mindset, if I was to overcome the guilt and become successful again. Whilst there was no one thing that worked for me, there were many things that worked together including:

Janet Beckers

1. Acknowledging the guilt and failure I felt
2. EFT and ZPoint energy therapies helped to move off the 'bad energy'
3. Listening to others share their stories and realising that I wasn't alone (thank you Janet Beckers)
4. Realising that people like Robert T. Kiyosaki and Alan Bond, who have been considered highly successful, have been in possibly far worse situations than I.

Ultimately, I realised that how I saw myself had the biggest impact on how successful I could be … I started recognising adversorial situations as opportunities to grow - no longer did I think "Why Me!", I started thinking "Wow, what can I do with this …" As Lenore Miller says - "When the world gives you lemons, make Margaritas'. The biggest single change was that I started treating my $1 million debt as my bill from the University Of Life … Be Prepared To Invest In Your Future. After losing so much money and being so far in debt, I was terrified of spending more. I couldn't see how I could justify spending money to build another business when I still owed from the last one. This meant I wasted a lot of time trying to do things myself. I also tried to use a number of free resources that were just flaky and required more of my time to resolve issues and potentially, the issues damaged client relationships. The big lesson here was that because I didn't value myself, I didn't value my time and ended up spending energy on tasks that provided little return to my business. It's funny how things change and I now see that spending $100, $200, $1000 can actually help me grow my business and realise far higher profits AND reduce stress. That's not to say that free resources aren't good, there are some excellent ones out there, it's just to say that sometimes spending money can move you forward a little faster. The other part of the investment, is to investment in myself. Taking time out, doing some personal development, believing in myself - it was all important.

Ignore the Nay Sayers

There are many people in our lives who are well meaning, but they don't 'get' our circumstances and offer advice that is contrary to our goals. When we walked away from our failed business, I had any number of friends and family suggest that I go back to paid, fulltime work. After all, I could earn a six figure income again and wouldn't that solve all my financial issues. However, it wouldn't resolve the life balance issues that started this adventure. A six figure income requires me to devote 6 figure hours to my new employer - something that I really wasn't prepared to do because I did have other options. (If I didn't have other options, then I would have done this). I love and cherish my family and friends, but there was a time that I had to distance myself from them so that their advice didn't have too much of an impact while I was reinventing myself.

Get A Mentor

This journey really couldn't be undertaken alone. I found that having 'mentors' - people who I respect and believe in but who are not emotionally tied to me were a key factor to achieving success. The type of mentor I needed changed as I developed in my business. Initially, I needed a Personal Development coach - if only to tell me to "grow up" or "get over it". Of course, my coaches used much nicer language and were far more tactful, but ultimately that's what it was about. As my business grows, I often seek advice from Business Coaches as to my 'next steps' and 'vision'. Often, a business coach provides a good sounding board to test my theories against.

My $1 Million Debt To The University Of Life

I hope you can learn from my $1 Million debt to university of life. Summarising all the points above the biggest lesson that I have learned is to focus on the things that are going well, don't give too much energy to the negatives and to be thankful for what I have.

Overall, I'm nowhere near as financially wealthy as I was, but I'm spiritually and emotionally far more wealthy - for me, it's not about the money, it's about the good that I can do for myself, for my family and for others.

3 Tips To Stay Focused On Your Dreams

1. Believe In Yourself - Do whatever you have to do to believe in yourself. Get a coach, get a mentor, use energy therapy and surround yourself with like minded, successful people who motivate you.

Never Give Up - if your strategy doesn't work this time: review it, adjust it and implement again. Just don't give up ...

Write down three Good Things About Yourself Or Your Life

Pin this list to your fridge or message board

Read it every day - or more...

2. Ignore The Nay Sayers My favourite phrase is "I'm comfortable for you to feel that way" (courtesy of Skip Ross) ... That helps me 'deflect' the implied criticism of my decisions.

Distance yourself from well meaning, but uninformed friends and colleagues. You can be friends, but maybe you need some space.

Don't try to justify your decisions to these well meaning, but uninformed friends and colleagues. Love and cherish them, by all means but understand - it's your life.

Develop your phrase to deflect the implied criticism's - by all means borrow my favourite phrase.

3. Get A Mentor - start today and find the mentor you need to achieve success.

Write down what you want to achieve

Write down the questions that you would have of a mentor - even if that is, "How can you help me?"

Engage today

About The Author

Charly Leetham's goal is to assist small business owners realise the power of the Internet as a channel to market their organisations in an appropriate and cost-effective manner. She helps solo-preneurs and small businesses map their business processes and plan their web presence. Charly has a passion for IT and helping people overcome their technology challenges. It is this enthusiasm that appeals to her audiences and makes Charly such an inspirational teacher. She has more than 20 years experience in the IT industry, ranging from hands-on technical, to high-level business management. She has installed and configured computing equipment and has managed business contracts in excess of $26 million dollars. This experience in IT and running a successful business from home is what attracted the Women's

Ecommerce Association International Board of Advisors to invite Charly to be an adviser for Women in Ecommerce. Charly has also won the MCEI Women in Business Marketing Award 2010 and was shortlisted for the Telstra Business Woman of the Year 2010 awards.

Special Gift

Need some help getting clear about your business processes - or staying on track? Book a free 30 minute consultation with Charly today:
http://askcharlyleetham.com/book-your-consult

http://www.askcharlyleetham.com

Janet Beckers

Follow Your North Star

Cherry-Ann Carew

"Eighty percent of success is showing up," Woody Allen, US movie actor, comedian, & director.

There is much truth in the above quote. We all know that time waits for no man, yet, many people take time for granted, and before they know it, they've not only aged, but haven't achieved a quarter of what they intended to achieve, or are capable of achieving. Regret surfaces, and they spend time pondering and wondering about what could have been. I learned a long time ago not to take this gift - for that is what time is - for granted, and do my best to use it to make it valuable, not only to me, but to others. Being an organized person helps me to accomplish my goals and intentions. For some people, I know this is a mammoth task, and I coach my clients to equate whatever job they are having problems with, to cooking. For instance, one doesn't throw all the ingredients into a pot, stir, and present a tasty dish. No, one has to have the right tools (pots, pans, utensils, etc.) organize time to shop for the ingredients, organize time to prepare the ingredients, organize time to cook the ingredients to make a wholesome meal. In essence, when you apply the same concept to a task at hand, it is easily manageable, and you use your time effortlessly, while accomplishing your goal.

To get focused in my business life and life in general, I use a desk diary to segment my tasks throughout the day. I prefer this, rather than an online diary more from habit. In addition, I tend to retain things better when I write. Given that my business is tripartite, meaning I coach clients, edit books - fiction and non-fiction - as well as write reports, e-courses, articles and books, I could easily get distracted and lose my way. Furthermore, I participate in on and offline events and do marketing, etc. Not to mention I have my domestic and personal life. As such, I have to micro-manage my tasks to get through each day, and I find that prioritising them in my diary and ticking them off as I go through them, gives me a sense of direction. In addition, I am able to gauge my production level and therefore, determine how successful I am at reaching my goals and intentions.

I'm more of a show rather than tell kind of person, in that I get on and do what I say I will do, and I put it 'out there.' By that, I mean I share my commitment with others, and people tend to respect and appreciate my efforts and support me. This I find leads to trust, which is important in any business.

Given that I am a solopreneur and work from home, I naturally experience feelings of doubts on occasions, as I do not have a support mechanism, i.e. anyone, or a team to lean on during the course of any working day. As such, I had to find an avenue to use as leverage. I sought a mentor whom I can interact with when I am tested, and have found that having someone to call on, helps to keep me focused so I can keep my vision alive. I do this with reminders, be it pictures or titles of what I'm working on, or hope to work on futuristically, around me. I also create images in my head, as well as say a mantra, and visualize things that I want, or places I want to visit, on a daily basis, usually before I fall asleep.

I am living my dream, which is writing books and programs that educate and entertain people. I read somewhere that, "There are those things in life that can never be recaptured: the spoken word, time passed and opportunities." These are wise words that we can all live by. So, set goals and intentions. Use time wisely to follow your 'North Star' and you will live your dream life.

3 Tips To Stay Focused On Your Dreams

1. Decide what your goals are and write them down. Review them daily.

Janet Beckers

2. Prioritise tasks. Deal with the ones that will bring you the best and quick return on investment (ROI), from your time.

3. When you face a new challenge. Plan accordingly. Seek help, whether it's tools, a group, or someone, so that you do not fall into the 'overwhelm' trap.

About The Author

Cherry-Ann, a former sports journalist and editor, is co-author of the bestselling book "How The Fierce Handle Fear - Secrets To Succeeding In Challenging Times" (Two Harbors Press) and author of "Whisper Of Lies," a novel (Outskirts Press).

Cherry-Ann is also The Power Writing Coach, Editor and Founder of Writetastic Solutions. She specializes in assisting novice writers prepare their books for traditional and self-publication by providing Coaching and Editing Services, along with creating programs and e-courses. She works with clients across the board, i.e. established and non-established writers.

Cherry-Ann is the proud mother of a son and daughter, and sponsor of a 5-year-old boy in Bolivia via World Vision.

Special Gift

To receive your complimentary copy of Cherry-Ann's popular Special Report "Discover The 3 Simple Steps That Will Help You Start And Finish Your Book", as well as her 7-day mini e-course, "The 7 Things You Need To Know Before Submitting Your Manuscript Proposal To An Agent Or Editor" and subscription to her "bi-monthly newsletter" through which she shares news, tips, articles and videos about the writing world that will inspire, motivate, educate and entertain you, visit: http://www.writetasticsolutions.com or http://www.cherryanncarew.com. Cherry-Ann will also gift you 30-minutes coaching session valued at US$125.00. Simply email her and quote 'Power of 100.'

http://www.writetasticsolutions.com http://www.cherryanncarew.com

Keeping The Vision Alive

Chris Georgopoulos

Keeping the vision alive - I was a very young girl when I decided that women were the most precious beings in this world. I had witnessed the oppression of women in my Greek culture and be it intentional or be it a way of life didn't really matter to me at the tender age of 9. I wondered whether I would be treated the same way when I grew up, to be denied the opportunities that boys had; to drive a car, to go to university, to have freedom of speech and the right to dress as I wished to. I knew of an unwritten law which showed me otherwise. It was right back then when I realized a feeling inside which I recognize now as being my passion. I work with women who have only known life as a mum and who now, after rearing their families, want more out of life but are afraid of the change they know they need to make; that of putting themselves first to discover the possibilities that lie beyond motherhood and the chance to re-claim their unique purpose.

It is my goal and vision for women to be empowered by their wisdom and their own creative ability. To help them gain confidence and to take pride in their achievements as they move forward to create the life of their dreams - a life of their choosing. This vision is kept alive in me via the path of life which inspired me to always want to nurture the spirit of a woman and to make sure that I used my freedom to choose wisely for myself. As we only get one chance in life I believe we

Janet Beckers

must take each opportunity as we see it. Sometimes that requires courage and it's in that moment of 'taking the plunge' where we have the ability to shine the most. I choose to live my life for me, for my creator and for those who touch me and for those whom I touch on this journey called life.

Focus for me means to actively search for and keep a visual of the greater goals I have in my heart and in my inner being. This is an activity which requires me to keep the vision very clear, vivid and colourful as I am a visual person. Thinking back, I have always drawn and written down my goals even before learning how to do this in theory. It was a natural ability which guided me and kept the dreams alive for me ever since I was a little girl. I have always had a vision board which held cut-outs from magazines and bits of paper with hand-written ideas on them. I had photo collages and bits of fabric to inspire me and I loved talking about my goals and dreams with my very closest friends. My artistry kept me going through tough times and helped me to get to the next level at whatever stage of life I was in. I cherished the little things I received as gifts and collected small trinkets and gift-cards. All these little things were 'special' to me. I used them to decorate my wall and they inspired me as I added pictures of the things I loved and wanted as well as poems, words of inspiration and my goals and dreams. A vision-board doesn't have to be big as long as the ideas on it are big. The reality is they work! I can honestly say that all of what I would call achievements in my life, were once a scene or a verse on one of my many such visual posters. For me, it made everything real. Many of my big dreams may have seemed ridiculous at the time but when they transformed into reality, well ... not so ridiculous after all. I encourage everyone I know to do this as an activity for themselves and to encourage others to try it also.

If what we focus on becomes our reality, then why not choose your reality? If you keep your focus on what you want rather than on what you don't want, you have a better chance of achieving more happiness and contentment in your life. It makes sense to have dreams and goals because it gives your life purpose and allows you to look towards the future with excitement and gives you the motivation to take action. Even if you take baby steps, remember, with each step you take, you are that much closer to your goal. So, dream, envision and create what you want to see in your life. Write it down and make it big and full of colour. See yourself in this picture and live it in your mind as if it is true. The mind doesn't distinguish the difference. It's as if you're there. Take this photo of your goal and place it on your vision board and watch as you attract into your life all the recourses and opportunities that will make it happen for you! Make this your daily ritual and remain focused on your vision. I would love to hear your stories and your achievements as you manifest the realities in your life as you move confidently forward, knowing that as you do, that anything is possible!

3 Tips To Stay Focused On Your Dreams

In summary: Dare to dream BIG. It takes just as much energy to focus on a big dream as it does to focus on a small one.

Make it visual so that your mind's 'eye' can see it on a daily basis. This keeps the vision alive and in the forefront. Make sure you use lots of colour and description so that your goal is specific and clear.

Examples of goals:

What you want your relationship to be like.

What career to choose.

How much money you want to earn.

Learning to play a musical instrument.

Going on a holiday.

Buying a new car. Etc.

About The Author

Chris Georgopoulos is the founder of COAL UNDER PRESSURE - Discovering Your Inner Gem. Chris is a Master NLP Practitioner and Life Coach who uses her skills to empower women to look within and to find the inner 'gem' which has been refined through years of life's pressures as a mum and all that comes through bringing up a family. With 3 grown kids of her own and a marriage of 28 years, Chris knows too well the issues which confront mothers the world over and is very equipped to guide her clients to designing the future of their dreams. She is known for her generous nature and her fun personality. Those who work with Chris achieve more than they thought possible by first learning the tools they need to succeed and then by being

Janet Beckers

coached by Chris to personally apply these tools in their own lives. Her passion for empowering women comes from her background where she witnessed the oppression of women and made it her life's goal to help other women in achieving everything they want in their lives by learning how to put themselves first, without suffering the guilt that comes with it.

Special Gift

A free audio on 'What and who do you value?' To assist you to prioritise your life and gain clarity as to why your life is as it is now, and how to begin your 'new' life. value: $67

Live well and dream Big!   Chris Georgopoulos

http://wwwDiscoveringYourInnerGem.com

Leap of Faith

Christine Hepburn

How are you viewing your world today?

This morning I woke with enthusiasm and an excitement for the day ahead. I am grateful for so much, including the opportunity to make a difference. Life wasn't always this way.

As founder and principal trainer for The Defining Edge Training and Development, each day is varied, where I feel privileged to work with wonderful people. I am also absolutely passionate about what I do. Let me tell you a very brief story. Growing up being told no one is interested in what you have to say, and if they ask, they are only being polite, did not lead me to where I am now. It did of course, like all of life's experiences shape the person I am. Being in a carefully controlled environment from childhood through my adult life, under circumstances most of you would never imagine, had me perfecting the art of being invisible, although that particular story is for another book. Let me just share that on the surface I always appeared serene, composed and in control, yet behind the scenes I was more concerned for surviving and not letting the cracks show.

Janet Beckers

Through life experiences, I refined a natural ability to remain calm regardless of what is happening around me. This earned me an honorary doctorate in dealing with difficult and demanding people or situations. Extending this skill into my professional life has been a bonus as I am able to empower my clients to handle any situation with a win-win focus. From childhood I consistently stated that I didn't do public speaking. One of my sisters excelled in this arena, yet if I was presented with having to address a group of people I would experience a heart rate almost guaranteed to bring about my demise, and a brain that would struggle to remember my name, let alone the topic. Allow me to tell you about the first time I addressed a group of almost 200 people. It was at a funeral, where I had been given the honour of being invited to speak for a beloved family member who was also my friend. Right up until the moment I had to stand and walk to the front, I was not sure how I would actually be capable of doing this. The celebrant had understood and gently offered to step in and read what I had written if I just gave her a glance.

When given the key to move to the front, I suddenly made the decision that I would not let Jill down, I would not let her partner down, I would not let family down and importantly, I would not let myself down. And do you know what happened? I did it. I managed so well, many people approached me to say thank you and to congratulate me on such a professional effort, thinking public speaking was something I did often. What is wonderful is that I have learned to not ever say, 'I don't do that' about anything. I have tried kayaking, rock climbing, and many similar pursuits once not on my radar. Aiming high and expecting to make it happen fits in here as well. I read somewhere "As long as you are going to go about your day thinking anyway, you may as well "think big". How true. The beautiful irony is that I now have a wonderful life and am paid for what I have to say! Speaking at events all over Australia and New Zealand, working with dedicated business owners and their people, are an everyday part of my world. How blessed am I! Since I started out with the information that I am the founder and principal trainer of The Defining Edge Training and Development, let me tell you what it is I do and how I came to be where I am today.

It started just under four years ago when I was presented with a life altering situation which appeared incredibly daunting at the time. Drying my tears and taking deep breaths, I dealt with the practicalities I was presented with, then set about making decisions for my future. Discovering strengths and a freedom I had not thought possible, I daily went about refocusing my thoughts. Although you are reading that in a short sentence, please don't underestimate the efforts required for me to do so. I shall be eternally grateful to friends and family members who have remained staunchly supportive and who always believe in me. Taking a long look one day at where I wanted to be and where I was, I considered those strengths, my expertise, experience, abilities and passions. To be truly successful, I believe we must apply ourselves with passion to whatever we set out to do. Putting each of those on a graph, I then considered how I could take these and put them to use in order to reach the goal of where I wanted to be.

It had been a long held dream of mine to one day utilise my skills to help others achieve success in their personal and professional lives and see businesses thrive with cohesive workforces. Putting the two together, seemed a perfect match, so off I went to meet with a small business advisor to gain their opinion on the viability of this dream. One business plan, further meetings, professional advice, further training and a huge leap of faith, saw me see this come to fruition. Has my journey of growth to this point been ... scary, stressful, disturbing, painful, exhilarating, fulfilling, empowering? Yes, all of these and many more. Am I still learning? Another yes here. I believe learning and growing is a lifelong opportunity and one to be embraced wholeheartedly.

My company helps change lives. We are passionate about people, the learning experience and helping people reach their true potential. Our love for our work is what drives our commitment to provide unparalleled personal service and professionalism. We understand the importance of each business, the role each person plays in it and the impact of exceptional customer service. We offer a complimentary range of customised training and services, designed to develop the true potential in people, creating experiences guaranteed to enhance your success. Priding ourselves in putting people first to achieve the most applicable, relevant and effective training outcomes on the market today, we develop the core of organisations and individuals alike. This also has the added benefit of boosting bottom line profits.

One program I am particularly proud of is working with a proactive employment organisation to give long term unemployed the skills to enhance their opportunities. We aim to not only see them in work, but in the right work, where their strengths can be utilised and their long term goals identified and achieved. The success of this program is immensely rewarding and seeing each person grow on a personal level is heartwarming. In order to give back a little, from every training workshop or speaker's fee, a donation is made to educate a child in an underprivileged environment, where they do not enjoy the basic opportunities we take for granted.

Janet Beckers

Do you regard obstacles or challenges in your life as defining moments that helped shape who you are, or do you choose to see them as reasons for why you have not achieved your dreams? You see, I believe our mindset matters here. It is not what happens to us in life, as life happens to all of us in some way or another. It is how we choose to view what happens and what we choose to do with it that makes the difference. Everything that is past is a learning experience to grow from, a beautiful memory to reflect on, or a motivating factor to act upon. We may not be able to change external factors, we can however change our responses which changes the outcome. My point is, whether your life is more nightmare than dream, more anticipation than action, whether you have a goal and have not been sure you have the courage or ability to pursue it, or whether you have your own business and wish to aim higher, it is all possible.

Being in business is one of the most amazing experiences. It challenges us in every way possible. It stretches our boundaries, makes us realise we're capable of far more than you ever thought. We each have within us the ability to create massive change. We can be whatever we want to be and do whatever we dream of if we just have the courage to pursue it. "We all have two choices: we can make a living or we can design a life" Jim Rohn

3 Tips To Stay Focused On Your Dreams

1: Think of your passions, skills, experience, what inspires you and where you really wish to be

2: Create a plan for how you can bring these elements together. A vision board helps keep your focus

3: Find a mentor, maintain focus on the big picture, yet continue taking baby steps each day in order to achieve your dreams

About The Author

Christine Hepburn is a Director and the Principal Trainer for The Defining Edge Training and Development. Christine has extensive experience in building successful small businesses from no more than just a concept, through to working within large corporations developing, training and mentoring staff. Her goal has always been to provide a standard of client and customer service, which creates an environment where both staff and customers feel elated by the experience. Drawing on this experience, she inspires her clients to discover what their customers really want and how to create an exceptional experience they can't get anywhere else. The results her clients achieve speak for themselves. With a passion and commitment to excellence shining through, this ensures she is a highly sought after presenter, speaker, author and was recently featured in an international television series.

As a certified Fellow of the Customer Service Institute of Australia, she practices her belief that "it is not what we know, it is what we do that matters."

- Judge for Service Excellence Awards Launceston
- Author 'Training Works, Better People Better Bottom Line'
- Author 'Passion For Excellence'
- Participant in the international television series 'Trainers on Trial'
- Featured in Enterprise, Tasmania's Premier Business magazine
- Keynote speaker TCCI Small Business Expo
- Mentor with Business Mentor Services Tasmania
- Regularly featured on 101.5fm business program
- As seen on Central News TVNZ

Special Gift

http://www.thedefiningedge.com

How To Keep Your Entrepreneurial Dreams Alive With Diamonds And Disco!

Cinaea Dallinger

You can feel excited as an online entrepreneur, a little alone, part of something big, focussed, exhausted, deflated, and then motivated, excited and empowered all in a single 24 hours!

It takes bravery to be an entrepreneur.

Courage.

Sometimes, raw dig-down deep courage.

But it is so worth it!

When growing up I constantly remember hearing my parents say when times were hard, two mottos. They were… 'Dig deep…you can do it!", and "Tough times never last but tough people do!".

A little motto I love, and have added to my family culture is "Fake it, till you Make it!", and I have to say in the beginning when I was first starting out, I called myself an online entrepreneur more as a 'dream term' than an actual reality.

When I first started an online business it was the allure of investing my time and skills into creating a business from nothing – just from sitting at my computer at home.

A business that sent me money whilst I slept – well that would be a dream!

A business that continued to operate even whilst I walked around the house in my pyjamas?

Unheard of.

A business that I could work on whilst the kids played on the floor in front of me.

A business I could personalise and call my own...

An enterprise I could grow from the ground up to give back to help and serve others –

...Well that would be both exciting and awesome!

There is something about being an online entrepreneur that excites me....maybe it is having a business that is completely different from the traditional format....I am hooked.

Now, when I first began online, I read a lot – and I mean a LOT. To be honest, I think I actually felt more comfortable reading about internet marketing than actually 'doing' internet marketing.

All the things I had to do as an online entrepreneur seemed a little overwhelming at times.

But so must training for the Olympics be– think of the swimmers, the triathletes, runners...it is a long road of ups and downs – but well worth it.

When I first started, I was bright eyed and bushy tailed, AND then the hard work hit. I knew I had a long way to go, and a LOT to learn.

Janet Beckers

Late nights, problems with software, internet servers crashing, email spam, spilling an entire cup of tea over my laptop so it sizzled, shut down and died, computer viruses, 3 little children tugging on my computer mouse, long distance phone bills, being told it would never work by close friends, ...and a myriad of other challenges that occurred along the way.

So what keeps my dream of being an online entrepreneur alive on difficult days?

What keeps me going when I think it is all 'too hard'? The answer I have found is in the acronym of G.E.M=S

A gem is something valued for its beauty or perfection, or a beloved or highly prized person. A gem sparkles like a diamond.

It is the combination of several 'Online Success Gems©' of people, wisdom, systems and opportunity that keep me going when 'times are tough'.

What do I mean by that?

Having - Goals, a Go-Getting Attitude, Excitement, Education, Experts, Momentum, Movement and Mentors in my life and when you put all that together it leads to Sparkling Success....

G.E.M=S

Goals & Go-Getting Attitude

Excitement + Education + Experts

Momentum, Movement & Mentors

=

Sparkling Success!

"Online Success GEMS"

G. Goals, Go-getting attitude
E. Excitement, Education, Experts
M. Momentum, Movement, Mentors
= S Sparkling Success!

www.OnlineSuccessGems.com

Yes, I will admit, there are days when I do not feel like an Online Success GEM, and you know what iI do on those days I feel flat, or I am not feeling like a shiny bright diamond?

I dance!

I put on great music and I create a disco in my kitchen. True!

Movement and music are very powerful. Dancing around the kitchen is fun and it changes my mood.

I also have visual pictures in a folder of my ideas and dreams and I really love to learn and get excited about being educated by smart savvy people. Each day I try to build momentum within a project I am working on and I get motivated by collecting great and inspiring quotes.

Here are some quotes I like to read frequently…

"The critical ingredient is getting off your butt and doing something. It's as simple as that. A lot of people have ideas, but there are few who decide to do something about them now. Not tomorrow. Not next week. But today. The true entrepreneur is a doer, not a dreamer." -- Nolan Bushnell

And…"In short: show up" – Seth Godin

I Love it! Because that is it.

That is half the battle –just showing up and putting in the hard work to grow and build your dreams and online business. That is what entrepreneurial women do – they show up, move forward with their ideas, do their core tasks and keep going.

Janet Beckers

I started with a list and some goals. It was a simple task but a necessary one.

Write a list of your goals and all the things you need to get done to achieve that goal. Work out which ones you need to get done this week, today, this morning – or ones that need to be done every single day.

I have a daily checklist of online things to do each day like remember to comment or post on facebook, twitter, read flagged articles, read my favourite blogs, edit my previous days article or writing, do some research, work on product creation etc

Work out the core tasks for your business– the ones that help your business to grow and then if you want to be an awesome online entrepreneur and a true Online Success GEM...

Become a doer, not a dreamer and ...never stop showing up.

So if you are in the trenches of your online business or just contemplating whether to dive in and start one.

I would jump up and down, dance and cheer wildly that you do.

Yes it takes work.

But anything worthwhile and wonderful does.... Doesn't it?

Keep Going towards greater online success!

P.S. If all else fails – just remember to have some fun, disco and dance around the kitchen.

3 Tips To Stay Focused On Your Dreams

1. G -Goals and Go Getting Attitude. Write out an idea or goal you want to reach and aim to do it within a maximum of 45 days. Write it down on a sticky note and stick it on the fridge, the front of your purse or on your bedside table so you look at it at least twice a day. Add a Go-Getting Attitude towards that target and mini targets. Write out a step by step list of things you will need to do to reach that outcome (break them into groups).

2. E - Create Excitement around your journey, if you cannot figure out a step or stumble in your progress, get Educated! Find and Expert - someone to help you, find someone to answer your questions, find the answer yourself – educate your mind and be excited by knowledge.

3. M - Build Momentum daily. Make sure you do more things to grow you online business today than you did yesterday. Find a Mentor -connect with those gems in your field. Movement - If all else fails – put the song 'Girls just wanna have fun' by Cyndi Lau

About The Author

Cinaea Dallinger is an enthusiastic Online Entrepreneur . She loves to teach, encourage and inspire others how to 'join the dots' and achieve online success. It is Cinaea's dream to inspire and connect people with true Online Success GEMS©. People, Training, Products and Systems providing solutions to people seeking freedom of lifestyle, through online success. Sharing the G.E.M stones of wisdom, information and inspiration she has gathered together. Cinaea lives in beautiful Queensland, Australia with her husband and three gorgeous children. She loves going to the beach, spending time with friends and occasionally disco dancing around the kitchen!

Special Gift

7 Sparkling Gem Secrets of Online Success Audio & FREE Workshop Tickets! (Value $1,067) In this audio, Cinaea would love to share with you how to become a successful online entrepreneur, and teach you the fundamental 7 Secret Gems you need to build a sparkling online business. She would also love to meet you at one of her upcoming OnlineSuccessGems workshops. So for a limited time, she is providing you with a fantastic gift, Two FREE Tickets to the total value of $997. So when you're ready to become an Online Gem, get yourself to this event. I know you're going to love it! To receive your FREE Audio and Tickets (Value $1,067!) go to www.OnlineSuccessGems.com/sparkle.html

http://www.OnlineSuccessGems.com

Janet Beckers

Connect, Connect; Give, Give; Rewards, Rewards¹

Claire McFee

Being part of the Wonderful Web Women Community for over two years now has not only opened my eyes up to many new and exciting ways of working but life changing ways of living my personal life as well. I believe the richness in life comes from connecting with others and in the joy of giving without expecting anything in return. The ways in which this belief has enhanced my life and expanded my business has gone beyond my wildest dreams. Below I will share with you some personal examples of how 'living' this philosophy can help your life purpose unfold in the most synchronistic of ways, as it has for me and hopefully inspire you to put yourself out there to do the same.

Meet the Author

A few years ago I was approached by a Publisher to review a new book called 'You Sexy Mother.' Little did I know then that within a relatively short period of time I would be aligned with numerous successful Authors both in Australia and Overseas.

I was chuffed to be approached and subsequently reviewed the book, which I instantly resonated with and was happy to promote. It struck a chord with my long held belief that it is imperative as Mother's not to lose ourselves to our partner and children. As I have always said to my customers "A happy mum equals a happy family.' It is not selfish to factor in your own needs along with your families. The truth is it is self defeating if you don't. What is good for you is also good for your family. Front cover promotion no less! To cut a long story short I felt compelled to contact the author Jodie Hedley Ward to introduce myself and to personally give her the review of her book. Thinking back I actually felt like this would lead to something 'big' which it certainly did! It may have been about 1 year later - but was worth the wait. Jodie and I really clicked and kept in contact via email and low and behold Jodie decided to kindly put my quote and business name on the front cover of her next book! Jodie has been featured on shows such as the Today Show; Sunrise and A Current Affair which has of course helped my Organize Your Life profile through our permanent connection. All from making the extra effort to connect and help her without expectation. Connected to Hugh Jackman —Yes Please! Similarly, I reviewed another great book called Naturally Better by Kristen Morrison. Kristen and I also gelled immediately - both being passionate about natural health solutions. Kristin added my quote to the second print run of her book and guess who was kind enough to give a front cover endorsement out of the kindness of their hearts —Hugh Jackman and wife Debora-Lee - so I am now forever linked with mega media personalities too. Not a bad outcome I am sure you would agree!

Doubts … .there were a few In the beginning, I had a few doubts around 'Who am I to be giving my opinion on this, that or the other?' but as Janet recommends - doing the thing that puts you out of your comfort zone most as that is where the growth and success lie – and it has paid off big time – and it does get easier. My association with other notable people has got to the degree that Publishers of best sellers in the USA have been approaching me to review their books as well. One such renowned Author, Linda Samuels, who wrote 'The other side of organized' and who has also written for the New York Times has in fact become a wonderful mentor. Linda is always quick to give helpful advice and goes out of her way to connect you with others who may be able to help. It never ceases to amaze me how generous people are with their time. Having a giving approach to life creates win/win situations. I wouldn't want to work any other way. Would you?

Now onto my own book! As my confidence has grown over the years (11 now since I came up with my idea for my Home based | Life Organizer full of ready-made lists), I feel I have enough experience and knowledge to share more of myself with others and am in fact writing my own book. The brilliant thing is before having even started it, I have a wealth of reputable contacts that are more than happy to put their name to reviewing my book and promoting it to their database as I have done for them. I will even quote some people in the book lending more credibility to it. As you can imagine I am very excited about it all! In the beginning, this wasn't my grand plan but it has evolved into these wonderful friendships and long term strategic alliances. In fact I recently won a Marketing Award for this and other strategies that have significantly increased by branding and all important 'List'. Several of my new lovely connections were referees for me in these awards helping with the win no doubt.

I am constantly amazed at what develops over time when you operate from a place of giving without expecting anything in return.

Full Circle

As it happens, a few months back I read an article in the Local Newspaper about a lady – Merrin - who has started a blog called Secrets of Motherhood and who is also starting workshops for mothers to help them cope with the often competing demands of parenthood. Merrin is basing the workshops on none other than Jodie Hedley Ward's 'You Sexy Mother' Principles and her Ten Day turnaround Plan. I contacted Merrin to offer my support to help promote her site/workshop as it is congruent with my work. Merrin generously gave my Organize Your Life Organizer a wonderful write-up on her blog, which got great traffic from her media exposure. We have kept in contact since then, which has led to an exciting development ... 100 Year International Women's Day celebrations.

Turns out, Merrin is on the Committee that is organising the upcoming Surf Coast Shire 100 year International Women's Day celebrations for the region and low and behold recommended me to be a speaker for the Event. I have subsequently been contacted by the Shire to be one of only two 'Ordinary Women Doing Extraordinary things' speakers on the day. I have wanted to increase the amount of Speaking I do in preparation for my book promotion as that rolls out during the year. How synchronistic is that? And all due to a being willing to help others without any agenda or 'What's In It For Me?' attitude. I love to see how events unfold as I carry this belief forward and relish the amazing people I meet and learn from along the way. I encourage you to step outside that comfort zone of yours and subsequently bring about wonderful new connections left, right and centre.

3 Tips To Stay Focused On Your Dreams

Actively search for Inspiring People that resonate with you and your life Vision. Make contact with these people or their Publishers/Agents – with a 'what can I offer?' attitude

Actively Promote these 'go getters' expecting nothing in return and see what exciting events unfold.

Keep track of your progress as your connections blossom and cross pollinate! Great to look back on and also to use for award entries when they really take hold.

About The Author

Claire McFee is the highly awarded Creator of the Organize Your Life Household e-Organizers – full of ready-made Lists you can type into on your computer or Print Out to use by hand. Basically Your Life in Lists. Everything you need in the short, medium and long term - right at your finger tips leading to more saved time for you. Claire has been extensively showcased on TV and other mediums enabling her to help thousands of people worldwide. Claire, who holds a Bachelor of Education, Majoring in Psychology has over 11 years experience helping people get more out of life by being better organized and improving their mindset. Claire is also a passionate advocator of natural health solutions, having overcome health challenges herself using these methods.

Special Gift

Special Offer Claire is offering a generous gift to all readers - a Free mini e-Organizer worth rrp$17 Once you see how easy it is to use and how much time you save using these popular readymade lists you then eligible to upgrade to the complete Organizer Set covering Your Home; Family, Self and Money for a Low $37 with the special code given in the mini-Organizer Simply Enter – 7878 – into the Discount section of the Order Form to redeem your free Mini Organizer.

http://www.organizeyourlife.com.au

An Inspiring Story From Our Partner Opportunity International and The 1 Million Women Out Of Poverty Project

Babuli's story (India)

At 6am each morning, Babuli and her husband Vasuda begin weaving baskets. This skill, passed down from Vasuda's parents, has proven invaluable for Babuli and her family. Despite not having an education themselves, they have been able to support their sons, Bapina and Biplab, who are now adults with small businesses of their own. Babuli and Vasuda work throughout the day, usually stopping at 10pm. During festivals, the business is particularly busy while during quiet periods the couple sells snacks and cleaning products.

Babuli was only able to expand the business effectively with a loan from Adhikar, the local microfinance institution. Starting with Rs.5,000 (A$125) and now on her fourth loan cycle of Rs.15,000 (A$375), Babuli used the capital to purchase raw materials in bulk. As her business grew, it attracted wholesalers as well as individual customers. With each loan cycle, her income increased and she is now earning Rs.5,000- 6,000 (A$125-150) a month.

Babuli and Vasuda were so determined their sons would have a brighter future, they never taught them how to weave baskets, preferring instead for them to focus on their studies. "Why should my sons take up this work? They have an education," says Babuli with a sparkle in her eye.

You can help families just like Babuli's by donating at
http://www.WonderfulWebWomen.com/recommends/opportunity

Work To Your Skills To Achieve True Motivation

Clare Kyle

I am a CV (curriculum vitae) writer. I don't have a degree in the English Language. But I do know what my skills are, although I stumbled across them quite accidentally. For years I'd informally written and re-formatted CV's for friends and family as the nature of my work as an HR Advisor lent me to the task. They'd always get great results when posting the new CV onto job boards or using it for applications. I'd never considered taking up CV writing on a professional basis, but now – having left my full time role after maternity leave and needing a source of income - it crossed my mind as a temporary solution. A leading UK CV consultancy accepted me onto a high-level induction through which only a small percentage of prospective consultants were hired. After a rigorous assessment period (and – much to my surprise – glowing critiques of my work) I was accepted into the fold of Consultants and worked from home, on my laptop, as and when required.

I learned tremendous amounts about the power of phraseology, aesthetics and compelling writing to maximise interview rates, and highly developed my knowledge in these areas to produce the best possible results for the clients I worked for. I then realised I wanted to specialise in working with specific groups and connect more fully with individuals to help them achieve their career goals and objectives. So I decided to branch on my own and start my own business as a freelancer. I love words, language, and I love CV writing. I have created an online brand with two very small children – one of whom is 2 years old and the other only 7 weeks. There's no doubt that the key to achieving anything in this world – no matter how big or small – is motivation. In becoming self employed and starting your own business it is of course very important to have a 'big picture' and ultimately be driven by your own idea of success and what that would mean for you. But to get motivated on a day-to-day basis and make working towards your ideal life a reality, you must uncover and use your innate skills to keep momentum. It took me around 6 months to do the groundwork for my business whilst managing a family and other commitments, but still I managed to keep motivated and my 'eyes on the prize'. The key is to work to your skills. You may already know what your innate skills are, or they may be waiting to be discovered. My story shows how you can stumble across talent by chance – or it may be something you have cultivated for a long time. It is important to be open to opportunity and acknowledge ability when you find it. Then you can use it to its fullest potential as a driver to achieve make your ideas of success a reality.

How do you know what your skills are?

1. Look at your parents or siblings. What are their gifts? They may be dormant or being used to their full capacity but, either way, you are likely to possess similar traits. Think about their activities or ask them if you can. For instance, my own father is an excellent artist and created beautiful drawings and paintings when I was a young girl. My mother is very skilful in the use of words and would write poems. I have a natural tendency towards each of these abilities and the acknowledgement of this isn't immodesty – it's simply being truthful! It's extremely useful that I know this about myself, whether or not I am actually utilising those competencies. You may be very good with numbers (financial planning) or enjoy working with people (a service business), or like building relationships and watching people thrive (the recruitment industry). The beauty of starting your own business is that you can pretty much do what you want – and you have a vastly increased chance of success if it is around something that you enjoy. You must identify your abilities and then apply them in a realistic and viable capacity.

2. What do you enjoy doing? What are you passionate about? Think about the following concept: I enjoy what I do because I am good at what I do. I am good at what I do because I enjoy what I do. Invariably people enjoy their work

because they are good at it, and vice versa. If you dislike your job it is likely that that kind of work doesn't naturally suit you and you are fighting against a downward current. It is quite common for people start their own businesses around a hobby.

3. Ask other people. Ask your friends and family for their opinion and when you get feedback DON'T modestly shrug it off! You will have natural abilities and skills that have manifested themselves so don't let self-confidence be an issue. It is important that you get to know yourself in this capacity. Alternatively, have you had an appraisal at work during which your manager has praised you for a job well done? It may be working under pressure, or delivering excellent service, or completing a piece of work to a high standard. These types of interaction give you excellent feedback from another, well informed, perspective and are another opportunity to delve deeper into your motivations and think about why you performed to a high standard.

I am in the fortunate position of enjoying what I do. CV writing also satisfies the perfectionist in me. Perfectionism could be viewed as a skill, but it is one that must be carefully applied. Fulfilling this tendency through my work takes the pressure is off me when feeling that I want to achieve perfection in other areas of my life. It is sometimes observed that being a perfectionist in life ultimately leads to rigidity - a stagnation of movement, keeping you stuck and unable to move forward. It is a form of control and once you are able to let this go you can progress very quickly towards whatever your goals are. That's not to say that you don't want things to be right but the key is to make decisions quickly and not agonise over every tiny detail. However, applied to the kind of work I do, perfectionism (or something like it) becomes a benchmark for my own standards. Therefore I also use my work as a very positive outlet for something that, applied elsewhere in my life, may not achieve the same constructive results. So consistently using and perfecting my skills fulfils me in two ways – and therefore succeeds in keeping my motivation levels at an all-time high.

Yes, it has been tough at times with 2 very small children. Support is vital and without a partner and friends and family around me it would have been much harder. Remember why you are creating your business and don't be too proud to accept offers of help. Otherwise you won't achieve anything at all – except, perhaps, a full head of grey hair and frazzled nerves before you've even named your venture. And make it easier for yourself by doing something you love. I can't

Janet Beckers

emphasis that enough. So... do you know what your skills are? If not, isn't it about time you found out?

3 Tips To Stay Focused On Your Dreams

1. Take time out for yourself. It will help refocus you and replenish your energy. Although it can be difficult, try and do this every day. Do something you enjoy or sit and focus on how you want your life to look in 12 months time. Remember you can achieve many things during a 12-month period – just ensure you are open to opportunities and try not to be a perfectionist when moving forward.

2. Connect with like-minded people, groups or online networks who are walking the same path – they will inspire and motivate you

3. Read 'Feel the Fear and Do It Anyway' by Susan Jeffers. Not just for business, but for life. An essential read.

About The Author

Clare Kyle is a freelance CV Specialist providing bespoke writing, critique, and advisory services to help job seekers move more quickly onto their next role, and promote increased confidence in the open job market.

Her primary background is within third-sector human resources and within commercial recruitment. She has worked regularly with a leading UK CV Consultancy and has a track record of crafting numerous multi-sector CVs spanning varying seniority levels. She lives in the UK (South East) with her partner and balances managing her online brand CV Tiger with caring for her two young daughters Chloe and Poppy.

Special Gift

Visit http://www.cvboutique.co.uk for a FREE CV assessment (valued at £25)

http://www.cvboutique.co.uk

When the "Why" is Big Enough, the "How" Takes Care of Itself When Selling in your Business

Colleen Lording

Why are you doing what you are doing everyday? Why do you want to sell to a Client? The answer to these simple questions will quite honestly determine your success. You need to have a true desire to do what you are doing. You need to have a real desire to assist your Clients. You need to have a desire to assist people in general. This is something that comes down to commitment. When you reach a certain level of commitment and become really clear on your reasons as to why you are doing something, the intensity of your vibration increases. Your spirit, your soul, your life force, or whatever you want to call it begins to operate at a higher frequency. These vibrations, like invisible radio signals, are picked up unconsciously by every single person you meet. The message is clear, but subtle, "I am committed". I can't put more emphasis on this point. You need to decide why you are doing what you are doing, and your reason "why" needs to be a big "why". It needs to get you out of bed every day. It needs to get you through the hard times ... and there will be hard times! If you have a big enough reason for doing something, you will endure pain and pleasure in the pursuit of it.

Now, this is also about congruency in who you are, in comparison to who you wish to be. Everyone is selling themselves to other people every single day. And, every person you deal with will pick up unconscious messages about what you think about yourself and how committed you are to whatever it is that you are trying to achieve. So be aware of this, and make sure you have a good enough "why". This one secret alone, will determine your success. Affirmation: "I have unwavering commitment to my outcome, and I will be consistent in my achievement of it, to ensure that I actualize it. The pain of regret far outweighs the pain of discipline." In order to sell, people will face a lot of rejection in their time. Therefore, you need to choose to face the rejections with Courage. Courage is not the absence of fear, it is doing something in spite of fear. And, it is a choice. What is Courage? Action + Fear + Commitment = Courage. It is acting in spite of fear, based on your commitment. This is another reason why you need a big enough 'Why'. You need to know that rejection is part of the process. The sooner you accept that it is just feedback that you will encounter on the way to your objective, the sooner you will be successful.

Rejection is also an opportunity learn and identify what is working and what isn't, which can be extremely helpful in reaching a flawless Sales strategy. A Great quote from Henry Ford: "Failure is the opportunity to begin again more intelligently". I don't actually really believe in failure or rejection...I believe you get outcomes, and really, it is all just a feedback mechanism to tell you whether you need to adjust what you are doing, and as Henry Ford says so eloquently, begin again more intelligently. The way I deal with rejection is to think of it like this; Rejection VS Opportunity Costs. What I mean by this is "What might it cost me if I don't take that action and risk possible rejection?" ie: the cold call, the setting up an appointment with a potential client, the completion of a follow up task from a meeting with a Client? What will it cost me if I don't do that? Will it cost me the next sale? Will it cost me my bonus? Will it cost me my self confidence because I am not making any sales and therefore won't meet my target at the end of the month? I never wanted to miss an opportunity to make a sale or do a deal in the future, and this is what always kept me going. If I didn't make that call, I might miss out on a Sale or opportunity. What might happen if I don't take action? Remember to ask yourself this important question and adopt this rejection VS opportunity cost psychology of success. It is a good perspective to have and it makes it easier to deal with so called 'rejection'.

NOTE: No matter how big the deal, don't, whatever you do, get stuck in numbers, or let the value of the deal frighten you. The larger the deal, the more you need to be yourself, apply the right psychology and build amazing relationships with your contacts. "I am fundamentally convinced that most of us will never understand the various talents we have because we never test ourselves enough" Paul. C Sereno – Palaeontologist

3 Tips To Stay Focused On Your Dreams

1. Define your 'Why'

2. Answer honestly, "Do I let the fear of 'rejection' stop me?"

3. If so, ask yourself, "What might it cost me if I don't take that action and risk possible rejection?"

About The Author

Colleen Lording has been in sales, forging business alliances, full-time, for 15 years as this book goes to press. One of her previous full-time Corporate roles was as a National Account Manager for a recruitment company ranked in the top five largest in the world. In that role, and throughout her career she managed and won Clients such as Australia Post, Visy Industries, all sectors of the Government (Federal and State, Local and not for profit), National Australia Bank, Origin, Optus, Cadbury Schweppes, Fosters, Linfox, Pacific Brands, and quite a number of others. So she has had a lot of exposure to a lot of big players out there.

She has also worked in smaller companies, such as the Hawthorn Football Club as a Corporate Sales Executive, selling Corporate Hospitality & Sponsorship. Colleen now runs 'Wisdom & Business' which teaches small to medium companies how to accelerate growth through Business Alliances.

Therefore, you are hearing from someone who has learnt 'by doing', interacting with Clients every day. With her experience and depth of knowledge, she can offer you some real insights and more importantly, strategies that you can use straight away that will make a huge difference to your results.

Special Gift

Go to www.wisdom-and-business.com and for a limited time, receive a full copy of the e-book "The Psychology of Dealmaking To Multiply your Results" 10 Secrets To a Successful Sale Read this e-book before you do your next deal...

www.wisdom-and-business.com

Design A Life of Rich Rewards!

Cydney O'Sullivan

How do I stay motivated and on track? I believe I am truly one of the luckiest women in the world....now! I have been very, very poor in my life and very, very rich, but for the longest time I was ambitious and driven, and lived with a deep feeling of being unfulfilled. I worked really hard for very little pay for years and years, and moved around a lot and tried to fit in and be happy with my life. I made some brave choices with my life at a young age, moving to Australia and following my heart to take over run down business that no one else wanted and rebuild them. I had a taste of living passionately, but knew I couldn't keep working at that physical pace, especially once I had babies. I continued to start and run home based businesses while raising my children, and while my husband built a small IT based business into one of Australia's most successful companies during the Technology boom. But I still didn't feel fulfilled.

For a long time I felt like I wasn't getting anywhere, and spent a lot of years investing in my education and planning my dream life. Now, staying motivated and on track has actually become a daily delight. All I have to do these days is say yes to wonderful people, keep everyone to the plan and continue my personal growth as openly as possible and live into the success. My business is connecting high integrity, successful people so they can have win win win relationships, and making

http://wonderfulwebwomen.com |

Janet Beckers

their best strategies and systems available to all the people who wouldn't normally have the time, the money or the connections to find out all these gold nuggets and get access to this level of expertise.

Developing this business model has put me into daily contact with over 200 high level super achievers like myself and Janet Beckers who are in the business of making magic happen. Do you think we hold each other accountable and keep each other in focus? Absolutely. Does it feel like work when I'm working with incredible mentors with the same vision to heal lives? Hardly ever!! I now know that the longing I was feeling for all those years, was the pain of holding myself back and not believing I could actually have all my dreams come true. I thought that if I dared to dream that high that I would surely be disappointed! A couple of years ago I nearly lost everything, and I realised that I had had everything I really needed all along – and that it was in me. The next 12 months will be a very exciting time. We just launched the new global interactive women's mentoring program that took several years of planning and 12 months of team work to create at www.MsIndependence.com.

The biggest challenge and billion dollar opportunity that most small business people need help with right now is taking their businesses online in a way that dramatically improves their lives and bottom line. We will be showcasing and teaching the cleverest and best strategies for Small and Medium Enterprises and enlightened managers, and sourcing the reliable 'done for you' solution providers. In March we celebrate International Women's Day with the Iconic Helen Reddy. In April we take a road trip to the US for a management intensive with Jack Welch, one of the world's greatest CEO's. This is the first of many amazing mastermind road trips planned for the year ahead so I'm bursting with excitement! We will be taking style and shopping trips to New York while attending the World Innovation Forum, and clearance retreats with some of the world's greatest yoga and spiritual teachers. We believe in nurturing the whole person. My dream AND goal is to help thousands of businesses and their families to flourish and I am committed and well on my way!

3 Tips To Stay Focused On Your Dreams

My three tips for staying motivated and on track:

1. Commit to Playing a Bigger Game. Create your dream board – make it as big as a whole wall in your garage if you want!! But focus on clarity of your heart's purpose. Take the time and make

the commitment to find a group of genuine, respected mentors and get clear on your personal VISION. What do you want more of in your life and what do you need less of, if you were to leave a legacy – what would yours be? When I started my first business there was literally one book in the city library for women wanting to learn how to run a business (that's how old I am!!). In my world there was limited or no perceived access to genuine mentors and world class cutting edge advice. Now thanks to the technology and reach of the internet mastermind advice is free and plentiful with resource centres like WonderfulWebWomen.com and Ms Independence. We've done the work for you and we're passionate about your success.

2. What You've Done So Far has Been Perfect, focus on what you CAN change and forgive yourself for anything you thought you did wrong – Now Plan Your BIG Game. All the super achievers I know, including the most successful people in the world, share one

3. Commit to Time with Mentors Living Delicious Lives. Will hanging out with successful people have a better chance of helping you lift your game? The odds are good. Is every successful person going to be a positive role model and mentor in your life? No

About The Author

Entrepreneur, mother and investor, Cydney has a depth of experience in a diverse range of industries; including founding and ownership roles in restaurants and catering, fashion and design, technology and social networking. She is an experienced real estate investor, and private and public company share investor. She admits openly that although she has enjoyed massive business success, she's made big mistakes too.

Janet Beckers

Her main areas of expertise and interest are Marketing, Customer Relations and Strategic Alliances, (in particular using joint ventures, Social Networking and mobile technology).

She is also a passionate supporter of micro-economic lending to provide greater opportunities for women in less enlightened cultures.

Through the Ms Independence Association she is blessed to enjoy the rewards of helping others who are committed to achieving dynamic results to develop profitable, sustainable businesses and find proven, qualified, ethical advisors. Members can join for free and greatly expand their access to outstanding, inspiring business experts and mentors.

Special Gift

Our gift to Gold Book readers: My 'get started' plan to set you up personally for success "How to Activate Your Inner Millionaire" plus 6 months free membership to our FastTrack program, a total value of over $300.

http://missindependence.com/wwwgoldbookbonus

http://www.MsIndependence.com

Big Dreams ... Big Life ... Living with Passion and Purpose

Dana Dunn

Pursue Your Passion "Every great dream begins with a dreamer. Always remember, you have within you the strength, the patience, and the passion to reach for the stars to change the world." - Harriet Tubman.

Today I am proud to say that I am living my dream, but not that long ago, my dream was a living nightmare. Like so many others, I had lost a job and career due to the unfortunate economic climate. When we lost our home, cars, and just about all of our material possessions, I began to question and ask myself, "what was I here for?"

It was truly in my darkest hour, that I had realized the adversity I was experiencing, was really a blessing in disguise. Very quickly I realized that adversity creates opportunity, and it was my chance to embrace it! It was my opportunity to break free. Free to be me, and live my life more passionately and purposefully! It was not the physical material things in life that really mattered, it was who was I in this world, and the difference I was meant to make in the lives of others around me.

It is my personal belief that we are masterfully created to live our lives with passion and purpose. You are here on purpose, your life has meaning, and most importantly, you were put on this earth to make a difference! What is your purpose? What do you feel called to do?

So often we get hung up on what other people think, or what they think we should do with our lives. The sad reality is that we almost become programmed to live someone else's dream or ideas for our life. The question you should be asking yourself is: "Who am I, and what do I want out of life?" I may not know you personally, but I would be willing to bet that for most of your life, you have been driven by the need, desire, and necessity of earning a living and getting a paycheck. I think this is probably true for most of us. The focus was not on what we wanted to do, but what we felt we had to do. Regardless of where your life has taken you up to this point, the exciting thing is that it's never too late to make a change. It's your life, and it's time YOU take control of it! Why not do something you love to do, instead of something you feel you have to do? It is time to ask yourself "do I want to make a living, or do I want to make a life?" It is far too easy to live an average life! To live a life of mediocrity was no longer an option for me, and it shouldn't be for you either. So the question you may want answered is: "What am I passionate about? Can I really make a living doing what I love?"

Why is it so important to pursue your passions? The answer is quite simple really. Passion is a very powerful emotion; it can become an unstoppable force. Passion creates energy, excitement, and breathes new life into us!

So let me ask you, "is your current career path providing that energy and excitement?" Do you wake up every day and jump out of bed ready to take on the world? If not, why not? I am telling you...life is just too darn short to live an unfulfilled life. Living life with passion and purpose will lead you to greater joy, and a life you've never even dreamed of.

Pursuing your passion in life can help you achieve your dreams. What do you have... if you don't have dreams? A very dull and average life! Dreamers are achievers. They push past all the negativity and live life to the fullest. The fact that you are reading this right now tells me that you are ready to pursue your passion, even if you don't yet know what that is. I am excited for you as you begin this incredible journey of self-discovery and life's purpose. Your life will be forever changed, and you will no longer be satisfied with just getting by. When you get to the end of your life, you will be faced with the one of two pains, the pain of discipline, or the pain of regret. Which will it be?

Pursing your passion will take discipline, determination, and the will to succeed no matter what! You have the power within you to make this happen. Don't fall back into your comfort zone, and let this beautiful life pass you by. It's time to pursue your passion! Pursuing your passion and purpose in life will take some hard work and determination. When times get tough, I just remember what my life was like before, and that keeps me pushing onward and upward. Most importantly, I have removed the option to quit! Never, never, give up on your dreams. You were made to do great things in this life! Now, prepare to go out and make a difference! For some people, discovering their passion and pursing it comes easily, while for others it is a challenge. As a life and business coach, I run into this quite often, and I have an exercise that might help you. Here it is below.

3 Tips To Stay Focused On Your Dreams

1. Name something you believe you are extremely passionate about. What do you believe creates the passion you have for something you care about? What causes it?

2. Take some time and get a sheet of paper out and answer the questions above, then list everything you can think of that you are truly passionate about. Then, for each item on your list, write a brief statement of why you are passionate about that.

3. See if you can find the thread that ties them all together. Once you do this, you will be well on your way to discovering what your true passions are.

About The Author

Dana Dunn has been a Sales and Marketing Professional for over 25 years. She is passionate about helping Business Professionals and Entrepreneurs harness the power of the internet and take charge of their life and business.

Dana works with Entrepreneurs, Service Professionals, Direct Selling Leaders, and Business Owners who want to get more Clients, and increase their profits, so that they can create the life and lifestyle of their choosing. She specializes in helping her clients create Visibility, Credibility, and Marketability by providing an online Marketing Solution that complements any business model.

In addition to her business training and experience, Dana is a Certified Life and Business Coach, Performance Consultant, an Online Business Strategist, Speaker, and Trainer.

Her professional experience currently includes: WordPress Coach/Trainer, Radio Show Producer for Wonderful Web Radio, Contributing Expert for Fast Video Results Training Program, Contributing Author for Social Media Woman Magazine, and Contributing Author for the Amazon Best Selling Book: "The Gratitude Book Project: Celebrating 365 Days of Gratitude."

Special Gift

My goal and mission in life is to help others discover their true potential by following their passions and purpose in life. In order to live big, you must first DREAM BIG! To learn more, please go to: http://DanaDunn.com   Register there for your free eBook and Audio: "Pursue Your Passion!"

http://DanaDunn.com http://WomenWithPassionAndPurpose.com

Career Journeys 101

Dana Hughes

Are you where you expected to be?

If you said "No I'm not" then you join me and thousands of others who have arrived in places they didn't expect. It's not to say you, me or they are unhappy, although some are, others have just taken a journey.

If you had asked me at 18 where would I be now terms of my career and life I would not have imagined that I'd be running an internet business, co-own an online training company, a career counsellor, be writing a book and developing career development tools and live in the country and that's now.

At 18 I had tried on many different 'career hats' which is important for any young person when trying to figure out what on earth they want to do for work, possibly for the rest of their lives. I'd looked at my parents and thought no way! I looked at people I admired and wondered about medicine, forgetting I hated the sight of blood and even thought about the police force, all perfectly good careers but not right for me. I began to panic.

My first career move was to become a teacher which I loved for a number of years. But still I felt restless. Then life happened and I found myself living is a remote community it was in fact the southernmost settlement of mainland Australia and the need to re-invent myself professionally.

Acknowledging that my work life was essential to my sanity. I discovered that I need to feel that what I do for work is contributing to the collective good. So I began some soul searching. I spent time identifying what I was good and as well as what I loved to do. I did simple things such as looking at the books on my bookshelf for indicators of what I was drawn to, I listened to myself in conversation and discovered what topics I gravitated to and then I began to **design a career**.

I didn't give it a name just listed what would be perfect, what would make me happy. I remember some people scoffing and saying that it was naive to start here and that I had to focus on making money. I was very aware I needed to bring in an income I just hoped that I could do it doing something I enjoyed. Many people never take the step to actually describe what they want. So armed with the belief that knowing what you want is the first step in getting it I soldiered on.

The result was a training company which gave me the opportunity to use skills I had, meet people I liked and required me to learn and build new skills. It also gave me confidence that I was on the right track.

Over time I kept adding to my perfect job picture. One thing missing in my first picture was the awareness that I wanted to work with a team. The next adventure was the serendipitous meeting of a woman with similar ideas who was a dynamo. Along with another IT savvy woman we started an online training company, developing resources to enhance the skills of staff in their day to day work roles.

I have loved all of my working adventures. Each one has given me at least one new skill and all have added to a more complete picture of the perfect career for me. The culmination of my work/life journey is my latest venture. Collecting the stories of people who have arrived in career and life destinations they didn't expect. It has entailed exploring the beliefs and behaviours that have brought these people to their unique destination point in their lives that they deem as successful, even if surprising. Sharing these stories on line, in hard copy and in conversation is an honour. Themes from these success stories include;

- **Say YES**! wherever possible and commit to make it work
- **Show up in every moment** – be a volunteer in your life, don't be a prisoner
- Remember that your role is to **create a happy life** so spend the time to discover what you like to do and keep sight of it always

- If you **follow your bliss** you'll get there
- Even what appears to be a disaster or procrastination if **thought of in a useful way** will bring insights and often opportunities

Your career journey is exactly that – yours. See it as unique and special. If you have to make the dollars in a job that does not give you much joy then do whatever you have to do to find aspects that you can appreciate.

I urge you to take the challenge, create the picture of the career of your dreams - shift it from a dream to reality. Once you have created the list then watch as components begin to come to you and above all have fun!

3 Tips To Stay Focused On Your Dreams

1. **Create a career picture** - add all that you can from the big ideas to the specifics e.g. what you want to wear to work. Describe what you will see, hear and feel when you are in your perfect career. Then place it on the wall so you can see it daily.

2. **Look for people who are doing parts or all of what you want to do.** Interview or talk with them. find out what they do or did to create their career and model the parts you want.

3. **Show up in every moment of your life**

About The Author

Dana's passion is career/life journeys. She works with people to create the bridges from where they are now to where they want to be. Her career journey has been as a teacher, facilitator and developer of resources to enhance skill development for work and an author. She lives in country Victoria where she never expected to be.

Special Gift

Free template for designing the perfect career can be obtained from http://www.careerlifesuccess.com.au

http://www.careerlifesuccess.com.au

Janet Beckers

What Are You Doing To Make A Difference?

Daryl Grant

First up let me introduce myself. I'm Daryl Grant. My gorgeous husband Andrew and I have an internet business where we sell info products. This is something we've done for the last 5 years, and it gives us a great passive income. It's allowed us to give up our 7-day-a-week consulting business, and pretty much do whatever we want with our time. Our business runs on autopilot, and because we have a world-wide market, we literally make money while we sleep. Now having passive income really is a wonderful thing. We travel, we hang out with the kids, we enjoy our beach-front home. But here's the thing (and you might be able to relate to this) - I find there is only so much sitting around I can do!

You see, even though I don't have to work any more, I still need to feel productive. To make a difference. And this is what motivates me. A couple of years ago, Andrew and I sat down and asked ourselves "now that we have all the time and money we need, what will we do with it?" It was a powerful exercise, and one which has shaped our current lifestyle. Here's what we came up with. We decided the best way we could make a difference, was to help other people to achieve the sort of life we now enjoy.

The Power of 100

Through our internet training program www.OurInternetSecrets.com, we now teach people all over the world how to make passive income the way we do - selling info products. Here's one of the reasons that we decided this would be the best use of our skills and time. We firmly believe that everyone needs to be responsible for their own financial future. The reality is, the government won't be able to look after you when you decide to finish work. With the baby-boomers retiring and living longer, there is a huge increase in the number of people needing support. And not as many people coming through paying taxes to support them.

If you're under 50, you're pretty much on your own financially. And with superannuation going backwards the future is looking pretty scary. So we're giving people an alternative to have a fantastic future – where you are in control, and free of financial fear. The other reason we do it (and this is what I find incredibly motivating) is because of the wider impact we can have. You see, we often ask people the question that motivated us: "If you had all the time and money that you needed, what would you do with it?" And you know what? Almost everyone we ask says the same thing: "I'd help other people".

We've heard some wonderful ideas – from helping struggling friends and family, to dreams of setting up charities and support around the world. I feel honoured to have played a part in getting these wonderful ventures under way. Many years ago I heard a story that sums up what we do, and why we do it. You may have heard it already, but I think about it whenever we help another of our members to financial freedom. Here's how it goes. There was a man walking along the beach. In the distance he could see a woman, bending down, picking something up, and throwing it out to sea – again and again. As he got closer he saw that there were thousands of starfish washed up on the shore. They were all destined to die – unless they could get back into the water.

So the woman was throwing them back, one at a time. It was a huge task, and the man thought what she was doing was a bit futile as there were so many starfish. He said to her "Why are you wasting your time doing this? Look how many starfish there are. You'll never make a difference." The woman reached down, picked up another starfish and threw it back. She stared the man in the eye and quietly said "Well I made a difference to that one". What would you do if you had all the time and money you needed? Together we can all make a difference.

http://wonderfulwebwomen.com |

Janet Beckers

3 Tips To Stay Focused On Your Dreams

1. Draw yourself a warm bath. Add your favourite fragrance. Pour yourself a glass of bubbles. Close the door and sink in.

2. Ask yourself this question: "If you had all the time and money you needed, what would you do?" Think about the things you'd do for you, your friends and family, and for people you don't yet know.

3. Now close your eyes and visualise the things you'd do as specifically as you can. Focus on the feelings you get as you do them. Congratulations! You're on your way to achieving your dreams.

About The Author

Hi I'm Daryl Grant. I live in a beachfront home on the beautiful Gold Coast in Australia with my hubbie of 22 years Andrew, and 2 gorgeous kids. But life wasn't always like this. Just 5 years ago Andrew and I were working 7 days a week in our consulting business. We never took holidays because when we did the money stopped. And we hardly ever saw the kids because we were so busy. We knew we wanted a better life – one with the freedom to do what we wanted, whenever we wanted. We tried loads of things to make passive income and achieve financial freedom – property, shares, forex trading. But nothing worked for us until we "discovered" the internet. Even though we're not techie (I could hardly download my emails when we started!) we ended up making over $250,000 in our first 12 months selling information products. This has now grown to a multi-million dollar business, most of which runs on auto-pilot. In fact our internet business is so automated that these days we'd have trouble turning the income off! We love to share our systems to help others become financially free. I hope you enjoy this article about how you can make a difference.

Special Gift

If you'd love some practical help to make passive income, please go to www.OurInternetSecrets.com to download your free copy of our "Quickstart Guide to Making Money Online". Enjoy!

http://www.OurInternetSecrets.com

Janet Beckers

Yes, You Can!

Dawn Z Bournand

Dreams are wonderful things! You surely have one glowing inside of you but perhaps for some reason you have not yet allowed it to come to fruition. Or perhaps you think you don't even have a dream, and that life would be so much better if only you did have one. Well, I can promise you, you do have one, perhaps you just haven't given yourself permission to bring it to your conscious mind…yet. We all have dreams; it is the beautiful human condition: our quest to continually progress, to grow, to make our lives better. So whether you have found your dream or whether it is waiting to be discovered within you, isn't it time that you started taking action to make that dream happen? No more what if's and wish I could's for you, if you have this book in hand (or on desktop as the case may be) it's a pretty good indication that you are ready to start making things happen.

Through my own life experience and work with clients both as a coach and a consultant, I have come to find that there are three essential steps to making your dreams come true. If you follow these three Realizations and carry them through on a regular basis, your dream will happen. A little caveat here though, there is one thing that could hold you back from creating what you really want: YOU! I do not mean that to sound harsh but until you realize that you hold the keys to unlocking all that you are dreaming of, those things will have great difficulty coming into your life. Believe me, I know, I have had to get out of my own way more than once. Don't let this idea overwhelm you, on the contrary, let it excite you and fill you with a sense of power that you have not fully tapped into, until now that is.

Realization Step 1: Define It

What is your dream exactly? You want to get very clear on what it is and when I say very clear I mean down to the tiniest detail. Let's say for example you want to start your own business. Ok, that was not too difficult but what kind of business do you want to start? Do you want to work from home or do you want to have your own company location? What will your company do and who will it serve? And most importantly how is it going to feel when you have that fabulous business? When I decided to move to Paris, I got very clear on how I wanted my life to be when I moved here. I imagined the kind of people I wanted to be around, the things I wanted to be doing and even the place I wanted to live. Nearly every idea became a part of my life here, along with so many more amazing things that I could have never imagined or dreamed of. It did take a little while to manifest that gorgeous apartment I had been dreaming of but even that came into my life in due time. A little side note here, if you are in that category that I spoke about earlier, the one where you are not sure what your dream is, take the time in Realization step 1 to figure out what it is.

Dreams do not all have to be big and grandiose. It could be something as simple as wanting to get a massage every week (easily done and quite cheap if you can find a local massage school) but find at least one dream that you can work on right now. Why? Well because once you get your dream muscle in shape, you will be amazed by all of the things she will bring into your life! Ok, now that you have named your dream, it is essential that you find the WHY of this dream. Your why will be your motivator when things get bumpy or even downright depressing. Your why will help you to realize that every unexpected turn in the road is actually a learning curve and a helping hand to get you on the right track. Your why is a very important element because it will help you stay the course.

The number one reason why certain people who strive for their dreams do not attain them is that they give up too soon. It is as simple as that. I love the story of the reporter who asked Thomas Edison about his famous 10,000 tries before he got the light bulb right. The reporter asked him if he wasn't disappointed by all of those

Janet Beckers

failed tries. Edison replied that for him they were not failures at all just steps toward understanding the right way to accomplish what he wanted to do! If only all of us could have the tenacity to try something 10,000 times and even better yet consider those tries successes and not failures for bringing us closer to our dream! Edison was determined to find out how to capture electricity and use it to create light. It was his driving force and he succeeded. He knew his why; it was crystal clear in his mind. Get that same crystal clarity with your dream and who knows what amazing things you could accomplish!

Realization Step 2: Make it Real

If your dream seems a bit far-fetched to you from where you stand right now, one of the best things you can do for yourself is a handy little trick called backward planning. You see, your dream is only too big to you from where you are right now. You need to get yourself mentally in the place of where you want to be. You then begin to plan from that point, only backwards. This allows you to be in the mindset of pure possibility because you are planning from a point of it already happening. Using the owning your own business example again, let's look at what backward planning could look like for this dream. Instead of planning from a place where you have no business, let's plan from 24 months in the future when you have a healthy, thriving business that is fulfilling to you and all those you serve.

Focus on this image for a few minutes and see the details: how many employees do you have, what is your annual revenue, how many regular clients do you have, how many hours are you working, who have you created joint ventures with, etc. Now that you know where you are, think about what came just before this. In other words if for example you are at month 24 with 4 employees, bringing in $450,000 in revenue, with 170 regular customers and numerous new customers, working a 35 hour work week and creating new joint ventures on a monthly basis, where were you at 21 months? Then continue to go back from there: 18 months, 16 months, 1 year, 9 months, 6 months, 3 months, 1 month, 2 weeks, tomorrow. You get the picture. The big out of reach goal of running a nearly half a million dollar business becomes very attainable when chunked down into easily reachable steps. You no longer have to bridge that gap from zero to 450,000. That is just too darn hard for most of us. But can you see yourself adding one new customer tomorrow, and then another one next week?

When the numbers and details seem more realistic you give yourself permission to go for it. You say to yourself 'Yes, I can do that'. And you know what...you can! If I had tried to jump from American businesswoman who barely spoke French to a woman happily living in France with three gorgeous children, a wonderful husband and a company that I am thrilled to be running, that might have been a bit too much for my imagination to grasp. Over a period of thirteen years, I have planned things in small backwards increments which helped me to accomplish each goal that I had. Just keep it real and you can accomplish all that your heart desires.

Realization Step 3: Put it into Action

You have surely heard the famous saying 'Success is 10% inspiration and 90% perspiration'. Now this may sound like a bit of a let-down and more work than you want to put in but you know what, when you are perspiring over what you love and moving in the direction of your dream, work feels pretty similar to play. So this action bit should actually be a whole lot of fun. Sure there will be learning curves, you will make mistakes and suffer some consequences but when those moments arrive, remember Henry Ford's wise words: "Failure is only the opportunity to begin again more intelligently". In other words there is no such thing as failure, just life lessons to be learned. The truly great thing about taking action is that you are subconsciously telling yourself, you believe you can accomplish this dream of yours, it really can happen. How exciting is that? Start with baby steps, the ones that aren't hard to do. Something as simple as buying a book on the subject that you are dreaming about will do. Just take action today, tomorrow and the next day, and the next day. Do not stop!

Now that the action ball is rolling you need to do a couple more things in this realization step to make sure you stay the course. You will have your periods of doubt and down moments just be prepared for that but in those down moments you will need someone to lean on and hopefully even lift you up. Therefore you need to get a coach, a mentor, an accountability buddy or even join a mastermind group who will be there to give you advice, motivation and even a gentle push when necessary. Just make sure you are setting yourself up for success by putting a support person or team in place. Last but not least, make sure that you are tracking your progress in some way and that you celebrate each victory.

When you are pursuing a dream it is so easy to get caught up in the details that you forget to acknowledge all that you have done and how far you have come. I must admit this is something that I still occasionally struggle with but it really does feel wonderful when you just allow yourself to bask in a moment of accomplishment every once in a while. Take the time to congratulate yourself and to be grateful for

Janet Beckers

what has already transpired. You can do this you know. Your dream is so close to realization. I have total and complete faith in you; it is my greatest wish that you do too! To your Fabulous Success!

3 Tips To Stay Focused On Your Dreams

1. Define your dream - get clear on your dream and your why

2. Make it real - create do-able steps from a mindset of having already accomplished your dream

3. Put your dream into action - a dream without action remains a dream but a dream plus action equals your new reality

About The Author

An American living in Paris, Dawn Z Bournand has pursued and achieved many lifetime dreams. Never one to take "that can't be done" as a final answer, she believes that reinventing yourself and personal transformation can take place anytime your soul desires. Happily married and a mother to 3 young boys, Dawn lives her message that your dream life is not only possible it is your right. She has seen how important it is to uncover your life purpose and then to pursue it with an inspired dedication and wants to help other women do the same. After 12 successful years in corporate America, Dawn took a break to study photography in Paris before the world of higher education came calling. Now an expert on Executive education and leadership, she has taken her passion for self growth and created Fabulously Successful to help women Live their lives on Purpose.

Special Gift

Specially offered for 100 Women, 100 Stories readers: A Fabulously Successful Action Plan Worksheet and Daily Checklist to get you on the path of your dreams and to help you stay the course. Additionally, you will have the opportunity to schedule a free 20 minute strategy session with Dawn to get clear on what you want and how to get it! To receive your bonus offer simply go to:
http://www.fabulouslysuccessful.com/100women

http://www.fabulouslysuccessful.com

Your Personal Mission Statement to Stay Focused

Debbie Allen

Personal development is the single most important thing you can do to improve your business or career. There is no faster way to make more money while you improve your business skills – and it will ultimately reflect your success or your failure. If you are going to be part of a best-of-the-best organization, you need to make sure that you have a personal laser-sharp focus. This will allow you to make a purposeful and significant contribution to building a higher level of success.

A personal mission statement is also extremely helpful in establishing and maintaining this focus in your personal life. Many business owners and managers have taken the time to create organizational mission statements. But few have gone through this process on a personal level. If you are one of the many who have not created a personal mission statement, now is the time to do so.

Five suggestions on how to write a personal mission statement:

1. Set aside some undisturbed time to think through and write your statement. Take some extended time away from the distractions of home and office to reflect on

where you are and how you desire to invest your life in the context of work, family, friends and your community. It is important to address all these areas of your life and to balance each. True success comes only when you have a balanced lifestyle of success, family, friends, true happiness and personal health. To become a highly successful leader, you must achieve this overall balance in your life.

2. Question yourself to identify your main purpose. What do you believe your sole purpose on this earth is? How will you achieve that by applying the right principles that determine how you live your life? How will you empower vision for yourself and others? What mentors do you admire, and what attributes does that person possess that you wish to obtain? What principles can you learn from other successful business people that you most benefit from within your own business? Your depth of thinking – not speed – is key to a strong focus. You don't have to actually write a statement at the beginning, simply answer the questions and you will begin to observe patterns and priorities in your life. By the time you have completed the questions, you should have discovered the essential elements of your life necessary to write your personal mission statement.

3. Collect your thoughts and implement your action plan. What are five goals you are committed to achieving in your business in the next year? In the next five years? In the next ten years? What specific actions do you need to take in the next year to achieve your one-year mission for your business? To achieve your five-year mission? To achieve your ten-year mission? Now, take a close look at your action plan, sole purpose, empowering vision and the right principles. Begin to write out your personal mission statement for your business. Then do the same for your family, friends and community. You personal mission statement may be short, but easy enough to clearly define and understand.

4. Enjoy the process and include others in your mission. Work on your mission statement and then gather the input of others to help you refine your ideas. Your business statement should also involve your team's input to crystallize your mission and its outcome affected by all.

5. Keep your mission statement available and visible at all times. You will continue to grow and change and your personal mission statement should grow and change along with you. Review and continue to plan with your mission in mind. Best-of-the-best leaders are marked by their clear sense of mission and strong vision. As a leader, taking the time to create a clear focus for your personal and professional life is the biggest gift you can give to yourself and your continued success.

3 Tips To Stay Focused On Your Dreams

1. **Be a Lifelong Learner** You can turn your commute time into life-long learning time. This is an incredible opportunity to help you stay focused, motivated and to help you advance your growth. Attend seminars often. Attendance at educational seminars focused toward your goals virtually guarantees your personal and professional development. Experts in your field will help you to stay on track, keep you inspired and offer you new insights, strategies and ideas. Stay after the event to meet the speaker in person, and ask questions that can help move you toward your goals.

2. **Network like crazy.** Meet people everywhere you go, and try to introduce yourself to at least three new people at every function you attend. Think of ways you can joint venture, send them business opportunities and build alliances with them. Arrive early

3. **Develop innovative thinking.** Most people know how to play a game that requires players to think only one move in advance. Many people manage their career in this manner, rarely investing in the future. Highly successful people, on the other hand, think five moves in advance. Forward-thinking people are much more likely to arrange training, and thus capitalize on their investment.

About The Author

Debbie Allen "The Millionaire Entrepreneur Business Builder" is one of the world's leading authorities on marketing. She is a best-selling author of five books and has presented before thousands of people in over 20 countries.

Sign up for Debbie Allen's Millionaire Entrepreneur Club and receive her 6 week e-Course Business Success Secrets Revealed plus audio download and business card quiz all for FREE ($200 value) at www.WealthAttractionMarketingSystem.com

Janet Beckers

Special Gift

Sign up for Debbie Allen's Millionaire Entrepreneur Club and receive her 6 week e-Course Business Success Secrets Revealed plus audio download and business card quiz all for FREE ($200 value) at www.WealthAttractionMarketingSystem.com

http://www.DebbieAllen.com http://www.ThePowerof3WorldTour.com

Illuminate The Path Of Your Dreams With Clarity, Focus, And Inspired Ideas

Debbie LaChusa

I was born a "driver." You know the type. Give me a task or a challenge and I'll make it happen, even if it kills me. Combine that with a Type A personality and you have the potential for huge success, and also burnout and constant dissatisfaction. I found this out the hard way. After burning myself out trying to manage my career and family, I was "forced" to quit my dream job and start my own business. When I say forced, I simply mean I saw no other way to find the elusive balance I was craving. So, in 1998, that's what I did. I started my own business, and guess what happened? I brought that same Type A, driving personality into my business and even though I was in control for the first time in my life, I found myself quickly heading down the path to burnout again.

I don't know why I was surprised; while I had changed my circumstances, I hadn't changed myself. Not wanting to end up chronically sick and burned out again, I knew I had to change. So I set out on a path of self discovery and personal development. And through that process I learned to live my life and operate my business in an entirely new way. It is through this new way of being that I have found the clarity, focus, fulfillment and peace I was so desperately craving. I also discovered it was the path – or should I say inspired path – to my dreams.

So what do I do differently now, than I did in years past that enables me to stay on this inspired path and in direct touch with my dreams?

• I recognize that I cannot, and do not want to, control things – rather I am open to what happens, knowing it is all here to serve me.

• I do not work hard to figure everything out on my own – I allow the ideas and answers to come to me instead.

• I do not fill my head so full with thoughts and my time so full with action that there is no room for anything else – I leave plenty of space for the Universe to bring me inspired ideas and to lay out my path in front of me.

• I take time to "check out" daily. For me, this means going for a run or just getting outside and NOT thinking about my business. I have solved more problems and generated more ideas, more easily, with this process than anything else I have ever done, and because they are inspired ideas they are ALWAYS in support of my highest goals and dreams. Oh, and this has helped my mental and physical health immensely!

• I trust that everything is happening in perfect timing and do not try to force things to happen more quickly than they are unfolding.

• I set clear intentions and I take consistent action.

• I am willing to change course when necessary and not be too attached to things.

• I am open to whatever shows up, and I continue to be amazed at how powerful the Universe is at making our dreams come true – much more powerful than we can ever be on our own.

If this sounds a little "out there" or "woo-woo" to you, let me just say that not too long ago I would have agreed with you. I was born a planner; organized in my actions, always mapping out my game plans and doing whatever it took to accomplish them. Letting go was one of the most challenging things I have ever done, and truth be told, it probably took me a couple of years to fully relinquish control.

But since that time, my life has been magical. My business has evolved and flowed in a way that has allowed me to continue stepping into my purpose and passion more and more every day. In the matter of just a few years, I was able to step away from a business that while very profitable, was no longer enjoyable, and instead design a new business that I love. I have created new programs and services that serve my clients better and that I love delivering. I trust myself more, my business has become significantly more profitable, and my life more balanced and fulfilling.

I would actually say that this new way of being has not allowed me to keep my dreams alive, rather it has allowed me to live my dreams. When you step onto the inspired path life flows and business flows. Yes, it requires that you take action (you can't just sit around and wait for things to happen), and in some cases it may mean a lot of work, but it is a joy, because you know you are following the path of your dreams and the Universe is lighting the way.

I personally couldn't imagine ever going back to living or operating my business any other way. If you're ready to follow the path of your dreams, here are 3 action steps you can take to get started:

3 Tips To Stay Focused On Your Dreams

Be willing to let go of trying to control everything.

Take time to "check out" every day and "listen" to the ideas that come to you. (This might mean going for a walk or jog, meditating, doing yoga, having a cup of tea, or just sitting outside in nature. Do whatever activity allows you to free your mind.

When something doesn't go as you wish, instead of focusing on it as a failure or mistake, ask the question "How can this serve me?"

Janet Beckers

About The Author

Known as The Business Stylist™ Debbie LaChusa is a business and branding expert whose focus is on making over businesses that aren't living up to their full potential, and helping business owners design a business and brand that "fit" them perfectly. An international speaker who has shared the stage with celebrity teachers from "The Secret," Debbie has inspired audiences in the United States, Canada, and Australia with her message of personal and business empowerment. Debbie shares her expertise frequently in the media and has been featured in Entrepreneur Magazine, Inc.com, Forbes.com, CNBC.com and Home Business Magazine. She was also chosen as one of five expert bloggers for the Yahoo! Small Business blog. Through all of her business ventures, Debbie has learned first-hand the power of clarity and focus and what it takes to build and market a successful and enjoyable business. Her message to you is, "Stop following in the footsteps of others, the best you can ever achieve is second place. Follow your own path and come in first every time!" Debbie is dedicated to helping people find that path and design a business that fits them to a "T."

Special Gift

Bonus Action Step and Free Gift: Get my Get Clear! Program for Free! This 3-week program will help you find and follow your inspired path (A $97 Value). Visit www.getclearprogram.com for all the details and simply enter the Coupon Code WWW2011 at checkout.

http://www.DebbieLaChusa.com

The chicken or the pig? It's time to get committed!

Dee Britton

The Chicken or The Pig? It's time to get committed! If someone had mentioned to me three years ago that I would be an author in a book on vision, focus and dreams I would have laughed at them. Oh, I had plenty of things that I wanted to do in my life, and I was managing to do a few of them, but I had never written down a goal and definitely had no big vision. You see, three years ago I was (or so I thought) happy just plodding along in life. I was a mother to 2 wonderful children, had a gorgeous loving husband, lived in a beautiful house, had just finished a double University degree and was running my own Personal Training Business. I didn't want for much more and was busy conforming to society.

I am not sure how it happened (fate, I believe) but I stumbled upon a Personal Development seminar and for the first time in my life I created a large vision for my life and learnt how to dream big (I mean really BIG). I came to understand how the laws of the Universe work and the reasons I was stuck where I was. Although I thought I was living a good life, I was living so far below my potential because of my thoughts and my lack of self belief.

Janet Beckers

All of a sudden I started to believe that I could be, do and have anything that I desired. That by focussing on what I really wanted in life and giving more back, I was able to attract new and exciting opportunities to myself in order to create it. I realised that I had a purpose in life and that the only way that I could live a truly full life is to fulfil that purpose.

My Big Vision My big vision is to work in 3rd World countries to help build schools for under privilege children. I am going to help these children obtain an education and believe in themselves, that they too can be, do and have anything they desire. Just because they are born into poverty does not mean that is their destiny. But in the mean time (while I am still raising two children of my own) I have become a Certified Life Coach and am working with women empowering them to be the best that they can be. I am helping women just like myself, dream big, believe in themselves, set goals and achieve a happier, healthier lifestyle.

Staying Focussed In order to stay motivated, inspired and focussed on my dreams, goals and vision I have a created my own vision board and mind movie. My vision board is filled with pictures of activities I will participate in, places I will visit, people I will meet, my dream house, my dream car, my ideal body and lifestyle. Every time I look at this board I get so excited that my heart flutters and my body tingles. My mind movie has very similar pictures and goals but it is in movie form and plays my favourite song throughout the movie (Woman on a Mission).

Most of these goals were once beyond my wildest dreams, but I now know in my heart that they will all one day be a reality. Life is never just plain sailing though and there always seems to be some obstacles that pop up just to make sure I am awake. But no matter what life throws at me the one thing that keeps me on track is my 'Gratitude Journal'. Every night when I get into bed and before I go to sleep, I write down at least three things that I am grateful for in my life. It may be something great that happened that day like speaking to a fabulous responsive audience, or something as simple as the beautiful flowers in my garden or the warm sun on my face.

So no matter what is going on in my life I am always able to feel grateful for who I am, what I have and the wonderful people around me. One of the most important things I have learnt over the past three years is to not to try and re-invent the wheel and to get a good team around me. There are so many other people who have already made mistakes and have so much wisdom and knowledge, so I make a choice to learn from them. I have mentors to help me achieve my visions, dreams and goals faster. I also have a team around me to delegate the tasks that I am not so good at. I share my dreams, goals and visions with my mentors and team and they help to keep me accountable.

By focussing on my vision board and mind movie, writing in my 'Gratitude Journal' daily, working with my mentors and team, as well as taking full responsibility for my life and taking massive action enables me to keep moving forward no matter how tough things get.

But it wasn't until someone asked me this question that I really started to move forward and create my success. During a conversation about what was happening in my life one day a friend asked me "Dee, are you the Chicken or the Pig?" I had no idea what she was talking about. She explained to me that in a meal of bacon and eggs the chicken participates but the pig is totally committed. So once again she asked the same question. It made me really think. Was I just plodding along still, just participating or was I really committed to my success and creating the life of my dreams?

I am totally committed to creating the life of my dreams and helping others do the same. Are you being the chicken or the pig?

3 Tips To Stay Focused On Your Dreams

Have a vision and know what you want in your life. Visualise your future and dream big. Feel the feelings of already achieving it and get excited.

Be Grateful. On a daily basis be totally grateful for the life you have. No matter what is going on in your life you are so much better off than millions of other people in the world.

Get a mentor and build a team. Learn from others who have gone before you and build a strong team of great people around you and your business.

Janet Beckers

About The Author

Dee Britton is a Weight Release & Body Transformation Specialist, as well as being one of Australia's Leading Lifestyle Coaches, Educators and Personal Trainers. With her extensive background in the fields of health, hypnosis, NLP, exercise prescription and personal development, Dee is widely regarded as one of this country's superior change specialists, having consistently produced outstanding results with thousands of people. Being an experienced Life Coach, Certified Hypnotherapist, NLP Master Practitioner, Primary School Teacher, Human Movement graduate, competitive triathlete, business owner, and a mum in her spare time(!), gives Dee a unique ability and skill-set to be able to communicate and connect with anyone, from any background, seeking to create life-long results with their mind, their body, their relationships and their lifestyle. Dee understands how easy it is to get caught in the trap of drifting through daily life and just existing. Dee specializes in empowering women to be the best that they can be and helps them create the fabulous, happy, healthy life they have always wanted.

Special Gift

Dee Britton has generously offered a FREE personal assessment, which will show you exactly how to create more health, happiness and success in your life - Valued at $97 - to all readers of this book. Simply email Dee at dee@feelingfabulousforever.com with 100 Women 100 Stories Offer in the subject title to book your FREE session TODAY! Be COMMITTED!!!!

http//:www.feelingfabulousforever.com   http//:www.deebritton.com
http//:www.7secretstoyouridealbody.com

Resistance, Confront And Staying Focused Through It All

Diana Vogel

Looking back over the past few years, I'm amazed how far I've come. I was a stay-at-home Mum, looking after my two beautiful children and supporting my husband in his business. I had serious health issues and had become convinced that I couldn't meaningfully contribute to society by going to work or even volunteering at the local kindergarten. Occasionally, I would venture out into the wider world, usually to attend a conference with our favourite business mentor. I was there in a supporting role – encouraging my husband to grow, both in his business and himself. Little did I realise that I was also growing. The moment my life changed, forever, still stands out vividly in my memory.

We were in Cairns, Queensland, at a special event held by our business mentor. He was discussing under-utilised products and how we could maximise them. When all of a sudden it hit me: I had a product that I was under-utilising. I had a market I wasn't tapping into! I lay there stunned (at the time I was at the back of the room lying on a banana lounge) as the enormity of the idea washed over me. I had

Janet Beckers

thought I was there to support my husband. The Universe had other ideas! For 2 years I had been educating my children at home. My eldest son had been falling through the cracks at school, and my youngest son had developed stress-related alopecia. Our eldest, had moderate dyslexia, and his difficulties in learning to read and write had been creating a very stressful, frustrating and overwhelming (for both of us) situation. I had initially attempted to teach him the way I'd learned, only to discover that approach made the situation far worse. In despair, I had rallied all my energy, suspended 'school-at-home' and launched into full-time research mode.

The more I studied, the more I realised that my son had been given a wonderful gift – if I could help him tap into it. As a result of all my research, I developed a system of teaching that involved movement, self-esteem development, auditory and visual cues. I developed aides that helped him develop his short-term memory and I was amazed that in one short year he had gone from not being able to read (3 ½ years behind his peers) to being on par with them. The next year saw him charge full steam ahead and he finished the year 2 years above his peers. People began to notice.

Enter "the confront." I was asked to tutor other children with dyslexia. I was very reluctant to do this – after all, it took all my energy just to teach my own children. But I couldn't say no, not when one of them was on the verge of suicide because she was convinced that she was a "failure – a waste of space" and only 9. In eight months of working with that little girl, I took her from being 2 years behind her peers, suicidal and very, very emotional to on par with her school year, and confident within herself. Her parents raved to other parents, the school, anyone who would listen... I had a business!

Enter "the resistance." I didn't want a business. I wanted to be a stay-at-home mum, I didn't want the responsibility. I twisted and turned and attempted every avoidance strategy I could think of to justify why I couldn't help more dyslexic kids believe in themselves. In the end, I realised that there wasn't an excuse that I could come up with that would, as the saying goes, hold any water. I knew that if I didn't speak up, that if I didn't reach out and help these kids, then I was condemning them to the possibility of a life filled with failure, low self-esteem, crime, gangs, or suicide. Very few of them would realise the gift that they had been given.

So, how did I overcome "the confront "and "the resistance?" First, I learned to meditate. To still my mind. Now, I begin every day with a 15 min session before I review my "To Do List". On my "To Do List" I have prioritised those activities that will make me money, and the ones I have the most resistance in doing. I do these first. No excuses. To make sure that I stay on top of all my projects, I have large pieces of paper stuck up everywhere on the walls of my home and office. They contain all the ideas, action steps and outcomes that I desire for each project. This way, I see them daily. Every day I review my vision – "To empower dyslexic children. To help them realise they are special, awesome beings that can achieve their dreams and goals".

I remind myself that no matter how confronting making a video, writing an article, or speaking from stage might be, if I don't, there are families and children out there who will suffer because of my lack of action. I am also part of a Business Mastermind Group – I have a Business Buddy to whom I am accountable. We talk each week and outline what we want to achieve for the week, challenges we've faced and give an accounting on how well we've met the previous weeks' goals. It has been invaluable – they are on the outside looking in, so they can see what I might have missed. Working on myself is critical. I have weekly sessions with a body worker (Reiki, Kinergetics, Network Care Chiropractor, etc) and I shift the emotional/energetic blocks that were contributing to my illness, low confidence in myself and my abilities.

I find that this helps immensely when my workload becomes hectic and I feel overwhelmed. Many people are afraid of taking the step and launching into their own business. I know I was. Developing relationships with successful business owners has been invaluable. These mentors have helped me understand marketing, business systems and client relations. But most of all, they have helped me to believe in myself and the gift I have to give. When I see the results that others get when they implement what I've shown them, makes the ups, the downs, the overcoming of fears and doubts all worthwhile.

3 Tips To Stay Focused On Your Dreams

Meditate daily

Do those activities which make you money or you have the most resistance to, FIRST!

Find a Business Buddy/Mentor that you can talk with weekly – someone who will hold you accountable.

Janet Beckers

About The Author

Diana Vogel is a sought after specialist tutor, speaker, parent educator and author who is passionate about teaching parents and their dyslexic children the life skills that they need to maximize their chances of success. The mother of 2 wonderful boys, one of whom is dyslexic, Diana has seen both the positive and negative sides of the dyslexia coin.

Special Gift

To obtain a free e-book entitled "How To Regain A Normal Life With A Dyslexic Child" valued at $47 visit http://www.TheWholeBodyLearningSystem.com

http://www.KinaLearn.com
http://www.LearnAtHomeSystem.com
http://www.DyslexicSuicide.com

http://www.TheDyslexiaMovie.com
http://www.FamousDyslexicPeople.com

Discover Your Hedgehog

Eve Grace-Kelly

'Look and you will find it – what is unsought will go undetected.' Sophocles

Plato's advice was "Know thyself." And it truly is the starting point in determining what we want to do in life and be happy doing it at the same time!

The Hedgehog concept, initially developed by Jim Collins and well described in his book Good to Great, has been around for a number of years, and was initially intended for business use, yet it is equally an amazing concept for everyone and is one that I use myself and with clients. As a coach, I've worked with several clients to help them articulate their Hedgehog as a cornerstone of a new business or new career.

I first came across the concept when I knew I wanted to start my own business, but having been on a traditional career path, I really didn't know where to start. I knew what skills I had but, beyond that, I really had no idea what I wanted to do or be!

For Jim Collins, the hedgehog concept "requires a deep understanding of three intersecting circles translated into a simple, crystalline concept (the Hedgehog concept)."

Janet Beckers

His book describes a distinct formula that great companies follow that allows them to be GREAT, not just good!

So what is this formula? Have a look at this diagram:

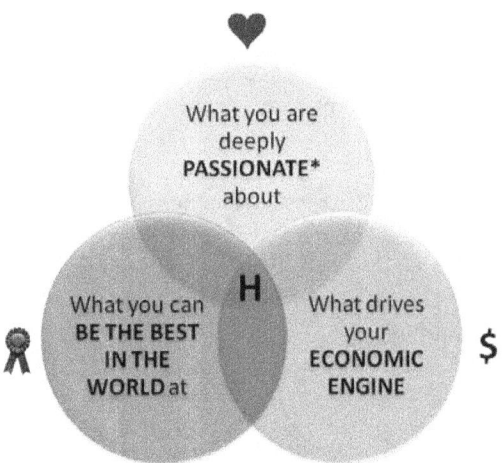

*Includes your core values and purpose

On the face of it, the concept looks easy. Find out what you are passionate about, what you can be the best at, and what you can make money doing.

Basically, your Hedgehog is the ONE key thing that can make a difference between loving what you do while making money, and all of the other alternatives. In addition, it's who you are. It's built into your DNA as what you can do as best in the world. Being your "best" may seem so natural to you that you don't even recognize it as a strength.

Do you know of someone who seems to have a particular knack for doing something but who doesn't know how or why she is good at it? The chances are she has found her Hedgehog.

My Hedgehog is to blast the glass ceiling when it comes to enabling women to succeed in what they want to do. I have recently set up the membership website: www.MillionaireWomenResources.com and want to make this the #1 site women go to for success strategies and other resources to help them achieve their goals.

So, let's look at the process in more detail. Each circle in the diagram above represents a certain characteristic.

1. What Are You Deeply Passionate About?

The first and most important thing is finding something that you are truly deeply passionate about. You may be good at finances, and you may know that you can earn a decent salary as an accountant, but do you love it? .....Really love it?

Being deeply passionate about something means trying and finding success in your life.

Success = Happiness

... so understanding what you are passionate about will lead to your happiness. If you understand the deeper purpose behind your goal, not only will you achieve it, but you will enjoy the journey!

Ask yourself this question: if you are making all the money you could need, and you were doing this job, would you still come to work? When you can honestly say to yourself, "I was made for this job and I am the luckiest person on earth!" you have it made.

2. What Can You Be The Best In The World At?

Secondly, identify what you can shine at – what you have a natural aptitude for. It is just as important to define the areas in which you are lacking skills.

What you could be the best at may be something you are not doing right now. Also, it may not be necessarily related to your abilities in a given area. You may be very good at writing, but that does not mean that you can be the best person in the world at writing, even with great effort.

In order to have a chance in a specific career field, you must first have a natural aptitude for it. For example, if I wanted to be a world-class singer, I'm pretty sure I would give up now! I don't have any natural acting or singing talent whatsoever – I don't even like to hear myself singing in the bath, so I know that there is no way that I can be the best in the world at it.

3. What Drives Your Economic Engine?

This sounds a very businesslike title, but really means: how can you make money? This is all about discovering the single denominator that will give you profits while allowing you to pursue your passion.

Once you have identified what you are best at, you can then determine whether it is economically viable. Very often, if you do what you love, the money will follow. This is the reason why we first look at what you are passionate about, and then what you can be the best at. If you look at the money first, you will probably be driven down the wrong path. But if you truly love what you do, this shouldn't matter. You should be thinking, "Wow, I can't believe I am getting paid to do something that I love!"

Your Hedgehog

The most important thing is at the intersection of all three circles. If you could live your life in that place, you will be doing something that works with your core competency:

Something you can be the very best in the world at; you are deeply passionate about your work and cannot believe you are getting paid for this; this combined passion and joy drives your economic engine – your ability to make money doing what you enjoy doing.

It is no good achieving two out of three circles – you need all three. If you are passionate about what you are doing and are good at it, but it's difficult to make money doing it, then this will only lead to disappointment and frustration. If you are good at what you do and you are making lots of money, but you hate what you are doing, it is not worth it. If there is money to be made in an industry that you are passionate about, but you are not any good at it, that can also be disappointing and frustrating.

So, what's your Hedgehog?

This is a process of discovery and I would firstly recommend you conduct a brief survey. Ask ten people who you know will be truly honest (e.g. this could be business associates, customers, friends, mentors, coaches) the following three questions:

1. What do you see are some of my greatest strengths? Can you give me a specific example?
2. What is the greatest contribution I have made to you personally? Again, can you give me a specific example?
3. What is, in your opinion, my single, greatest strength if you had to narrow it down to one? Can you give an example?

You will probably find you have pages and pages of results, which can seem quite daunting. A great resource you can use is called a word cloud. Go to www.wordle.net and create your own. Then print it out and put it in a prominent place (on your mirror, fridge door – anywhere you will see it on a regular basis) and look at it frequently to see whether it 'fits' you. If not, go back to Wordle and make some changes.

Secondly, look inside yourself. Start by thinking about what you do naturally that others admire. You are probably on the right track. If you want an outside stimulus for this phase, there are a number of Strengths Finder applications you can use.

I have a big A3 poster on my wall in my office with my Hedgehog diagram filled in – my passion, what I am best at and what my money activities are. It's sometimes very easy to drift off track - whenever this happens to me, I simply spend a few minutes looking at my Hedgehog chart.... that brings everything back into focus!

Enjoy the journey

Visit www.UltimateLifeLessons.com for some other great success stories

Go to www.MillionaireWomenResources.com to access tried and tested resources for women

Sign up at www.QCCigroup.com for a free workbook on how to develop your own personal mission statement and a free workbook on how to develop your core values

> "By believing in yourself, you open the door to the art of possibility.
> By not believing in yourself, you close the door to your own potential."
> **Eve Grace-Kelly**

3 Tips To Stay Focused On Your Dreams

Create a "Word Cloud". Print it out and put it in a prominent place (on your mirror, fridge door – anywhere you will see it on a regular basis) and look at it frequently.

Look inside yourself. Start by thinking about what you do naturally that others admire.

Janet Beckers

> Create a Hedgehog Diagram of your passion, what you are best at and what your money activities are. Refer to it regularly and it will bring everything back into focus.

About The Author

Eve Grace-Kelly CWC MBILD MAPM MISMA is "one of the UK's leading Success Coaches" (Jonathan Jay, founder of The Coaching Academy), and is CEO and co-founder of Quantum Coaching and Consulting Group (a leading Personal and Business Success Coaching, Consulting, Training and Wellness organization). She has wide-ranging experience of setting up and running businesses including a recruitment company, a management consultancy, Internet businesses, a personal and business success coaching company and even a gym!

She has decades of success in Project and Programme Management Consultancy and Performance Coaching for major, leading clients. Corporate clients include Lloyds Bank, Legal and General Insurance, Fidelity Investments, NatWest Life, WH Smith, the NHS, J Sainsbury's, Her Majesty's Revenue and Customs, KPMG, Glaxo SmithKline, National Power, NASA, 3UK, the European Commission in Brussels, and the pan-European aviation organization, EUROCONTROL. Eve is a qualified and experienced Success Coach, Personal Coach and Business Coach. In addition to her qualifications as a Weight-Management consultant, she is also a Certified Wellness Coach. She is also certified in Neuro-Linguistic Programming (NLP) and Stress Management.

Pursuing her constant interest in personal development, Eve has achieved Member status of the British Institute for Learning and Development. She's also a certified Work-Life Balance consultant and endeavors to follow her own advice in this regard, but admits that she doesn't always succeed! As a member of the European Mentoring and Coaching Council, she upholds high standards in ethics and integrity in all she does.

http://www.QCCGroup.com *http://www.MillionaireWomenResources.com*
http://www.UltimateLifeLessons.com

Special Gift

Visit http://www.UltimateLifeLessons.com for some other great success stories.

Go to http://www.MillionaireWomenResources.com to access tried and tested resources for women.

Sign up at http://www.QCCigroup.com for a free workbook on how to develop your own personal mission statement and a free workbook on how to develop your core values.

http://www.QCCGroup.com   http://www.MillionaireWomenResources.com
http://www.UltimateLifeLessons.com http://www.QCCigroup.com

Janet Beckers

Keeping your Sanity while pursuing your Dream

Fabe Keily

WHEN THE GOING GETS TOUGH, THE TOUGH GO SHOPPING....OR DO THEY? Did you know.....If you put a frog in boiling hot water, it will jump out immediately, but if you put a frog in cold water and gradually turn up the heat, until it's boiling....it won't jump out, it will just explode! Are you doing things in your life that are slowly but surely turning up the heat and putting pressure on your health and your relationships? Are you in danger of exploding? Well you're not alone! In 2008 I was National Events manager for one of the largest investment education companies in Australia. We ran events all over Australia and the South Pacific. The more successful the company became, the busier I became.

I loved my job but I didn't have much flexibility with my time and while I don't mind working hard, the consistent long hours were taking their toll on my health and my relationships. The definition of insanity is doing the same thing over and over again and expecting a different result, so I knew that something had to change.........or I would end up like the frog – exploding!

I decided to use my 20 years experience in Event management and combine it with what I'd experienced the hard way about the importance of keeping a healthy work / life balance. So in April 2008 I decided to leave my safe, comfortable, secure job and What Working Women Want was birthed. I have come to realise that birthing a business is not without it's labour pains. A friend once told me "Fabe, the road to success is full of ups and downs" and how true he was. There have been many ups and down along the way, times when we could have given up, got sidetracked or lost our way.

So how does one keep going, when the going gets tough? Well I've heard it said "When the going gets tough, the tough go shopping"....if only! There are three key things to remember when the going gets tough.

1. Be willing to ask for help: If there are areas you don't have expertise, then ask for help from those who have the expertise you need. Most people are happy to help, they just need to be asked.

2. Don't give up: If you make a mistake – don't give up, just try again, and again, and again if necessary. The most successful business women of our generation have been women who have made a decision to "stay the course" and not give up.

3. Enjoy the journey: In the midst of pursuing your dream, and being a busy working woman, make sure you make time for yourself and those who matter most. See the Smart Weekly Planner for how to be Smart with your time.

3 Tips To Stay Focused On Your Dreams

THE SMART WEEKLY PLANNER:

Time for You: The night before your work week actually starts, sit down with your diary and a freshly brewed cup of coffee or a glass of wine or champagne and make a plan. The first thing to do is schedule in time for yourself.

Time for the Crew: Next schedule in time for your partner and your kids (if you have them). Your significant other and your kids need quality time with you. Quality here is much more important than quantity. Just ensure that when you do spend time with

Janet Beckers

> Time at the Zoo: Okay last but not least is work. Once you have your priorities sorted, work will fit into it's rightful place, and you will be able to feel happy and fulfilled knowing that the most important things have been taken care of. And remember.... "A woman is a lot like a teabag. You never know how strong she is, until she gets into hot water!"

About The Author

Fabe Keily | CEO & Founder | Speaker | Author | What Working Women Want Fabe Keily is your typical working mum. A mother, lover, wife and friend; as well as taxi driver, counsellor, financial controller, masterchef and the list goes on! As a busy working mum she knows firsthand what it's like trying to juggle everything. With over 20 years experience in Event management and a love for educating people how to make money work for you, she spent nearly 4 years as National Events Manager for one of Australia's largest investment education companies. After experiencing burnout as a result of things being out of balance in her life, she decided to use what she'd learnt to make a difference and launched What Working Women Want in April 2008.

She has three beautiful children (29, 27 and 16) and a loving and supportive husband of 30 years!

Special Gift

Receive a FREE All Natural Eye Gel mask when you sign up as a Member to receive our Free Monthly newsletter full of great articles on how to be Smart with your finances, your health and your relationships.

Go to http://www.whatworkingwomenwant.com

http://www.whatworkingwomenwant.com

How to Ignite your Vision and Keep it Alive in 3 Easy Steps

Gabriela Rosa

I used to get so caught up in the question: "What is my life's purpose?" I used to spend hours thinking about what is it I was put in the world to accomplish; what is God's plan for me? Until one day I was fortunate enough to attend an amazing personal development seminar based on the generalised principles taught by Buckminster Fuller. That was a turning point for me, because I learnt about precession and finally realised that in order to fulfill my purpose in life, it wasn't so much what I was doing that mattered but rather HOW to do it.

Precession, as described by 'Bucky' and how I understand it in my life, is about the ripple effect my actions have on other people's lives; and that as long as I am serving to the best of my ability, I am already serving my life's purpose. How making honey makes the world go round... A bee's life purpose is to produce enough honey for her and the entire colony to survive and in the process of going about her business - the business of making honey and collecting food for her young, the bee sustains an entire ecosystem as it cross pollinates flowers; flowers which some become fruit; that feed animals, which in turn feed other animals, which eventually keeps the human race alive. An entire chain of events unfolds from her commitment to that one seemingly "small" job; that one mission. The bee has been blessed with just enough instinct so that in its own way it can make such a huge contribution.

Just imagine what you are capable of by working to fulfill your vision. Realise the contribution you can make, the people you will touch and the lives you will change; lives which will be better because you choose to exercise your right to fulfill your purpose in life, ultimately guided by your clear and strong vision. The world can indeed be a better place from the moment you choose your mission and with all your might, enthusiasm and vigour go about sowing the seed of your message whilst being of service (in the best possible way you know how) to those who come your way. You are not destined for a life purpose; you choose one and make it your own I used to think that was some mystical way of "discovering" one's life purpose... but I don't anymore. In time and with more life experience, I grew to realise that ANY endeavour can enable one to fulfill his or her life's purpose because who we are is not what we do in life but how we go about doing it. Also, as it turns out each person has an intrinsically tuned set of innate strengths that guide our natural predispositions and choices.

So the '"what" to focus on', part of your life purpose, can be anything; it's always best though for it to be something you LOVE. Really LOVE. Something that when you are doing it, you simply lose track of time and you could and would like to do, even if you weren't paid a penny for it. Because in that way you will be in your very best state in order to be of service. Coming from that place you cannot help but fulfill your life's purpose. I've chosen a purpose, how do I keep going in the face of adversity? From time to time we are all faced with challenges and sometimes these difficulties come to help us prove or strengthen our resolve to our chosen "cause". The key to maintaining one's inspiration in the face of challenges is a clear vision.

A powerful vision keeps us going; it helps us pick ourselves up when we fall. Falling is a definite reality along any journey, how quickly we pick ourselves up after a fall is what differentiates winners from learners. And what helps us pick ourselves up quickly is the clarity and the strength of our vision. For me finding my BIG "WHY", my major reasons for continuing to choose my vision is one of the biggest things that keep me strong on my journey. And I found it really helped me to pick "whys" that go far beyond the material or monetary reasons to be in business and that far surpass the merits of this world.

My "WHYs" mean everything to me, they are about me being the best I can be in this world, for me, those around me and God. I am not a religious person however I am a deeply spiritual person and for me these values permeate my vision and keep me highly focused on "collecting pollen and making honey".

Do you believe in yourself?

Another deeply important factor for helping me stay on track is the belief I am consistently developing on myself and my abilities. I often see people with low self worth and poor self belief struggle to "stick with their vision". My suggestion? Change it. Do whatever it takes. For me I love the works of Louise Hay, particularly 'You Can Heal Your Life' and 'The Power is Within You' because they provide the working blueprint for assisting one's development of self belief. So vital for successfully staying focused on one's vision. Another amazing book that in my opinion no one should go through this life without reading is 'The New Psychocybernetics' by Maxwell Maltz. And in the end applying what you learn is the key. Some of my friends think I am crazy but if there is one thing I do in my life is apply good strategies when I learn them. For many years now, based on a recording of one of Brian Tracey's famous audio programs I have had several colourful A4 laminated pieces of paper stuck with bluetak everywhere in my home (and particularly my bathroom because it guarantees I see it for an extended period of time at least 2 times daily). Their message ranges from "I love myself" to "I can do it" to "I am a genius and I apply my wisdom" (one of Dr John Demartini's favourite sayings).

What does this do for me? It reminds me to tap into my inner core so I can be the best that I can be. It motivates and strengths me and in turn my vision for my life—and as a result it give those around me permission to do the same: Step up and be the best they can be. The option to stay focused on your vision and keep choosing it no matter what comes your way is a moment by moment choice but one decision is all it takes. Have you made yours?

3 Tips To Stay Focused On Your Dreams

1. Decide - are you in, are you out? Choose what you want your life purpose to be; make it about something greater than yourself; Choose to be of service to others… overall, just make a decision.

2. Develop a deep belief and love for yourself. This is not about being conceited, it's about being happy to be you and understanding the value that only you can add to this world. Do whatever it takes; use visualisations, affirmations, self-talk—anythi

3. Keep choosing it daily. Like many other things in life, motivation towards keeping our vision strong is not permanent but then again neither is eating or bathing—we need to do these things daily—and often more than once daily! The same applies to you

About The Author

Leading fertility specialist and naturopath, Gabriela Rosa (BHSc, ND, Post Grad NFM, DBM, Dip Nut, MATMS, MNHAA) has gained international recognition as an expert in her field. Gabriela devotes herself to natural fertility treatment, the management of women's health issues (puberty to menopause) and men's health—via the web and through her busy private practice in Sydney. Gabriela is the author of three books on natural fertility and she is a sought-after expert contributor on topics of holistic health and natural fertility. For more information or a FREE subscription to the Natural Fertility Booster please visit www.NaturalFertilityBreakthrough.com

Special Gift

FREE Natural Fertility Advice from 'The Bringer of Babies'   Leading natural fertility specialist, Gabriela Rosa (aka The Bringer of Babies) has a gift for you. As a thank you for purchasing this book get your FREE "Natural Fertility Booster" subscription and discover

- Easy ways to comprehensively boost your fertility and conceive naturally, even for women over 40;

- Natural methods to dramatically increase your chances of creating a baby through assisted reproductive technologies such as IUI, IVF, GIFT or ICSI;

- Simple strategies to help you get pregnant fast and take home a healthier baby;

- How to prevent miscarriages

You will also receive the FREE audio recording "The Natural Fertility Solution: 11 Proven Steps To Create The Pregnancy You Desire And Take Home The Healthy Baby of Your Dreams" a total value of $397!
http://www.NaturalFertilityBreakthrough.com

http://www.NaturalFertilitybreakthrough.com

Janet Beckers

Women With Empowering Secrets

Helen Brougham

Do you sometimes feel that just as you have it all together something comes out of left field (unexpected surprise) and you're left wondering how to deal with the problems you now face? When this happens a number of times over, we can end up feeling unable to enjoy life when it does flow along nicely because we expect the next round of chaos to hit us at any moment.

Yet this very way of thinking "don't get too comfortable, the good times won't last" is actually contributing to bringing about the next round of chaos! Your mind is focused on being a victim of circumstance and that is a very powerful mindset to try to break free from.

There will always be challenges in life but in order to deal with them you need to approach them from a place of powerful positivity rather than allowing the circumstances to have power over you. An attitude of "I am focused on having an amazing life and can deal with anything" will bring about an assured change in your outlook and the severity of challenges that arise.

Peace became more common in my own family with the conscious decision to stop chaos from entering our everyday life. If you're wondering how you can change your attitude that will allow you to live a unique life that is stronger, happier and freer, the answer lies in learning how to deal with our inner voice that is programmed to give us all of the reasons why we can't do something. Its intention is to try and protect us from making mistakes.

Unfortunately it is over zealous in nature and stops us from enjoying new experiences in life; from stepping out of our comfort zones and taking risks. It berates us if we want to say 'no' to another's request. Unless we deal with quieting it, it can take over our lives and imprison us in a downward spiral of excuses, guilt and stress. This stress can be so toxic and overwhelming that it can cause us to shut down our feelings, become numb to others and prevent us from taking action on anything in our life.

The inner voice stops us from living the life we deserve; it prevents our enjoyment of being the unique person that we truly are and therefore we need to find ways to dull it down by getting clear about who we really are as opposed to what we think we should be, what we truly want in life and what we are going to do to get it. As a Massage practitioner, I know that looking after yourself by having regular massages really opens your heart and mind to the unique you and changes the way you do everything.

It's so important to make time to use massage as a tool to reduce the stresses in our life yet it is too often considered a luxury that we don't have time for or could be better spent elsewhere. But look at it this way; do you honestly have the time to be sick, injured, short tempered and lacking energy? Having regular massages helps you to be strong in your mind, helps your muscles to relax and prevents fatigue and overwhelm. After a Remedial Massage, you will feel recharged, taller, lighter and revitalized. It gives you the confidence to be yourself, energy for those already busiest days, a clear mind, the power to have great relationships, be productive and ask for more money and get it because you are the one that makes the difference in what you do for others.

If I did not look after my mind and body by having regular massages, I would not have the energy or strength to help others like I do. As we free our mind and body and become our unique selves, we realize that as women we must come together and be friends, work together in harmony and be on the same side. When we act as separate entities we can feel isolated and alone. For women who want more out of life, acting as part of a group and investing time with each other we find that while there may be differing levels of age, needs and wants, we now have a community of women who can share skills and talents in real estate investing, parenting, entrepreneurship, mediation and much more.

Be careful though when addressing relationships, work or money issues within these groups. If you are in a group that becomes solely based on complaining, you will never move through the issues to achieve the results you desire. This is where coaching with a practitioner with a down to earth attitude who can see your blind spots and help you is far more effective. It's this attitude that has allowed me to confront my own fears and to turn what could be negative situations into positive ones! I discovered that the feelings we all experience can be interpreted by us all in different ways and we can learn to react differently. Now if I begin to experience a negative feeling, I stop, reverse the situation and turn those feelings into excitement and fun! We experience a myriad of feelings every minute of every day and night. These feelings are all the same until we subconsciously class them as good or bad. What often happens when a person has classed a feeling as sad is that they start to analyze that feeling, they try to find answers or try to push the feeling away. They get angry or upset.

This is one of the oldest chaos techniques that we use for survival and this does not work anymore; it just brings on more panic and anxiety. This is empowering to know this and we must learn to stop ourselves from reaching this point. When you experience a feeling like this, allow yourself to let it in. When you try to remove something, it just gets worse. Instead, let the feeling sit and just be with it. This helps it fade and it will soon vanish on its own. When you have feelings of doubt, let doubt be doubt; on its own it will disappear.

If you add meaning, it will take off and become negative, disempowering story. Move if it is a real physical issue of a bus coming toward you of course! But in a non life-threatening situation, an exercise to use would be to close your eyes, imagine the worst it can be, now open your eyes. You are safe. Stay calm, stay happy. Always remember, the better you are at controlling your emotional intelligence, the more you create the life and the lifestyle you want.

Many women are now making extra income by going forward beyond their comfort zones to create an entrepreneurial business which serves by building self pride. Their accomplishments lead into helping others by making a difference in an area they want to contribute to. Pride in what you do always brings new feelings of excitement in your life. I have found this throughout my own life and each time it has been a freeing experience. My empowering secrets bring me the freedom to do and be what I want.

3 Tips To Stay Focused On Your Dreams

Plan your big steps to your dream lifestyle as an entrepreneur. Starting from where you are right now, plan your goals and walk the little steps forward 3 months, 6 months and 12 months into the future.

Book yourself in for regular Remedial Massages to bring calm and balance to your life.

Choose the right kind of down-to-earth coaching to clear blockages; creating a happy and relaxed family and the health and wealth to achieve a full and abundant life.

About The Author

Helen Brougham has been a Remedial Massage Practitioner for 21 years and is also a 7-figure empowerment coach, author, wife to Des for 33 years and mother of 4 children. As a young Mum, she experienced the wonderfully positive affects after her first massage and has now created Down To Earth coaching whereby she now dedicates her life to helping women, mums and their families. Helen provides empowering individual and group coaching programs to clear away blocks so that you can enjoy the happiness, abundance, love and freedom to be you. She brings the experience of achieving her own results of freedom for herself and her family to her many clients so that they can achieve the freedom, lifestyle and abundances in life that they want through a direct path of love, peace and joy. Helen owns a Remedial Massage and Reflexology Clinic in Kensington Park, Adelaide, Australia specializing in Remedial and Pregnancy Massage. She also offers Freedom and Empowerment Coaching Programs through her online business. Helen's book will be out mid-2011.

Janet Beckers

Special Gift

3 steps to Empowering Yourself
"Letting go of your limitation being ready for left field"
Video and map to get there faster and easier with long lasting success. Gets you results straight away valued at $197.00

http://www.Helenbrougham.com.au

Abundance Comes in a Rainbow of Colors

Jandra Faranda

Isn't it exciting when you discover something that opens up a whole new world to you! For years I have been dipping in and out of various ways to create and attract abundance. I guess that I was really hoping for the 'big one' – amazing wealth that would just land in my lap somehow!

It all started forty years ago when a clairvoyant told me that I would accumulate extraordinary wealth, starting with a huge lottery win. Well I invested in a lot of lottery tickets and have had lots of very small wins but the 'big one' is yet to happen. Really what I was doing was purely wishful thinking. Apart from buying the tickets and madly hoping, I wasn't doing anything to achieve an abundance mindset. And it's the creating and nurturing of that abundance mindset that really gets you into the wonderful flow of life's gifts.

There are many wonderful ways to create your abundance mindset, and I am so thrilled to be able to introduce you to an amazingly powerful source of abundance that uses a natural resource that is everywhere, is free, is entirely natural, is available to everyone, and is of course, abundant! It's not new either. The ancients were onto it millennia ago! I'm sure that they were far more tuned into their natural world than we are with all today's distractions. Ancient Egyptians, Greeks, Indians and other civilisations used it for medicinal and spiritual purposes.

I'm talking about COLOR. Because color is such an integral part of our lives it's easy to take it for granted and not be aware of what it actually IS. Since I became aware of the extraordinary powers and influences of color on our lives I'm flying from strength to strength.

I've done a course on color therapy, and read voraciously about the possibilities and uses of color to enhance an amazingly broad range of areas in our lives. And I'm hooked! One thing I've discovered is that "color therapy" as a name doesn't begin to describe the extraordinary things that color can do to attract what you want into your life. And I've found that there's a wonderful multiplier effect too. For example if I'm dressing for a particular occasion I'll choose to wear a color that has the properties I want – and the very act of choosing also sets my intention. Maybe I'm heading off to a meeting that I suspect will be fraught and heated. By choosing and wearing something green I am announcing clearly that I am in harmony with myself and others. The other attendees don't have to know anything about color to receive that message, and I am empowered too, both by the green itself and also by having my intention set clearly, my subconscious is working for me. Try it, you'll be amazed.

It's the same in your house. If there's an area that doesn't really work for you, that you don't feel "quite right" in, have a think about the color and lighting in that space. Transforming it into somewhere you love to be may be as simple as a coat of paint or effective lighting. In fact feng shui practitioners say that color is one of the quickest and most powerful ways to move energy around.

Color is an integral part of our world and has many amazing powers and properties, but most of us truly take notice of color only in an aesthetic sense. Yet there's so much more! Color has a profound effect on our wellbeing, our health, our emotional state and our effectiveness. Let's first consider what color actually IS. COLOR IS SIMPLY VISIBLE LIGHT. That's right, color forms the tiny part of the electromagnetic spectrum that the human eye can see. We have no trouble accepting the power of the invisible ultraviolet and infra red rays – science has made that knowledge perfectly clear and indisputable.

Overexposure to UV is known to be dangerous –people in all warm countries are continually reminded of being careful in the sun, and there's a huge business in UV sunscreens, sunglasses and clothing. Infra red light has healing properties, and is widely used medically.

We humans are strange creatures at times. None of us question the power and effects of the invisible UV and infra red rays. And yet so few of us understand how to harness the powers of the colors, or rays, that we can see!

Most of us have favourite colors, and our speech is full of colorful expressions, such as 'I saw red' or ' I felt blue'. And yet on a day to day basis, few of us consider color on anything but an aesthetic level – such as when choosing a color for furniture, clothing, a car, accessories etc. And that means that we're ignoring a fabulous resource that can achieve so many positive effects in our lives.

Our bodies inevitably absorb light, and that light is made up of the color spectrum. It's accepted scientifically that each color has a unique vibrational frequency, wavelength and energy associated with it. And the qualities of each frequency have a strong influence on what occurs around it. This knowledge has been used in medicine for literally millennia.

I'm not asking you to take a leap of faith with your eyes closed here. There's a whole body of scientific evidence around the effects of color. For example it's known that the colors we absorb can affect both the endocrine and nervous systems, influencing the hormones released into the body. And we all know how powerful hormones are. There's also the spiritual element. For the ancients each of the colors that make up sunlight were literally aspects of the divine, and were considered to have a profound influence on the lives of humans. Some of the Ayurevedic color treatments are still being used effectively after five thousand years.

One of the things you'll really love is how enjoyable and easy it is to harness the power of color. If you're like me you're already juggling a myriad of roles, and the last thing you need is to take on something else that will drain your energy. The beauty of color power is that it's actually energising. Truly there's just so much I could tell you but unfortunately space doesn't allow. That's why I'm delighted to offer everyone a free copy of "Color in your Life" – all you have to do is email me at info@colorfulpowers.com and ask for it.

Janet Beckers

As well as attracting abundance and wellbeing into your every day life there are heaps of business applications for color too. The color of your stationery, your office, your marketing material, can literally raise or lower your bottom line by many thousands of dollars. Every day big corporations and brand names are using color to extract the most out of the marketplace. They know it works and prove it over and over.

There is just so much to explore and learn and to help you I am developing a website called colorfulpowers.com It will offer classes, articles and talks across a broad range of fields where color is used. Emotional and physical healing, the laws of attraction, feng shui, marketing and sales, relationships, romance, psychology, decorating, design, art, creating abundance, intention setting and so much more. There's a lot of amazing information out there, and I am combing the world for experts in their fields and inviting them to submit articles and to be interviewed so that you can learn from a broad cross section of experts. This will make http://www.colorfulpowers.com a unique site and I'm very excited about its launch in April 2o11.

Attracting abundance is so much more than just landing the big one! Its true wealth lies in the little moments in every day that we can feel and be abundant in. I promise you that color will help you achieve, many, many of those magical moments. Color is our birthright and belongs to us all. Poetically it has been described as the soul of nature. And when we tune in to color we are tuning in to nature's soul.

3 Tips To Stay Focused On Your Dreams

Start experimenting with wearing different colors and really taking note of how you feel in them, and how others respond to you.

Each day as you choose your colors, firmly set your intention for the day. Intention is an enormous part of attracting abundance.

Frame your intentions in positive, active language, eg "Today I will be fully present to receive knowledge"rather than I hope I can concentrate in my lecture today"

About The Author

My name is Jandra Faranda and that's my greatest claim to fame! I'm sure I'm the only person in the world with that name. Aside from that, the roles in my life that mean the most to me are those involving people. I adore being a wife, a mother, a grandmother, a friend – to me the people in my life are where my true wealth lies. And I have a HUGE appetite for fun. I am a marriage celebrant and love helping couples fulfil their dreams of a perfect wedding. I also teach bridge and run a small country bridge club. Both of these are people oriented occupations that I love! My career has been varied – I've been an advertising copywriter, a farmer and a restaurateur. I love meeting people, travelling, and collecting fascinating snippets of information. I have a degree with a double major in psychology and counselling and mediation and have worked as a voluntary telephone counsellor.

Recently I have completed a diploma in Color Therapy and I'm so excited about all the applications that color can have in people's lives. It's far more than just aesthetics – the correct use of color can have amazingly beneficial effects on our physical and emotional health and wellbeing, as well as attracting abundance into our lives.

I am currently developing a membership site, due to be launched in April 2011. Called colorfulpowers.com it will be like color central – with classes and interviews and articles on a whole range of color applications – from medical to spiritual to emotional to style to feng shui and more. I'll constantly be combing the world to find color experts in as many fields as possible and bringing you their wisdom and expertise.

Special Gift

I'd love to share with you some of the ways that you can use color to bring abundance into your life. Simply email me at info@colorfulpowers.com and I'll send you a special report called "Color in your Life" valued at $39, completely free.

http://www.colorfulpowers.com

Passionate Pet People

Jane Hinchey

Hi, my name is Jane Hinchey and I'm the founder of Adelaide Pet Sitters and also host of My Pet Problems.com. You guessed it, I'm an animal lover and in 2010 I took the first step in realising my dream of owning my own business and working with animals by starting Adelaide Pet Sitters. As the name suggests, I provide pet sitting services to people in Adelaide, South Australia, who go away on business or holidays.

Starting my own business from scratch has been a hard slog, there's no getting away from that, but it also forced me into examining what it was I wanted out of my business. And could I expect to achieve it? This takes us into goal setting territory, and it is the tool I use to keep myself focused and motivated, now. But when I first started I had goals floating around in my head, the "I'd like to … " type, but no clear definition and no tangible outcome. For example, I had a goal of replacing the income from my "paid" job, so that I could quit and focus full time on my business.

That's ok as a goal in itself, but what I didn't do was work out the details on how I was going to achieve that, and break it down into smaller goals. For example, how much do I need to earn per month/fortnight/week? How many pet sits would I need? How many clients? And what sort of time frame could I expect to reach these

The Power of 100

goals in? I had been working in my job full-time, and running my pet sitting business part-time, for six months and was exhausted and nowhere near reaching my goal. I was tired and frustrated!

My vision was more than having my own business. While I had successfully started a business, and it was working with animals, it wasn't giving me the lifestyle I wanted. That's when the penny dropped. I wanted to be able to work from home for a few hours each day, take time off when I wanted, but still make bucket loads of money! I'm sure you've heard this before – I wanted to make money while I slept! I re-did my goals. I have a copy of them stuck up on the wall next to my computer so I can see them daily and stay focused. I've found that breaking the goals down into smaller, manageable chunks, makes it easier.

I'll look at my lists and see that today, to help me reach my goal of attracting 100 new clients this year, I have to arrange for my advert to go in my local directory and post a new blog on my website. That's all I need to do – for TODAY. So I may have a new blog each week, a newsletter once a month, advertising campaigns, but I've worked out a timetable for all of these things that tells me when I need to do them. Not overwhelming at all. What this process did for me was highlight that it was going to take me a whole lot longer than I wanted to reach my financial goals. I needed multiple income streams, and after some research and signing up for Wonderful Web Seminars, http://www.mypetproblems.com was born!

I'm passionate about animals, so to set up my own series of live tele-seminars talking to experts on pet health, first aid, nutrition, training and behavioural issues, was awesome. While this was going on I was also battling with negative self talk, you know the stuff, "who am I kidding, I can't do this" and a big one "what if this doesn't work?" This was really scary stuff for me, and had the power to stop me in my tracks. Every now and then I would feel totally overwhelmed and I wouldn't do any work on my business for a few days while I battled my way out of the dark thoughts. It was getting to the point where I needed help – I was in danger of sabotaging myself and my success.

After listening to the live tele-seminar between Janet Beckers and Kim Castle about "Clearing the path" I knew I had found the answer! I signed up for Kim's course, and have been using the Clearing the Path techniques to rid myself of the fear that kept holding me back. I'm no expert at it, but I have nowhere near as many negative thoughts. When they do pop up, I know how to deal with them. Another strategy to keep me focused and my dreams alive is by sharing them with like minded people.

Janet Beckers

I have some cynical friends (and family) in my life that think I'm chasing some sort of pipe dream. So I choose not to share my dreams with them. I don't need them brining me down! I use a lot of social networking sites and forums to connect with like minded people, both pet sitting business owners and other entrepreneurs from around the world. Connecting with these people stops me from feeling isolated and helps me to know I'm not on my own.

One word that I have heard repeatedly during my entrepreneurial endeavours is action. If you want to succeed, you need to take action. That's what I've done. I took action in signing up for the courses I needed so that I had the knowledge to move forward. I then took action using that knowledge.

3 Tips To Stay Focused On Your Dreams

Write out your goals – if you've already written out your goals, update them, break them down into chunk size, manageable pieces, with actions and due dates.

Take action. Sign up for a course, or download a tool (and use it) that will help you toward achieving your big picture goals.

Network with like minded people – I'm sure you'll find plenty in this book, myself included. Find me on facebook and send a friend request, I promise I'll be your friend!

About The Author

Jane Hinchey is founder of Adelaide Pet Sitters, a local pet sitting business in Adelaide, South Australia. Jane or one of her team of sitters stop by your house while you're away on business or holidays and feed and play with your pets, while also checking up on your house. If you live in the Adelaide area check out Jane's website www.adelaidepetsitters.com.au .

Jane also hosts My Pet Problems, an online series of live-teleseminars helping pet owners find the solutions and information they need to address problems they may be experiencing with their pets, which can sadly lead to pets being abandoned or needing to be re-homed. Visit http://www.mypetproblems.com to sign up for free membership and to become part of the "My Pet Problems" community.

Special Gift

My special offer for readers is my eBook called How to give your dog a checkup that usually sells for $19.95, but you can have it for free! It takes you through, step by step, how to check your dog for illness and/or injury, along with photo's to show you what you should be looking out for. This is a wonderful resource in maintaining the health of your pet. The same principles apply for cats, so you could easily use the same techniques in this book to asses your cat's health.   Click on this link http://mypetproblems.com/free-ebook/ for instructions on how to download your free eBook.

http://www.adelaidepetsitters.com.au   http://www.mypetproblems.com

Awakening the Goddess Within

Janelle Manton

After ten years of marriage, living a compromised version of myself in order to feel accepted, I decided to leave. My children were only 3 and 5 years old, so the decision did not come easily but I knew I had to fly, I knew there was something I was not doing in my life, a path I had to follow – which had not yet been revealed ….

The deep yearning in my belly was so profound, it didn't make any sense at all but I trusted what I felt. I knew, should I stay, I may die a slow and painful death by getting lost in the make believe world I was living. 8 years ago I became single and followed a calling to help other women find themselves amongst the rubble of life. I did my first Coaching course, became class dux and started to fly for the first time.

You see I'd never achieved an intellectual merit, I left school as soon as I could and worked successfully in the cosmetic industry for over 15 years. The one thing I learned, working with primarily women during that time, is how similar we all are. Regardless of what colour or size we are, what demographic we come from, what we have achieved or not, women suffer from the same insecurities, the same lack of worthiness and the feelings of not being enough. As a coach and mentor who is adopted, the more women I coached the more I realised this to be true.

The more years that went by overcoming my own adversities as an adoptee and single mum, the more I realised what it really takes to make it in the world. It was sometime about 5 years ago when I facilitated my first women's workshop that I found my purpose in life and discovered the path I have never left. Even though I have taken side paths at times, my persistence and the draw to my purpose always brings me back. I have been drawn to assisting women achieve innate confidence, self love and acceptance ever since. I know deep within each woman there is a Goddess just waiting to be unleashed. As a single working mum who is the provider and primarily running on masculine energy to make my life 'work', it wasn't until near burnout I realised just how important doing things like a Woman really are.

The more I studied women, energy, polarities, goddess history and feminism, the more I discovered the importance and strength of divine sacred femininity. Being an awakened, conscious woman is the most powerful force in the world. Slowly I started to take notice of which 'polarity' I was in. Was I operating from a feminine space or being masculine? Masculine energy while being equally part of who we are, when we are out of balance and over working this muscle can lead to exhaustion and in some serious cases, adrenal fatigue.

No wonder I was exhausted all the time. I was the hunter of my family and trying to do it all! How many other women were experiencing the same thing? How many other women thought that being feminine was weak? How many other women didn't realise how powerful and sexy they really are? The more I went down the rabbit hole the more women I attracted that needed my help. The more women I helped, the more my workshops and retreats started to take flight and eventually Top Secret Women's Business was born. My life's purpose is to assist women to find themselves, the gorgeous sexy goddess within - living life as balanced and energetic, super sexy, vibrant woman full of zest, confidence and spunk.

My life's purpose is ironically the very things that I needed to awaken in myself to fulfil my deep yearnings for being a real and raw, authentic woman. The very things I avoided as a young 'unconscious' woman. When I woman decided to leave my marriage it was because of a lack of emotional fulfilment – a lack within myself, not my husbands. When a woman lives passionately and reveals herself for who she really is, she lives with integrity, passion and authenticity. This I learned the hard way at a very dear cost ...

My message to all women is be yourself, awaken to your deepest yearnings and live your life as an empowered Goddess, the one that is your birthright ... You asked me how I keep my dreams alive? I persist every day, without ever second guessing who I am (ever again)... And when I do, I stop, observe, re-align myself to my purpose and proceed with caution at first... Then with full gusto BUT I remain in my feminine – with flow, creativity, discipline, nurturing those around me, with softness and quiet determination and with my friends close by. If you truly want to feel the power of 'woman' that dwells deep within you, awaken your Goddess within and celebrate your feminine complexities as your greatest gifts...

3 Tips To Stay Focused On Your Dreams

How can you find more energy and personal power in your life, living like a Goddess? Firstly, I know what your dreams are. It seems simple enough but setting goals and understanding what you want is critical to your getting it. This is a good time to seek coaching - if you are not sure and need objective neutral assistance.

Do things daily that inspire your feminine energy to be present – take luxurious baths, use gorgeous fragrance, make your home beautiful, dance, sing, have girl time, shop, eat chocolate, be creative and nurture your relationships. And when you feel exha

Wear sexy knickers! It's that simple, sexy lingerie makes you feel powerful, loveable, super sexy and alive... And sexiness cultivates confidence, confidence takes your life to the next level and has you playing a greater game...

About The Author

Janelle Manton is the peoples Goddess. Her mission is to turn every woman into a Goddess, where she is sexy, confident and powerful, so she can enjoy better quality relationships, especially the one she has with herself. Janelle believes "at the core of your femininity lies your ability to be sensual and sexy and from that energy comes enough innate inner strength and power to achieve anything in life – herein lies the secret to true self-worth, confidence, personal pride and ultimate happiness". It's been a lengthy and deeply personal journey for Janelle, a single mother and adoptee, to move through to the other side of adversity to a place as an

The Power of 100

International Facilitator & Speaker, Healer and Coach of women and men. A journey she openly shares in her unique Real and Raw personality through her Writing, eBooks, Audio and Coaching Programs, Retreats and Trainings with Top Secret Women's Business. Welcome!

Special Gift

To Receive your BONUS - THE SEXIER SEX GUIDE eBook valued @ $27 visit my site and enter your details to receive the download. You are only a few chapters away from developing a deeply connected and sensual relationship with yourself and your lover. http://www.topsecretwomensbusiness.com/

http://www.topsecretwomensbusiness.com/

Janet Beckers

'Fake It 'Till You Make It - Life Is A Game'

Jedha Dening

There are many different things I do to stay focused and on track in my business and personal life, so today I would like to share a few of those with you. And I would also like to share a couple of motto's that I frequently use to keep me moving forward in my life. One of the motto's I use is "Fake it 'till you make it". When I have feelings of doubt, or I'm a bit scared about taking on a new challenge, I just think about this motto in my mind. It really does work. I built my whole massage and health business around this idea.

In the beginning I had no business skills and not a lot of clinical experience but I faked it, I convinced people I was the best and that my business was the best. I faked it all the way, learning as I went along. If I had a problem I didn't know how to deal with, I would just get out the books that night and work it out. It's like fast track learning. It's nerve racking but exciting all at the same time.

But what I've proved time and time again is that just by putting yourself out there, you can achieve anything you want. I built up my massage and health business to be very successful in only a short amount of time. Recently my partner and I decided we wanted to take a new path and would start a new company doing Internet marketing and management for businesses. Sure we know quite a bit about it, we have some fundamental skills, but we certainly don't know everything and we've never done business in this arena.

So off we went to business meetings with our fake caps on, nervous, excited, and ready to take on the challenge of getting new clients for our business. We have only just started and we've already got a few clients. And we've already confronted a few interesting challenges, but we'll just work out all the details and learn the rest as we go along. So I say if there is something you want to do and you are not ready to do it, it doesn't matter, just jump on in and fake it 'till you make it.

Another motto I often use is "life is a game". I think in my mind, this is my life, and my life is a game. I think it when difficult or challenging things happen. It helps me from getting too caught up in irrelevant emotions and negativity's that might pull me down. It helps me to keep a positive mind frame. Like many people I also have an inclination to procrastinate sometimes, but if I just think, my life is a game then it gives me the energy to move past procrastination. I had a great realization not so long ago that it takes a lot more energy to procrastinate than it does to actually do the thing that you are procrastinating over.

Think about that…say it is exercise you think you want to do. You could just make a decision to do it, plan a time you want to do it, and then just do it. Or you could just think about how you should really do some exercise, it will probably make you feel better, and you will try to start on Monday. Problem is, Monday comes and the cycle just keeps on going and going. I realized if I just make that decision, set a plan, and just do it, it's actually a lot easier. But I'm just human like everyone else, I get stuck on lots of things and I think that it's really hard to do a lot of things without support. So when this happens I get some help.

I find someone who can keep me accountable, or I find something to keep me motivated or inspired. Although I like being healthy and fit and I could do it on my own, I don't. I have a personal trainer twice a week to keep me highly motivated and accountable. With my businesses I have always done a course, looked for mentors when needed, or been a part of a subscription program where I can have access to resources I can use to keep me motivated.

On a personal level, I have a wide selection of personal development books and audios that I use when I need a bit of inspiration. I've been using these for years and they really are a great way to get my thoughts back on the right track or inspire some deep reflection when needed. And every day I practice gratitude, even if it's just for 5 minutes. Usually I practice it first thing in the morning when I get up. I sit down by my window, with a cup of tea and I look out on the view and just quietly think about all the things I am grateful for in my life. 'Thank you for this wonderful morning'. 'Thank you for my great family, my kids'. 'Thank you for a body that is healthy'. 'Thank you for this wonderful warm cup of tea'. It doesn't matter what it is but the practice of doing this every day makes me appreciate how lucky I am and it reminds me not to take too many things for granted. It makes me show more appreciation for the people around me and value the circumstances I have. And it also seems to bring more great positive people and experiences my way, so it's a win-win all round.

Another thing that helps to keep me motivated is I try to stay as healthy as I can. This really makes me feel better on an everyday basis in all areas of my life. I've always had an interest in natural health and wellness and I've worked in the health and wellness industry for many years, so I see what a difference it makes to your life in the long term when you take care of your health. We often take it for granted but health is the very most valuable thing that we own. No amount of money or any possessions can replace health once it has been lost. So in order to achieve anything in life, health must come first.

I really love to be full of energy and vitality on an everyday basis and I think it would be great to end up at 70 or 80 years old and still actively engaged in my life on many levels. So I eat good healthy food and try to do exercise most days and stay as fit as I can. Like many women, I have sometimes struggled with self-esteem issues but I find that if I am kind to myself and if I feel good about myself, then everything else in my life naturally falls into place a little better. Feeling good about myself also helps me to feel more confident in the things that I want to pursue. I have found that eating well and staying fit are a great way to feel good about yourself, boost your energy and really enhance your overall productivity.

3 Tips To Stay Focused On Your Dreams

1. If there is something you really want to do this year but have been too scared just remember "Fake it 'till you make it"- jump in headfirst and think about the details later. You may just surprise yourself by what you can achieve. Your life is a game, so play it.

2. Get some help when you need it - we all need support, guidance and accountability in order to achieve our goals.

3. Boost your energy, confidence and productivity by being as healthy and fit as you can.

About The Author

Jedha Dening is a health coach and educator, pain and injury therapist and aspiring internet marketer. She is the creator and health coach for the Paleo Weight Loss Program, which is a revolutionary lifestyle program for ultimate weight loss, excellent health and unlimited energy .http://paleoweightlosscoach.com

Jedha has a passion for helping people improve their health so they can experience a better quality of life and more happiness and joy in their lives. She also has a passion for constant self-learning and personal development. In fact Jedha believes that when it comes to improving health and wellness, no matter what it is, there is always a component of self-learning and personal development involved. When we are ready to honestly look at the underlying issues, only then can we make a permanent change.

Jedha also runs a massage and health business on the Central Coast Australia. And she is helping her partner establish a new Internet marketing and management company to help local businesses with all things internet. Outside of business she is the mother of three wonderful teenagers, one by birth, two by default, and partner to a wonderful man.

Special Gift

"Weight Loss Resolutions & Ultimate Solutions"- Get your FREE report that reveals many important tips on how to kick start your weight loss journey and explains why The Paleo Weight Loss Program is 100% the program for you to use. To receive this special offer please visithttp://paleoweightlosscoach.com/100-women-special-offer

Websites:

http://paleoweightlosscoach.com
http://internetexpressions.com.au
http://elitesportsmassage.com

Janet Beckers

Changing My Mind: A Journey from Employee to Entrepreneur

Jenni Proctor

When I was first exposed to the concept of creating an internet-based business I considered the options very carefully. After all, as a Career Counselor and Coach my professional skills lie in helping people recognise what work or business is going to enable them to shine using their skills, interests and strengths, and then planning to achieve that. So I became my own client! I evaluated my skills and experience against the skills that I thought would be needed in different internet business models, created a plan for how this new work could fit into my work timetable, and confidently started learning all I could.

I'm a positive and self-motivated person and loved the idea of using my creativity to build a business that would, without any doubt, bring in millions of dollars.

Although through much of my working life I'd been employed in education I had always considered myself an entrepreneurial person who just needed the right vehicle to allow my latent business skills to burst forth into fruition.

An internet business seemed to me to be the perfect combination of an outlet for my business creativity, supported by my combination of skills and my eagerness to learn.

What I failed to recognise was the major handicap that I was bringing with me from so many years of being an employee.

As an employee I'd always had a strong work ethic, taking pride in ensuring that my qualifications and ongoing professional development kept me at the forefront of my profession. I was in a helping profession and would joke about the fact that giving 110% effort, with no extra salary, was only just enough to keep everyone happy. Simply continuing to do my work kept the salary coming in without me ever having to ask anyone for the money or change my strategies to increase my salary. Money just came in and went out without me thinking about it.

If I'd been working with a client I'd have identified and examined these beliefs, but they were so much a part of me that I failed to recognise their significance and to realise that they would prove to be a major problem for me as I made the transition from employee to entrepreneur.

As I embraced this new venture my self-motivation, work ethic and resilience proved to be invaluable, and I recognised the value of many of my existing skills in building my business. But despite my best efforts no money was flowing in through my internet endeavours.

My career practice supported what had become my obsession to make money on the internet, and I purchased new programs, new training, new ideas............each offering the promise of financial success.

Everyone else that I had met through internet workshops seemed to be making money, why not me? My resilience faltered, my confidence reached an all-time low, and for a short time I considered accepting that I had spent all this time and money in vain. Conventional wisdom was telling me to just give up and focus my efforts on my offline business. But I am a tenacious person, perhaps a little pig-headed when it comes to achieving something I really want, and I just could not accept that I was unable to achieve what so many others seemed to be doing effortlessly.

Reflecting on my offline business I realised that although I expected to be paid for my professional work, I wasn't confident in asking for the money and still monetarily undervalued my professional expertise. So I put my fees up and nobody even commented, let alone complained!

That was a good start but still the problem remained for my online ventures. I paid other people to rewrite my copywriting; I presented my work for public "hot seat" scrutiny and constructive criticism; I made all the changes that were suggested to me. I was so frustrated, working long hours, doing everything that all of the "experts" said I should be doing, and still the money was not coming in.

It seemed like something was blocking me, putting a huge impenetrable barrier around anything that I did online. How could I break down this barrier?

As most women know only too well, if you want to change your body you have to change your diet and increase your activity. I decided to see if the same concept could apply to the mind.

My healthy mind diet started with reading everything I could find about having a positive money mind set. I worked through the activities suggested in the books I read, thought hard about the concepts and embraced the notion that it was possible to change the way you think, even if the ideas were deeply ingrained.

I attended a couple of workshops where we actively engaged in strategies to change the thought processes that were impeding money flow. I experienced some revelations and some mental shifts, but perhaps I was seeking a miracle and they aren't commonly found instantaneously in seminar rooms.

Meditation seemed like a good way to adapt my thought processes, so I purchased a few positive money mindset mediations and put them on my iPod. I started listening to them every night when I went to bed, but I usually fall asleep quickly and it seemed that I only ever heard the first five minutes of the meditations. I think the ideas continued to impact on me, but I'd often wake as the mediation finished, disturbing just enough to turn off the iPod and remove the earphones. The idea of working online was a foreign concept to most of my friends and as a social being I needed to be able to talk about my work with other people who were heading in the same direction.

I consciously developed a network, offline and online, with people I had met through workshops and seminars, so that I had friends with whom I could discuss my work or who I could turn to for suggestions or encouragement. This fed my need for a community. Email, Skype and Facebook became the equivalent of my "staff room" where I could stop work for a while and chat with friends before starting work again, refreshed from the break.

Just as increased activity is essential to support a healthy physical diet, so too are activities which expose you to attitudes and environments where making significant money from your online business is the expected outcome. I found that being around people who were financially successful in this sort of work was important in changing the way my mind was programmed, so over the last couple of years I have made a point of seeking these opportunities. I have gone to many workshops and seminars, which included two amazing seminar cruises.

Mixing with other people who are already very successful, or who are equally determined to succeed, is like putting yourself on a physical training regime. Everything you do in that environment takes you closer to your goals.

Similarly, deciding to focus on some issue usually makes you become acutely aware of related activities. So it has been with changing my mind about money. I now check my business account regularly, watching expenses and income far more closely than I have done before. By paying attention to my income I believe I am reminding my mind regularly that the outcome of all my work is going to be financial success.

Changing my mind from an employee to an entrepreneur with a successful money mindset has been a slow process. My mind quickly accepted the concept that making money online was possible, even relatively easy for some. My employee mind is long gone, and my entrepreneurial mind is well focused on a successful future.

Has the money started to pour in? The impressive income stream that I anticipated hasn't eventuated yet, but the flow is increasing all the time and I remain optimistic that momentum will build. When you make a significant change to your physical diet and activities you don't expect the results to show immediately, but once the changes become obvious the improvements seem to become more clear, more intense, every day. I take heart that this is how it will be.

Janet Beckers

The work to develop a deeply engrained positive money mindset continues, as do the practical strategies for online success. Resilience, perseverance and optimism remain undaunted. The journey has been amazing. Now I look forward to enjoying the results!

3 Tips To Stay Focused On Your Dreams

Feed your mind with books, CDs, and meditations that encourage positive money attitudes.

Attend lots of seminars and workshops. Network, offline and online, with people who are on the same journey but choose your mentors carefully.

Focus on the money that is coming in, even when it isn't much.

About The Author

Jenni Proctor is a career practitioner, professional speaker and entrepreneur with experience in Career Development, Education and Training, and Internet Marketing. She is the founder of Career Clarity, which specializes in mid-life career change. Through her practice she has worked with many mature workers planning the most significant transition of their lives, wanting to leave the security of a job behind them but unsure about what to do next. Very few intended to follow the traditional path of working until retirement age and never working again. Most were motivated by passion, dreams and the desire to love their work , and wanted to create a worklife that enhanced their desired lifestyle www.RedesignRetirement.com was developed specifically to assist Baby Boomers to reignite their dreams, revitalize their plans and help them redesign their future.

Special Gift

Readers of the book can access a 30 minutes personal coaching session with Jenni Proctor by emailing jenni@careerclarity.com.au.

http://JenniProctor.com   http://CareerClarity.com.au
http://www.RedesignRetirement.com http://RedesignRetirement.com.au

An Inspiring Story From Our Partner Opportunity International and The 1 Million Women Out Of Poverty Project

Mariam's story (West Timor, Indonesia)

Mariam's rujak (fruit salad) and cendol (beverage) stand is well-stocked with an array of fruit and attracts a frequent flow of customers. Her husband Usman is helping her support their two children with his motorcycle taxi business. Mariam works from 8am to 6pm each day and considers herself fortunate for the opportunity to do so.

Prior to joining TLM (Tanaoba Lais Manekat, the local partner in West Timor), Mariam's life was less promising. She struggled as the primary income earner for her two children Agil, 16, and Fritria, 14, her cousin Nona and her previously unemployed husband. Despite working long hours selling fried banana and tofu popsicles at the local market, Mariam earned barely enough to support the family, with infrequent contributions from Nona.

With her first small loan from TLM, Mariam established the rujak business for a more secure income. Her increased income enabled her to help Usman start his motorcycle taxi business. Now on her second loan cycle of Rp.2,000,000 (A$256), Mariam has purchased additional stock for her business. She has also been able to buy a cupboard.

Mariam now has the flexibility to save part of her income, creating the foundation for a brighter future for her family. Along with school fees and medical costs, she would like to spend her savings on repairing the family home. With continued assistance from TLM, Mariam is planning to expand her business to sell rice and other food. This will result in a higher and more consistent income - giving Mariam the security to plan for her family's future.

You can help families just Mariam's by donating at
http://www.WonderfulWebWomen.com/recommends/opportunity

A Fish, A Tantrum and A Choice

Jennie Harland-Khan

Everything was seemingly perfect. Until I threw a fish at my husbands head and my life changed forever. We were camping with our two young children and my frustration had reached a boiling point. As he began to cook the fish he had caught that day on the camp fire he said: "Come on Jen, out with it, what's the problem?" "Nothing" I retorted grumpily. "You're in a strop because I went fishing…" That was all I needed to unleash about how it was alright for him to do the things he wanted but I was stuck because I had to look after the kids (love them dearly, but I am sure you know what I mean!). And then it came. "Stop being such a bloody martyr Jen, and choose to do something!"

With Olympic accuracy I flung his fish squarely at his head. That night, during a fitful, tear strewn night, it dawned on me that he was absolutely right. Choose to do something. I wasn't doing that, I was simply complaining about my circumstances. The flood gates opened, feverish goal setting, training, certification with Bob Proctor and researching different business strategies, my business was born. The concept of 'Choice' is the thing that keeps me going through the ups and downs of

The Power of 100

starting a business from scratch and holding onto my vision. It is also the very thing that will give the life that you truly want.

To fully comprehend this, I would like to introduce you to the most simplistic framework I discovered during my training with Bob Proctor (of The Secret). It has been transformational for both me and my clients when it comes to both creating a vision AND getting through difficult times to maintain momentum during those times when you wonder is it worth it. Please welcome....The Stick Chick.

STICK CHICK

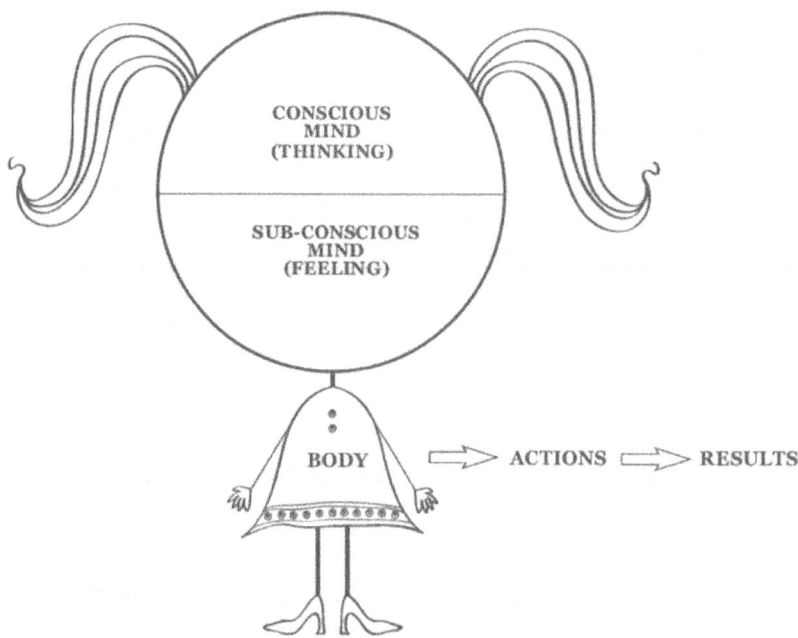

The head is deliberately drawn bigger; as it represents the mind and everything we do or create manifests firstly in the mind. The top part is the conscious mind, the bottom the subconscious mind. The conscious mind is where we think, the crux being that we have the ability to accept or reject any thought or idea that comes into our mind. The subconscious mind is where our emotions lie, it is where we feel. When we accept a thought in our conscious mind it gets impressed down onto your subconscious mind. This part of the mind has no ability to reject a thought, whether it is a constructive or destructive thought.

So at any given time you can chose whether you accept or reject a thought you are having. Clearly in reality not many people think! If they did they wouldn't accept the thoughts they were having. If I had been actually thinking at my fish moment I wouldn't have been blaming my husband for my frustrations. Here is the really important bit. When you chose a thought, and get emotionally involved with it in, it literally moves your body into action and that action is what creates the results in your life. In a nutshell, if you want to know what you have been thinking, simply take a look at the results in your life. The critical thing to realise is that our current results are not a reflection of our potential. Our current results are merely a reflection of our thoughts to date. Our potential is actually limitless. Let's face it though, that is all very well in theory but it is easier said than done to constantly be 'choosing your thoughts'. Why is it so difficult to hold onto our vision?

From day one we have been conditioned to gather information from our environment through our five physical senses. We listen to news, we gossip, we listened to what we were told by our parents and teachers. All these have created many of our beliefs regarding what we believe we can and can't do to date. So how can we improve our ability to control our thinking, hold our vision, and step over our fear? We can achieve this by becoming aware of, and training our mental facilities. These are: perception, will, imagination, memory, intuition and reason. By developing we have more control over the way we think; it just needs practice, like building up a mental muscle. Here, very briefly is an insight into how you can use these:

Perception

Perception enables us to look at the same thing from a different angle. And when you change the way the look at things, you can change the way things are.

Will

Our willpower is our ability to focus, and focus to the exclusion of all outside influences, so it is training our mind to switch off to negativity that tells you why you can't do something.

Imagination

Imagination can be the most destructive or brilliantly powerful gift that we have. So instead of imaging all the failures and what could go wrong with our business it should be used to create a vivid picture of what you truly want so that you can get emotionally involved with that idea.

Memory

We all have perfect memories, we can remember all our successes and failures but we tend to remember the failures and the bad things and drag them from our past into the future. You need to start retraining your memory to remember your successes.

Reason

We can reason all the reasons why we can do something, or reason why we can't do things – again it is a choice.

Intuition.

The last is intuition. This is about training yourself to start to tap into what you really do know, and allow yourself to be open and listen to the inspiration that comes to you everyday and act on it. So when I am facing challenges I literally picture the Stick Chick in my head and stop and think. How could I perceive this situation differently? Am I allowing external influences sway me? What am I imaging right now? What is my heart really telling me?

3 Tips To Stay Focused On Your Dreams

Think! Burn the Stick Chick into your mind to remind you what is causing the results you are getting

Create a vision board to train your subconscious mind to accept this as truth, remembering it can only accept thoughts that are constantly impress it with these thoughts

Build your self awareness by consciously using your mental faculties in a constructive way

Janet Beckers

About The Author

Jennie is the founder of Jenniehk.com a business born out of an insatiable desire to jump up and down and give people a shake and say "Noooo! You don't have to spend the rest of your life believing that your circumstances are stopping you having the life you want!" Having come from a place of overwhelming frustration herself by feeling limited by how she could live her life when she had children, she is passionate about working with people with kids to help them create a lifestyle with more freedom, more adventure and more purpose. Trained and certified as a Life Success consultant with Bob Proctor, Jennie has combined this knowledge with practical strategies to help clients firstly design their ideal lifestyle and then build it by introducing business strategies and tools that enable you to leverage your time. She fits this around her two beautiful kids and her husband Babs, currently splitting their time between the UK, Australia and Italy.

Special Gift

Go to http://www.jenniehk.com/wonderfulwebwomen for my special offer

www.jenniehk.com

My Time to Shine

Johanna Baker-Dowdell

I am working on two dreams right now. Both are related to business, but they are also intensely personal.

Johanna the Author

The first is to publish my book for mums in business, Business & Baby on Board. I never thought of myself as an author of more than articles and eBooks, but after speaking with many mothers who started their own businesses around children, about how they couldn't find advice that was right for their circumstances, I thought why couldn't I do it? After mulling over this idea for years and allowing a few hiccups to get in the way, I decided it was now or never and submitted my book proposal to three publishers. One of those publishers is currently considering my idea, but instead of waiting for their answer I've started writing anyway. I will self publish if they pass on my proposal. Researching and telling stories of great business mums have inspired me to run with the idea.

Each business mum profile is posted on my blog http://www.businessandbabyonboard.tumblr.com/ and tweeted via @bizbabyonboard, so I have now built some momentum behind the dream. From these profiles I will choose a selection of amazing women to interview for the book. I'm not planning on stopping until I'm holding that book in my hands – I even know what the cover looks like! I make sure I stay on track with this dream by sharing my goals with as many people who will listen - this way they ask me what is happening with it each time we talk, so I have to do something, but it also means I know others are interested, which keeps me motivated.

Johanna the Farmer

The bigger dream is to become a hazelnut farmer.

After spending most of my life living in a comfortable coastal region (aside from four years in the UK), my husband and I decided to sell our home, and move our family of four (plus two cats and a dog) to Tasmania to start a hazelnut farm. We had to give away our beloved chickens, rabbits and goldfish, as well as move away from family and friends, but we knew this was what we wanted to do and set about making it happen. We'd talked about having a farm 'somewhere' for two years before we actually made the decision to sell up and just do it.

In April 2010 I suffered a head injury that rendered me pretty useless in my business for three months. While struggling with little income (my business, Strawberry Communications, supports the family), I was forced to think about what was really important – my family, health and following my dreams because life is too short to waste. So we stopped talking and just did. The house was sold within weeks and we found a home to rent in Launceston while searching for the perfect property. We intend to grow hazelnuts so amazing people will travel to get them!

We are still looking for that farm, narrowing our search area each week as we find more prospective farms, and have decided 2011 will be the year we find our patch of land. In the meantime, I have been blogging our adventures at http://t-changers.posterous.com for friends a family to see what is happening. I also want the blog to be a document our two sons can read as they get older, so they see where we started and their role in the dream.

The blog has been a motivating tool for me because I am putting our plans for the farm out there for all to see, but the biggest factor in keeping the farm dream alive has been to stop talking and just do it – this attitude started with selling the house and will continue right through to planting the trees and then selling our finished hazelnut products. Despite personal and professional difficulties that could have spelt the end of these two dreams, I am still charging along the road to making them a reality. After all, I am mistress of my own destiny and 2011 is my year to shine!

3 Tips To Stay Focused On Your Dreams

Clarify exactly what steps you need to take to make your dream a reality - and then take action.

Don't let the hiccups turn into roadblocks – just see them as part of the ride.

There is no timeframe for dreams – they will happen as they should.

About The Author

Johanna Baker-Dowdell owns and runs Strawberry Communications, a writing and public relations service that generates amazing publicity. Strawberry Communications was launched in 2007 to help businesses tell their story. The business is based in Launceston, on the Tamar River, Tasmania, but services clients all over Australia (and sometimes the world). Johanna is also a freelance journalist, author and blogger.

Special Gift

Want to generate amazing publicity for your own business? Secure hundreds or thousands of dollars worth of publicity by using the strategies outlined for you inside Johanna's eBook, The 21st Century Guide to Promoting Your Small Business. Use the code "WWW" for a $10 discount off the AU$37 purchase price. Buy your copy at http://strawberrycommunications.com.au/ebooks

http://www.strawberrycommunications.com.au
http://www.businessandbabyonboard.tumblr.com/
http://t-changers.posterous.com

Janet Beckers

Your Money Personality

JP Miller

A note from Janet Beckers: OK so you may be wondering why we have one lonely (brave?) man in our book. Believe it or not, our community of Wonderful Web Women attracts men as about 10% of our members. They are our "enlightened men". So when JP submitted his article, including a photo of what he would look like if he was a woman, I thought "Why Not?". So JP represents those men in our community who tell me they are drawn to the collaborative way women do business. Besides, I really like JP. He is one of my favourites who has been an active part of our community for years.

When it comes to Money it's important to know yourself (your money profile) and others (their money profile). The wisdom of self knowledge has been revealed to us throughout the ages. At the entrance to the Temple of Delphi was inscribed the words "Know Thyself". In Sun Tzu's book The Art of War he gives the advice, that by knowing your enemy you will win the battle and by knowing yourself you will win 100 battles.

Understanding yourself is the most important step when you want to become wealthy. As an Accountant and Financial Coach/Educator for the last 25 years I have seen people make a lot of money when they align their financial activities with their personality. They do what they love and the money comes. When Warren Buffet was a child he enjoyed calculating the fastest way to get from one city to another in the USA by studying the train and bus timetables. This was his hobby that he would spend hours researching. Now Warren Buffet uses these innate personality traits to make money in his company Berkshire Hathaway and he is one of the richest men in the world.

Both Donald Trump (Real Estate Entrepreneur and Dealmaker) and Robert Kiyosaki (author of the Rich Dad Poor Dad books) have similar personality traits. They have the entrepreneur profile which makes doing the deal a great joy to each of them. They have both gone broke and then have come back even stronger. They could go broke again because it's not about the money for them; it's about doing the deal. On the other side of the money profile is someone like J K Rowlings (author of the Harry Potter books) who is one of the richest women in the world. Not a business woman per say but a creative soul. She lived in poverty while writing the first Harry Potter book. Her association with Amazon and Hollywood has taken her on a road to riches. Had she not teamed up with other different personalities, she may still be living in her council flat.

When you focus on that one thing that aligns with your personality and your passion, you will be setting yourself up for success. By getting to know the personality and passion of others, you will find the right person to assist, guide, and partner you on your way to riches, both internal and external riches.   If you are a JK Rowling personality type and you are trying to follow the Donald Trump personality type Model of Wealth creation (which is the most common model), you will just become exhausted and disappointed.

Following your own personal model of wealth creating, which is aligned to your personality, will lead to you to a financial life of ease, grace and success.   One of the most relevant aspects of your money profile is understanding how you function under stress – particularly financial stress.   When we are stress free, we can follow our strengths, which leads us to what we love to do and to our personal success. When stressed, we have a tendency to use our weaknesses to get ourselves back to a stress-free state – we think those behaviours will get us out of trouble.

BIG mistake!!

Why do we do this? Why do we think that doing something that doesn't, and never has, worked in the past will work this time?   The experts still don't know, but the fact is that we do. A 'JK Rowling' type would be likely to become overly logical - over planning and controlling when under stress. Not great for the creative process of writing novels, at which she is so good.

A 'Donald Trump' type would likely become quite intuitive, going with this gut feeling when under stress. Not the ideal way for someone who likes to, indeed needs to, touch, see, smell and taste (plus number crunch) a good property deal! By knowing your money personality, you can identify your strengths, weaknesses and challenges around your behaviour and choices with money.

This sort of awareness gives you the wisdom to change the things that you can. So where do you start?

3 Tips To Stay Focused On Your Dreams

Take the time to understand Your Money Personality.

Find someone to help you define Your Money Personality.

Continue to be aware of Your Money Personality and how you can use it to play to your strengths.

About The Author

JP Miller. JP started his career as an accountant with Delloites, an international firm. After 10 years in the accounting industry, he opened a practice in Pitt Street, Sydney. Having studied counseling, psychotherapy and adult education, JP joined All Money matters in 2000, adding his depth of industry and training expertise.

JP's interest and focus is on how our personality affects and influences our financial decisions, habits and behaviours. He studied under Australia's leading expert in the Myers/Jungian personality profiling and continues to research the application of this profiling model to money management and wealth creation styles.

He has developed an exceptional money personality profiling tool for exclusive use for Your Life Your Money and All Money Matters clients.

JP sits on the boards of The Australian Society of Clinical Hypnotherapists and the NSW branch of The Australian Association of Psychological Type.

Special Gift

We want to encourage and support you to take your Action Steps, so here's what we're offering. Choose either or both!

1. Your Life Your Money E-course. Just follow this link to our web site http://yourlifeyourmoney.com.au/products-and-services/your-life-your-money-ecourse scroll down to "Purchase the Full E-Course" and click the "Add to Cart" button. The 'coupon code' is GoldenOpportunity. The full cost of the e-course is $Aus 279.00 - you will pay just $Aus 249.00.

2. Do 'Your Money Personality' Profile with us and we will give you a Wealth Check for free! Value: $Aus 220 Just email goldenopportunity@allmoneymatters.com.au telling us you're ready to take your first Action Step. The Wealth Check will help you with Action Step number 2 – for free.

http://www.yourlifeyourmoney.com.au

Janet Beckers

How To Achieve Your Dreams With Ease And Speed

Judeth Wilson

So many people in this world are wonderfully passionate about people, about sharing what they know and wanting to help others. I am passionate about equipping people to do exactly that. I take the natural talents and knowledge that people have and fine tune their teaching and training ability so that they are then able to share their knowledge and passion with others. For some, this is starting their very own training businesses or becoming professional speakers and for others it is being able to give back to, and develop, their communities and those closest to them.

My dream is for anyone with a passion for sharing information with others to be able to learn how to do this most effectively and to be able to benefit financially from doing so. I have trainers, who had never trained people in their lives, come through my program "The Trainers Ultimate Toolkit" and are now earning $35000, even $70000, a month delivering people-skills training courses in businesses.

Over the years I have seen how many people are stuck in jobs that they are not passionate about, simply going through the motions in order to pay the bills. It is the most rewarding feeling in the world to know that I can help liberate people to be able to do more than just think about how things could be different for them, and their families, and actually make it a reality.

After doing it the long, slow and hard way for nearly fifteen years in the business of training and professional speaking I now find it hugely rewarding to show people exactly what to do in order to succeed. They don't have to make the same mistakes that people doing it on their own make. I have the systems and know-how to give them the training skills and marketing and business tools to truly do it with "ease and speed." To keep this dream alive means I have to keep perfecting the training I offer and also to stay ahead of world trends in training, education, marketing and business so that the trainers in my coaching program are being constantly stimulated and developed and assisted to run their own businesses in the most effective way. This means, as a mentor, I can never take my eye off the ball and, whilst I enjoy the challenge, it can be hard work.

Some mornings I can't wait to jump out of bed when I realise, with excitement, what the day has to offer. Other days I am not nearly as enthusiastic and it takes a great deal of encouraging self-talk to get me to leave the silky sheets. It is this self-talk that I have come to master over the years and I now have a little ritual that I perform every morning and it stands me in very good stead. Instead of having to leap out of bed I give myself a few minutes to firstly acknowledge that I am truly grateful for the new day and to think about what I have planned for the day. Then, instead of letting myself feel unenthusiastic about the more tedious tasks that may need to take place, I consciously think about each activity, such as a business meeting or training session, and I put a 'thought projection' onto each activity – picturing it going exactly as I would most like it to – perfectly! This lightens the feeling I might have towards the activity and makes me feel much more enthusiastic about approaching it.

I have come to be aware, over the years, that my attitude to the tasks I have to do is crucially important. I have big, exciting goals in my business and many of the things I want to accomplish can seem daunting or tedious in order to be achieved. One way I deal with these feelings is to tell myself that I will be able to do each task with "ease and speed." All too often we tell ourselves the tasks will be laborious and take weeks and weeks to complete, whereas, if you go into them with an attitude of "ease and speed" I always find things coming together quickly, smoothly and remarkably pleasantly!

Janet Beckers

I know that my dream is going to grow from strength to strength and I am excited that it will help others to realise a dream of being their own boss, of choosing when and where they work and that it is possible to become financially free doing something you love. How much fun we can have when we are able to achieve our goals in a way that we enjoy the journey and know that each step towards learning the skills or building our own business can be done in the most enjoyable way possible – with "ease and speed!"

May an air of "ease and speed" be with you in whatever you turn your hand to.

I wish you every success!

3 Tips To Stay Focused On Your Dreams

1. Commit to spending 5 extra minutes in bed before you get up each morning and consciously think about how grateful you are for the day you have been given.

2. Think about each of the activities you have to do that day and put a "thought projection" onto each one, thinking of the activity going exactly as you would most like it to.

3. When you have a task you would rather not have to do decide to get it done with "ease and speed" and keep that thought in mind as the task pleasantly comes together!

About The Author

Judeth Wilson, Managing Director and Lead Trainer, Upfront Communications Pty Ltd and founder of "The Trainers Ultimate Toolkit." In the past fifteen years Judeth Wilson has started, and successfully run, four training organisations on three different continents. This is impressive considering she is only in her thirties! With the coaching and mentoring programs she now offers she has earned the reputation as Australia's Ultimate Trainer of Trainers. She is the author of three highly acclaimed books including "The Inside Secrets of Powerful Presenters Revealed – How to get enthusiastic applause, even a Standing Ovation, every time you speak", "Become a Millionaire Working Just Two Days a Week" and "Training Works – better people, better bottom line." As a professional corporate trainer, when she talks the likes of Cambridge University, Sanofi Aventis, Minter Ellison, Grant Thornton and Women on Boards to name but a few, listen! Judeth has a passionate belief in people and developing the skills they have. With this in mind, she delivers outstanding keynote addresses and runs dynamic training sessions around the world. She believes that people have the power to make an enormous difference - as a trainer, coach and mentor she helps to wake up the difference that people make to themselves and others and ignites a passion for what they do. With qualifications to complement her years of experience, Judeth has a degree in journalism, is an Advanced Toastmaster, a certified Neuro-Linguistic Programming (NLP) practitioner and holds an Australian Certificate IV in Training and Assessment.

Special Gift

Special Offer for Readers To receive a free copy of my book "Become a Millionaire Working Just Two Days a Week" please email info@trainersultimatetoolkit.com Free Bonus – Worth $1791 If readers mention this article when enrolling for The Trainers Ultimate Toolkit program they will receive 3 months membership to my Mastering Business Acceleration Coaching Program for Trainers and Speakers absolutely free.

My website is www.trainersultimatetoolkit.com

Janet Beckers

Single Minded Focus

Judi Mason

I'd like to tell you about Joshua, he is my Son and one of 4 children. Josh was not a real believer in the law of attraction, however, Josh is one of the most amazing manifestors I know, why? Joshua has the ability to really FOCUS on what he wants- even when everyone around him is saying it's not possible. If he wants something – he knows exactly what he wants and he is very single minded about it. When Joshua was younger, he wanted a black holden ute, he knew what he wanted, the exact make and model, all of the details of what the car would have right down to the magwheels and the price he wanted to pay for it (all he could pay for it) was under $20,000 at the time.

We (his parents) tried to dissuade him and said maybe he should look for something cheaper, but no, we looked all over Brisbane and were told that model, especially in black, was as rare as hens teeth and there were none around, if we did find one it would be closer to $30,000. Again we tried to tell Joshua that he should look for something else- but NO, he knew what he wanted and that was that. We picked up a little local newspaper and in it was a very small add for, word for word, the car Joshua wanted, however the asking price was $24,000. Joshua looked at it, loved it and offered $19,000 for it, the seller accepted and Joshua drove home in his dream car.

I knew and believed in the law of attraction but I still had at that time doubted - I really think that is the secret, and also why some things seem so easy to manifest and other things seem so hard ...

"It is as easy to create a castle as a button, It's just a matter of whether you're focused on a castle or a button."

Abraham Excerpted from the workshop in Boca Raton, FL on Sunday, January 12th, 1997 Abraham-Hicks Publications © Jerry and Esther Hicks

It is our focus and some things seem to have less importance and also less resistance and therefore we state it and release it and it flows to us. Something that seems hard or even impossible has us hoping but doubting, wishing but listening to others opinions.

If we could really just stay in the belief - regardless of outside influences, we could and in many cases do create whatever we want.

So to create what you want you need:

1. To know what you want- exactly with as much detail as you can.
2. To know that you will have it- end of story!
3. Trust and release all resistance, doubts and negative thoughts from well-meaning friends and family.
4. Receive – be open to receive it with gratitude.

3 Tips To Stay Focused On Your Dreams

Create a vision board or book and describe what you want with as much detail as possible, but have fun with it, let your inner child out. Visualise yourself having it, feeling it, again stay in the lightheartedness of the moment, do not get into the place of neediness or wanting.

Stay in the focus of what you want, if you are feeling doubtful, change your focus, look at your vision board again or just go for a walk.

Be open to receive and spend time appreciating everything else.

Janet Beckers

About The Author

Judi Mason is a successful Property Investor, Author, Reiki Master and Coach. Judi Mason has travelled throughout the world and studied with many great teachers learning about and understanding the principles of the law of attraction. She lives on the Sunshine Coast in Australia. Judi is currently writing a book - 'Stories From The Law of Attraction, The Good, The Bad and The Funny.' (this story is an excerpt from that book.)

www.storiesfromthelawofattraction.com

Extreme Life Extension - At Ageless Zoom my Vision of Living to 120 becomes Real

Judith Sherven, PhD

Ever since I was in my teens I've known that I would live to be at least 120 or longer. Most of the time when I told people they'd laugh at me. But no longer. Today there's a swiftly growing community of widely diverse people around the world who are dedicated to exploring the science and technology of living to 150 and beyond – otherwise known as extreme life extension and age reversal. Some even believe that aging and death are the result of disease processes that when overcome will lead to immortality. Is My Teen-age Vision Now Being Brought To Life — Or Are We All Nuts? Hardly nuts. In fact, my informal research indicates that approximately 80% of men and women of all ages are eager if not hungry for the opportunity to live what my husband is calling a Second Lifetime — as long as they can be healthy in body, mind, and bank account.

To that end, in the fall of 2009, my husband Jim Sniechowski, PhD and I, along with our two partners Sy Joffe and Brian Johnson, DDiv, began putting together our company AgelessZoom.com. It is now the central authority-hub for all facets of extreme life extension. Through AgelessZoom.com which is dedicated to the science, philosophy, spirituality, and creativity of living to 150 and beyond, my adolescent vision of living to 120 has now found full expression. I can now see how I've been guided — through a variety of careers that taught me diverse skills — to prepare for this time in my life (in my late 60s) when I can finally express my deepest vision. In fact, I believe it's been my life's destiny to now be the President of our fast growing international company Ageless Zoom, Inc.

I want to underscore the role of "vision" throughout my life, and walk you through the journey that led to AgelessZoom.com It will give you a kind of blueprint to help you stay on your own magnificent path, instead of getting safety-stuck or veering into someone else's vision. The Type Of Vision That Takes You Forward — For your vision to actually stay alive in you, it must move you forward, always helping you break new ground that supports where you're headed. In my young life, when I was 12 (and looked 18) I experienced the first significant breakthrough into my future vision. I won a beauty contest for adult women.

That started me on what would be a 15- year career modelling and acting in Hollywood and New York. Little did I know that the media skills I was learning would support decades of later radio and television appearances. I was also developing my passion for adventure, travel, and living outside the bounds of the "typical" or "normal" lifestyle. In my mid-twenties, having no vision of a career as a movie star, my future-vision nudged and prompted me to return to school and earn my PhD in clinical psychology. That led to 12 years in full time private practice in Santa Monica, CA before I met my husband Jim on a blind date in 1987. From there we fell in love, became engaged and married 13 months later. And even before our wedding we'd started specializing in relationship work with couples and singles, doing workshops, speaking, and even sketching themes that found their way into four best sellers that were purchased by major publishing houses.

Prior to our meeting, Jim had been a professional actor and earned his PhD in philosophy and psychology after we met. He then began running men's groups and coaching. So we now had media skills, writing skills, speaking and workshop skills, and were fast developing our depth-psychology approach to the every-day psychological burdens that plague men and women — together and apart. But that wasn't really our deepest vision.

Neither was being "out of work" 18 months after we'd moved to a tiny mountain town in upstate New York in 2000. After losing a well-paying radio show we hosted — what to do? While neither of us knew a thing about marketing, sales, or business — much less Internet technology, that didn't stop us at ages 61 for me and 63 for Jim from jumping into Internet marketing and the most frustrating years of our lives — learning about it, making a living at it, and finally teaching it through our unique brand of Soft Sell Internet Marketing.

Despite often wanting to throw our computers out the window and wondering what on earth we were doing in such foreign "land" --- we pressed on. We developed our Soft Sell approach to Internet Marketing, produced the very first Internet marketing conference for service providers — people like us who hated to sell but had gifts they needed to get out to the world (and make a living), and we call it "Bridging Heart and Marketing" with:
http://www.BridgingHeartandMarketingIII.com and
http://www.BridgingHeartandMarketingIV.com still available online.

Next, in 2007, we moved to Las Vegas, where we created our 12-CD program "Overcoming the Fear of Being Fabulous" and met one of our current business partners Sy Joffe. That definitely was the hand of destiny guiding us forward into what is our deepest and truest vision — creating a home for all extreme-life extensionists at Ageless Zoom.com How? Sy was 80 at the time and he introduced us to Brian Johnson, (56), and the four of us — over Thai dinner one evening — realized that there was a missing voice for all of us who want to live well past 100. So we set about creating it. All of the skills of my several careers came to bear on my role in the company as President, and without the Internet skills Jim and I brought to the table Ageless Zoom would never ever have been born.

3 Tips To Stay Focused On Your Dreams

What Can You Do To Identify And Follow Your Vision? There are three keys for evolving your full, vision-based expression:

Reflect back on an early Truth, that you knew would come to pass, and perhaps you've been ignoring it.

Evaluate how your life has been leading you back to that early "knowing" — back to your very personal early vision.

Janet Beckers

> Open your vision to what is needed on the planet today that you've been guided to prepare for — and expand your imagination to show you what you can do that will also make you a good living as you express your vision. Above all, trust your vision

About The Author

Judith Sherven, PhD, clinical psychologist and best selling co-author of five relationship books, has, in partnership with her husband Jim Sniechowski, PhD, pioneered a visionary approach to personal growth which they call "Overcoming the Fear of Being Fabulous." Judith and Jim have also broken new ground in Internet marketing which they call Soft Sell Internet Marketing. Judith worked in private practice in California for twenty-two years. When she and Jim got involved online (in their early sixties) it came as a rude awakening to realize that nothing in her background prepared her to sell and market their relationship programs. In fact, as a psychotherapist, it had been unethical to even have an ad in the phone book. Now six years after entering the online marketing world, having established themselves as leaders of the Soft Sell Marketing movement, and producing their "Bridging Heart and Marketing" conferences, she and her husband and two partners have created Ageless Zoom, the international authority site for the "Why" and "How" of extreme life extension — where you learn all about living to 130, 150, and beyond — http://www.AgelessZoom.com

Special Gift

Get your Free Ageless Zoom Alert: "10 Dangerous Beliefs About Aging and How To Avoid Them" by going to http://www.AgelessZoom.com

http://www.AgelessZoom.com http://www.JudithandJim.com
http://www.BridgingHeartandMarketingIII.com
http://www.OvercomingTheFearOfBeingFabulous.com

How Could I Keep My Dream Alive, When I Became An Emotional Eating Machine?

Julie McDonald

Revelation

When things were good, I would eat, when things were bad, I would eat. I would get together with my friends for a coffee and a chat and say "it is hard to lose weight and keep it off" and we would agree and order another pastry with our latte. We would console ourselves with delicious cakes and pastries'; telling each other and ourselves it was just too hard.

I would read the articles and follow the weight loss plan they laid out, regardless of whether it made me feel good, or whether or not I lost any weight. I would persevere if it killed me. Then disillusionment and boredom would set in, so when something unexpected happened in my life - for example, if I had money problems or self esteem issues, all the weight I had lost gradually piled back on. And then some!

Once, I did lose 30kg by careful dieting. I just loved hearing everyone was telling me how amazing I looked and I loved hearing it! I felt wanted and loved. But after a few months, people became used to my new size, and my old bad habits and self-destructive behaviours just seemed to take over and it wasn't until I stopped and had a good look at myself in the mirror, I saw the old 'me' back again. Fat and frumpy!

I was once told that being overweight was due to underlying emotional problems that hadn't been resolved. For me, when situations in life happened that I couldn't cope with, I sought comfort in food. I'd always done this. I would start a new diet then whenever I became stressed, angry or felt lonely I would seek comfort in food. But to make matters worse, even when I was celebrating something I would eat the wrong food, almost like I wanted to extend the happy feeling I was enjoying.

I think I had tried every diet on the market. You name it I tried it. I would see the word 'diet' on the front cover of a magazine, I would look at the before and after pictures and decide if they could do it, then so could I. This new "diet" would be my weight loss magic wand. I would succeed this time. It was definitely going to be my pot of gold at the end of my weight loss rainbow.

I had become an emotional eating machine. I knew that if I wanted to stop the yo-yo weight loss / weight gain I had to gain control of my emotions. It was time they worked for me, not against me. It was time to get control of my mind and my love / hate relationship with food. Maybe if I could do this, then I could finally stop my diet cycle of despair.

Enough was enough

At the lovely age of 40, I decided enough was enough, I needed to regain control of my life, I had spent thousands of dollars over the years and I think I had only bought dreams never solutions.

So I quite surprised to read a major research initiative from the USA involving more than 30 studies and thousands of slimmer's that concluded that dieting does not work. I had personal evidence that dieting didn't work, and I blamed myself every time I fell off the weight loss bandwagon. I didn't try hard enough. I didn't try long enough. I'm just not programmed genetically to lose weight / be thin / stay thin therefore I must be genetically programmed to be overweight. It was such a relief, to me, to read and discover thousands of other people were having the same weight loss problems as I was.

If I created my problem in my head, then surely I can solve it there?

The light bulb moment came after reading this research as I asked myself, "what if my weight loss problem could be solved in my mind?" This now made a lot of sense to me. After all, this is where it started. If I ate because I was emotional, then where did these emotions come from? If I could overcome these emotions, then I could work on our mind to start thinking and behaving like a thin person!

For the next 8 years, I researched and tested everything I could get my hands and eyes on, to discover how I could lose weight using my mind and guess what? It worked! I became naturally motivated to eat the right food; I naturally exercised my body and the best part, I started to like myself again, it seems improving my self-esteem and sense of self worth played a huge part in my losing three dress sizes! Was I a happy girl – and better still, I have kept it off now!

MindSlim is born!

MindSlim is the 'head stuff of weight loss'. Its purpose is to assist people with the psychological and motivation aspects of weight reduction and focuses solely on the alleviating the bad habits that are the source of overeating and obesity.

I now run the MindSlim Day Spa Seminars, Workshops and one on one therapy. There have been hundreds of people discovering the Mind Tools for Weight loss and this is so very exciting!

Whilst there isn't a magic wand, there most certainly are very practical, easy to follow steps I can share to help you keep your dream alive and you remain focused, that are proven to work with using your mind to lose weight!

Practical Mind Tools to keep you focused No. 1

Be aware of what you are thinking about at every given moment?

Towards and Away from Language

 Away	Away from language is moving away from what you don't want and because your focus is on what you don't want, then you still have it and can't get away from it. e.g. I can't stop eating mars bars (focus is mars bars) I eat too much when I go out (focus is on eating too much)
 Towards	Toward language is moving toward what you want. With the language on where you want to go and do. e.g. I am enjoying eating healthy food. (focus is on healthy food) I am eat healthy snacks. (focus is on healthy snacks) I am allowing time to exercise. (focus is on exercise)

Practical Mind Tools to keep you focused No. 2

1. Grab a book and be the Dialogue Police.
2. The role of the Dialogue Police is to be as honest as possible and report on yourself.

3. Make up a page with three columns. Every day, write down EVERY negative word and statement you use, internal and external dialogue.
4. At the end of the day, reflect on your eating behaviours in the last column.
5.

Words I use inside my mind	Words I say out aloud	What were my behaviours towards food
I say stupid things I wish my backside wasn't so big I don't like myself	I look fat in these clothes Do I look fat? Are my arms fat?	I ate chips for morning tea and biscuits after dinner.

6. From this exercise, you will gain awareness from the negative words your use and how this has programmed your mind to perform accordingly.
7. Therefore, adjust your words to TOWARDS language and watch the difference in your behaviours toward your food.

Practical Mind Tools to keep you focused No. 3

This practical tip is worth everything!

Focus only on One Day at a Time

Otherwise we will become overwhelmed and fall off the wagon, so to say.

1. Wake in the morning and think only about your food for the day.
2. At night, reflect and compliment yourself on your positive behaviours and achievements
3. Then, the next day, do the same thing again,

You see, we only have the NOW, the past has gone and the future will evolve from what we do in the NOW.

Janet Beckers

3 Tips To Stay Focused On Your Dreams

Your thoughts create your actions, your actions create your behaviours and your behaviours become your habits! Be careful what you think about because you are about to create it!

It's not what you put in your mouth, that is the concern, it is what you put in your head! Create the 'Mindful Police', this will keep you on track!

If you don't have a healthy body, then you don't have anywhere to live. Weight loss isn't about 'losing', it is about keeping you healthy and staying alive!

About The Author

Julie McDonald B. Design (Vis Com), Grad Dip Ed, Mas. Trainer NLP, Dip Hyp. Therapist, Author and Speaker   Julie is the owner of Julie Mac and a world leader in assisting people in breaking their bad habits and overcoming personal adversities and professional challenges.   She has developed the academic and applied skill set, which enabled her to be who she is today. She is very passionate and committed with assisting people to create the life they truly desire and deserve.   Julie is the founder of MindSlim the No Diet program. MindSlim is a comprehensive and powerful program that has benefited hundreds of people. It was designed for those who are seeking the 'mind' knowledge to achieve effective and long lasting weight loss. MindSlim's purpose is to re-engineer the mind to take control of bad eating habits, behaviours, attitudes toward food and eliminate self sabotage.   Julie works as a Therapist and Professional Speaker. She has two clinics; at St Ives in Sydney, and the Central Coast, NSW. Julie also faciitates MindSlim Workshops and is the author of two books: "7 Habits to Break and How to Break Them", "Recipes for the Mind". Julie particularly enjoys reading and researching how the mind works and testing these 'learnings' on her three 'Y' gen children and husband. She finds inspiration in observing the life of her three legged dog, Prisais, whose self-acceptance is an example of how uncomplicated and joyous life can be. She is also an accomplished artist.

Special Gift

Are you ready to lose weight? Take the FREE test to discover what will make you feel good with your body and stay motivated to exercise. http://www.mindslim.com.au/cds-and-mp3s/ MindSlim helps you figure out the real reasons for the ingrained behaviours that are no longer serving you. It provides the tools to reprogram your thoughts, attitudes and beliefs about yourself, the food you eat and your health. Take control of your mind and take control of your diet. Lose weight permanently.

http://www.mindslim.com.au

Success Can Be Yours

Kandee G

The richness of whatever you do lies in your willingness to be in your own life – to really be "in" it. The success that you have in your life is your responsibility; your goals, your results, your failings are all your responsibility- regardless of the past, regardless of what others may want for you, you are accountable for your life, your actions, your reactions, and those things that you bring into creation. You wield real clout when you accept responsibility. There is power in owning your destiny. There is power in reclaiming what was meant to be yours in this life.

How many times have you heard to live your passion…live your dreams? But, how do you get there? The magic is in believing. Why is belief so important? What does it really mean to believe? Passion fuels our desires. Our desires fuel our drives and creates fulfillment. And it is belief that drives our passions. It is up to us to take the time to unearth, to dig deep and discover what it is that we want in our lives. With real belief we can utilize incredible laws and principles that can help bring these unearthed dreams and treasures to life. The ability to consciously, deliberately manifest those dreams and desires live in that place called belief. Henry Ford once said, "The man that thinks he can and the man that thinks he can't, they are both right."

It is so vital, it is so huge, it is so important that you understand the power in your ability to be in "real" belief. It is about having faith and belief in yourself, your universe, your God, whatever is important to you. The thing is, you cannot "play pretend" at belief. You cannot perform a task or activity or work towards a goal on the outside, while your insides are telling you all the while that it won't happen. Or that maybe it could, sort of, kind of….maybe. That is doubt at play. And being in doubt is a great way to seriously slow down or stop the creative process from happening. What I mean by "creative" is the ability to bring into creation; to manifest.

You are either in belief or you are in doubt on some level. I want you to know that you can build belief. One of the ways to build belief is to "focus forward". You can train yourself to stay focused on what you want out in front of you. Look ahead always to what you want and not what you think will go wrong. The problem with most people is that they continue to focus on what they don't want or what is going wrong. Or perhaps, what could happen wrong.

Just take the time right now to decide something that you truly want and choose to focus on that. You can take the time to create tools that can keep you focused in the right direction. You can build powerful mental images and thought processes. As you build those thoughts and images, you can build your belief in you. If you continue to focus on what you don't want and can't do, you will build more belief in what you don't want and can't do. If you are in a place of saying to yourself, 'Nothing ever works out for me" you help to build your belief that that is so. See the thoughts flowing in your mind, picture what you want. Forget about how is will happen. Forget about all the things you might have tried before. Just take the time with you to uncover what YOU want.

Decide, truly decide on a direction. Begin to define mental images of what that looks like and hold onto those, no matter what. Remember, to make them powerful, positive thoughts and images. And for those folks that fight with the conversation that says I can't, well just put that conversation away for a while. Try just holding onto the "I can".

Make a conscious, deliberate choice to focus on those powerful positive images. Choose to stay in positive productive conversation. "I am" that thing that I choose to be. "I have" those things that I want. Make the choice to stay away from negative conversations and naysayers. Arnold Schwarzenegger, when once asked the secret to his success, he replied, "I never listen to anyone that tells me I can't do it." And that goes for your own inner voice of doubt. Just don't listen. What will happen is that the more you can have these powerful mental images and productive thought processes is that you can build your belief.

Remember; don't get hung up in the how of things. Another great way to build belief is to create tools to keep yourself on track; listening audio tapes that can keep you focused, reading books that can help you develop a positive personal message, listening to music that is inspirational or watching TV and movies that make you laugh. Turn off the national obsession of 24/7 negative news; turn on Kandee G Radio: Nothing but Good News and be part of a weekly message of inspiration, hope and creativity. Read Nothing But Good News magazine, a publication designed to give you tools and ongoing stories of inspiration and hope.

Habituate gratitude; one way to build belief is by staying in gratitude. When you are in gratitude, you can not be in a negative emotion. You will see the good begin to move toward you and a natural by product is a belief in the good things. Finally, be sure that the conversations that you share with others are always positive and productive. When you share negative conversations with others, you fortify the belief that things are not necessarily good for you.

Help those around you to focus on the good stuff, whether in your personal or professional life. Never criticize or blame anyone, ever. Negative judgment is not the path for you as you move towards building power self- beliefs. You see, there really is magic in believing. Start now to see what you truly want and who you truly want to become. We are not meant to merely sit around dreaming about things we can do and be. That's a good place to start, but a poor place to stop. It is up to us to turn our dreams into action.

We all have untapped gifts and talents inside us, and the way to develop our potential is by stepping out in faith and making the most of every opportunity. It's not how much you have, but it's how you use what you have that matters. Are you making the most of your gifts and talents? It is our beliefs that bring our dreams to light. When we step out in faith and use the talents and believe in ourselves that is when we create the actions that cause us to succeed. Do the work that you need to do today, so that you can become the person that you are meant to become. And then watch magic and miracles start to happen. I really believe in you.

3 Tips To Stay Focused On Your Dreams

Look ahead always to what you want and not what you think will go wrong.

Habituate gratitude; one way to build belief is by staying in gratitude. When you are in gratitude, you can not be in a negative emotion.

Never criticize or blame anyone, ever.

About The Author

Kandee G is an author, speaker, trainer, coach, talk show host and founder of Nothing But Good News Media. http://www.kandeeg.com

Special Gift

Go to my website http://www.kandeeg.com where you can download interviews I have done with Les Brown where I tell how you can reinvent yourself, claim your life and how to live from a place of power.

Are You Serious?

Karen Thomson

When it comes to planning out your daily or weekly routine, all too often women business owners, especially those who work from home, end up throwing time away through lack of proper preparation. How do I know this? Well apart from being a business owner myself, and a single mother of 4, I've made plenty time-wasting mistakes and I know my clients have too!

You would be surprised how many don't have a proper business plan in place and ping around from project to project like that little silver ball in a pinball machine. And at the end of the day, all that wasted energy leaves them depleted and no further forward in their business. When I started my first online business in 2004 as a life and business coach, I found that my clients were often stuck in a rut simply because they were trying to work in office or a house full of clutter. As I'm pretty much a hands-on kind of girl, I visited quite a few houses to see for myself how exactly they were trying to cope in the disorganised muddle that surrounded them. I often took on the job of de-cluttering and one woman, to my amazement had a substantial amount of cash stuffed down the back of her office cabinet that she had completely forgotten about!!

That was certainly a joyous day for her! Think to how you start off your day. Are you walking into your office to find your desk covered in all kinds of papers, coffee mugs, books, children's toys and school newsletters? Or is your desk clear and prepared for the day ahead? Do you have a clear plan or goal to work towards today? When you finish a job, do you clear away and file all of the relevant paperwork, folders and any other related materials from your desk and computer desktop before starting on the next project? If you don't, you're causing a stagnation that can lead you to really feeling unable to move ahead in your day.

Clearing away the clutter keeps your mind focussed. As you are working, do you continually check your Facebook wall, emails and Skype messages? I class these as the virtual office water cooler – a place where you hang out with your mates when you know you should be doing something else! Work out when you are most productive in the day. For instance, I am absolutely on fire early in the morning but by the end of the day, my head can be one big fuzzy mess plus I've got children to attend to. I go to bed early but am often at my desk for a few hours before the kids get up.

This makes me a perfect assistant for one of my clients; often she's just going to bed as I'm getting up so she feels like her business is now run 24 hours per day! As she awakes, all the tasks she's left for me have been done! Also, do your family and friends truly understand that you are running a business from home? Do they realise that it's a business and not just something to fill the hours of the day? Are you serious enough about your business to make this lifestyle decision work viably for you? I ask because I know how hard it can be to get your family and friends to understand that just because you are home doesn't mean that you are up for a coffee and a chat on a whim.

As difficult as it can sometimes be, you have to be firm and clear that you are not to be disturbed during your working hours except for emergencies. Working with a clear desk and a clear intention helps to keep distractions to a minimum and as each task is finished and properly put away, you get a sense of closure which leaves your mind free to completely focus on the next project to hand.

My dream goal for this year is to write my first book and home study program to teach Virtual Assistants to raise their service offerings to a higher level and become Online Business Managers. What I have found is that the clients that I have who use my services to run the engine of their business have the most profitable outcomes and I'd like to teach more business owners and their clients the benefits of

Janet Beckers

employing one person to take care of running and marketing their online business while they do what they are best at whether it be as a coach, consultant, speaker, author or personal trainer etc. After all, how much time do you think you waste trying to get clients and keep up with all the bookkeeping and marketing of your business when you could be earning more money actually doing what you're passionate about and talented in?

Wouldn't you rather that all the boring and stressful stuff was being dealt with by someone else who loves that side of the job and gets it done? Even better, when you get a fantastic idea for a new product, it's presented to you packaged and ready to go a few weeks or months later depending on the scale of the idea!

3 Tips To Stay Focused On Your Dreams

Clear your desk of clutter, ONLY have on your desk what you need to perform the task that you are doing at that time.

Work out when you are most productive and do the tasks then that require the most concentration – leave other tasks for when you're likely to be more tired or otherwise distracted.

Employ the help of an Online Business Manager to free you to do what you love to do best – serving others with passion and purpose!

About The Author

Karen is CEO and founder of VisionaryVA, a Virtual Assistant & Online Business Management Company which helps both offline and online companies to manage and grow their business presence online through the provision of VA services, Planning/Research/Creation of Products, Website Creation, Graphic Creation, Blog/Content Management Systems, Copywriting/Ghostwriting/Editing /Proofreading/Transcription, Shopping Cart Management, Online List Management, Hiring and Management of Multiple Contractors in Multiple Time Zones, Project Management and Strategic Marketing Consultancy. In late 2010 after a personal consultation with Janet Beckers, Karen realised that her range of services went far beyond the average task assistance of a Virtual Assistant and that largely she was not being compensated for her talents. Now in her newly named role as an Online Business Manager, she sees her clients businesses as a whole rather than as a sum of tasks and creates and manages projects from conception to completion and then beyond with her strategic marketing and virtual assistant services. In 2011, Karen will complete her first book and home study program designed to train Business Savvy Virtual Assistants to provide the range of services that are being sought by online businesses today and therefore charge higher rates for their skills.

Special Gift

Karen is giving away a FREE report on why you should hire assistance to help you run your home based virtual assistant business. ""Women In Business – Why You Should Hire A Virtual Assistant" can be downloaded from http://VisionaryVA.com/goldbook2011gift

http://VisionaryVA.com

http://empressmarketing.com

Dream Often And Dream Big

Kathleen Gage

"Dreams are for others, but not for you. Who do you think you are to dream so big? Dreams come true only in the movies."

If I had a dollar for every time these words have been spoken by well-meaning friends and family to dreamers around the globe, I could likely retire today. Yet, retire is not in my vocabulary. You see, I'm a dreamer.

A dreamer, who at one point believed well-meaning family and friends who cautioned me to get my head out of the clouds. A dreamer, who put my dreams on hold for years, believing I had to conform to the norm. A dreamer, whose life was diminishing day by day.

That is until conforming and giving up on my dreams no longer worked. What worked was letting myself dream about the life I could live, the business I could have and the impact I am meant to have on the lives of others.

There was the slightest glimmer of hope when I realized my life was growing emptier by the day due to continually complying with the rules of others. The calling inside became stronger than the fear of judgment. It became apparent I was meant for more than simply showing up to a meaningless job in exchange for a steady paycheck.

So how did I go from someone who believed the stories of others steeped in fear, disguised as safety, to an entrepreneur who has a highly successful business I love, working with clients who pay me well for my knowledge and guidance, writing books that impact countless men and women around the globe, being a featured speaker at conferences and living a life filled with joy, passion and expression?

It happened when I was willing to trust Source. In trusting Source I was able to risk and not fear failure.

Did it happen in a day? Not by any stretch of the imagination. It took vision, planning, action and persistence. It also took a realistic view of uncovering truth from the fantasy.

Fortunately, I had mentors who taught me the difference between dreaming without a plan and dreaming in such a way that I could day-by-day build a business and life I daily give thanks for.

Is it always easy? No, but when I honor who I have become and continue to be, even when things are difficult, it is far better than the life I would be living had I chosen to deny my dreams.

To assure I stay on the path, I simply do the following:

- Surround myself with possibility thinkers and doers

- Strengthen my faith daily with prayer and meditation to know I am on my path

- Recognize the talents I have been given were given for a reason – to use them

Life is too short not to honor your dreams. There are plenty of people who will support you to live fully who you are meant to be. Dream often and dream big. Surround yourself with possibility thinkers. Strengthen your faith in whatever way resonates with you. Recognize you have been given your talents for a reason – to use them.

Janet Beckers

3 Tips To Stay Focused On Your Dreams

Dream often and dream big.

Surround yourself with possibility thinkers.

Strengthen your faith in whatever way resonates with you.

About The Author

Kathleen Gage, The Street Smarts Marketer™, has owned and operated her business for nearly two decades. Kathleen is recognized as a creative and effective Internet Marketing Advisor who works with spiritually minded coaches, speakers, authors and consultants who are ready to turn their knowledge into moneymaking information products and life-impacting services.

Kathleen is an award-winning speaker, writer and entrepreneur. She has been a featured speaker at conferences and conventions. Kathleen is the host of Daily Awareness radio show and has been a featured guest on hundreds of teleseminars and radio programs.

Her signature series, Street Smarts Marketing and Promotions, is a favorite of thousands of clients around the globe. Kathleen's greatest passion is working with those who realize and accept their role in raising the consciousness of business.

Special Gift

Visit Kathleen's website and blog at http://www.kathleengage.com and http://www.themarketingmindset.com

Access Kathleen's FREE 3 Part Video Series – How to Build a Successful Coaching and Consulting Business – http://www.kathleengagetrains.com

You Can Control Your Financial Future!

Katie McDonald

Imagine for a moment if the money that you receive on a week to week or month to month basis ... STOPS. Do you have enough savings for the rainy days? What will the money you have allow you to do? What will you have to give up? How long will you be able to survive?

Now, imagine if you were fully self sufficient. Think that you are earning from more than one source. Think Cloudy With a Chance of Meatballs! This time believe it is raining money and it's pouring effortlessly into your hands. With that money you are able to have everything you desire.

Given both scenarios, I think it is a no-brainer on your part which of the two situations you would rather find yourself in. If you would rather find yourself in the first predicament, then we have a huge problem with the kind of mindset you have around money.

Now that I have your attention, I want to outline a few critical issues I have discovered about women and money.

Being financially unaware is dangerous, especially considering the following statistic: 49% of 50+ women are single through choice, divorce, or death. For the first time since World War 1 there are more single women in Australia than married. Women are expected to live on average 10 years longer than men, with female baby boomers expected to outlive their husband by 15 to 20 years. It is important to take control of your finances and there is no better time than NOW. It doesn't matter if it was your choice to become independent or it was forced upon you. It doesn't make any difference whether you are in a happy and healthy marriage or single. Whatever situation you are in, taking control of your financial future is significant especially when you are a woman.

We already have what it takes to look after our own financial future. As women we spend our life looking after everyone else, from our children, husbands, our home, grandchildren to our career. We are very good at budgeting, paying off credit cards, paying bills and saving. We are blessed with skills and faculties that will make us good money managers. And believing you can take control of your financial future is the first and most important step you need to take.

The following five steps are the simplest set of rules to follow in order to start on the path of taking control of your finances.

1. Know where you are now

The famous quote by Zig Ziglar goes, "If you don't know where you are, how are you going to get to where you want to be." It is important to know your full financial position. What are your expenses for the month? How much is your income for the month? What do you own and what do you owe – house, shares, investment property, furniture? Knowing where you are now lets you understand if you are under financial stress. Is your income greater than your expenses? Do you own more than you owe? This serves as a Financial Health Check for you. For instance, I cannot talk to you about putting up multi-income streaming if you are still at the phase of your finances where you need to get out of debt. In other words, before you go to step three, know if you are at the second phase. Knowing where you are now provides a benchmark for moving forward. Download your [free budget and essentials expenses workbook](#) and start taking control of your finances.

2. Understand the power of your mind

Do you believe money grows on trees? Do you say to yourself constantly we will never be able to afford that? Is it affecting your finances? You may not know it, but what you focus on is what you get. That's right! You need to understand the power of your mind. Start building your confidence about money and tap into your intelligence. We learn the majority of our money literacy from our parents. This is the foundation of our beliefs and our confidence about money. If you saw your parents fighting all the time about money or watched your father hand out the weekly housekeeping to your mother, this will have an effect on your beliefs about money today. Much of the conditioning women have stems from generations of men controlling the money. Cast your mind back as far as you can and try to remember? Are these memories hindering you from taking the next steps? Are they valid beliefs to still be holding onto today?

3. Setting financial goals

Where do you want to be and by when? This is quite a large and daunting task. Therefore start by breaking it down. Find a purpose for wanting more money. Focus on the purpose and develop goals in order to achieve your purpose. For instance, I want more money because I want to get a cleaner so I can spend more time with my kids. Then find out how much money you need to afford a cleaner. Set goals around how to earn the extra $80 per week. All you need to do is look at your expense section of your budget you have completed through the budget and essential expenses worksheet (see below for our free download). Set goals around earning a passive income equal to your outgoings. You can also set up a Freedom account. Work out what your expenses are for a month and start putting aside money in a freedom account to cover those expenses. Use the budget you downloaded to work out your essential expenses. Start putting aside money to cover you for one to six months for emergency only. If your purpose is to be financially secure download the Goal Setting Workbook.

4. Invest in your financial education and start taking action

You are probably oriented with the saying that you cannot teach an old dog new tricks. Well, it isn't as scary as you might think to educate yourself and start taking action. For example, you can invest in understanding how shares work and what they can do for you. It will increase your confidence tremendously to discover new ways of trying to increase your wealth. You can also discover about property investing and how it could work for you. Even if you use a financial planner it is important to know what risks you are taking with YOUR MONEY. When you are financially safe and you have educated yourself, set your next goal of creating a passive income that covers your freedom account.

5. Surround yourself with the best

The most successful people have mentors and other great people who work for them. You can't be everything for everyone. Find a great financial planner and uncover a property investment mortgage broker. Get a great accountant. These people will help you become financially free. Some steps may be tantamount to breaking a simple habit. Some other steps may be uncomfortable and what we may call giant leaps. However, you must remember to go out of your comfort zone. Otherwise, you're probably doing what you have always done. And you'd be getting what you've always gotten with a hundred and one percent certainty. Remember all of these are possible. Thousands of women have done it before you and thousands more will do it after you. Just take one step at a time.

3 Tips To Stay Focused On Your Dreams

Build up a can do attitude to investing and looking after your finances

Create positive beliefs about money – Once you start taking control you will have a great capacity to help others. There is more than enough money in the world for everyone

Put together your budget – this may seem daunting at first but you may be surprised by the results, Set financial goals and educate yourself about both shares and property

About The Author

Katie McDonald is a successful share trader and property investor. At present, she looks after a multimillion dollar property portfolio plus a multimillion dollar share portfolio – consisting of a personal share portfolio and several super funds... and growing. Katie's business, "Freedom for Women" educates others through workshops, online courses, one on ones and seminars on how to control your financial future. She bought her first investment property when she was 23 and since then she has never looked back. At 29 she had her two beautiful boys and needed to create an income that enabled her to stay at home with them. She turned to share trading. She went to every seminar she could possible get her hands on and read lots of books. When the Global Financial Crisis (GFC) hit a lot of people lost a substantial amount of their retirement income. One of these people was Katie's Aunt who had recently become widowed. Upon further investigation it turned out her aunt could see her retirement fund going down but didn't have the confidence to tell her financial adviser to get out. She felt inadequate when it came to money matters even though she paid all the household bills and ran the administration side of her husband's business. This is one of the real life experiences which prompted Katie to start Freedom for Women. And to this date, Katie has lived up to her ideal to help women increase their confidence and education about their finances.

Special Gift

To receive You Can Control Your Financial Future ebook with bonus free access to a budget excel download and a goal setting sheet. Please visit http://www.freedomforwomen.com/wonderfulwebwomen.html

http://www.freedomforwomen.com

Janet Beckers

A Travelling Destiny

Kerrie Jeffreys

I am a terrible employee. I worked that out very early in life. I couldn't stand the frustration of taking directions on how to (or not) make someone else's vision a reality. I wanted to concentrate all my efforts on my own plans, my own vision, creating my own destiny. Not someone else's. I've always had a destiny in mind. The path took some curves – even some u-turns and the destination changed slightly from time to time, but it was always there in front of me; a glowing nimbus surrounding a vision of a successful me in an exotic locale competently juggling a truckload of challenges with a smile on my face. And the really important part of that vision? The exotic locale – travel. As a very young single mother, I loaded my daughter into a Kombi and for many years travelled the east coast of New South Wales and Queensland, taking on roles in tourism and hospitality.

I loved the continually changing landscape, lapped up the backpackers' travel stories, marveled at the excitement of overseas tourists as they saw something so different to their country. A tiny flame was lit inside me but it burned untended for quite a few years. I took a detour that saw me become a qualified Herbalist, teaching at Newcastle College of Herbal Medicine, and in my spare time developed and manufactured a range of skin and body products based on herbs, natural clays and essential oils, selling them at markets on the weekend.

I'd travel (there's that word again) long distances hunting out the markets that specialized in natural and alternative wares. Then, fifteen years ago my brother got married in the Cayman Islands and my family, now expanded to include a husband and a son, travelled there to witness the ceremony. Oh my goodess! There was this incredible world out there, an exotic, enticing world. I had to have more of this. I knew then that I needed to build a business that could fund my passion for travel. My weekend markets expanded into a shop that, as well as my products, stocked a whole range of fashion and handicrafts from Bali.

I was buying this stock from local wholesalers, but knew I had to get to Bali myself to source a range of products that was unique.

All it takes is a decision ....I firmly believe in "say yes then work out how. " Being open to opportunities that may present to you. This attitude saw me in Bali for the first of many visits. After that first time, I visited Bali regularly to purchase more stock for my shop (I've been there 19 times). I spent most of my time there talking to small stall holders, explaining what sort of clothing, footwear and handcrafts I wanted and seeing if they were interested in producing them for me. After several visits I became comfortable in moving around in a strange country, working in a different currency, dealing with the language barriers and most importantly reveling in the exotic surrounds, immersing myself in their lifestyle and customs and making friends far and wide.

I then started taking Australian friends with me on these trips and loved showing them this beautiful country with its wonderful people. Watching them try new experiences and stretching their comfort zones was exhilarating. And another piece of my destiny puzzle fell into place. Not only did I want to travel, I wanted to help other people travel. I wanted to take them on their adventures – or at least plan them.

Networking has been pivotal in my business expansion. It is amazing the generosity of like minded people   willing to share advice and support and the all important sounding board for times of uncertainty. So, 7 years ago I studied to became a travel agent and, after a brief period of working for someone else (still not a good employee), I became a mobile agent. To provide an income stream while I got some experience under my belt I purchased a hairdressing salon (stocking my own products of course) and as well as providing income, it also provided a wonderful pool of people wanting to travel.

Janet Beckers

I started taking groups of women on what I affectionately referred to as "broads abroad" tours. Bali, Vietnam, Thailand, Cambodia. Tours that stepped outside the normal resort stays and incorporated an element of adventure – a true immersion into the countries we visited. I got real enjoyment watching others as they took tentative steps out of their comfort zones and realized what they could do and achieve. Whether it's sampling new foods, striking a bargain, swimming with elephants – every new experience helps people realize that they are capable of much more than they may have believed. If you're a traveller, rather than a tourist, then travel is the fastest way I know to grow as a person. Then I was asked to organize a really large group of people to go to a conference in the United States – with a lot of sightseeing and extraneous travel thrown in. What a challenge! What a buzz when it all came together.

Okay, so I was now travelling to all sorts of interesting countries and introducing others to great travel related experiences. That was my dream, wasn't it? My vision? Seemed my dream had grown. I was addicted to challenges – big ones. So now I have my own company – BG Travel and Events. Yes, events. I also organize conferences – not just people's travel to the conference. I come up with the concepts for the conference, I find the guest speakers, I put together the promotions, I build the websites. And I've found another passion; fundraising for charities. A passion I'm integrating into my events by donating the profits from elements such as trade shows to organisations such as Opportunity International.

To keep on track I work with a DMO (daily method of operation) which I review monthly ensuring to schedule time out (me time) and a to do list is always on my desk. I've discovered I'm a real ideas person, and more importantly I've discovered that I have the determination to take my ideas and make them succeed. I need to always have another project on the horizon once I've put my latest one to bed. And always, always I have to have a ticket to another travelling adventure in my bag. "The World is a book, and those who do not travel read only a page."

3 Tips To Stay Focused On Your Dreams

Find something you have a passion for and build a business around it. Be prepared to be flexible…. allow growth and move forward.

From my favorite mentor Loral Langemeier "Say Yes first then sort out how" always be open to opportunities.

Lend a Hand ... the greatest gift you can receive is in the giving to others and I don't just mean donate ... you need to jump in boots and all.

About The Author

Born with a wandering soul and itchy feet, Kerrie Jeffreys has always craved new sights, new landscapes, new people, new experiences. It's taken her a while but she now has her own travel and events company where she organises great trips for her clients or, better still, takes groups of women on tours of other lands, sharing her passion for the travel experience. She also organises business conferences, pulling together people who can share their skills and experiences with attendees. Along the way to achieving her dream, Kerrie was a lecturer in Herbology, an importer of exotic products from Bali and a retailer. She thrives on challenges and has a mind that never stops and feet that are never still.

Special Gift

Visit www.bgtravelandevents.com register your details before 31st May 2011 and you will be in the draw to win 5nights accommodation @ BG Bali Luxury Villas. Every entry will also receive TRAVEL DIVAS ... Stories from the Road Less Travelled E-Book complied from women travellers full of inspiration and motivation with many hints and tips for women on a journey.

http://www.bgtravelandevents.com

Janet Beckers

3 Easy Steps To Achieve MILESTONES

Kerry Weymouth

What milestones have you achieved in your life? Take a look at the Milestones you achieved in the past four years – 2007, 2008, 2009 and 2010. What do you see? What were your personal highlights? What are your big milestones? Time goes so very quickly, one moment we are making New Year's resolutions and then in a blur of days into weeks, into months then with a blink of an eye, it's almost the end of December.

After another birthday, we are another year older; another year wiser right? Milestones are defined as "a significant event in a life or history" Significant events in your life don't happen by accident. The way you think, more specifically what you think especially; your daily focus and the action you take helps you to achieve milestones.

One of the easiest methods to move towards achieving your next milestone is to work out specifically what you want to achieve. Most people don't know what they want. Some say "oh I don't know. I have no idea what I want to do with my life". Sometimes it is easier to live in the land of confusion, or 'Limbo land'. Taking each day as it comes, putting up with the daily frustration and getting annoyed because "nothing good happens in my life. My life is crap." They get consumed by the frustration, bitterness and become over powered by negative thoughts which imprison themselves into a tiny jail cell; which is their mind. If they only knew that the power of the mind is the key; the way you think and actions you take are the keys to free themselves.

Here are my Three Golden 'Tools' I use to achieve milestones in my life:

1. What is it You Visualising?

Tell me or write it down what you would visualise? What picture in your mind do you see? What does your future look like? An excellent way of doing this is to look at your time line, what milestones do you see in 2011, 2012, 2013 and 2014? Visualising is absolutely free; it won't cost you a cent to visualise. However, it can be very costly if you don't visualise. Nothing happens.

2. Identify Your Thinking

What are you thinking about? (Voice in my head: "Kerry, I'd love a coffee right about now. How about you go and put the kettle on") Identify what that voice in your head is saying. Your future and future milestones depends on that voice inside your head. Let me ask you; what are you thinking about today? What are your plans for tomorrow? Have you thought about what you are doing this weekend? What are you looking forward to achieving this month? "I think I can..." "I think there is absolutely no way..." "I don't think I'm good enough" "I think I should just go for it"

3. Take Action

Take massive action, every day, do something that brings you one step closer to your milestone. brb Right where was I? I am back now with my coffee. See, what was I saying? Taking Action; I had to get up, put the body in motion, move to the kitchen, put the kettle on, find a clean cup and spoon, add coffee then add boiling water, open the fridge, add the milk, 2 teaspoons of sugar and stir. Now, I am drinking this lovely cup of instant coffee. Making a coffee would never have 'happened' if I didn't commit to taking action. Take action on your thinking. Never lose sight of the big or small milestones in your life.

Janet Beckers

A milestone could be going to college, graduating from university, getting married, career change or even finishing project at home like starting home compost. Ultimately your thoughts, the way you think and the action you take equal the milestones achieved in your life.

3 Tips To Stay Focused On Your Dreams

1. What is it You Visualising? Tell me or write it down what you would visualise?

2. Identify Your Thinking; What are you thinking about?

3. Take Action; What action are you going to take every day that brings you one step closer to your milestone?

About The Author

Hi, I'm Kerry Weymouth, Lead Trainer and Founder of Milestone Training Australia Pty Ltd. My responsibility specifically is to inspire individuals and regional businesses to create something extraordinary. I'm committed to providing intensive training that empowers individuals with essential leadership and communication tools, to help build new foundations. My dream is to inspire thousands of people living in regional Australia to take action. I survived a ton of "reality bricks" that came crashing down on me. At one point there, I was at a total loss. I had no plans, no goals and no direction. At that time, I didn't know what it was called but I knew I had to use my strength and determination to take control of my life. Milestones in my life are a direct result of the dreams, plans and action I have taken. From the BIG milestones - trekking in Nepal, getting acceptances in national and international photography competitions to the SMALLER goals, cooking one recipe a month from Delicious Magazine and starting a home compost. My commitment to help others from regional areas achieve their dreams, use the same 'tools' that I have used to achieved my dreams is extremely important.

Special Gift

This is my exclusive offer to you as a dedicated "The Power of 100" reader. When you book a one Full Day leadership training course for 12 people. Your seat, valued at $300 is absolutely FREE! Yes absolutely FREE. Note: Full Day Training Course maximum 12 participants, so gather your colleagues, friends or family. This offer is limited to the first 10 customers. Fist in, first served Go to my website www.milestonetraining.com.au and enter promotional Code: milestonewebwomen Hurry Offer closes: 31st May 2011

http://www.milestonetraining.com.au

YOU Can DO Anything - The Challenge Of Believing That Being A Generalist Has Value In A Specialist World.

Kim Lambert

My first reaction when I thought about writing a chapter for this book was "I'm not very interesting" (how's that for a typical response ?!).

Then I thought about it, reread my own Bio and decided maybe I did have something to say. So, here are some concepts that have been key learnings for me, in achieving things, and dealing with the expectations of others in the workplace, in business, as a woman and as an individual. The challenge in my life has been in trusting myself, and forging forward with doing things in a way that is true to myself – my personal values and ethics – in a world where there is so much pressure to do business the way "it has always been done".

By telling my story here, I hope to encourage others to believe in their own ability to be a success, doing things with authenticity, no matter how discouraging those around you are being. More and more, we are living in a world where there is so much information that it is impossible to keep up with everything. This has lead to a situation where it is possible to become so focused on an incredibly specialized field that you know very little about anything else. Such knowledge is valued highly (and rightly so), but an unintended consequence of this is that broad based knowledge has become less valued in the process.

In past generations there was the concept of the polymath – a person who knew a lot about a lot of fields – most early scientists, highly successful business people etc were in this category until late the 19th century. Now no-one wants to believe that you can be good at more than one thing. But you can. I discovered very early in my life that I was quite capable of doing pretty much anything I set my mind to, and was lucky enough to have parents who made no gender based judgments about what I should do, in an era when 'women's work' was still a very strong concept. That was both a good, and a bad thing.

I remember clearly being sent to the school careers counselor (as we all were) in about year 7 and having them look at all of my records, exam results etc etc and come to the oh, so helpful conclusion of "you can do anything you want to, dear". So much for guidance! So I studied what interested me, and then dropped out of it when it turned out to not be what I expected or wanted. I started working and was continually amazed by the fact that people expected me to have a set career path picked out and to only look at jobs on that track. I could not conceive of doing the one thing all my life. So I did a lot of different things, and even in my early twenties, interviewers would look at my resume and say "my, you've done a lot" whilst looking at me suspiciously, as if I had made some of it up.

By the time I was 31 I had already been an admin clerk, a reporting clerk, a personnel clerk, a warranty clerk, a switchboard operator, a vehicle service administrator, an audio visual sales rep, a real estate sales rep, a party plan sales person, a wholesale sales rep, run a bookstore, run a camera store, been a professional photographer, a riding teacher, a receptionist, a secretary, owned and run a florists/plant nursery shop, delivered leaflets, been publicity officer for a couple of organisations and been published (small articles in a couple of magazines). It never occurred to me that I should find it difficult to switch from one thing to another, or do a pretty good job at any of them. But people would ask about what I did and expect an answer of the "I am an office manager" kind – something with a nice neat singular label. And I never had that kind of answer. I was, absolutely, a generalist, have a go at anything kind of person.

I started to wonder if there was "something wrong with me" that I could not/had not settled to a nice neat path, "like everyone else". And then, in an admin job, I hit a situation where, when I had been there 3 weeks, people who had been there 3 years would be coming to me saying things like "Kim, the printer won't work, can you fix it?" And so IT as a job arrived in my life. We had computers at home (in the mid eighties) but I had never done much more than use them for word processing and playing games. So at first, I just fixed the printer, was puzzled that they couldn't and thought no more of it. But, after about 2 years of that, I decided that maybe I should get some qualifications in that space, if it was going to be what I ended up doing most of the time.

Over that two years I had been studying things I was interested in on a purely personal, as far from IT as you could get, basis and had completed an Associate Diploma.

So, knowing that I could study, at 33 I went back to Uni, by correspondence, and did a Grad Dip in Applied Science in Computing. I don't think that it helped my work much, apart from looking imposing on the resume for other people's reassurance, but it was interesting. The real life day to day hands on stuff taught me a lot more than the study. At that point I, for a little while, thought "OK, I've got me a label, I'm an IT person". Then people started asking " Oh, yes IT, but what do you DO ? Are you a programmer, an operator, a support person?". Hmm here it goes again. People wanted a label. And, as usual, I didn't.

Since I started in IT I have done 26 different IT related job roles (and probably a few more things that don't leap to mind right now). It's fun, I learn new things in every role. I'm still a generalist. And people still want me to have a nice neat label.

I have come to the conclusion that this is very much a female thing. Of all the people that I know, especially in IT, those who can, and do, multitask in every aspect of their lives are usually women. There are a few exceptional guys that I have met who can, but, on the whole, most men specialize, and become more and more deep specialists in their field as time goes by. I don't want to. I still think that it would be boring to spend all the rest of my life doing one thing.

I am more interested in leveraging all that experience that I have, to create new businesses and help others. So, the challenge for me, especially over the last few years, has been finding ways to work that allow me to make use of that broad base of knowledge that I have developed, by being a generalist, and having a go at many things. For a short while, I tried to force myself down the path of specialisation, and hated it. There was a point where I despaired of being able to keep advancing and working, whether in employment, or in my own business, without having to sell out on my personal values to do it.

After lots of soul searching (and a lot of very targeted personal development work) I worked out how I could do things in a way that was in line with my values, and help others to do the same. This has been especially important in the latest stage of my life where I am getting myself out of doing a "day job" for someone else and into being fully supported by running my own, mainly internet based, businesses. The business through which I am achieving this is www.business2live.com which is specifically aimed at helping people in small business get clarity about exactly what is happening in their business so that they can "get their life back" and improve their business profits at the same time.

There are a number of key things that I have identified which have allowed me to change the way I relate to work, and change my life as a result. Being in a business or job that lets me function based on those understandings works for me, without forcing me to specialize. But, if I look at working for others, I still have the question of, if I want to advance, how to find roles like that.

They are still rare. And unfortunately, given that corporate culture in general is very much still built around the concept that people specialize, and that deep specialisation makes you more valuable (and therefore able to be paid more money...) than generalization across a strong knowledge area, I don't expect that to change soon. So the answer that I have come to is that the only way for me to continue to move forward, being authentic to myself, is in my own business and that business has to be one that helps others.

But I do expect it to change over time. So, I encourage you, if you are one of the people like me, that does not have such a depth of passion about one area that it calls you to specialize, to do what interests you, all of it (but maybe not all at the same time....) and keep reinforcing to others (and yourself) just how much value that generalization brings to an organisation or a project, and how valuable that makes YOU, as someone who can adapt on the fly, fill any gap, problem solve and deliver regardless of what happens around you.

Janet Beckers

Every one of you has some knowledge that could be a business for you, and help others in the process!

3 Tips To Stay Focused On Your Dreams

The 3 key things to do to ensure that business or work is in line with your personal values are:

Understand what you really like doing - I discovered that I like building new things, things that are needed, but do not yet exist, or have barely begun. This works well, because for something new, there is no exact path – broad knowledge is useful (and gets broadened more in the process) and people appreciate my ability to have a go at anything and solve problems on the fly. This has been key for Business 2 Live – I see, and can structure a way for others to see, multiple aspects of what happens in a business. *What do you enjoy most ?*

Understand your work and management style - I manage people in a very 'mentor and support' fashion, not a dictatorial one. I want them to be there because they want to work for me. If I am working for someone else, the person who is my boss, and the company culture that backs them, is more important than the tasks, in terms of how long I am likely to be willing to stay/how long it will take me to get bored (so I treat others as if that is equally true for them..). I hate being micromanaged, and therefore won't do it to someone else. *What matters most to you as a worker? as a manager? how effective are you at acting in accordance with that?*

People are people, whatever role they are in - relate to them as valuable human beings, not as embodiments of a corporate idea. Build your networks by relating to people as people, regardless of where they are in the business.

I respect the requirements that the role may place on the person, but they are still just a person, with whom I should be able to have a civil and ordinary conversation. (and very often, someone in an important role is immensely grateful to be treated as a person, rather than the embodiment of some grand idea.) I build people networks in a meshed fashion throughout an organization, or an industry, and outside it – if you expect me only to go via a rigid chain of command, it won't work (and meshed networks is why I am effective at getting things done). *Do you see the person behind the label? Do you treat the "lowest" person in the organization with the same respect that you treat the "highest" with?*

About The Author

Kim worked in a wide range of private industry and government roles, as well as running a number of small businesses, from wholesale sales, through retail management, administration and financial management, to an extensive range of IT industry roles. Within these roles Kim has delivered results in complex environments, through effective people and business management. She has had some ventures and roles which are more successful than others. She has consistently learnt from her less than successful moments and used those lessons to grow. Through working in organisations from micro businesses through to huge government departments and global corporates she has identified that there are some key areas of understanding required to allow a business to be successful, and to grow beyond a certain point.These key areas are rarely applied to small businesses, even though they are in a position to benefit massively from applying this information. In her business – Business 2 Live (www.business2live.com) Kim is making that knowledge accessible to small business owners through clear information and structured workbooks, hands on workshops or ongoing mentoring to allow any small business owner to leverage the type of tools and concepts that the big corporations use to ensure their survival!

Janet Beckers

Special Gift

Special offer for readers – 50% discount (offer valid until 30 June 2011) on the Business 2 Live "12 Steps to Business Sanity" Full work book system package – normally $299 – for readers $149. – Coupon code 2011BOOK50. Claim by going to http://business2live.com/12-steps-to-business-sanity-full-workbook-system-package/ click on the "add to cart" button to buy, then enter the coupon code in the checkout to receive your discount.

www.business2live.com

Escape of the Corporate Zombie

Kim Morris

When I was thinking about writing the chapter for this book, there were so many things that came to mind as to what I could have wrote on, but when I sat down and really reflected on what had impacted and influenced me the most over the past 12 months to really push though my comfort zone, I realized that three things stood out the most as being really big motivators for me in moving towards achieving my dreams and my vision for the ultimate lifestyle business. But before I get into that, let me first introduce myself.

My name is Kim Morris and up until mid 2010 I had worked in a corporate cubicle for 15 years. I also had a not so secret life for many of those years as freelance fitness trainer and small business owner. Whilst it had always been in the back of my mind that I would one day pursue a deeper entrepreneurial path, I literally woke up one day, back in 2008, after a life-changing trip to Vietnam and decided that my life would have to change.

Janet Beckers

So, I set in motion certain events, at a very conscious level that would take me from my windowless corporate cubicle to my comfortable home office where I could see the trees and sky. From that point on, of setting that intention of change I have been on a whirlwind ride of trial and error, pass and fail, right and wrong and all the while, I have been following my passion.

You see, I am on a mission to help small business owners achieve the business they set out to create. I am passionate about, and fortunately also have a natural talent for, solving problems and working out how to make things work more efficiently. It is these gifts that I use to help tired and frustrated small business owners to streamline and systemize their business, without them having to do all the work themselves. I help them to bridge the gap between the big picture they are trying to create and the foundation, structure and systems needed to deliver their vision. In a nutshell, you could say that my vision is to help small business owners tangibly realise their own vision. So, how do I stay motivated, excited and passionate about keeping my vision alive?

Well, there are three big things for me that have been really key in helping me to break through old habits and limiting thought patterns, and have allowed me to cultivate a healthier connection with both myself and my business. My first strategy has been to find a great coach and mentor. Right from the very beginning since I started out designing how I wanted my business to be, I always knew that I couldn't build what I wanted to build on my own. Having a coach and mentor by your side is like being in the fastlane. Sometimes you'll find yourself doing things that you're not quite sure of on the advice of your mentor, and then all of a sudden the reason why you needed to do it becomes crystal clear, and you know that without your coach and mentor you wouldn't have taken that step forward.

Your coach and mentor is like your guiding light, keeping you on the straight and narrow and the catch-ups, brainstorming and mastermind sessions will always be a source of inspiration, motivation and excitement. I would not be where I am now without the unwavering support of my coach and mentor, and of course the other fabulous people that I have been introduced to along the way – you know who you are!

My second strategy for keeping my vision alive, has been to keep an ideas journal. This is a pretty little hardcover notebook (A5 size) that I carry round with me in my bag, and it contains all my radical, out there, far fetched, even ridiculous ideas and thoughts that I might "one day" do, some personal, some business. But the real power of this is that simply by writing these ideas and thoughts down you are actually incubating each one, at a subconscious level, turning it over, weighing it up, and either moving it forward, or putting it on a shelf for future consideration.

I write in my ideas journal almost every day and I find that when I am most relaxed, not even in "business mode" is when my most impressive ideas come. Without a doubt my ideas journal has been a source of inspiration to me that I have been able to look over when I feel like I have nothing left in the tank. It has been my comfort and my mate since I have stepped out on this journey and I wouldn't be without it. It is the source from which all my products, services and marketing strategies are born.

My third strategy, is a very practical one and no doubt many people currently use, but it's how to do it effectively that I think sometimes challenges people. It's about lists. I love lists and I have lists for everything. Keeping lists helps me to keep my vision alive because it helps me to plan, stay focused and keep organised with the million and one things I have to do. I have a Master List that I keep in Excel which has all the things I need to do. Even when I have done things, I don't delete them from the list, I just grey them out because it gives me a feeling of satisfaction to look back over what I have achieved. This Master List is where I get my weekly and daily lists from.

To be as organised as possible and to get the most value for my time, I have to plan ahead. So, each week, I use my Master Plan to create a list of the things that I will work on for that week, and I do this on a Friday afternoon so that I can rest easy over the weekend knowing that I have clarity around what is on my plate for the coming week.

On Monday morning, I create a plan of what I'll do on each day. I'm not too pedantic about things getting done on certain days, just so long as what I have planned for that week gets done in that week. I find that this is a nice balance between not being to structured, but not being to abstract about what needs to be done. As a result of this approach, I find I have developed a disciplined and focused way of working that really motivates me because I can see results! And there is nothing like seeing the fruits of your labour to get you going to want to do more!

Janet Beckers

3 Tips To Stay Focused On Your Dreams

Find a coach or mentor. This can be done in a number of ways depending on how much you are ready and willing to invest, both financially and mentally. At one end of the scale, from afar you can choose to follow, learn from and model just about anyone who has the success you want. And at the other end of the scale, you can consciously seek out a business coach and mentor who will help to take you to the next level, to keep you accountable to deliver on what you say you will. The question is: are you to play that big?

Start an ideas journal. Buy a nice book that you can fit in your handbag. Your objective is that over the course of one month, you consciously spend 10 mins twice per week thinking about and brainstorming your business to come up with ideas. Ideas abou

Create Your Master List. Write down all the tasks and activities that are outstanding in your business right now. Doing this in excel is ideal, but if you prefer the old fashion way, using a notebook is fine. Once you have all your tasks written down, prioritise them using A, B and C, with A being the most important, followed by B being next important, with C being the least important. This will give you a great starting point from which to create you weekly to do list from.

About The Author

Kim Morris has over 10 years experience in Project Management, Human Resources and Information Systems working with businesses of all sizes helping them to maximise efficiencies through simplification, streamlining and automation, increase productivity and reduce staffing levels, reduce duplication, waste and rework, and introduce best practice processes for service, delivery and turnaround.. Kim is a Business Systems Expert and Business Improvement Coach, who now works exclusively with small business owners and entrepreneurs to help them to systemize and streamline their business. The beauty is that Kim uses a unique system which means business owners don't have to do all the systemizing themselves!

Special Gift

To find out more about Kim's proprietary system and learn how you can go from being a stressed out, time poor business owner to having an efficient and streamlined business where you can concentrate on what you love doing and not what you have to do, go to http://entrepreneursystems.com for your FREE 50 page Business Boost Blueprint.

http://entrepreneursystems.com/

Janet Beckers

Awakening Awareness

Kim Townsend

After a lifetime of so many big ideas that have never happened, it is wonderful to have a vision that I am finally putting into action. And this vision is huge!

I have always wanted to experience and achieve so much. Despite successfully dealing with many personal demons, I felt my life had not added up to anything worthwhile. I had always felt there was a deep purpose to my life but could never grasp what it was. I was spinning my wheels. Then, I went to my first personal development seminar – it made sense of so many things. Mostly, I was not alone! I was able to connect with many others who wanted more out of life. That's when I started to wake up – to become totally aware, conscious and responsible for myself and my life. I began to unearth the courage to be my true authentic self, and be the person I knew myself to be, connect to my power and get results.

The difference has been like night and day. I am now engaged in deeply rewarding work.

My vision is to create a global community of like-minded spiritually aware individuals and businesspeople dedicated to making a difference to others. Out of this community are growing events and projects which are sharing information, education and support to community members enabling them to create and live their dreams.

The current focus is to make Sydney, Australia, the global hub for aware businesses. Aware businesses are run by people connected to their higher purpose, and making a difference at all levels of the community. The Aware Business Community allows people to connect, collaborate and create from the same values and shared purpose. Our global launch is slated for 2012. We are planning a global initiative which will link with many other organisations out there working to change lives and our world for the better.

How do I keep my focus? On a day to day basis I am utilising my NLP (Neuro-linguistic Programming) training combined with ancient wisdom (eastern and western), quantum physics and science, and these tools enable me to teach people to get the results they really desire.

What have I learned from working with vision? Firstly, dare to dream big. Then, having the end in mind, create a solid foundation. Get a clear picture of what it is you would like to achieve, then imagine being in the desired result in full sensory perception - see, hear, smell and really feel how good it feels to be there. Ask yourself, 'why do I want this?' If the 'why' and the vision are congruent, start on "the how". Set realistic and measurable goals, with a 'by when' date and an intention of how you need to show up in order to achieve this goal. Then chunk down into bite size pieces to find the next simple step. Choose wisely, when selecting your team. Pay particular attention to who resonates with the underlying vision, sharing the same values and purpose, and adds something unique to the mix. Pay attention to the practical, a vision without a practical action plan is a fantasy. Set monthly, weekly and daily tasks/goals and hold each other accountable.

Be open and honest – always. Reassess and alter the plan if required. This process works for any time frame – 10 years down to 10 minutes.

Practice. When I am feeling stuck, or getting a bit frustrated, I sit quietly, take a few deep breaths, still my mind and ask 'what do I need to do now?' A really simple next step pops up. I also check my life balance. Have I been working too much and not getting enough rest and play.

When I'm lacking motivation, I check whether I am operating from my intention or whether old unconscious fears might be creating a hurdle. Motivation is always more powerful working towards an outcome. So, as in the beginning, I visualise the

Janet Beckers

outcome and remind myself of how good it will feel being in that place. However, sometimes, as a last resort I remind myself of what I don't want! Taking time to remind myself what I don't want and the pain I have endured can be a great motivator!

Regular sessions with a coach are critical. We all lose focus and having an "outside eye" is really beneficial. A coach is being paid to keep you on track – unlike your friends and family, who will sometimes unknowingly project their 'stuff' onto you. Their purpose is to coach you to be the best you can be, to achieve what you desire. A good coach will tell you what you need to hear, not what you want to hear and hold you accountable.

Above all, if it doesn't feel right, don't do it or at least question it. If something is out of alignment you need to check in with yourself: are you on purpose, is it about values, integrity or an old belief? Talk with your team or coach, as soon as the discomfort arises. Trust your intuition, listen to your body. Learn to pay attention or you will pay with pain. This could be physically, mentally or financially.

I think the 'biggies' that keep me moving are: I actually have a goal, I now believe in myself, I know I do not have to do it alone, I take action and maintain a balance – nurturing the mind, the body and the spirit.

3 Tips To Stay Focused On Your Dreams

Have a clear vision & know why you are doing it

Set realistic, measurable goals & take action towards them every day

Have support – a partner, life or business, who shares the vision and a coach, who works with mindset, the spiritual and the practical

About The Author

Kim is a passionate life coach who works primarily with women to help them to 'embrace change today, for a brighter tomorrow', to live their love & achieve the results they long for, in all areas of life. She does this by working closely one-on-one

in person or over the phone. Her extensive life experiences, including single mother of three, overcoming substance abuse, divorce & working in many different industries, combined with formal qualifications in Neurolinguistic Programming (NLP), Results Coaching, Hypnosis, Small Business Management & Fine Arts equips her with experiential knowledge to connect with her clients. She is passionate about education, health, caring for our aged and adventure. She has a rare ability to combine creativity & practical business sense. She is a Spiritual Entrepreneur and a founding member of the Aware Business Community. A developing online, global community that assists and supports businesses making a difference through connecting and collaborating to create events & projects to improve the quality of peoples lives. Kim loves working on Community projects & is a member of Lions Club International. She works with Community festivals & public artworks. Her grant writing expertise is a valuable asset. On International Volunteers Day, Hurstville City Council formally acknowledged her volunteer contributions.

Special Gift

My gift to you is a special introductory coaching session. Please contact me at mindsetmastery@yahoo.com.au. I look forward to hearing from you.

http://www.awarebusiness.com.au   http://www.mindsetmastery@yahoo.com.au
http://www.womenliveyourdream.com

Janet Beckers

The Secrets To Creating Your 'Magical Sparkle'

Kirsty Greenshields

To start my story, I want to share a quick synopsis of a movie I love, called Mr Magorium's Wonder Emporium. 23 year old Mahoney is the manager of Mr Magorium's Magical Toy Emporium. Everyone who enters the store knows that there is something magical about Mahoney too, but Mahoney doesn't BELIEVE it herself.

When she was a girl, everyone thought she would become a famous concert pianist because she was really good. After work at the Emporium every day, she practices the piano. But she gets stuck EVERY day. She can't get into the flow of her masterpiece after hours of slogging away at the keyboard. When 243 years old, magical Mr Magorium dies and leaves the store to Mahoney but she doesn't want it because she doesn't feel good enough to manage it without him around. So she puts the store up for sale and goes to play piano at a local hotel, doing requests.

After a little while, she realizes that her heart is really sad, because she isn't loving what she is doing. With that, Mahoney returns to the store and uses her 'SPARKLE', her own unique talent, to bring magic back to the Emporium.

Why did I tell you that story? Because I really relate to Mahoney – to that little girl who doesn't want to embrace what she knows, deep down, she was born to do, because it doesn't 'fit in' with the pictures she has in her head of what her life is supposed to look like. Can you relate too? In my quest to construct the perfect life for myself (and protect the little girl inside) I joined the army, an environment that promises stability and security, but not one known for its ability to encourage individuality! During that time I also married, at 22, to a man who also had a vision of my so-called perfect life. At 24 years of age, just 18 months into my marriage, I left him. My 'head' vision was so out of alignment with the dreams in my heart, and my heart was sad.

My construction was far from my perfect life. I was in a job that I really disliked, I had painfully broken my ankle 12 months earlier and I was on the verge of serious illness, due to weight loss caused by stress.

I believe that it is at that point, when we back ourselves by taking a leap of faith that the magic happens. No matter what it is, when we stand up and allow ourselves to sparkle – even just a tiny bit – we are saying to the universe. "Yes, I am ready to take the next step. Bring it on!" And the universe will do it in such a way that we are ready for it. At first, baby steps are usually the best way but, as we continue to back ourselves and build our own self-confidence, we will allow ourselves to face bigger and bigger things, so our inner light becomes progressively brighter.

When it comes to growth, the lessons I have learned in my personal and professional lives are intertwined. My biggest lesson, I believe, has been about never believing I am good enough for whatever it is I am doing, despite outside evidence to the contrary. Therefore, I must try to be 'better' than others, rather than just be myself – because myself isn't enough. It is a scarcity mentality – like this world is only big enough to support the unique talent of a few people! My choices reflected that deeply held belief, so that I found myself emotionally and physically ill again by the time I was 27.

As you know, that mentality is debilitating and, in today's world of co-operation and partnership in business, it serves no-one, especially me! When you can get to a place where you trust your decisions and choices, and you know that what you have to offer is enough, you are embracing your own holiness, accepting your own gift to the world. As a health practitioner, this is a beautiful feeling because, like most other health practitioners I WANT to help and serve people! When we live in a reality of scarcity, rather than abundance, we limit the number of others we can serve.

So what do I do each day to nurture my sparkle, cultivate abundance and fertilise the dreams in my heart?

1. Every morning (except Sunday) I wake at 5.30am to meditate. I usually meditate for 30-45 minutes. Meditation is an incredibly beneficial time for me. My mind is very active and, in the past, a lot of that activity didn't serve me. Meditation allows me to get in touch with those thoughts and witness the 'loop' of negative thoughts, so I can be more aware of them throughout my day.

2. Every morning after my meditation I practice Surya Namaskar – Salute to the Sun, a yoga sequence. It only takes about 15 minutes, and it clears my head in preparation for the day.

3. At least three times a week, I go for a walk or a run for about 30 minutes. Walking and running in nature is another form of meditation for me, and I often find that inspired ideas come to me when I am doing it.

4. A little while ago I introduced a gratitude ritual into our family dinner time. Every night before we eat, we light a candle, hold hands and each say what we are grateful for in our day. This raises the energy of our entire family, encouraging health and happiness.

5. Every night before bed I tell my husband something about him that I am grateful for. Those closest to us offer us a consistent opportunity to look inside of ourselves. If I am consistently finding things about my husband to be grateful for, I am reinforcing my own grace, and nurturing my heart.

Two other activities that are really important to me:

1. Whenever I feel a 'niggle' in my body – it may be a tickle in my throat, a catch in my hamstring or lower back – I always ask it what its purpose is. What is it here to teach me?

2. When I sit down at my computer, or when I am about to meet with a client, I use an 'anchor' that allows me to focus on the here and now, and not get swept

away in reacting. I can then retain my connection with my intuition and inner balance.

As you have noticed, most of these are not focused specifically on my work. They are focused on my connection with my spirit, on nurturing the love in my life. Because when I LOVE my life, I am healthy and happy! Like Mahoney, I have discovered that my talent isn't necessarily what I thought it would be, but every day I am living my dreams by embracing my unique sparkle.

3 Tips To Stay Focused On Your Dreams

1. Make a time every day – preferably the same time – to do something you love. It will nurture your heart-head connection.

2. Take a deep breath – yes, right now – and notice how you are feeling in your body. Where are the sore spots? What else can you feel? Ask your body what it wants to tell you. You may not get an answer straight away – don't worry. Keep trying. Make it a habit three times a day, or whenever you sit down at your computer. You will be amazed at what you start to notice.

3. Find out more about how you can nurture your body, rather than fight against it, so you can get out of 'your head' and into your heart, so they can work TOGETHER to keep you healthy and fulfill your dreams.

About The Author

I am a naturopath and coach, and I'm passionate about empowering women with the resources and knowledge they need to take control of their health. I use the philosophy of the ancient Indian medicine, Ayurveda known as 'The Science of Life'. It teaches that it is our level of 'consciousness' - our ability to listen to our body and how it is FEELING - that influences our degree of health at any given moment.

When we are trying to 'figure things out' all the time, we are living in our head and distancing ourselves from our heart, which often results in a feeling of confusion, or frustration – STRESS! - when things don't go the way we planned.

Janet Beckers

After years of working with professional women who are overcome by stress, anxiety, depression, pre-menstrual syndrome, and other debilitating conditions, I have developed a system that empowers individuals to take control of their own health, raise their level of awareness, and develop a nurturing relationship with their body. I call it Create Perfect Health. My clients have overcome chronic anxiety; relieved debilitating pre-menstrual syndrome; shed kilos that they have been trying to remove for years; stopped smoking; and exponentially improved their energy levels!

My qualifications include an Adv Dip Naturopathy, Dip Nutrition, Dip Medical Herbalism, with postgraduate studies in endocrine function, women's and children's health. I am a Master NLP practitioner and instructor, Reiki and ReconnectionTM practitioner, teacher of meditation and yoga, as well as a qualified success coach.

Special Gift

You can take a free 10 minute self-health check AND Download my report, "Six Simple Steps to Create Perfect Health" AND Register for a complimentary 90 minute health check with me, where we will talk about your health, and ways you can start creating Perfect Health for YOU. Head to www.youcanhaveperfecthealth.com to claim your free gifts

You can find out more about Kirsty at http://www.kirstygreenshields.com

Sweet T.E.A.

Kris Lafferty

The universe if full of dreams for the taking, yet many of us struggle to find time in our multi-tasked, over-scheduled lives to turn our dreams into reality. We convince ourselves that we must have blocks of time to work on our goals and put off getting started or moving forward until we are free of other commitments. Too often we never see our vision fulfilled because we never get started. The reality is all you need is five to ten minutes a day!

I call it my "T.E.A. time". For you it might be a quick solo walk around the block, time in the shower, or waiting in the car for the children to finish soccer practice. For me, I like to grab a glass of my favorite guilty pleasure, sweet tea, and sit on the porch. It is amazing what you can do with a just a few moments of time if you focus on the joy of unlimited possibilities. But you must focus and you must have a specific plan. Here is my strategic plan.

T. Success is already in your mind all you need to do is listen to what you already know. Think about your vision. Think deeply, without distractions, and let your intuition speak to you. Be only positive in your thinking and distinguish the present status of your vision or goal as clearly as you can. Think forward. You know where you are in your project so don't waste time replaying that information; rather focus on what will move you to the next step. What do you want to offer that is new and different from other programs, plans or ideas? What is the value that you bring to your niche? Most importantly, what is the next immediate step you need to take to reach your goal?

E. Now take the one best "what" or idea you have had today and shift your mental focus to explore the possibilities of making that one thing happen. Explore creatively. Do you need to find a resource, write an article, find a mentor, or do some online research? Do you need business advice, a second opinion, or to buy a number two pencil? Sometimes the "how-to" of completing a "what" is not in the expected place or even in a place. Be open to novel solutions.

A. Do something right now! Big or small doesn't matter. You can have the best idea, goal or vision, but if you do not take action, you will never share your gift with the world. Take at least one positive action every day toward your goal. Even if your next step appears complicated and overwhelming. Break larger steps into smaller more manageable chunks and keep moving forward. However small, any action is superior to letting weeks go by until you can find the perfect time. Look up a phone number to call later, write a quick email requesting an informational meeting, draft an outline, or organize your notes while you watch tv, you will be one step closer to your dream fulfilled.

Get into the routine of having T.E.A. time everyday until it becomes an energizing habit. Accomplishment is the result of actually doing something and it is the doing that sets successful people apart from the rest. You can do it! Go to sleep thinking about your vision and your mind will have its own T.E.A. time while you rest. You will be amazed at the new possibilities and refined intuitions that will emerge at your next time for T.E.A.! It's sweet.

3 Tips To Stay Focused On Your Dreams

T.E.A. Time

1. Think positively
2. Explore ideas creatively
3. Act in some way everyday

About The Author

Kris Lafferty is a speaker, facilitator, and coach with an extensive background in corporate training and leadership development. She started her professional life as a school psychologist, completed law school, and joined the Navy to practice law and see the world. Her work experience also includes cross-cultural trainer for Disney Cruise Line and seminar facilitator and keynote speaker for the renowned Disney Institute. Presently, Kris is a college adjunct faculty member, life coach and internet marketing mentor assisting both individual and business clients to define and reach their goals. She is busy constructing a new website focusing on eldercare information for caregivers, serving as a guest blogger, and helping her clients become catalysts for change.

Link In with Kris at http://www.linkedin.com/in/klafferty for progress updates on her new website and blog. In your invitation to connect with her, mention tea! If Kris's strengths match your personal needs visit www.increasedonlineresults.com or contact her at lafferty.k31@gmail.com.

Special Gift

Kris will provide a free 30-minute time management coaching session to readers. Please email her at lafferty.k31@gmail.comto schedule a time and mention tea time offer in the subject line.

http://www.increasedonlineresults.com

Janet Beckers

Dream BIG!

Kristi Sayles

I have a dream… Haven't I heard that somewhere before? Oh, yes, Martin Luther King begin his famous equality speech with that. He was a cool guy with a big dream. But, wait, he dreamed big and look what happened to him! No, I'm not talking about his assassination, I'm referring to his amazing success in helping to liberate people! You see, most of those people didn't really consider the possibility of being treated as equals. They just accepted their low station in life. That's what I don't want you to do.

Don't just settle for what you're handed, improve it! I want you to dream big! Imagine what you would do if money was no object - and then go for it! But, you can't just lie around wishing upon lucky stars. You have to make success happen. "The harder I work, the luckier I get," stated Samuel Goldwyn. Ever heard of MGM Studios? The "G" stands for Goldwyn-Samuel Goldwyn. Enough said. OK, I'm no Samuel Goldwyn. I'm just little ol' Kristi Sayles, second grade teacher and internet entrepreneur. Everything I sell can be downloaded in an instant. It's fun to create cash from thin air! I've grown rather addicted to seeing those "Notifications of Payment" in my inbox.

But, it's not always easy to stay motivated, even for me. You see, sometimes I get refund requests when customers aren't satisfied with my products. It hurts, so I always reply that the refund is on its way, but could they please be kind enough to let me know exactly what they were hoping to find? More often than not, these customers reply that they expected the software to actually write the whole article, essay, story, business plan, or document for them.

My software provides a step by step process for writing these and other things. It needs your input. Most people find it helpful, but it's not a "cheater" tool. I AM a teacher. When I get down in the dumps about my business, I go to my site and read the testimonials people have sent. That always puts a smile on my face and reminds me that it's only a small percentage of the thousands of customers I've had that have been unsatisfied. I'm excited about a new business venture I'm embarking on. It's selling software created by Joe Clayton and his team. Joe used to create software for NASA, so it's quite professional and seems to have a profitable business plan. By the time you read this, I should be able to enroll you into the business too, if you like the sound of it. Simply join my newsletter with the links below and you'll hear all about it soon.

I don't have to stockpile lotions, potions, or pills. Been there, done that, and have the t-shirt. If it works for you, that's fine and I'm tickled for you. It's just not my thing. If it's not yours either, contact me about the software business. I have high hopes for it. Hostgator hosting had to create a special package just for this program because the "unlimited" bandwidth they usually offer just won't cut it with the expected traffic for this software business. Am I millionaire? No, darn it, not yet. But did you notice that I said "yet?" That's because I have a dream-a big one-to become a millionaire. Is that being realistic? Sure it is! I've interviewed dozens of internet millionaires, so I know it is possible.

I love the rags to riches stories like Joshua Shafran's, Stephanie J Hale's and Ross Goldberg's for example. Each of these people experienced near poverty before climbing up out of their bad financial situations into millionaire status. They told me all about it when I interviewed them for my Mentored by Millionaires World Talk Radio Show. Why do I want to be a millionaire? Other than the obvious reasons of enjoying being debt-free, working only when I choose, and security, I have other reasons. I have a dream... I want to be able to coach people into becoming self-sufficient internet marketers.

I live in a low-income area with few job opportunities, and it hurts to see decent, hard-working folks have to rely on government assistance just to provide for their families. How I would love to be able to afford to set up a grant for internet marketing training purposes! My dream is to provide motivated individuals with computers, internet access, and the training to provide not just necessities, but luxuries for their families.

Most of all, I want to provide the luxury of freedom. I want everyone to have the freedom to choose their lifestyles. I want moms and dads to have the luxury to stay home with young children, if they so choose. I want everyone that wants to attend college online to have access to the internet. I want to provide the means to achieving whatever goals people have that seem impossible at this moment. I told you. I dream big. I'm sure if I gave up my teaching position and worked full time on my internet businesses, I would be a millionaire by now. But, there's one snag - I love teaching!

I love my kids and they love me! In many ways, I'm more blessed than many millionaires. So, now you know my biggest roadblock to realizing my dream - ME! I've convinced myself that I can either be a millionaire or a second grade teacher! But not both. Am I sabotaging my own success? Can I be a millionaire second grade teacher? I don't know. But, I'm going to try.

I want you to think about the beliefs that may be holding you back. Is it possible that you are sabotaging your own dreams with silly nonsense and excuses? Maybe you're afraid to fail? Or maybe, just maybe, you're afraid to succeed! Think about it. That's not as crazy as it sounds. Your life would change if you achieved your utmost desires. Could you handle it? Of course you can, Silly! Go for it! As soon as you're finished reading this chapter, I want you to follow the action steps below. Then, I want you to send me a message on Facebook about what you did to take action! If you're not my friend, why not? My ID is kristisayles. I'd love to make friends with you! Remember this and write this down somewhere you will see it every day...it's become my favorite motto...

"Always shoot for the moon. The worst thing that can happen is that you land among the stars!"

3 Tips To Stay Focused On Your Dreams

Go to http://askkristi.com/?p=2009 and find the post that says, "Tell Me About Your Dream Lifestyle." Shut your eyes, create your perfect day, and share it with us through the comment section. Just writing it down will make your goals more concrete and achievable.

Do something every day to move closer to your goal. Write a chapter, buy a domain, research a favorite niche, ----do something and then go back to the blog and use the comment section to let us know what you did. Brag a little - it's time to feel good ab

Start a blog of your own! Use either Wordpress.com or Blogger.com - they are user friendly! Be sure to update us at http://AskKristi.com of your progress so my member list and I can all visit and come back and comment on your blog!

About The Author

Kristi Sayles is a second grade school teacher, author, internet marketing consultant, copywriter, and talk show host. Her books include "Accomplishing Goals-Not Just Setting Them and Jacob's Monkey-The Trouble with Lying. She lives in Camden, Tennessee, with her husband Terry and her rat terrier, Max.

Special Gift

Sign up for your FREE Article Marketing E-Course at   http://WriteThatArticle.com

http://SmartAuthor.com
http://SmartAuthor.com/affiliate.html
http://TalkwithKristi.com
http://YourChildandYou.com
http://DogsintheNews.info

http://SmartAuthor.com/blog
http://TalkwithExperts.com
http://MentoredbyMillionaires.info
http://ICanMakeCash.com

Just Start and Don't Stop!

Kylee Legge

The biggest problem I see these days is people telling me they want to publish a book and then not publishing one. Saying they want to write a book and not writing one. If you want to do something and for whatever reason you don't achieve your goal there is only one thing stopping you and that is yourself. There are the usual excuses; 'I don't have time', ' I don't have money', ' I don't know how to' etc. but you will notice the reoccurring use of the word 'I'. 'I' is literally in the middle of ach'I'eve so if the 'I is not right you will never achieve you desired outcome.

But enough about how you can get in the way of fulfilling your dreams and let me share with you how to overcome this obstacle once and for all. When it comes to publishing and distributing a book I refer to a successful author as an up-side-down traffic light. What I mean by this is someone who is a) ready to go now, b) radiating a bright light of extreme passion about their book and c) never wanting to stop. This description could be used to describe successful people the world over as if you simply start and are extremely passionate about what you are doing nothing will stop you fulfilling your goals.

The question is not so much what is an up-side-down traffic light? but more how to become one. The answer is quiet simple. Once again start in the middle with the passion. Are you extremely passionate about what you are trying to archive? What motivation do you have to stay focused and achieve your goal? If the motivation, the need, the want or the outcome is not strong enough chances are you won't ever start what you are wanting to do and will spend all your time thinking and planning but never actually creating. I call these group of people the 'thinkers'.

What about the people who have no trouble starting but can never finish anything? I call those people the 'entrepreneurs' as they have the passion and take action but aren't necessarily best equipped to manage or fulfil any of the creation steps in their own project. Get a good team behind you and an 'entrepreneur' can quickly become what I refer to as the 'creators' meaning they are continuously creating and continuously fulfilling goals and achieving their desired outcomes. Sometimes the 'creators' move so fast that they are fulfilling goals quicker then they create them – now wouldn't that be a bad problem to have.

The secret however is just like the 'I' in the middle of achieve is you, the radiating light in the middle of the traffic light is your success. Find something that you are extremely passionate about and get a good team behind you and a thinker can easily become an entrepreneur and an entrepreneur can easily become a creator as suddenly it is not your own passion, thinking or creating but by relying on the strength of numbers the 'I' can quickly become a 'we' and that is how to be truly successful. On your own you can only achieve so much but if you treat your goals like a team sport you will find you can achieve, set and achieve again whatever you set your mind to more easily then you ever imagined.

3 Tips To Stay Focused On Your Dreams

Just Start

Be Passionate

Don't Stop

About The Author

Kylee wrote her first book at age 2 and opened her first business at age 8 however it took her a few more years to learn how to link the two to allow her to follow her dreams, while earning a passive income publishing books at the same time as becoming known as the expert in her field. Kylee now services all of Australia

Janet Beckers

educating people on how to make self publishing as easy as 1, 2, 3! She has a series of books educating on various areas of the 7 stages of the publishing process. She also runs free seminars and intensive 3 day bootcamps named after each of the books. Kylee enjoys walking people 1 on 1 through the publishing process via phone consultations where she creates customised publishing plans for people designed to get any individual from where they are now to where they want to be as easily, efficiently, economically and as effectively as possible. As an independent publisher and distributor Kylee's personal goal is to help as many people as possible by educating them on everything they need to know to ensure their publishing success.

Special Gift

To learn more about how you can become an up-side-down traffic light when it comes to publishing and distributing a book register for my FREE 7 day ecourse 'How to Write your First Book' and begin setting the right goals for you and your book today: http://www.thepublishingqueen.com/7dayecourseregistration.html.

http://www.thepublishingqueen.com

I Am Not A Cockroach

Lee Martin

I believe that others perceptions and how you actually see yourself are two totally different things. I could always relate to the Gary Larson 'Far Side' comic which saw a man and a giant cockroach sitting at a bar and the cockroach says something like 'you know, I used to have a great life, a high paying job, a great car and a beautiful wife and then one day someone turned around and said "Hey, he's just a giant cockroach!"'.

I think many people feel that they don't have enough knowledge. That, they don't know enough to do something great, or different to what it is they are doing now. They feel that there are others out there that know so much more than them. I myself sometimes feel that way. What conclusion have I come to with all of that? Who cares! What if there are other people that are more knowledgeable than me, most people do not act on it anyway!

Everyone is so "stressed", "too busy", or have let some other facet take over their life and they are stuck in the mouse wheel, just going around and around and not getting anywhere.

They are not happy that way but they don't believe they have time to get off to act on anything else or change the way things are. Well I have a secret to tell you. It is the secret to my success and it may not actually be much of a secret, as they have it printed on t-shirts. Just do it! If you have something that you have always wanted to do, just do it! Now I am not saying if you have always wanted to travel overseas and you are already in debt, that you should put it on your credit card and get packing. What I am saying is, get things happening, start the wheels in motion, make a plan. If you have always wanted to go to Paris, work out how much it will cost, get researching on the internet, reading books about Paris or go by the travel agents and pick up a brochure, pick a date and MAKE A PLAN!

My life has not been charmed, but I have often had people say to me "Wow, stuff just always works out for you" or "No matter what you always land on your feet" or "things just always happen for you!."

I moved from Sydney to Melbourne about four years ago for my husband's job. We did not know anyone and I had given up my job as an art teacher at a school in Sydney to move here. Within three months, I had made a new circle of friends, started a new job and had booked in my first solo art exhibition, at which I ended up selling not only my first piece of artwork, but five other pieces. Again, friends said "Wow, stuff just happens for you!". But the truth is it doesn't.

It was my attitude and my willingness to just get in there and do it that made the difference. I could have sat around feeling homesick and just easing myself into my new life. But I thought if I am going to do this, then I am really going to give it a red hot go. I had always wanted to exhibit my own work, but had gotten too caught up with teaching other people art to find the time, the energy and the passion to create my own work and put something together. Well, that is what I told myself but the truth is I was just too scared to do it. Where would I put it on? What if no one came? Worse still, what if they came and everyone hated it? Are you still an artist if everyone else thinks your artworks stink? I believe I let all these things hold me back. I let the fear of being found out as a "giant cockroach" preventing me from doing something I had always wanted to do.

I cannot say that fear does not sometimes still hold me back and that sometimes I find new things too hard or overwhelming, or that I feel like I will never have enough knowledge or the skills. I just break it down into manageable bits and chip away at it until I make a break through.

3 Tips To Stay Focused On Your Dreams

Decide what it is you do want. If you don't know where you are going, how are you going to get there?

Make a plan. Set a date, start saving, ask for time off. Work out what it is you need to set in motion for you to achieve what you want. Oh, and stop making excuses.

Just do it

About The Author

Let me introduce myself. My name is Lee Martin and I have been teaching art for 11 years in high schools, community centres, art galleries and the occasional primary and infant school. I have had one solo art exhibition and have exhibited in three group exhibitions, one exhibition for each year I have lived in Melbourne. My greatest passions in teaching art is introducing students to new materials, new ways of seeing things, great artworks and artists and one of my greatest frustrations teaching art is finding new and interesting ways to engage students and pass on that passion. With that in mind I have set about creating a new way for the classroom and artists to connect and it is called My Artroom Online. It will be a place that will help bring technology into the classroom, help with tight budgets and provide new and innovative ways for creating connections between artists and people that are keen to learn more about art. Art buffs will be able to connect directly with the people who create the work and hopefully go away with a sense of excitement and a plan to fan their own passions for however it is they use art in their own life. If you are interested in art or know someone who is join me at www.myartroomonline.com.au and let's stART a conversation!

http://www.myartroomonline.com.au

An Inspiring Story From Our Partner Opportunity International and The 1 Million Women Out Of Poverty Project

Ester's story (West Timor, Indonesia)

In the village of Sikumana, 40km from downtown Kupang, lives Ester Hurint and her family. Ester, 38, lives with her husband, Joni, her brother-in-law, Philipus and her three children—Silvester, 15, Paulina, 11, and Maria, 2. Ester always wanted to contribute to the household income - which was reliant on Joni's wages as a grocer and Philipus' occasional contributions from his pay as a bus driver. In 2003, Ester established a small kiosk - selling snacks, beverages and other goods - which she strategically placed by an intersection to attract drivers' custom. However, with her husband's income going towards their children's education and daily essentials, there were few funds available to buy stock for her kiosk and Ester's business struggled.

One of Ester's friends was already a TLM client (Tanaoba Lais Manekat, the local partner in West Timor) and spoke highly of the benefits of the Community Group program. Ester was intrigued at the prospect of a loan with small weekly repayments and applied to join. Since her first loan of Rp.500,000 (A$64), Ester has graduated through four group loan cycles of increasing amounts. Her latest loan was Rp.2,000,000 (A$256) and she has also received business training through TLM's partnership with a local university. The loans and support have enabled Ester to expand the range and quantity of goods in her kiosk and double her daily income from Rp.50,000 (A$6.40) to over Rp.100,000 (A$13).

With her increased income, Ester has saved Rp.600,000 (A$77) for her children's education. Ester and her husband are also planning to build three extra rooms joined to their house, which they will rent out.

In just four loan cycles, Ester is making a major contribution to her household income and is creating a more stable and secure life for her family

You can help families just Ester's by donating at www.WonderfulWebWomen.com/recommends/opportunity

Death, Resilience and Success – a Vision for Living!

Lenore Miller

My vision in life, no matter what I do, is to be an inspiration to others and an example of what's possible. The challenge is to be true to my vision when life throws me the most challenging of life experiences. In this chapter I want to share with you part of my story, and the strategies I have used in life to stay true to my vision. I am not looking for your sympathy I want to show you that everything and anything is possible regardless of your circumstances.

On the 4th August 2007 I was sitting in my home office taking stock of all I had to be grateful for, my two beautiful healthy children, a thriving business, a lovely home and the partner of my dreams. Within hours I found myself sitting in my local hospital being told that my eldest son Ryan, just 19 years old, was gravely ill and may not live through the night.

I was handed a phone and left make calls to our family so they could come and say their good byes. It was 1.30am on Sunday 5th August 2007. The next few weeks were a rollercoaster ride of hope and despair. This part of my story does not have the happy ending we all would have liked, on 28th August 2007 Ryan died from an hypoxic brain injury he incurred when he had a serious asthma attack, that came out of the blue. Life had changed forever there was no going back, no amount of hoping or dreaming or positive thinking would change my new reality.

There were times in the early days I could have just curled up and faded away too but I am not that woman. I started on a journey of putting one foot in front of the other. I was looking for hope, what I found were books that focused on the unbearable grief of losing a child or talked about the stages of grief, they did not give the hope I was looking for - that I would one day feel normal again. I wondered if that was possible. Honestly I felt I had, had my share of things to deal with that would prove my strength, the death of my father to suicide when I was 18, 6 weeks before my final senior school exams; divorcing at 30 and raising my then 2 small children (aged 3 and 5) by myself.

Of course I had lost all my grandparents as well, although that seemed less cruel, as you are meant to outlive your grandparents. I had, had cancer scares and major surgery and a business partnership break-up, all of which paled into insignificance compared to losing one of my babies.

The thing about the most dreadful experiences of life is that they put us in a place of questioning our values and choices and ultimately allow us the opportunity to become more of who we are, of who we were meant to be. They may humble us enough to ask for help when we have been too proud or independent to do that before, they give us the opportunity to choose to live a life on purpose and with passion. I realized over time that the strategies I had used to deal with all kinds of situations in my life, I used here too. As human beings we are so very resilient.

So let me share 3 key strategies

1. What you decide

In our most challenging times we make decisions about what things mean. For example you have a business partnership break-up and you decide you can't trust others in business. You get divorced and decide that all men/women are the same – clearly neither of these things are true but you could decide it means that you will never trust others in business again in the first instant and in the second that you will not have future relationship – how limiting is that. Similarly I know parents who have lost children who decided they would never smile again! My decision was that

I would not let my grief define me, nor would I become my grief. I decided I would go on to learn and grow and become an example to others of what's possible

1. Who Will you Show Up as?

Have you consciously decided who you're going to show up as in life? Many of us wonder through life being buffeted around, bouncing from one way of being to the next or playing the 'ain't it awful game' , you know the one where someone tells you how sad or bad their life is and you tell your story of how you or someone you know has a worse situation. Does that empower you? Does that propel you toward the quality of life you desire? Or does it give you more of what you already have. Who are you showing up as in Life? Make a choice, take a stand! At each point in my life when I have been faced with one of Life's challenges, we all have those right, I decide who I am going to show up as – am I going to be the victim or the victor!

2. Are you in Interested or Committed to your Vision?

I couldn't tell you how many times people have comment that 'it's all right for you Lenore' or 'you're so lucky', sometimes I have an internal smile to myself and think if only you knew my story. But you see I am NOT my story and I only ever use it to demonstrate a point, in fact most people I do business with have no idea and when they find some of this stuff out it leaves them with no more excuses.

So my question to you is – 'Are you Interested or committed to realize your vision?' If you're interested you will do what's convenient however if you're committed you will do what it takes to fulfil your Vision and to live the life you desire. When it's all said and done it's your choice, you can step up and into your visions or you can chose to play victim and become your sad bad stories about why life isn't working out for you, or why success isn't possible.

There is no doubt that each big challenge I have faced in life has had me reassessing who I am and what I want from life, however I have always stayed true to my vision or mission in life to inspired others to find the best in themselves.

3 Tips To Stay Focused On Your Dreams

What decisions have you made in the past that now limit your success, in business in relationship, in life?

Janet Beckers

> Who have you been showing up as in your life? Is how you're showing up, going to lead you to fore filling your visions?
>
> Are you Committed or Interest – Be honest? What do you need to commit to, to be living your vision?

About The Author

Lenore Miller is an experienced business woman, who understands the day-to-day challenges and demands of running your own enterprise. Her book Ignite Your Business Mojo – Get the spark into your business was released in November 2010 and has created a buzz amongst business owners looking to reinvigorate their business mojo. This experience combined with her skills as a speak, mindset and business development specialist means she has a unique ability to really engage an audience, she can inspire and motivate while delivering practical real-world advice that has immediate application. Lenore is the owner of inspired for Life Pty Ltd, a company she has directed for 12 years. She was co-director and General Manager of Rent to Own Housing Pty Ltd, a property investment company specialising in vendor finance, before she moved on to start the first Contours women's fitness franchise in the Hunter Valley (November 2005). This successful operation was highly profitable for Lenore, was at running at arms-length within 18 months, and sold as a profitable going concern in July 2009.

Special Gift

Go to http://www.IgniteYourBusinessMojo.com/VisionforLiving to download your Vision for Living Audio and Guide. Find out what it takes to constantly move toward your Business, Relationship and Life Goals no matter what life throws at you!

http://www.IgniteYourBusinessMojo.com

Move Beyond Resistance to Your Path of Creation

Linda Philip

It is usual to get stuck in limiting patterns of thinking, feeling and behaving which can inhibit us in moving forward and creating change in our lives. Maybe we have set our sights on a goal but no matter how hard we try it's hard for us to manifest what we want-instead we get more of what we don't want. We are generally motivated to seek pleasure and avoid suffering so in the case of procrastination or not taking action towards a goal, it is most likely we are moving outside our comfort zone and are seeking to avoid something we don't like to feel such as rejection, fear of change, or fear of failure or success. The problem is that the energy in the motivation away from that feeling often leads us to create what we don't want. In other words 'what we resist, persists'.

The exercise below I find very helpful to separate fear –which keeps us entrapped, from what our heart or our higher self wants and is motivated toward. This enables us to keep focused on taking action towards what we want.

Here is an exercise for you to do: On a piece of paper draw out two columns. On one side write- "Avoidance or fear". On the other side write "Heart or higher purpose".

Janet Beckers

Now, in the fear column answer the following questions:

1. What am I wanting to avoid?

2. What behaviors do I do to avoid this?

3. What reality does this create for me?

Notice how the pattern of what you don't want is created-how you entrap yourself.

Now, in the higher purpose/heart column write

1. What is it that you love, are passionate about and want.

2. What obvious action could you take to create more of this in your life?

3. What sort of reality would this create for you if you had it?

Then ask yourself where you have been putting your energy and your focus, in the fear column or in the heart column?

Now draw out two big circles on the ground each representing these columns. Stand in the circle that represents fear, get the picture of yourself there and what you are saying to yourself and how it makes you feel. Notice how much energy you are giving it.

Now stand in your heart or higher purpose circle and notice how you look there and notice your self-talk and how it makes you feel to have that a reality in your life. Now go back to fear circle and say: "what's the worst thing that could happen if I went for what I want and love-maybe that I would feel like this-BUT- I'm feeling like this anyway so I may as well go for what I love and want".

Go back to heart circle again and get the feeling state of having what you want. Then bring those feelings across with you into the fear circle and notice how the feelings in the fear circle-change, the fear collapses and it feels more neutral, it doesn't have the same power over you anymore. You can stay focused now and take action on what is truly important in your heart to create. It's called "following your bliss"!

Remember to stay focused on the outcome and completely let go of how it will be achieved. You can never know the how and this is where many people get stuck

The universe takes care of the 'how'. Your job is to focus on the outcome of what you want and just take action.

3 Tips To Stay Focused On Your Dreams

Become aware of what feelings you are wanting to avoid

Know what it is that you want and love your higher purpose

Separate the two lists you create in steps 1 and 2. Put them in two circles. Stand in and feel the difference of the two circles then bring the wanted feeling into the unwanted feeling circle. Stay focused on the wanted outcome, take action, and let go of the how

About The Author

Linda Philip is a counselor and psychotherapist . For the past 10years she has been seeking and studying powerful, cutting edge, personal change tools to facilitate change in people's lives. Her website Your Healing Hub is a healing community full of resourceful information and powerful tools for healing and change. Interviews with teachers from all over the world contribute to this site.

http://www.yourhealinghub.com

Janet Beckers

Fridge Magnets, Melodies and Mum

Linky Muller

Keep your sense of humour alive at all times. This would be my best advice to anyone, no matter what their circumstances.

Humour makes it easier for you to deal with anything and everything anyone throws at you. Even when times are rough, people can look up and say, with tears in their eyes and smiles on their faces, "Yes I am ok," and point out some rare irony to their current situation.

I myself am a Foot-in-mouth-specialist, who often says inappropriate things, or tells the truth at inappropriate times. There's a slight possibility this means I have no tact, but my point is, that it can get you into a great deal of trouble sometimes. Deciding to be a therapist, then, to try and help others with their issues might not seem like the right place for someone like me, but somehow, I've found that is exactly what most people come for, a good dose of the unadulterated truth. And when they are ready and in the right frame of mind to listen, being somewhat forthcoming is not such a bad attribute. It helps with those first few steps needed to change. Life is sometimes challenging to us all and each and every one of us, yes you too, has some or other favourite thing to keep them going.

My mother, for instance, always has an answer for the frustrating things we have to endure in life. We have a Dutch/South African background and her thing, being a great linguist and knowing all the idioms that make a language rich, would pull one, relevant to any given situation, seemingly out of thin air. If life is driving you nuts, she would say, in Dutch, "yip, Heaven is not here below, leave the earth and climb up a tree." In other words nobody said life would be easy, let's get a different perspective on the problem and move on.

I used her wisdom in my therapy sessions many times as it was perfectly applicable to so many of my clients. The added bonus to her wisdom is that it's always a little humorous and grounds you when your head is spinning out of control with whatever life decided to dish up for you this time. Living in South Africa also gave me the opportunity to work alongside many different cultures and poverty was constantly right at my doorstep. There was always someone telling me their life story and how hard life was treating them and, yes, asking for bread money to stay alive. These people were often very desperate, but they would still smile and have something funny to share with you if you took the time to engage them in conversation.

Fear was a great part of our lives then; I remember when our domestic helper came to me one day, in tears, saying that she was pregnant and couldn't work for much longer. If she could not work, they could not eat, so what was she to do? Well, my mom told me that every child brings his place along with him when he is born and, when I told Damaria what my mom had said, she was smiling again. Yes, she did go on maternity leave, but she was back after three months with her baby in her arms, ready to work, and full of elaborate, hilarious, tales about how they coped while she was away.

Out of all my mom's wise sayings, I created an eye and an ear for interesting sayings and in the process became quite hooked on Fridge Magnets. They are great when your sense of humour completely fails you. My fridge door can be really nurturing. There is always one to remind me that maybe I should not eat everything in sight: "No, I'm not fat! I am just a nutritional overachiever!" Or if the computer drives you nuts, as it keeps freezing up, my fridge is there to remind me that the only way to make "windows go faster is to throw it harder." Since June 2010 I have been trying to get my internet connection cancelled at (dare I say this) Telstra. Well, after the third try I thought 'it's taking them awfully long time,' but by the twelfth time, yes twelve times with no guarantee at all and mind you seven months later, I now know my fridge magnets by heart. Another thing I love about them is that I can choose which one suits me best at any given moment. Is it "Out of my mind, back in 5 minutes," or "I think, therefore I am obviously over qualified," or "Of course I am sane, the voices told me so"?

Learning to play the harp, and growing up in a musical family, also greatly influenced my life. Instead of having to picture the audience naked in order to get over my fear of stages and performing, there are always a few songs popping into my mind. Granted, sometimes this happens at very inappropriate times—it's still me we're talking about. At a funeral, for instance, you don't really want to hear the song "Great Pretender" in your mind, or "The Entertainer"; it makes it very hard to keep a straight face. But, music can be very encouraging when the right song comes to mind. I hear the Halleluiah Chorus in my head when there is something to celebrate. Although, I have heard that one when someone got a fine as well—not so nice. Not to mention all the fridge magnet wordplays on harp: "harping on the same point again," "harp along Cassidy," oh and don't forget "you are pulling my harp strings," and "you are breaking my harp." Really guys, I think I've heard them all. It becomes a great coping mechanism in hard times and I have tried to teach my clients to use these humorous affirmations by sticking them in the places they go to when they are upset. One lady told me that her best place for affirmations is in the bathroom and she even put a whiteboard and a pen in there to write the new ones down as they pop into her mind in the shower.

Change them often, but keep the good ones, because you seem to need them again. When I had my Personal Fitness Centre in NSW, the one action that my clients really enjoyed was the affirmation my colleagues and I put on the white board. After a while the clients participated in the theme of the week. It was also very interesting to see which of the clients could not get into their training before fixing the grammar; we had so many discussions on how the sentences should read that it often took everyone's mind off the hard work they were doing and made the sessions a great deal of fun.

When certain, specific, people come to visit, you can display the one that says, "this is a self cleaning bathroom, you have to do it yourself." Or, "Press this button for service, if nothing happens, get it yourself." Instead of buying books with Sudoku puzzles to keep my mind active, I make a point of finding affirmations or names or some humorous idea from the numberplates on the cars in front of me when I drive. This keeps my mind active, helps me cope with "pretend" drivers and even alerts me to the fact that I see some cars every day at the same time, going the same way. Something I might never have noticed otherwise. Humour is really the medicine for most situations in life. It has certainly helped a great deal with the natural disasters we have experienced since we moved to Australia, and the trauma we experienced because we left our home country. It is as Barbara Streisand sings in the song "The Way We Were": "what is too painful to remember we simply choose to forget. So it's the laughter, we will remember whenever we remember the way we were."

It is amazing, the number of jokes and humorous situations that are created when people are put in difficult situations. It gives us inspiration and motivation to do what we have to do to get to the next moment. Thinking back on how difficult things often were in South Africa, a mere five years ago, when my family and I left, it seems almost strange that what I remember most, and want to go back for, is all the love and laughter we experienced there. We were constantly outside of our comfort zones, and so we turned to jokes, companionship, and shared laughter to carry us through the frustrations and dangers. And I know I can rely on that same sense of humour to help in future tough times. So here are my ridiculously easy action steps for using humour as a coping mechanism every day and especially in the challenging times life produces so often.

3 Tips To Stay Focused On Your Dreams

Option 1:

If you see a good fridge magnet, buy it. It's a great gift to yourself.

Keep it in the place you go to when you are upset, or where you spend a great deal of time, so you have to see it often.

Reorganise them often and get new ones to keep your mind sharp. And so they don't just become an overlooked part of the décor.

Option 2:

Make a mental note of the cars in front of you in the traffic by looking at their numberplates.

Janet Beckers

> See if you can make up a word, or a formula of some sort, to keep your mind off the frustration of sitting in traffic.
>
> Option 3:
>
> See if you can think of a song that would sum up the situation that you are experiencing, to make it more bearable, or just to create a small measure of kinship.
>
> If you can, sing it out loud, but beware not to sing it everywhere. It could get uncomfortable.

About The Author

Linky Muller (BA, Kinesiologist, Harpist and Personal Trainer) Linky is married with three beautiful daughters. She loves being available for her family and helping them get closer to their goals and dreams. Lived in South Africa and moved to Australia in 2005. With children grown and leaving home she is creating a new business on the internet. With her active interest in health and wellbeing, she has written an ebook on Hemochromatosis (Iron Overload in the body) which is currently being published on www.TheIronOverloadEbook.com . Up to now Linky kept her businesses close to home in order to be there when the family needs her. Writing ebooks on topics close to her heart will enable her to travel between South Africa and Australia for the family and have a mobile business. Playing the harp and sometimes singing for special occasions such as weddings, church services, dinner parties, big events, golf events, Valentine's day and Christmas dinner parties, is Linky's other passion. The harp has always been a great way to bring in some extra cash. Becoming a Personal Trainer fulfilled the dream of keeping fit and helping others to rehabilitate and become fit again at any age.

Special Gift

Go to http://www.TheIronOverloadEbook.com to get a free MP3 recording of beautiful harp music.

http://www.TheIronOverloadEbook.com

Gorilla Glue Dreams

Lisa Robbins

Did you ever have a dream of something better? I know you have! Did you hold onto it? Or did you let it go? Or did it change? Some dreams change, some drift away, but some stick like gorilla glue, embedded in your subconscious, creeping up and nudging you, rooting a little further into your reality every time they visit. When I was a little gaffer I used to dream about talking to animals, and being an animal doctor. But when I got a little bigger my dream changed because I realized I would have to euthanize them and that just wasn't me.

So I dreamed about being a nurse. But I quit school when I was 16, to sell ice cream at the Scarborough Town Centre mall in Toronto. School wasn't important then. I guess being a nurse wasn't that important then either. Then I grew up a bit more and planned out my career. I would eventually work for a CEO or President of a large company. I would drive to work in a nice car and park in the underground lot of a tall office building in downtown Toronto. I would bring my boss and his associates cappuccino and thickly layered sandwiches on trays. I would type up his dictations, while wearing beautiful wool suits, and silk blouses.

But then I realized that a career working for someone else meant I had to be a slave, and I thought I had more to give. Soon I had three children and became buried in

Janet Beckers

life, babies, laundry, cooking, cleaning and working ... always working. Sometimes I hardly saw my babies I worked so much and so far away. So I quit. I realized my babies were more important than anything else. But ... I always kept my dreams alive, in the quiet and darkness of my bedroom, when everyone else was sleeping and all I could hear was the sound of my dreams dreaming.

As my children grew, I grew with them and again my dreams changed. This time I dreamed of living without struggle, without being chained to a job I hated, without debt, and mostly, without my father and then mother being diagnosed with cancer, suffering grueling treatments, and then dying anyway. So out of the raw emotion, the anger, the resentment, a new dream started to form, and I kept it alive; a picture of my future, fastened to my path ahead, unwavering, steadfast ... always there ... waiting for me to catch up.

This dream was of a world without illness, without cancer. A future where we actually allow our bodies to heal, and do not suppress that innate ability with toxic drugs or poisonous radiation. Where we cleanse instead of remove gall bladders. Where women realize that breast cancer is just a symptom of being stressed and clogged up. A symptom than can easily be reversed with knowledge and action. I began to dream of Incredible Healing Hospitals where people are healed with love and caring, delicious healing foods and herbal medicines. I dreamed of a place, where people come together to share their true stories of natural healing, teaching others to feeeel their way to health and heal themselves with conscience.

A place where people gripped by fear or devastated by a horrible diagnosis; feeling frustrated, misinformed and manipulated; could find helpful, truthful and inspiring information; real information that they could actually use to heal themselves! This dream was different from the others. This dream was stuck with Gorilla Glue. It was my destiny, held with passion and emotion. No matter what I did, I could not shake it. So, finally I did something about it. I went back to school. Wow ~ what an experience! I quit my job. Hallelujah! The biggest relief EVER! I began to take control of my future and plant many new dreams on my path. Now I spend every single day doing exactly what I want to do ... catching up to my dreams!

My Gorilla Glue Dreams: TheGoodWitch.ca My hangout ~ this is where I post about what I have learned ~ delicious healing recipes, simple herbal medicines, quick tips, important and controversial information about vaccinations, illness and healing; and my proudest achievement yet ~ adding my own audio and video interviews with people who have healed themselves naturally! IncredibleHealingJournals.com Born out of incredible interviews with people who have healed themselves naturally, this is the world's first online healing community: our mantra ~ Healing The World With Truth!

This is where anyone including you, me, our children, our friends, natural practitioners … anyone with a true healing story, experience and knowledge can share and help others. This is where people can go when they are frustrated, fed up and finally willing and ready to make the changes necessary to heal themselves! A place where you choose who to follow and who to listen to … a safe haven … an online healing community! The Cancer Journal ~ Heal Yourself! A tribute to anyone and everyone that has ever suffered from the ignorance surrounding any illness called 'cancer'.

This book will smash your fears forever and give you the tools to heal yourself! It includes: The journal of my life as it pertains to cancer, and the incredible discoveries I made; making my own amazing medicines that kill every lump, bump and cancer I try them on; suppression of natural cures; new scientific information proving the healing power of certain foods; the amazing world of healing plants and how to make your own remarkable medicines; true healing stories; the 10 key healing principles others use to heal themselves; the new revelations about cancer, polar opposite charts for your refrigerator, Heal Yourself! (everything you need to do!) and What Initiates and Promotes Cancer (everything you don't want to do!), and much much more; including exactly what to do to protect yourself and your family, whether you have cancer or not!

CAnswer The 10 Key Principles Of Healing This book, to be released in 2011, focuses on the 10 key principles of healing, inherent in The Cancer Journal ~ Heal Yourself! A small paperback book, with only the tools you require to heal yourself ~ just simple, accurate and easily applied knowledge. Incredible Healing Hospitals This dream is strongly embedded in my future path. I am planning, working and scheming toward this dream right now. p.s. I just gave it some Gorilla Glue by writing it down and telling you about it!

3 Tips To Stay Focused On Your Dreams

Keeping Your Dreams Alive! Choose a quiet time. Sit in a comfortable chair. Close your eyes.   Breathe deeply, extending your exhale each time you breathe; relaxing, focusing on nothing but your breathing and the space around you. Continue until you

Janet Beckers

are fully relaxed. What is your dream? Hold a picture or movie of your dream in your mind. Imagine what it will be like in detail. This may be difficult at first, but as you repeat the process of imagining your dream; layer upon layer, it will become more clear, until it can do nothing but become your reality.

Stick your dream on your future path Now image you are holding that same picture in your hand and imagine floating along the path that makes up your life, the past behind, the future in front, you in the middle. Are you still holding the picture?

Use Gorilla Glue Give your dream some Gorilla Glue. Each time you dream your dream, add more detail to it; the colour of your new car, the clothes you are wearing while you are speaking to a room full of people, the people who surround you on your vacation of a lifetime; more Gorilla Glue! Take time every day to see your dream, deeply embedded in your future path, waiting for you to catch up; more Gorilla Glue! Now focus on actions toward your dream. Do something, anything towards it … every day, plan, develop, work, organize, talk and network; more Gorilla Glue! The more laser-like you stay focused on your dream; the more Gorilla Glue you use; the less distractions you allow ~ the faster your dream will become your reality!

About The Author

Lisa Robbins, BScHN, RHN, CTT, is a Registered Holistic Nutritionist, with Highest Honours, Bachelor of Science Degree in Holistic Nutrition. A teacher at heart, she delivers effortless ways to heal from any dis-ease with whole delicious foods and simple herbal medicines. She excels at motivating you to heal, by cutting through all the rubbish, and making difficult concepts clear and understandable, in a friendly, engaging and approachable style. Lisa has dedicated her life to transforming harmful beliefs about illness. She teaches you to become the leader in your life, to adopt a safe and health-promoting environment, without harmful experiences, to feeel your way back to health. She delivers these empowering messages through a varied medium of writing, audio and video, using real life stories and experiences.

Special Gift

Special Offer for 2011 Gold Book Readers Only! For every The Cancer Journal ~ Heal Yourself ordered with the following secret code, your order will gift another copy to the person who you would like to receive a copy. Please note: We reserve the right to cancel this special offer at any time. After placing your order through www.TheGoodWitch.ca, email us with the following information:

To tgw@TheGoodWitch.ca

1. Place the following code in the subject line of your email: 2011GoldDoubleOffer

2. Don't forget to include the name and email address of the person you want us to send the free copy to. We will notify you as soon as the email has been sent to them.

http://www.TheGoodWitch.ca http://www.IncredibleHealingJournals.ca

How to Keep your Freelance Dream Alive

Lisa Taliga

There are countless ways of making money from home and one of the easiest ways is online freelancing. If one of your dreams is becoming a freelancer then read on. My name is Lisa Taliga and I've been freelancing from home since 2004. I've been involved in lots of different projects including website design, copywriting, graphic design, creating newsletters and Powerpoint presentations, formatting and typing documents and helping businesses market themselves on the internet. I am known as a Virtual Assistant and I have marketed myself as such, however, these days I don't restrict myself to a label such as this. I'm a freelancer above all else and I love what I do.

One of the stumbling blocks to your freelance dream may be that you have no idea how you're going to get enough work to support yourself financially and the thought causes you anxiety. Or maybe you've already tried to get freelance work but hit a brick wall. Or you may have started working from home but don't have enough clients to make this an ongoing business and are not sure where the next client is coming from. When it comes to marketing your freelance business, you can read up on tons of marketing strategies until your eyes get dry, but in order for you to be successful, you'll need to work on your "mindset" first.

When I say mindset, I'm referring to your level of self belief. I'm also referring to whether you are operating from a place of fear and scarcity or from a place of confidence and abundance. This is a fundamental part of the process which many people overlook. Think of this as your foundation for keeping your freelance dream alive. Without a positive mindset you will falter at the first hurdle of finding clients, that's if you muster up enough courage to try in the first place! However, with a sturdy, optimistic foundation your "house" i.e. your business will be built on solid ground. You will find it much easier to persist even if things don't go your way from time to time and you will grow from strength to strength.

Let's explore various aspects of mindset and how it could be affecting your success right now. Scarcity   The scarcity mindset is quite insidious and can catch us unawares. You can tell whether you have a mindset of scarcity if you find yourself believing that there is "too much competition", "the market is too saturated" and that there are "not enough clients" around.

None of these beliefs are true! Opportunities are abundant for good freelancers. There are lots of clients and exciting projects out there. We have to work on nurturing a mindset of abundance rather than scarcity before we start marketing our business. Self belief   Each one of us has had "successes" and "failures" in our lives. How we perceive these events affects us in terms of how we perceive ourselves. If we are hard on ourselves and beat ourselves up about our perceived "failures", this will be detrimental to our sense of self confidence and will affect how successful we are when marketing our business. For example, you get a call from a potential client. For whatever reason, the prospect does not end up using your services. This could be because he or she is not ready to use your services rather than anything to do with you.

If your confidence in yourself is not as strong as it could be, you are likely to blame yourself for "doing something wrong" just because this particular prospect did not turn into a client. However, if your level of self belief is strong, you would just put it down to "one of those things" and move on, without beating yourself up about it. It's normal and healthy to have fears and doubts   Some of these thoughts and doubts went through my mind when I first started my business. It's important to realise that it's normal and healthy to have fears and doubts like these, although they do make us feel uncomfortable. After all, we are human beings with emotions! Sometimes our emotions are "positive", sometimes "negative".

Having fears and doubts is a sign that we are moving out of our comfort zone into the unknown. It's our subconscious way of protecting ourselves. It's nature's way of saying "Hang on a minute, it's dangerous out there, this and that could go wrong. Maybe it's best and safest to stay where I am".

However, can you see how negative self talk does not help you build a solid foundation for your freelance business? Actively working on your fears by challenging them with positive statements will reduce procrastination and have you feeling inspired to work towards your goals in spite of any "obstacles" you may encounter. So how do you "overcome" feelings of fear and anxiety? In my mind, it's not really a case of "overcoming" these feelings in the strictest sense of the word. I think it's about acknowledging your feelings, appreciating them for what they are and then, most important of all, it's about challenging your doubts in a logical way. Only by acknowledging your fears and working through them will you get to the other side and bring your freelance dream to fruition. Turn negative self talk into positive self belief I encourage you to write down any fears that you have, in your own words.

By recognising and acknowledging your underlying doubts, you gain the power to turn them into positive beliefs. Here are some examples of negative thoughts I had when I started my freelance business, along with positive statements to strength en my sense of self belief:

• Will I actually get any clients or is this going to be a waste of time? I will get all the clients I need so that I can work from home full-time. Each hour that I invest in marketing and building my business will pay off in the future.

• Where am I going to get clients from? Is anyone really going to need my services? I know that suitable clients are everywhere. I just have to market myself in a way that will attract the right clients to me. There are people out there who need my services to help grow their businesses.

• It might take me ages to get my first suitable client. I will get my first client within six weeks, as long as I go about my marketing the right way and stay determined and optimistic.

- Will I really get enough clients to fill each week? I will get enough ongoing clients to fill xx hours a week. It's just a matter of having a good marketing strategy, investing time and taking consistent action.

- I'm not confident enough to "get out there" and meet people face to face. Maybe I'll just stick to putting a few ads in the local paper and see if I get any business. If that doesn't work, then nothing will work! I am ready to try various ways of marketing my business. I will put an ad in the local paper and start from there. Some marketing methods will be more successful than others. I am confident enough to get out of my comfort zone and educate people about the services I have to offer. When a particular marketing method works then I will do more of the same!

- There might be a lot of competition already. If the market is already saturated with Virtual Assistants / freelancers, how will I get any business? My fellow freelancers are all unique and have different skills and services to offer. The market is not saturated because there are many potential clients that have not heard of virtual freelancers! I am confident that I will get lots of business and be able to use my unique skills to help other businesses.

- How much money do I need to market myself? I might not have the budget for it. I have all the resources I need to market myself. There are many ways to market my business without spending a cent. I have enough money, time, determination and persistence to be successful.

Once you have formulated your positive statements, take a fresh sheet of paper. On your blank sheet of paper, write out ONLY THE POSITIVE STATEMENTS. There is no need to write down your fears again because you have already got these out of your system. There is no need to focus on them again. Going forward, you only want to focus on your positive statements. Each night before you go to sleep, read through your positive, affirming statements so that they are absorbed into your subconscious mind. Every morning, read through them again. Really FEEL the statements rather than simply reading them through. In time, you'll be amazed at how confident and optimistic you feel. You'll be able to face any obstacles and challenges (and we all have them!) with faith and resilience. Having faith in yourself is vital to keeping your freelance dream alive.

Janet Beckers

3 Tips To Stay Focused On Your Dreams

Write down your fears and express your feelings of self doubt

Challenge each thought with a positive, empowering statement

Read through each positive statement every night before you go to sleep and every morning when you wake up.

About The Author

Lisa Taliga has been freelancing from home since 2004. She has worked on many different projects including website design, copywriting, graphic design, creating newsletters and Powerpoint presentations, formatting and typing documents and helping businesses market themselves on the internet. She markets herself as a Virtual Assistant however she is a freelancer above all else and she loves what she does. Since 2006 she has helped many virtual freelancers through three ebooks that she created. She "gives her all" when it comes to helping others because she gets a great deal of satisfaction from it. She is now launching a 6 week teleseminar course called "How To Attract Clients To Your Freelance Business" in early March. As part of the course she will be helping you develop a positive and optimistic mindset which will enable you to market your freelance business with confidence and joy, instead of operating from a place of fear and scarcity. She will be giving you concrete steps and strategies that you can apply on an ongoing basis, to help you build a freelance business that you will be proud of. Find out more here:

http://www.freelancingathome.com/mktg-teleseminar/priority-list.html

Special Gift

FREE Ebook - The 7 Things You Must Know Before Starting Your Own Successful Virtual Assistant Business   http://www.virtualpabusiness.com/free_ebook.html

Lisa Taliga's Virtual Assistant website   http://www.virtualpa.com.au FREE Ebook - The 7 Things You Must Know Before Starting Your Own Successful Virtual Assistant Business http://www.virtualpabusiness.com/free_ebook.html 6 Week Teleseminar Course

Letting Joy Be Your Guide

Liz Raad

Have you ever experienced a moment of consuming joy? A moment where everything seems perfect, you are completely at peace and you feel a rush of gratitude and love? It may be only just a fleeting feeling, perhaps on a beautiful day when the sun is shining, there is a light cool breeze and you are totally free to be out enjoying it. Or perhaps when you gaze onto the face of your child sleeping peacefully, and you realise how blessed you are to have them. Or sometimes when a business project you have been working on comes together perfectly. These are the moments that come upon you unexpectedly, like butterflies – you can't force them to land and you can't make them stay, but when they happen they deliver an important message – you are on the right path and you are living your dream.

My husband Matt and I have been travelling through life together for over 17 years, and in that time we have always known whether we were on path to our real dreams in this way.

It is interesting that we say "real" dreams ...

Most of us when asked to list our dreams and goals automatically put down more money, more time, less stress, more health. And yes, Matt and my goals include increasing our income and systemising our business so we can have more time (which we have been very successful at), but what really motivates us is knowing what we will DO with all that money and time, and how the moments of joy will come when we are living that life. And just to clarify - our joyful moments aren't only happening in our free time, joy can come from achievement and challenge too.

When we first started presenting from stage, we both faced some big challenges and it took a lot of guts and determination to overcome the fears we had around getting up there and speaking to large groups of people. But let me tell you – the half hour of consuming joy as we drove home after our first event was absolutely awesome!

Now our events have helped hundreds of people realise how to make the most of their business and get the best possible value from the time, effort and energy they put in – which brings us great joy too.

Joy can guide you no matter what your goals are …

In the course of our business life we have worked with many different business people, and as a business broker selling multi-million dollar businesses, Matt was working very closely with people who were worth not just millions, but tens of millions of dollars.

We found that some of these people worked long hard hours, night and day, and were stressed and worn out just like everyone else! They had spent their lives building up their business and paid what we think is a hefty price in their health and happiness. By the way, this wasn't just the wealthy owners of large businesses - a lot of small business owners were in this same category but making a fraction of the money with the same levels of stress and struggle.

Then there were the wealthy business owners who were the total opposite - they were happy and joyful and free! Their businesses still had huge turnovers, but they had been smart in the way they set them up. These businesses supported their lifestyle, rather than destroying it and they used their money and time to enjoy life. Often we would be on the phone negotiating a business sale, and we could hear seagulls in the background – they were at the beach negotiating multi-million dollar deals!

What made the difference is very important, it is what keeps us motivated in our business now and keeps us on our path no matter how many distractions and challenges are thrown in our way.

These people know what brings them "consuming joy", and they only make decisions and accept opportunities in their business that will bring them more of those moments.

This is an issue we see with many business owners – they are so excited by the prospect of an opportunity that they try and take on every one that is presented to them. This means they get busier and busier and it feels like they are making lots more money and are becoming more successful ...

But when we look at their results and the real situation, often it is just the opposite. They are running round like headless chickens, and actually making less money than they were when their business was half the size and a great deal less stressful!

Over the last 6 years, we have been helping business owners get out of this vicious circle. As brokers we are called upon to get businesses in great shape very quickly, so they will sell for as much as possible. The first thing that adds big value to a business is the ability for the owner to step aside and only do the tasks that they are best at and enjoy doing.

We often had business owners come to us who were desperate to get out of their business, then after we helped them get their business ready for sale and structured in the right way, they realised that they were back on path and decided not to sell! This led us to create our "12 Week Turnaround" program, which takes business owners through our prepare for sale process. Even if they are not thinking of selling right away, they end up with a business that is easier to run, easier to grow and often much more profitable.

Or no matter how big the challenge ...

When faced with big challenges that I know I want to overcome, or if I feel overwhelmed, I take some time out to focus on the joy that successfully overcoming them will bring. I ask myself how I can deal with the situation in a way that makes me feel calm and confident rather than stressed and worried.

This always seems to bring up new creative ways that I can view the challenge or approach a situation, and that in itself makes me happier!

Janet Beckers

Even day-to-day, Joy can be your guide ...

I find great happiness in completing a task, no matter how small. When I write out a list of the tasks I want to complete, I am far more productive and I feel much happier and fulfilled at the end of the day – I have a little moment of consuming joy as I tick each task off my list!

This is what motivates me each day, and what gets me through the challenges – when I can see that the end result of my actions is going to create a situation that attracts joyful moments.

And the more joyful I feel, the more the right people are attracted to me and my business, the ones who can help me achieve what I am aiming for, and the ones who will benefit and appreciate what we can do for them.

What is our dream?

Our joy has led us to this business, where we get to share our knowledge and experiences and help a whole lot more people create businesses that support their joy too.

And now in the next phase of our journey, we are going to start sharing a business model that makes creating passive and highly leveraged income far easier and faster than anything we have seen in the traditional "bricks and mortar" business world.

We buy up underperforming websites and renovate them, and now own a portfolio of sites that bring us wonderfully passive income. Each one is a little business that takes very little time to maintain, very little effort to grow and has amazing potential to grow quickly and easily.

I now get a little moment of 'consuming joy' when I see a deposit for $1,000, $2,000 or $5,000 suddenly appear in one of our accounts!

We have taken our offline business strategies for buying and selling business into the online world, and I'm really excited about sharing this and helping other people achieve the same.

In summary, knowing what really brings me joy has guided me in a direction that makes pursuing my goals and dreams a fun, enjoyable experience. Matt and I let our joy tell us if a decision was right or wrong.

It's much easier to keep your big vision and goals alive when you are enjoying the journey and being rewarded with moments of "consuming joy" along the way!

3 Tips To Stay Focused On Your Dreams

Write down your TRUE passions, what does your life look like when you are experiencing moments of "consuming joy"?

When presented with an opportunity, always ask yourself if it will take you closer to your joy or if you are only tempted because you can't bear to pass up the money or fame

Find little things that you can take joy in daily – ticking off a task, feeling the sun on your face, calculating how much money you made – whatever gives you a little moment of happiness!

About The Author

Liz and Matt Raad are advisors and experts in buying and selling businesses. They have bought and sold their own businesses, and as business brokers worked closely with high net worth buyers and sellers. They know first hand the keys to creating an irresistible business that is worth top dollar.

Matt and Liz also own a range of money-making websites and use their buy and renovate strategy to create fast passive online income, as well as automating their offline businesses.

They have condensed their insights and knowledge into a system for creating wealth through buying and selling business and websites, and give a unique, "at the coalface" perspective in their mentoring program and workshops.

They love helping people realise the value in their business, and achieve their business and lifestyle goals.

They do this by giving simple, practical yet powerful strategies that set up a business or website for sale right from day one, and grow it into a highly valuable asset and income generator.

Janet Beckers

Special Gift

As a special gift for readers of this ebook, we want to offer you the opportunity to hear our strategies for creating a business that supports your lifestyle. Go to http://www.MattAndLizRaad.com/inspired where you can book in for our information-packed "How To Buy And Sell Websites" webinar.

http://www.MattAndLizRaad.com

Ask Quality Questions to Get Quality Results to Keep your Dreams Alive

Lorrah Berg

'The quality of your life depends on the quality of the questions you ask yourself'.
John Demartini

• Have you ever thought about what kind of questions you ask yourself?

• Have you ever thought about how the questions you ask yourself contribute to the results you get in life?

My vision is to heal. Heal myself and heal the planet by creating a 'space' where professional women (and enlightened men) can heal and empower themselves by understanding the soul purpose of life and how to collapse pleasure and pain experiences to live a balanced and fulfilling life.

Janet Beckers

With a history of pleasurable and painful experiences I've learnt that asking questions has resulted in me getting good and bad results. When I've asked good questions I've achieved good results and when I've asked bad questions I've gotten bad results. The above two questions are worth exploring if you want to change the results you are getting in life and stay connected to your dreams. Asking the right questions to get the right answers will get you the right results. However most people ask weak questions and therefore get weak results and then wonder why. Weak questions will turn your focus away from what you want and towards more of what you don't want. And since we ask and answer questions every day, the questions we ask exercise great power over our results.

Dis-empowering Questions. Weak questions are dis-empowering and will keep you stuck in a situation. They keep you focused on your own ego, your problems, and your shortcomings. Weak questions keep you focused on what's wrong... on what isn't working and all they do is further reinforce the situation you'd like to change. Weak questions will lead your brain to come up with answers that are useless, circular, or even destructive. Weak questions contribute to tortured thinking, depression and are addictive.

Everyone including myself often ask weak questions such as a 'why' question and this leads to circular thinking and often results in destructive behaviours. Take depression for example, you might think that if you're depressed, the best thing you can do is to ask, "Why am I so depressed?" Perhaps if you could diagnose the problem, you could cure it. But when you're in a negative state or situation, you aren't thinking clearly to begin with. You're in no position to accurately diagnose yourself. Effectively you're blind. So the answers you get back will be misleading and worthless. At best you'll merely come up with a temporary solution, but the underlying condition will remain, and the problem will simply submerge and appear again later, sometimes in a different form.

Asking why you're depressed merely feeds your depression and gives you every reason to stay depressed. In answering the 'why' question, you've just added a justification story on top of your depression. That goes way beyond acknowledging your depression and trying to do something about it.

Empowering questions. Strong questions are empowering. They keep you focused on solutions, on what you can control. When you focus on what you can do, you avoid falling into analysis paralysis. Ultimately the way out of any negative situation is forward thinking. Wrong or dis-empowered thinking leads you in circles. Right or empowered thinking leads to action. Going back to the depression example, the first thing you need to do is to get yourself to a more positive emotional state. There are many ways to get yourself into a positive emotional state quickly but asking empowering questions can really start the process if you don't have any other tools to work with. Empowering questions will help you shift your focus away from depression or other sources pain and the thoughts that reinforce it and move towards action.

When you focus too much thought on what you can't control and don't like, depression is a natural consequence. When you ask different questions to focus on what you can control and what you do like, depression or any other negative state will lift. Mediocre results largely come about from asking mediocre questions. Great results come from asking empowering questions. If you don't like the results you're getting, think about reframing your question and ask an empowering one. Ask questions that turn your focus towards your vision and goals instead of away from them. Ask questions that allow you to enhance the pleasure in your life instead of creating more or greater pain.

We all ask weak questions in our life but the key is having an awareness to quickly observe what is happening and reframe them.

Having recently worked with a personal life coach around a negative state and recurring pattern of perceiving not having my needs met and then feeling resentful and thinking like a victim, I've been able to break the pattern by reframing my question. I changed from 'why is this pattern coming up again' to 'what do I need to do to overcome my resentment' to 'how do I have my needs met' to 'what are my needs'.

When I got to the core of what I needed, my inner energy shifted and I got the result I wanted in my external world. Asking empowering questions is just one of the strategies I use for staying connected to my purpose and keeping my dreams alive. Once you have a vision and written goals to be working towards, the following actions will help you keep your dreams alive. The more often you do these actions, the quicker you will see a change in results. 'By changing your perceptions, you can change your life. Through daily practice, you will transform your life'. Lorrah Berg

Janet Beckers

3 Tips To Stay Focused On Your Dreams

1. On a regular basis, either daily or weekly in your journal write down an empowering question that will move you closer towards your goal. (Visit my website for a free copy of empowering questions for various states www.lorrahberg.com)

2. Be alert and look and listen for the answers and be ready to act on them

3. Regularly reflect on your day and week and keep a record in your journal

About The Author

For over 20 years Lorrah has been involved in the Human Potential Movement, learning about universal laws and how they apply to everyone in business, career, relationships and everyday life. Today Lorrah openly shares her education, wisdom and experiences to help her clients live with gratitude, joy, success and abundance. Lorrah is an inspirational Life Facilitator and Empowerment Coach, the creator of the 5 Step ANGEL System and the CorporateANGEL Program for Professional Women (and enlightened men). She leads her clients to break through walls of limitations and step into a world of infinite possibility. She has the ability to gently guide clients to a 'safe space' where they can dissolve fear, guilt, doubt and limiting beliefs that prevent them from moving forward. After spending many years working at senior management level positions in the corporate sector feeling like a 'square peg in a round hole' Lorrah now lives her dream of doing what she loves and loving what she does – inspiring professional women to honour themselves in living the life they so truly desire. If you are truly committed to a life of happiness and joy, then you are committed to experience a journey of pleasure and pain to grow in fulfilment, and transform your dreams into reality. Lorrah is the person to help you get there and she is available to personally coach you either by phone, skype, email or face-to-face.

Special Gift

Free Mp3 Daily Activation Practice

http://www.lorrahberg.com

Every Milli-Second Makes a Difference.

Louise Brogan

Every Milli-Second Makes a Difference. Isn't it extraordinary how your whole life can change in a milli-second? One minute, you're just sailing along, enjoying life and getting things done... then WHAM! Everything changes. No going back. It feels like someone has taken a great big black pen and just crossed out your whole life! Yes, it's a shocking experience – literally – however, it can be an incredibly liberating one too!

Hi, my name is Louise Brogan, co-owner and co-creator of Your Life Your Money and the All Money Matters Group. I'm blessed to have 2 passions. Investing and money management education and financial coaching. Perhaps they could be one really – 'doing' and teaching the 'doing'! My whole working and business life has been in the finance industry. Oh, except for a brief, and wonderful, sojourn when I worked with one of Australia's leading alternative health companies. Not only was that 3 years of learning about the fascinating world of alternate therapies, it was also an intense time of personal discovery and development.

Janet Beckers

Back to my passion! After getting the foundational number crunching skills of money through working and studying in the accountancy profession, I moved into the exciting, high-energy world of stockbroking. Yes, it was a man's world alright, but I managed to carve my niche in that world and had my own investment consultancy together with being one of 5 female members of the Australian Stock Exchange. My adrenalin 'high' lasted for 12 years when, of course, the inevitable happened. Complete burnout! I decided it was time I went on a holiday; so I took 2 weeks off… and never went back!

Thank goodness the business had others to pick up the reins. I couldn't; I was exhausted! But that wasn't my life changing milli-second! Nor was working in the alternative health industry – although I learned so much about myself, others and the world of healing. Even though I had burned out from my previous foray in the financial world, I just couldn't help myself, I had to go back! But this time, it was going to be on my terms… or so I thought! That's when I started up my financial coaching and education business, All Money Matters. I loved it! My own boss again, working in an industry that I knew and understood, but adding that dash of passion, and compassion, by helping others with their money 'stuff' rather than trying to squeeze the last cent out of every share trade. The business grew and I was enjoying it, but oh goodness, it was becoming more and more of a struggle!

Why? Why was this work that I enjoyed and which was helping people so hard? I couldn't understand it, I couldn't see. And yet, I couldn't stop! I just had to help everyone who asked; I couldn't say 'no'. At times, some couldn't afford to pay me much, if anything, but still I took them on and worked with them. After all, I didn't need the money – this was my calling… wasn't it? It felt like I was running through treacle! Sweet but thick and sticky! I was exhausted. Again. Around that time, my mum had sold the family home to move into a retirement village. My husband and I were at the house, doing the final clean up and throw out; ready for settlement. I will never forget it! From another room, his voice reached me "Ah darling, there's something here you need to see… now!"

I got there quick smart. As I looked over his shoulder, my heart stopped, my vision blurred, my legs gave away and I half sank, half fell to the floor. There, in his hands, were my adoption papers. Yes, that's right, my adoption papers! At the age of 45, I discovered I was adopted. As I said earlier, it felt as though someone had a great big black pen and just crossed out the first 45 years of my life.

I was beyond shock, I was numb, completely blank. Who I thought I was just disappeared! I needed time out. Time to think and try to make sense of it all, to make sense of me. The strange thing was, as those feelings – or lack of feelings – dissipated what took their place was relief! Relief, that I finally knew. A great weight lifted from my being. And ten years on, that weight hasn't returned. Now, that's liberating! Over time I collected all my adoption papers and documents. My heart stopped – again - when I read the reason for my adoption: "The birth parents are unable to financially support a child at this time" My birth parents were not able to keep me because they couldn't afford to. They couldn't afford to. What an insight! No wonder I was pushing myself to exhaustion to help people with their money issues. I didn't want them to be forced to give up something precious in their lives because they couldn't see how they could afford it and could see no other option. Finally, I was understanding more about the underlying reasons behind my driving need to push myself, and the business, so incredibly hard. That's when I was able to step back, take a long hard look at my business (and my life) and make some very necessary changes.

Instead of 'acting it out' through the business, I worked it out - with a lot of help - and moved to a much more sensible, do-able and sustainable way of working. It became fun again, much easier and more fulfilling. Now, I know why I react the way I do, and I have strategies in place to support me and also to alert me when I fall back into those 'old' patterns. Now I won't say that business, and life, still don't have challenges. They do, but now, it's a positive experience because those 'ghosts' are not driving me, whipping me on, via my unconscious. Everyone has their own story; their own 'milli-second'. I have shared this part of my story to encourage you to continue doing your 'inner' work. That has made the difference for me. Personally, I have found it to be the key to success in my investing and business life, as well as enjoying a happy and fulfilled personal life.

I guarantee it will have a huge, and positive, impact on your business and life. Here are a few ways that positive impact can manifest:

• Enjoying your business again, • Your business will support you (not the other way around!),

• Work and clients will be drawn to you and your business,

• You, and the business, will be supported and respected,

• The business will be more profitable,

Janet Beckers

• The business will be able to make a wonderful contribution to the community,

• The business will be a lasting legacy,

• You'll have a balanced life. Self-understanding is the key – everything else flows from that… Happiness, wealth, health, fulfillment, achievement, contribution – Abundance!

3 Tips To Stay Focused On Your Dreams

Keep doing your inner work. Not only your personal work but also understand 'Your Money Personality' or your financial profile. This is the key!

Ensure you have your business and financial boundaries in place. Then you will stay profitable and continue to appropriately help others whilst still having fun.

Get the help of a great mentor to guide you, encourage you and alert you to those unhelpful attitudes and behaviours.

About The Author

Louise Brogan is the founder of All Money Matters and co-founder of Your Life Your Money. Louise studied and worked in the accounting and stockbroking industries, giving her extensive experience in investment advising. She ran her own investment consultancy business and was one of five women members of the Australian Stock Exchange. This, plus years of counseling and psychotherapy study has given her a solid foundation for an integrated approach to money issues. Louise believes that our attitudes towards money can be used as "signposts" to guide us to achieve financial literacy, financial independence and an abundant life. She encourages and supports a full exploration of those attitudes whilst still learning the 'number crunching' skills necessary for all your financial decisions

Special Gift

We want to encourage and support you to take your Action Steps, so here's what we're offering. Choose either or both! 1. Your Life Your Money E-course. Just

The Power of 100

follow this link to our web site http://yourlifeyourmoney.com.au/products-and-services/your-life-your-money-ecourse scroll down to "Purchase the Full E-Course" and click the "Add to Cart" button. The 'coupon code' is GoldenOpportunity. The full cost of the e-course is $Aus 279.00 - you will pay just $Aus 249.00.

2. Do 'Your Money Personality' Profile with us and we will give you a Wealth Check for free!

Value: $Aus 220 Just email goldenopportunity@allmoneymatters.com.au telling us you're ready to take your first Action Step. The Wealth Check will help you with Action Step number 2 – for free.

http://www.yourlifeyourmoney.com.au

Janet Beckers

Breakable Bones - Unbreakable Spirit

Malissa Thorpe

"Life isn't about finding yourself - life is about creating yourself" George Bernard Shaw famously said. Our dreams are definitely part of creating our lives. Everyone, at some point of his or her life, has dreamed of being somebody special, somebody big, but few believe that they can actually achieve them. Who hasn't fantasised about being the one who hits the game-winning run? Who hasn't dreamed of living the life of a movie star or being the most popular person at school? And how many times have we dreamed of being rich, or successful, or happy with our relationships?

Nevertheless, some people achieve their dreams while others live lives of regret. Some are inspired and follow through, while others delay or give up entirely on their dreams in exchange for whatever excuses they comfort themselves with. Often, we dream big dreams and have great aspirations. Unfortunately, our dreams remain just that - dreams. And our aspirations easily collect dust in our attic. This is a sad turn of events in our life. Instead of experiencing exciting adventures in self actualisation, we get caught up in the humdrum of living from day-to-day just barely existing.

What are the factors that make the difference between the person who achieves and the one who regrets? I believe it's a combination of the language you use when having a conversation with yourself, how quickly some people give up when they come across a challenge and understanding the simple system to conquer challenges in your life. Noticed I said challenges and not problems? I learnt at about the age of 14 there was a difference.

Problems have a mental block that basically implies that you can't get past them. A challenge implies that there is already an answer out there and you just have to find it. Easier huh? But you know what? Life could be so much better, if only we learned to aim higher.

The most common problem with dreams is the word impossible. Most people get hung up thinking I can't do this. It's too hard. It's too impossible. No one can do this. However, if everyone thought that, there would be no inventions, no innovations, and no breakthroughs in human accomplishment. Remember that scientists were baffled when they took a look at the humble bumblebee. Theoretically, they said, it was impossible for the bumblebee to fly. Unfortunately for the bumble bee no one has told it so. So fly it does. On the other hand, some people suffer from dreaming totally outrageous dreams and not acting on them. The result? Broken dreams, and tattered aspirations.

If you limit yourself with self-doubt, and self-limiting assumptions, you will never be able to break past what you deem impossible. If you reach too far out into the sky without working towards your goal, you will find yourself clinging on to the impossible dream. Don't forget if you told someone two hundred years ago that it was possible for man to be on the moon, they would laugh at you. If you had told them that you could send mail from here to the other side of the world in a couple of seconds, they would say you were out of your mind. But, through sheer desire and perseverance, these impossible dreams are now realities.

I don't want to get too sidetracked (see bio for more info) I use a wheelchair to get around and am only 3ft 10" tall (120cms). But DON'T feel sorry for me. I live a very "normal" life. I have my own business in Executive Resilience Training, two Beautiful children (boy 6, girl 8), I drive, travel, clean the house(!) and all whilst being a single mum. I achieve goals regularly and miss a few too so I know I'm not super human, but I've learnt my limitations and more importantly learnt how to get past challenges quickly and easily. In 2009 I put a photo of snow-covered Europe in my diary for the month of December. Then out of seemingly nowhere – I was booking tickets in October to celebrate Christmas and New Years in a snow capped Europe with my kids and family in tow.

Ultimately there are three simple steps you can take to help you live the life of your dreams:

1. Motivation. Everyone has their own motivations for their dreams. Consider what motivates you towards your goal. It could be financial freedom, more free time, or a home in Paris. Whatever it is, remind yourself of it on a daily basis.

2. Planning. Although developing a plan may seem obvious if you want to achieve your dreams, many people overlook or downplay this process and then wonder why they aren't moving forward toward their dreams. Be sure to take the time to plan your path for greater success!

3. Action. Lastly, no dream or goal can be achieved without action. If you've developed your plan as recommended, you will see that there are a number of little steps you must take on a daily or intermittent basis that will further you on your path to your ultimate goal. This is critical to the whole process. Believe me when I say if I can do it – so can you. So dream on, friend! Don't get caught up with your perceived limitations. Remember – Live to Love, Love to Live

3 Tips To Stay Focused On Your Dreams

When you suffer inevitable setbacks or frustration, a visible reminder of your dream will help motivate you to do what is necessary to get back on track toward your goal.

Giving yourself a reward here and there along the way will reinvigorate your motivation with its positive result.

Each step you complete brings you closer to your dream. Your little action steps show your more of the map to your treasure.

About The Author

Malissa is a woman who has a disability who often forgets that she does have a disability! She was born with a condition called 'Osteogenesis Imperfecta' which in plain English means she can break bones easily and has had over 400 broken bones and 22 operations for roding in her bones. She doesn't believe in the word "problem" and choose to replace it with the word Challenge, because the language you use contributes to your outcomes. She has two Beautiful children and enjoys the learning's they bring to her life daily. She calls a spade a spade and won't tolerate verbal "fluff". Malissa constantly strives for more challenges in her life so she can continue her learning and improve her resilience and persistence. She was training people on an international level from the age of 20, starting with 300 university students from 23 different countries in Ireland. Malissa loves showing others how to be resilient in their life and over come challenges with a simple system that they've never been shown in their instruction book of life.

Special Gift

Rush over to www.malissathorpe.com/100women now to grab your free gift bonus - two chapters of my book "Unbreakable You: How to Quickly and Easily Conquer the Crap in Your Life".

http://www.malissathorpe.com   http://www.facebook.com/malissathorpepage

Janet Beckers

Keep your Dream Alive by feeling Fabulous, Frisky and Focused – the Feminine Way!

Maree Lipschitz

Do you try and go at the same pace all month, every month? Have you ever found that sometimes it's a huge effort to get things done and other days it's a breeze? Are you aware that you're probably not using the most important stress-sensitive feedback system available to all women? That was me too until about 15 years ago – and I'm 50 this year. I'd push myself to get everything done on my list, work long hours, maximise my time multi-tasking, run from one thing to the next, but never managed to 'get it all done'. And feel incredibly stressed about it all as well. And after I became a working mother it only got worse – more things to do, to organise, to 'fit in'.

My adrenals were running on overload - big time. And then I met a woman who changed all that for me – Alexandra Pope. Bless her cotton socks (she's English and she actually does like her cotton socks!) Alexandra introduced me to understanding my cyclical nature as a woman – so that I can use it and work with it rather than go against it all the time! I've found this has helped me remarkably over the past 15 years to stay on track and be in sync with my body's natural rhythms and cycles so that I can maximise them and use them to my advantage. If only I had learnt this when I was 14-15! Life would have been SO much easier and I would have looked after my body and my health as well!

So let me tell you what I found out... Understanding Your Natural Female Rhythm So here's what I learnt – and it's been invaluable. We are cyclical beings – all of us, men and women (e.g. day/night; summer/winter; asleep/awake, birth/death, etc) but particularly we women. We have our own inbuilt cycle every month, which gives us feedback as to how we are going in life. If things are getting on top of us – guess what? It shows up in our cycle – our stress sensitive system! Our culture expects us to be 'ON', productive and on an upward curve – available 24/7 all the time. But nowhere else in nature does this happen.

Everywhere things birth, grow, blossom, decline and die. For things to be able to focus, thrive and flourish – there must be also be some fallow, reflective, resting time. And that's also how our female cycle works – and all the four phases (or four weeks) of our cycle has different gifts or attributes that we can use to our advantage skilfully and consciously. Focus is only one of them. Our cycle is our secret power source! Let me explain using the seasons as a metaphor.

1. Week 1 - Winter – Menstruation – Reflection & Chilling Out – New Moon – Days 1-7 I'm starting here because this is usually the time of the month where every menstruating woman becomes aware that she has a cycle! Many are not even conscious of it at all the rest of the month, until they start their period. Most in our Western culture see this as a nuisance, some dread it because of painful, disruptive symptoms (which was my own story until I learnt how to accept it and work with it) - but very few see it as a time for reflection and renewal. A cleansing time – the womb is being emptied out and so are we.

We have the chance to start anew again soon. But I've learnt that we need to be restful now in this phase - to take things more slowly. The 'Feel Good' hormone estrogen is very low in our body – making us feel anti-social, grumpy, tired, tracksuit pants and ugg boots territory! It makes us very dreamy, fuzzy thinking, unable to focus on one thing, often very low in energy - but also highly intuitive and psychic, very attuned to all the nuances in relationships around us (that's why we want to be away from people 'cos we can feel everything going on for them!).

Yes, we still have to go to work, look after our family, etc. BUT we can postpone any extra social commitments or strenuous exercise until that estrogen starts kicking in again!

GIFTS and ATTRIBUTES of this phase: intuition, wisdom, insight, inspiration, reflection, bliss, release and relief. Good time for: Meditating on problems/issues to gain insight; dreaming/visioning up goals/plans; slowing down and going easy; gentle exercise; love and accepting yourself!

2. Week 2 – Spring – Pre-Ovulation – Focus and Clarity – Waxing Moon - Days 8-14 A new beginning - spring has sprung! Yippee! Most women say they feel a lovely sense of being refreshed and reborn once they have stopped their period. The key feeling here is one of clarity – of thought and of direction. We have increasing energy – and lots more brain power 'cos that wonderful hormone estrogen has started filling up into our body again and we feel SO much better! (Estrogen also helps our brain and communication function better so we can think and talk more clearly – our focused phase! (Check out Louann Brizendine's book - The Female Brain – easy to read and fascinating!)

GIFTS and ATTRIBUTES of this phase: focus, enthusiasm, clarity, freshness, lightness, activation. Good time for: Initiating ideas and plans; focusing; goal setting and reaffirming; resolving recurring issues; vision boarding; writing journal notes; stepping up the exercise slowly

3. Week 3 – Summer – Ovulation – Energy and Friskiness – Full Moon – Days 15-21 Yes – the frisky phase! The female brain is now flooded with estrogen – our highest level all month. This makes us feel very expansive, social, sexual (the egg is popping from the ovary so Mother Nature wants it fertilised!). This is also our 'nice girl' phase – the high level of estrogen makes us very accommodating to all – not much seems to aggravate us. We are like mothers of the world – we can nurture everyone and everything. We feel very much in control – multi-tasking a million projects at once, saying 'yes' to everything, superwoman, we can do anything here! It is usually the highest energy point of the whole cycle (some women do get some painful ovulation symptoms but they are the minority).

GIFTS and ATTRIBUTES of this phase: Drive; Energy; Articulate Communication; Sexy; Social; Playful; Nurturing; Having It all Good time for: Networking; Manifesting Goals; Birthing Projects; Going on that Hot Date; Doing Presentations; Asking for Pay Rises; Negotiating (anything!); Weekend Away with Partner (with contraception unless you're wanting to become pregnant!); Falling Pregnant; Shopping (cos you look great now); Dinner parties and Socialising; Testing new ideas; High energy exercise workouts – run that marathon now!

4. Week 4 – Autumn – Pre-Menstruation – Creativity and Intuition – Waning Moon – Days 22-28 The estrogen is starting to fall away and our bodies become much more sensitive and vulnerable - physically and emotionally. Now's the time we start to say 'what the !!!! was I thinking saying Yes to all those things! We start to see what isn't working in our lives – this is maximum 'feedback' time from that little voice in your head. Warning – do NOT go shopping in this phase – your bum will always look big here. That inner critic can be VISCIOUS here! To us and everybody – if we are feeling overwhelmed here our inner bitch comes out! We start feeling more inward turning, anti-social, coming back into our body – and feeling every bit of it! Cravings and addictions are highest here – chocolate, red wine, alcohol; food; coffee; cigarettes – anything to make us feel better! And our dreaming gets more intense – and our creativity goes through the roof! Use all that tension and frustration that often occurs in this phase to design something new and sort out what isn't working in your life.

GIFTS and ATTRIBUTES of this phase: Creativity; Intuition; Sorting; Assertiveness; Provocation Good time for: Slowing down; Pampering Yourself; Body work – Massage/Facial; Analysing what works and doesn't work in your life; rescheduling unrealistic tasks/projects; focus on your core purpose; behind the scenes work in business ; cleaning out stuff; taking on challenging situations; getting real; doing your own creative thing that soothes you – cooking, sewing, knitting, painting, writing, beadwork; working smarter not harder; gentler exercise regimes and then we're back to Week 1 - all over again, the cycle continues.

I know you might be saying – well I just can't structure my life to be this planned to do all these things only in that particular week! I know – but somehow even knowing or being conscious of which cycle phase I am in will help me select certain things that I can naturally do well – and if I am able to postpone some things until my optimum time for working on them – then I do that! No point trying to get my project up and running in my reflection phase – it just doesn't work and I struggle and struggle. Better to keep visioning that week – and sure enough - I have much more clarity after 'bleeding' on the problem (bit like 'sleeping on it' but the feminine version!) And guess what – if you don't look after yourself through your menstruating years – then menopause will likely be the mother of all wakeup calls! And since I came to understand so much more about the menstrual cycle and how it affects our lives - my dream is to assist 40+ midlife women to understand the fabulous opportunity that menopause is - to rediscover their purpose, reclaim their power and recreate their life! So contact me if that speaks to you.

3 Tips To Stay Focused On Your Dreams

Track your cycle and know what phase you are in – reflective, clarifying, energised; creative

Use the natural gifts of each phase to determine what tasks you will do that week.

Love your body's wisdom – learn about it, nurture it, accept it and listen to it!

About The Author

Maree Lipschitz is one of Australia's best 'Transitions Coach' for women – the 'Midlife Midwife'! She is a specialist coach in Mid-life & Menopause and her business 'The Midlife Midwife' offers Group Mentoring, Webinars, Events, Seminars and Personal Coaching to assist women 40+ to rediscover their purpose, reclaim their power and recreate their life. Maree is also a Senior Facilitator and Co-founder of 'Working Mothers Secrets' for corporate working mums; 'Pathways into Womanhood' residential programs for 13-15 year old girls and their Mums; 'Let's Talk Growing Up' puberty weekends for 9-12 year old girls and their Mums. She is passionate about helping women and girls navigate with grace and ease through these major transitions in their lives. 'Come have a chat with me on Facebook - I'd love to know what's happening for you and how I can help!'

Special Gift

Special Offer: All readers can grab a FREE copy of my special report 'The 5 MUST KNOW Secrets to Avoid the Menopause from Hell!' by going to http://www.facebook.com/TheMidlifeMidwife

The Power of 100

Keeping your Day Simple and Staying Motivated and Focussed

Margaret Ann Beth Saunders

Hi, I'm Margaret Saunders the founder of four successful websites providing advice to parents of young children and I'd like to share with you how I stay motivated and focused in my busy life.

As a proud mum of two teenage girls, and running my parenting businesses from home. Often when I told my best friend what I had done in just one day she would say "You did ALL that?" and I didn't think I'd done a lot!

The Beginning Of The Day

First thing in the morning I have a morning routine. I love routines and this probably stems from when my daughters were a lot younger and I discovered the joy of routines. I get up, put my porridge on to cook slowly, have a luxuriating shower then I do some light exercises, a short yoga relaxation and then read two pages from

"You Can Heal Your Life" by Louise Hay and two pages from "The Secret" and then one Daily Teaching from The Secrets Daily Teaching Series. This really starts my day. Here is an example of one the daily sayings … "There is a presence inside you. It is the life force that breathed your first breath when you were born. It is the life force that is breathing you now. It is a presence of unbelievable harmony, peace, and love, and it is inside you.

To connect with and feel the life presence, stop, close your eyes, relax, let go of thoughts, and focus deeply on the inside of your body for a couple of minutes. The more you do this exercise, the more the presence of pure harmony, peace, and love will arise within you." Day342.

During The Day

To keep me focused during the day I write a list of things to do for that day and appointments. This helps me to focus on what I need to do when. This helps me to be action orientated in school hours, and getting my girls to and from their school and work on time. I then now exactly how long I have and when and can then easily prioritise my day. I always do my phone calls between 12 and 1pm and check my emails early each day. If I haven't completed a task that day I write it on the list for the next day. I also keep a book on my desk to write any bright ideas I have when I think of them. I also have a pen and paper in my handbag at all times. I have often had a bright idea when I least expect it. For example, I was one the bus on the way home from the airport the other day and I had a bright idea for an advert to promote a service of mine that I hadn't promoted before. A fellow passenger on the bus noticed me writing the advert and asked what I did. This then lead to a fabulous discussion on my parenting expertise.

At The End Of The Day

At the end of the day, the minute I get into bed, I write down in a journal the things I was grateful for that happened that day. I do at minimum of five, often a page full. Then I write down the things that I am going to be grateful for that are to happen tomorrow. This builds the intention and the feel of the coming day. I also complete my day by writing down my wins and how the universe supported me. These activities at the beginning and finish of the day motivate me to be positive and learn something new about myself every day. Having my day mapped out in segments of what I am doing with and for my family and the time slots for my working hours, keep me focused on that particular activity and helps me to concentrate on the activity at hand. I believe by keeping it simple reduces my stress load and keeps me focused on one thing at a time, and also keeps me balanced, mindful, appreciative and eternally grateful for everything and everyone.

3 Tips To Stay Focused On Your Dreams

Start the day with some positive input. This can be something like reading a few pages of a motivational book, listening to affirmations or writing your intentions for the day.

Map out and plan your day in advance. This way your day flows and you know what you are doing as the day progresses. You will be surprised by how much you can accomplish.

Finish your day with something like journal writing, writing down the things you are grateful for, your wins, what you accomplished, how you were supported during the day and what you are going to be grateful for in the coming day.

About The Author

Margaret Saunders is proud and enthusiastic later in life mom. She had her two daughters when she was 39 and 41. They are now two beautiful teenagers aged 15 and 19. She lives in a beautiful small seaside village called Dromana which is 1-1/2 hours out of Melbourne Australia, on the Mornington Peninsula. She is an international Parenting Expert, specialising in toddler bedtime and sleep and toilet training. She is an author, speaker and the host of the Children Are Everything Radio Show. Margaret is also passionate about the dynamics of our families and has studied intensively and is now a Family Energy Coach. She believes that the energy we have as a mom permeates into those around us, especially our children. Her family energy coaching sessions are designed to align your energy, revitalise, calm and renew you so that the energy you put out around you calms all those you come into contact with; as well as healing your own deep family issues.

Janet Beckers

Special Gift

I'd like to offer you all two special offers.

1. A 15 minute complimentary Family Advice Coaching Session, valued at $57. Is the energy or some of the behaviours of your family not quite how you would like them to be? Have you been feeling frazzled and loosing your cool? Are things not how you think they should be? Then why not enjoy the benefits of a complimentary session with parenting and family energy advisor and expert Margaret Saunders. Find out more and to register for your complimentary, 15 minutes, (no charge to you, valued at $57) go to http://www.FamilyAdvice.com.au

2. Half Price, Bedtime And Toilet Training Solutions Packages. You save 50%. Packages include: The Ultimate Bedtime Package – how to get your child to happily go to bed and fall asleep fast. The Ultimate Toilet Training Package – How To Toilet Train Your Child In Just One Day. The Ultimate How To Have Your Child Be An Angel – how to bring out the angel behaviour in your child. The Ultimate How To Have More Time – how to have more time as a family, as if you lived in the country, no matter where you live now. Single packages usually $57.00 now $29.00 total package value $107 you save $80.00 Your Price =$29.00 Buy 2 get one free offer usually $87.00 now $45.00, total packages value $214 you save $177.00 Your Price= $45.00 To get this offer, you must order by midnight February 28th 2012 please go to http://www.BedtimeAndToiletTrainingSolutions.com.au/WWWomenOffer

http://www.BedtimeAndToiletTrainingSolutions.com.au
http://www.ChildrenAreEverything.com.au   http://www.BabySleepAdvisory.com
http://www.FamilyAdvice.com.au

Give Up. Give In. No Way!

Margaret Sims

Looking at me from the outside, I look like a successful business woman. After all, I am an Image Consultant and that's how I am supposed to look. But dig a bit deeper and it's a different story. I almost did not write this. The tears of past shame were close to the surface. It has been over 10 years since I walked away at 53 from my teaching job. Have I made millions from my business? No. Have I made six figures every year? No. Actually I earn less than the unemployment benefit. In the eyes of the world, I should have gone back to teaching, got a job as a checkout chick or spent all my days waiting hand and foot on my aging mother. All of these have at various times been suggested to me. But I am still here. I have a dream and a vision that I am stubbornly holding on to. And all the time I am re-committing and re-focusing.

When I left teaching, the rest of the staff said it would be easy for me to do something different. And I agreed with them. I was smart, adaptable, very good at teaching and I related well to people of all ages. It couldn't be too hard to become successful. (I am an optimist. We judge ourselves on our potential. Very harsh). I discovered very quickly that I had to start again as a complete beginner. It had been a long time since I had been a beginner and experienced all those fears and fragile confidence. Here's three things I have learnt about life and starting a business in your 50s.

De-clutter

As I lived my last 10 years I had to spend a lot of time deciding what I would keep in my life and what would go. At first I did not even know what I wanted from my life and my business. I had to re-discover myself before I could move on. I read lots of books, did courses, joined business groups and Wonderful Web Women – all to find out who I am and what I want at this stage of my life. It was Helen Keller's quote 'One cannot consent to creep when one feels an impulse to soar' that started this journey and kept me going. Everything stayed that would help me soar. Everything went that was keeping me creeping on auto-pilot. And a lot had to go.

Re-vitalise

This was a rough stage as I repaired and altered my thinking and actions. I had let 'fun' disappear. I had to bring it back into my life. I had to let go of doing everything myself. God is pleased that I have resigned from my self-appointed position as one of his General Managers of the Universe. Thank you Marci Shimoff for that one.

Now I trust that others want to share my journey and my successes. And I let them. It took a number of years to repair and alter my relationships with my mum and my husband (letting go of all my untrue stories). My mum passed away last year at 90. We were wonderful friends for the last years of her life. I changed. My mother and my husband stayed as they are. More importantly I repaired my relationship with the teacher in me. I finally took it back with renewed pride and a re-vitalised sense of fun. Always I was re-committing and re-focusing.

Modernise

I love learning new things, then applying them, then teaching them to others. Teaching, writing, speaking and big-picture organising are my passions and my strengths. Now I honour and develop them. Over the last ten years, I have learnt new Business Skills, new Computer and Internet Skills and especially Modern Marketing Skills. It took a long time to realise that Marketing is the most important skill of all for any business woman. It's a big subject. I now concentrate only on three aspects of it each year so that I master a little at a time.

The judgmental optimist is now a happy beginner as I have learnt not to overwhelm myself with impossible expectations. With every step I am re-committing and re-focusing. And when it all gets too much, I have my own motivation – 'I have done it before. I can do it again.' My business dream is now more than simple personal colour and image consulting. I want to help women over 45 have the courage to de-clutter, re-vitalise and modernise your wardrobes and your lives - however long that takes you. Will "Your Future Direction" soar to become a million dollar business or a six figure one? I have no idea. I am more confident and much calmer than 10 years ago. And I'll see where my opportunities, including this one, take me and everyone who shares all or part of the journey with me.

3 Tips To Stay Focused On Your Dreams

De-clutter – Whatever your business or personal goals, decide what actions, thoughts, beliefs and skills stay and which ones will go

Re-vitalise - Take some of the things that you have kept and repair or alter them in a more positive way. You have done it before. You can do it again in a new, fun way.

Modernise – Pick one skill. Learn something new about it and spend one year applying it in 3 different ways. Always be re-committing and re-focusing.

About The Author

At the age of 53, Margaret Sims left a long career teaching business and computing skills to high school and adult students to go into solo-entrepreneurship. It took her a number of years and three changes of direction to discover what she's really passionate about. Courage as a mature-age businesswoman is something Margaret is still developing. Margaret is the owner of "Your Future Direction". As a Business Image Teacher, Margaret teaches all aspects of dressing to business and professional women over 45 so you have the courage to be who you are now and tackle anything in life that appeals to you. Margaret lives in sunny Brisbane in Queensland, Australia and is a proud member of Wonderful Web Women. With two adult sons and no grandchildren, she's joining the 'Too Young to Retire' brigade.

Janet Beckers

Having decided to let her hair go grey, Margaret's goal is to inspire women to confidently show your individuality whatever your hair colour. Margaret firmly believes that the world benefits from the wisdom and insights of people of all ages and she sees the Internet as a wonderful force for connecting people all around the world. Margaret is now developing Internet Image Products for women over 45.

Special Gift

My Special Offer My Gift to You: Go to http://www.yourfuturedirection.com.au to sign up for your '10 Tips in 10 Days to Look Younger & More Modern' Auto series. Each day you will receive a simple tip with some actions steps to implement the Tip of the Day. The series contains Modern Dressing Tips, Simple Insider Secrets and 'Aha Moments' to help you revitalise and modernise your looks. The aim is to help you look professional, modern, approachable and individual.

http://www.yourfuturedirection.com.au

Unleash The Power Within

Marguerita Vorobioff

What is it you most want to achieve in life? What are you deepest, inner most dreams and desires? If you could have anything you wanted in life, what would that be? And finally, why haven't you got those things in your life right now? Most of us settle for mediocrity simply because we don't know any better. However, if you could even begin to understand your true power and that you are have unlimited potential, what you could achieve would blow your mind.

So why do we settle for mediocre? Because that's what we are programmed to do from the day we are born. Not because of any dark conspiracy theory by our parents, loved ones, teachers or other influential people in our lives. There is nothing sinister about it. It's just because they didn't know any better. You see, there are 2 distinct parts of your mind: the conscious and the sub-conscious. (Actually three, but for our purposes the unconscious is not relevant here.)

Most of us live under the illusion that we are living primarily consciously, making conscious choices and in control of the outcomes in our lives, when in fact, our sub-conscious mind is running our lives automatically ninety-six to ninety-eight percent of the time. I know! Hard to believe isn't it? When we are born, and up to six years of age, we are primarily operating in what is called a Theta brain wave state, which is the realm of the imagination, and this brain state is incredibly impressionable.

This is the ultimate state in which to program the most powerful part of our brain, the part the runs the show, the subconscious. So during those first six years of our life we take whatever is fed to us by our parents, teachers, care givers, the media, and other influential entities in our lives as ultimate truth. Everything we see, hear and experience during those formative years ends up running the rest of our lives automatically. The record button is on and everything gets uploaded without any filters or discernment. Then as we grow into adulthood, we operate primarily in the alpha brain wave state, which is playing the programs that we recorded automatically all those years ago and causes us to make decisions that are in total alignment with those programs. The 'record' part of the brain is now switched off, and the 'play' part is switched on and playing the same programs over and over and over.

So, if you are conditioned to have dysfunctional relationships, you will automatically create dysfunctional relationships. If you have negative belief systems around money (e.g. money is the root of all evil, money is hard to come by, you have to work hard for money, there is never enough money, etc, etc), then you will create lack and limitation around money within your reality. If you believe that you are not very intelligent and you will never amount to anything because someone imposed that upon you when you were very young, you will create your life based on those BS (belief systems).

The good news is, that once you realise the lies that have been running your life year after year after year, you can change them, and you can transform your life into being, doing and having whatever you want. Your deepest dreams and desires can become your reality. But how do you do that when your life is being run automatically by deeply ingrained programs in the core of your subconscious processing centre? We are living in a time of great change, and incredibly powerful energy transformation techniques are becoming more and more widely accepted within our community.

Emotional Freedom Technique, or EFT for short, is one such phenomenon. Based on the ancient Chinese medicine, acupuncture, EFT utilises the energy meridian points of the body to reprogram the subconscious mind and literally create miracles in peoples' lives. Physical and emotional pain disappears in minutes. Destructive, life long behaviours are reversed. Negative belief systems about any aspect of your life can be completely eliminated from your life using this incredible technique. And the exciting part is that this therapy is now beginning to be embraced by main stream medicine and is infiltrating the world of psychology, therapy and even hospitals because of its amazing ability to transform people's lives simply and effectively in just a few minutes.

By combining this technique with another incredibly powerful emerging vibrational medicine, sound therapy I have positively transformed my relationships, my career, my financial reality and I have helped many others to do the same. The possibilities are infinite. In fact, your potential and your power is infinite. You are the creator of your life. The question is; are you creating it by design, or by default? Are you allowing all those automatic programs to run the show, or are you embracing responsibility for being the director in your play and rewriting the parts of the script that don't work for you? Stop living the lie that you were sold when you were growing up, because if you fail to see yourself as a magnificent and powerful being with infinite potential and possibilities, then you are living a lie.

Step into your truth, start living your extraordinary life and share your genius with the world. You will be amazed at what you can achieve, and how many peoples' lives will be transformed because you had the courage to step out and shine.

3 Tips To Stay Focused On Your Dreams

Set aside 30 minutes to an hour to write down all your hopes, dreams and aspirations. There are no limits here. If your life were perfect, what would it look like? What would you be doing? Who would you be doing it with? Where would you be? How would you fee? Let your imagination run wild!

Look closely at your life and start to uncover the limiting belief systems that are preventing you from realizing those things in your life. You are powerful beyond imagining and capable of having whatever you want in life. You are the only one holding youself back. Why? And what do you intend to do about it?

Focusing on your insights, use EFT, Emotional Freedom Technique, and Sound Healing to release these powerful programs from your subconscious. We are incredibly complex creatures with thousands of automatic programs, so this won't happen over night, but with consistent and regular use of these techniques with honesty and true commitment to change, you will start to see results within weeks, days, or possibly even minutes.

About The Author

Marguerita Vorobioff is a Life Coach, Vibrational Healer and Motivational Speaker. With a background as diverse as having performed as an opera singer, to transforming peoples health and fitness as a personal trainer, Marguerita now expresses her unique talent and training via the powerful combination of Sound Healing and EFT (Emotional Freedom Technique) which is transforming many peoples lives. Sound healing is considered the vibrational medicine of the future with infinite potential to transform people physically, emotionally, mentally and spiritually. When combined with the proven, seeming miraculous results achieved through EFT, Marguerita has created a healing system with the ability to transform the lives of thousands of people around the globe. As a Life Coach, Marguerita has an acute understanding of the subconscious mind and how it dictates the results we achieve in our lives until we learn to master it through awareness and dedication. She is committed to helping increase consciousness and awaken people to their infinite potential to be so much more than they ever imagined. Dreams become reality when Marguerita's unique and powerful healing system is used daily.

Special Gift

A free CD incorporating EFT and Sound Healing - the ultimate tool for clearing blocks to success and abundance.

http://www.marguerita.com.au/thepowerof100specialgift/

Storm Survival Skills

Marney Perna

Storm Survival Skills Warning! Warning! A Storm is approaching; please ensure you are well prepared! Hi my name is Marney, the year is 2011 and I live in Queensland, Australia. As you may well be aware my home state has been subject to some frightening and deadly weather and storms for several weeks. We have experienced the heartbreak and loss of human lives, pets, businesses, homes, infrastructure, wildlife, the environment and sanity.

However as our State Premier has declared... "We breed them tough North of the Border, knock us down and we just get up again" You may wonder what this has to do with success. So please allow me to share with you my personal journey, which starts off in 2004 with the tragic death of my niece. I was a stay at home mum, loving and totally enjoying my life as a wife, mum and home maker. I had left school at 15 and was quite content to never study again. Whilst travelling home from my nieces funereal, the car I was in was involved in an accident, and I was left with whiplash and shoulder damage.

Mainstream medicine was unable to make me feel better so I looked elsewhere. I discovered Kinesiology and from that moment I took yet another fork in the road of life. I became so fascinated with this form of healing, which encompassed the mind, body and spirit that I enrolled in a course so that I too could become a qualified practitioner. I was fast approaching 46 years young and here I was about to start my career. Remember I left school over 31 years earlier and have to admit that I had never liked school very much. However what I had going for me on this occasion was my passion. This time I wanted to learn and was extremely passionate about the subjects and the more I learned the more I wanted to learn! I was also in the very fortunate position of having a family that backed my desire to learn by supporting me emotionally and financially, so that I could give my attention to my studies.

There were however two aspects that were making life somewhat difficult, the first being my complete and utter unawareness of the more untraditional aspects of natural health care. By this I mean I was suddenly confronted with concepts like chakras, auras, vibrational energy medicine and the metaphysical mindset. These were totally foreign ideas to me and I can tell you took some time to embrace and accept. The second aspect was the dreaded "M" word...menopause!

My brain could only hold limited information and I was being overloaded. I would sit in Anatomy and Physiology classes and listen to the lecturer talk and only understand one word in thirty and when reading through my notes wonder who wrote them as I certainly didn't remember doing them. It didn't seem to matter how often I would read and re read and write down, again, again and again, still I would not retain the information.

Then one day I had an epiphany, I had my books, notes and heaps of charts so why was I being so fanatical about remembering everything. There was no need to so long as I retained enough to pass my exams, when I was in my own clinic I could use all the tools that the universe had supplied. Phew what a relief, with that I gave myself permission to relax and to know it was OK to not be perfect. My Diploma of Kinesiology took me several years to complete and I had an absolute ball.

I embraced learning and was very fortunate to always get very good and extremely passionate teachers and lecturers. I was now ready to start my very first business, my Kinesiology Clinic. So with great excitement I approached a local natural health clinic and asked if they would like a kinesiologist to join them and to my great joy they did and so my clinic life began. Slowly I began to build my business content in the knowledge that I could take my time and learn all the business tools gradually. I was still being supported by my family and my primary focus was not the financial side of business, which I found very comforting.

The Universe however had another plan for me! As a part of our family's retirement plans we had invested in a managed share fund with a finance company called Storm Financial. Well this Storm was very similar to the weather, it had many stages starting with the excitement and building of investment stream, followed by the calmness of the "eye" followed by the crash and thump of the storm and lastly the aftermath as it petered out whilst leaving in its trail utter destruction and despair!

Suddenly and without warning our retirement plans and our financial security was gone. Here one moment gone the next, and with it my slow building of the clinic. It now it had to be a financial concern. When one wishes to be successful, you must mix with other successful people, so began my next stage of learning. I found others who had already mastered the business side of life and mixed with them, I joined network groups who inspired and led by example. I began to embrace technology as a means of promoting myself and my clinic, learning to use social media tools such as FaceBook, Twitter and LinkedIn all the while building my profile as an expert in my field. I looked for and found mentors who would hold me accountable for my goals and vision for my clinic.

Kinique Kinesiology is now a successful busy home based natural therapy clinic and I am still learning as I travel through life's journey. We have weathered many storms some natural and some man-made, the key is love, faith and hope. Love who you are and what you do and this keeps hope and faith alive.

3 Tips To Stay Focused On Your Dreams

Always align yourself with your core self beliefs. Love who you are and what you are achieving.

Make yourself and your goals accountable and declare your intentions out aloud to others.

Give yourself permission to not always be perfect, allow room for growth and learning. It is far better to take action and have a go than to regret doing nothing.

Janet Beckers

About The Author

Marney Perna is principle of Kinique Kinesiology, a boutique natural therapy clinic. Her formal qualifications are Diploma of Kinesiology, as well as many advanced Kinesiology and Nutrition subjects, however many of her skills have been learned from the University of Life. Marney specializes in trauma recovery especially emotional trauma which in turns affects structural integrity. A passionate practitioner Marney encourages everyone to be 100% responsible for their own health care journey and to assist with this holds regular workshops to teach self care techniques. Marney is a keen family person and loves spending her time with her husband and her three young adult children. Marney's parents also live in a granny flat on their family property along with two dogs and a rainbow lorikeet. As well as learning new skills, Marney's also loves and enjoys regular episodes of Retail Therapy especially when accompanied by close friends and family.

Special Gift

Please accept this complimentary report on how to "Ten Simple Steps to De-fuse the Stress in Your Life" go to http://www.kinique.com

http://www.kinique.com

The Authentic You

Meg Ringrose

Some of the words defining authentic in the Oxford English Dictionary are "real"; "actual"; "reliable"; "trustworthy"; "sincere"; "genuine". Are you able to apply any of these definitions to your own personal characteristics? You'll know if you do because there'll be a feeling of peaceful determination in your day to day life knowing that every connection with someone, and every act you do comes from that good place in your spirit and is serving everyone you connect with to the best outcome. Not only is it an empowering way to live and interact with family, friends and acquaintances day to day. But did you know that an authentic approach to your business is a rewarding route to guaranteed long term success.

Do you remember a time when you saw a movie that you absolutely loved to the point where you wanted to tell everyone you cared for to go see it?. Why did you want your friends and family to see that movie so much?? Because you genuinely wanted them to have the same uplifting (or enlightening as the case may be) experience as you. Or maybe you tried a product that really worked for you and you just couldn't wait to tell your best friend about it. Why? Because you want to share your experience of the fantastic results and feel the same emotion.

In these examples you are able to thoroughly recommend these products and services because you know without a shadow of doubt that they had a positive impact on you. Now think about how you feel when you recommend a product or service that you're not really completely happy about – perhaps it doesn't quite come up to your expectations, or maybe - a quick fix that didn't quite go the distance – but there's a dollar or two in it if you can convince someone else to purchase it. Can you imagine these two different scenarios?

In the first instance your motivation for recommending the product or service is a genuine desire to make a difference to someone's life and/or for your friends and loved ones to get that same wonderful feeling that you did from the experience. The second is to make money. The first example will leave you with a rewarding feeling of having improved someone's life, perhaps by empowering them to greater heights ,even if in a small way; of sharing an experience; and of developing an ongoing relationship with that person on common ground. As for the second example, well sometimes, for one or many reasons we are loathe to let others see our real selves.

The most common reason I've found for this is that we don't feel we are good enough. Perhaps we try to "fake it till we make it". I'm not a big fan of this philosophy. I've known many people who find it easier to continue to "fake it" than to make the decision to do take a look at themselves and make the decision to find their genuine persona. I've come across many people over the 20 or so years that I've been a Multi Level Marketer who work in this way. I've found that, sure, they might rapidly build a large business but alas many of their good people fall by the wayside when they see that their uplines aren't as genuinely committed to the business as they would have their networks to believe. In my experience the successful leaders are those who are committed to the people in their business and also to the authenticity of their products.

I personally have been marketing a range of Australian skin care products for over 20 years. Before I committed to these products I researched not only the ingredients, but the company behind them and their corporate philosophy, and I visited the manufacturing laboratory to see how the products were formulated. I've been using the range now for all that time and I wouldn't trust anything else. So you see I can stand by my product and the marketing company 100% and every person I speak to about my products can feel that trust and commitment. You'll find my product range here If you don't feel you can stand behind your product or service 100%, in other words, if you can't truly confess that you use it and live by it every day, then don't promote it. I'm always mindful of one of Oprah Winfrey's favourite sayings –"doubt means don't".

The Power of 100

If you have the slightest doubt about the authenticity of an idea or product you are considering promoting – then don't. If you genuinely feel that you can expect for others the success that you've had for yourself then go ahead and promote to your heart's content. Your authenticity, your genuineness will shine through. If you decide you want to live a more authentic life you may need some assistance or encouragement to lift your self esteem, become more empowered, find your inner peace. You are fortunate to have lots of help right here in the pages of this book.

Whether you feel you need some coaching or mentoring, or to become part of our community of successful, supporting women you'll find the right path for you. Success will be so much sweeter if you know in your heart it has evolved from you being the authentic you.

3 Tips To Stay Focused On Your Dreams

Find a mentor or supportive friend to encourage you to find your true self.

Research and market your product or service thoroughly - use theinternet to tap into blogs about similar products to find out what people arre saying about them. phone manufacturers and quiz them about their ingredients and practices. If you find a product doesn't fit with your true ethics then keep researching until you find the one that feels right and let customers know that this is your practice.

Mix with likeminded people who will encourage uplift and support you. For example join and online community like wonderfulweb. You never know you might become a published author one day - like I have!

Janet Beckers

About The Author

Hi I'm Meg, I became involved with an MLM company marketing their beautiful Aloe Vera based natural skin care range around 25 years ago on a part time basis. My life has taken many twists and turns resulting in several career changes. I'm a qualified hairdresser and have owned hairdressing businesses, I've dabbled in real estate, event management, wedding reception coordinating and more recently over the last 15 years been involved in administration within the legal profession and the justice system. My life has been truly blessed with two beautiful children and now a gorgeous granddaughter. I need more hours in my day, I have so much more that I want to achieve! So I continue to promote my skin care range whilst developing my internet lifestyle business. I live with my husband John in a beautiful bushland suburb of Sydney and I just love my life.

http://www.thebestyears.com.au http://www.bbeautiful.promastore.com.au

The Woman Entrepreneur

Melinda Boyer

The Woman Entrepreneur

The obstacles in life can sometimes hinder you from where you really want to go. In 1995 I had decided to go back to school and take classes that I felt I would enjoy.

I am a people person and had always enjoyed working with numbers so when I went to work for a bank it was a natural fit for me. It seemed to me like a perfect environment, I got to work with numbers which was fun and had a chance to mingle with the public which I highly enjoyed. However, that all changed the day I was robbed. That experience began to change my perception of my job and the environment I worked in completely. When people would walk in the bank I would now look at them as if they were there to rob the place. Fear had taken my perception of reality and began to distort it so that my actions and judgments were affected. In essence, fear started holding me back from enjoying my job and life. I share this story with you to help you understand that fear cannot only distort your reality but hold you back from pursuing your dreams.

Janet Beckers

My Dream

My working career started at the young age of 16 years old. For the next 25 years I found myself working for someone else. Howbeit, I worked for a number of great companies never the less; I was building someone else's dream. There are many great advantages to working for good companies or corporate America, and for some that is a perfect fit. But for millions of women like myself, there is an Entrepreneur inside wanting to be let loose and express itself. If you are a Women Entrepreneur or desire to be one, no matter how great a company you work for, there is still that deep longing inside that something is missing. That something is your inward desire to make your entrepreneurial mark in the world. The global way the world does business today makes being a successful entrepreneur easier than ever before. The opportunities are endless. Unlike 25 to 30 years ago where breaking out on your own usually required a big monetary investment and very high risk, today you can start a profitable business for $500.00 or less and turn that into a six figure income in a very short time.

What does it take to be a Woman Entrepreneur? The first step is to change your mindset from a pay check mentality to a profit mentality. Having worked the majority of my life for corporate America, my paradigm was that you had to have a JOB to survive in this world. To venture out in your own business was so scary and out of my comfort zone that I was paralyzed in my mind even though my heart knew that is the direction I wanted to go.

When my husband and I started our company, because he had been an Entrepreneur all his life, the first area he had me work on was my mindset change. Even though our company was making more money in one month than I was making in an entire year, I still had that fear. For 3 months I worked harder on myself, changing my paradigms and mindset than I did on our business. But once my mindset went from a pay check mentality to a profit mentality I felt right at home and I have never looked back.

Follow your Dream

Following your dreams may require you to do some real soul searching. There will be no doubt that as you purse your business dreams or even your life dreams, there will be times when that journey seems too hard to follow and everything inside you cries out to stop and to give up. That is when you need to dig deep within yourself and realize that you made a commitment that no matter how many times you get knocked down, you will arise and keep going forward. Is following your dream always easy? No, but I have found that the reward of your dream is worth the price of every valley and hard spot you must face. When your dream is big enough and your passion strong enough you can find a way to overcome every fear and obstacle that stands between you and that dream. The last year on my job, right before I decided to come home and really take on the role of a Woman Entrepreneur and help build our business to a million dollar corporation, I had 10 years of the corporate world under my belt.

Although I was fed up with that work environment, and I was in a position where they kept changing my position and department every quarter, there was a fear to leave it. I found myself addicted to misery due to my thoughts of "What if this Entrepreneurial venture does not work?" All my benefits will be gone, and that nasty thing called a weekly pay check will be gone too! What I now realize was all that misery and change that was going on in my job was really the Universe giving me the signs that it was time to get out of that environment and follow my dreams. How about you? What sign is the Universe giving you today? One of the best things I can share with you is that having success in life, whether it is in the arena of finances, business, home, health or relationships, is not a by-product of luck or good fortune but the end result of understanding the basic laws of life.

If you are going to achieve your goals and attain your dreams you will have to implement 3 important factors.

1. Upgrade your associations

Ask yourself, "Is this the team that will get me to my dream?" If the answer is no, you must upgrade those you surround yourself with which include your mentors, associates, business partners and friends. An important element you must understand is, "Who you listen to will determine what you have, what you get, and where you will end up" and that is a powerful thing!

2. Enlarge your thinking

You must see yourself mentally as a successful Woman Entrepreneur before you will ever experience it in your physical world. Remember, you cannot think like a poor person and expect to live like a rich person. You cannot think small and expect to live large.

Janet Beckers

Being short on money or resources does not prevent you to think like a millionaire. And thinking like a millionaire is what will change your bank account balance to a positive mode. The power of your thoughts can change every negative condition in your life to a state where your conditions reflect that which you truly desire. All success begins in your thoughts; however, your thoughts are where all failure starts as well. Enlarge your thinking to only think on things you want, and not allow them to focus on what you do not want. Your thoughts belong to you...choose them wisely.

3. Be visible in the market place

It is not the size of your product, but the size of your market presence that determines the size of your bank account. Do you realize that there are millions of people who want what you sell? No matter what you do, someone is doing the same thing and getting rich from it. The only reason people are not knocking your door down and stuffing your bank account full of cash is they do not know how to find you. You are walking around in the market place of business like the invisible man. To make matters worse, you are making yourself visible to the wrong people, those that do not want our product, or do want it but cannot afford it. The best way in my opinion and from our experience in business to turn a huge profit in your company or finances is to make yourself well known so that people that are pre-sold, (those who want and can afford your product) can find you. Every co-author in the Power of Mentorship book series has leveraged their market presence to maximum exposure.

In the last 18 months we have put over 49,000 Power of Mentorship books into the market place worldwide. Do you think your business might increase if your contact information, photo and story were put in front of 49,000 people who would qualify as your target market?

This is the epitome of being visible in the market place in order that your pre-sold customers can find you and fill your bank account to overflowing. In closing let me just say, if you have the desire, are willing to muster up you the courage and surround yourself with good mentors, you can be a successful Women Entrepreneur! Dream, Believe, & Achieve

The Power of 100

3 Tips To Stay Focused On Your Dreams

1. Upgrade your associations
2. Enlarge your thinking
3. Be visible in the market place -   Dream - Believe & Achieve

About The Author

Melinda Boyer is an outstanding business entrepreneur, writer and speaker. She co-founded Real Life Teaching Inc. which created the best-selling Power of Mentorship book series and produced three hit movies "The Power of Mentorship-The Movie" and "The Art of Business for the 21st Century" and the recent movie production of The Journey featuring such prominent leaders as Brian Tracy, Bob Proctor, Marie Diamond, Vic Johnson, and Lisa Jimenez.   She has appeared on numerous radio shows and is a frequent guest on the Wright Place TV show that airs into more than 3 million homes in the greater Los Angeles area. Using her education in accounting, her interior design skills and sound business principles she was able to build the Power of Mentorship Training Center which is the hub of their teaching and seminar division hosting boot camps and training seminars in the area of success and personal development.

Special Gift

Audio download, Make your Money Go Up as the Economy Goes Down. Contact info@donboyer.org

http://www.thejourneymovie.net/   http://www.realifeteaching.com/
http://thepowerofmentorship.com/

Janet Beckers

Leap of Faith

Melissa Groom

I am the Founder/Host and Producer of Toddlers To Teens Parent TV Show. A web-based show that provides free parenting advice on our weekly shows which you can watch in your own time. I have three beautiful children who are the love of my life. Nicholas has a lifelong kidney condition, Grace is Anaphylactic, and Matthew has Aspergers, ADHD, and ODD. We have a few extra little challenges which have been the major catalyst for me re-educating myself to take the leap of faith and become an entrepreneur.

To overcome childcare costs we hired a live in aupair in exchange for childcare. I did a mortgage broking course and went out to work full time. I brought a home on my own, renovated it and added a granny flat for some extra income. I needed a second job at night as a waitress. The children didn't see me and when they did I was cranky and tired. I ended up selling the house. The stress was having a negative impact on my health. I started a business teaching children etiquette and manners and I spent a lot of money setting up a web-site, and getting all the marketing material together.

I soon realised my business did not fit around my family circumstances. In 2010 Nicholas' kidney condition deteriorated and he had to have a life saving kidney transplant. We spent six weeks up at the Mater Children's Hospital and Ronald

McDonald House. The transplant was a success. Without my other two children to care for and no chores to do I had a lot of time on my hands to think. I jumped on the Women's Network Australia Linked In Group and asked, "I'm starting an on-line parenting TV Show, who wants to contribute?"

Within hours I had my panel of experts. And that is the story of how Toddlers To Teens Parent TV Show was born. In 2 ½ months Toddlers To Teens is now being watched in 8 countries around the world. We have had over 50,000 views on our Facebook page and are growing bigger daily. We support other mums in business. I do guest interviews with mums who have their own home business. We hope to help others grow their business or help start an online business.

We support parents who need advice, or feel isolated, whether they live in remote areas, have children with health issues, or work-fulltime. No one should ever feel alone. Tips and Tricks to Keep Myself Focus and Motivated I printed out a time management plan which I have synchronised with my diary and blackberry. I review my following day in my diary the night before. I check it first thing in the morning. I have set times I check my emails, Facebook and Linked In. I break down my task into smaller tasks. I have to say with all honesty that my biggest motivators for keeping focused are my past experiences of having to live off government payments and having to sell my home to feed my children.

What Do You Do In The Morning To Stay Focused?

I stay focused by having structure and routine in my day. I rise before everyone. I then quickly review my list of things to do, go for a walk, and I remind myself of what I am grateful for. I visualize where I want to be in my life and what I am aiming for. I have a very clear picture of what I want my life to be like in 1-2 years and that is, to be in my own home, travelling the country speaking at events, having multiple forms of income streams to support my family, taking my family on holidays, specifically the kids to Disneyland and winning Telstra Business Women of the Year. I visualize these things every day. They are on my vision board. I eat a healthy breakfast, make lunches and prepare dinner. I have a shower and dress for success. It puts me in the right mindset.

Janet Beckers

What Do You Do When You Have Feelings of Doubt?

I typed up some positive affirmations, printed and cut them out, and laminated them. I read them in times of doubt. It really works. I look at my vision board and remind myself of why I am doing this.

1.To help others

2. To provide financially for my children and

3. I remind myself of the times I worked two jobs to put food on the table and pay the mortgage and then had to sell our family home.

I also go and read my book. They are all inspiring stories of people that I never get sick of reading about. I am currently reading Ms Millioanaire which is so inspiring. Do You Have A Way Of Keeping Your Vision Alive? I keep my big vision alive by visualizing the end goal. I also work backwards from visualizing my end goal and then breaking it up into parts. E.g. I want to go on a holiday, it's going to cost $5000. I need to put away $100 a week into a bank account. I am going to do X, Y, Z to find that $100 a week. I am doing the same with my business. I go to inspiring and motivating events and take action after them.

How Do You Get Organised?

I am the organizing queen. Everything has a place. Having three children with their own medication and dietary needs and having to rush off to the hospital unexpectedly in the past have made me become super organised. I do most of my shopping on-line. There is a file for everything. I pull out the meat for dinner the night before. I prepare all meals in the morning, ie. Lunches, snacks and dinner. I do the washing and ironing everyday and break the housework up and get the children to pitch in and do their share to earn their pocket money. My Dream is to have multiple income streams, do public speaking and get paid to do it. Win Telstra Business Women of the Year in 2012. To own a retreat for people with major health issues and low incomes to come and have some reprieve.

3 Tips To Stay Focused On Your Dreams

Get a business coach - they keep you accountable and on track.

Build Your Profile on-line constantly - Network on and offline, especially with your mentors, write articles and submit everywhere, ask and answer questions on blogs, collaborate with other people on their projects.

Put Systems in place, be consistent and persist.

About The Author

Melissa is the mother to 3 children who all have special needs and partner of Glen Spargo. Through her many challenges in life Melissa has managed to turn them all into a positive, learning and growing from each one of them and wants to share her life skills with others. From adoption, to incest, to taking her perpetrators to court, moving frequently during her childhood, to mis-carriage, divorce, to being blessed with children with a life-long kidney condition, Anaphylaxis, Aspergers and ADHD, to re-uniting with her natural mother and siblings after 30+ years and now to searching for her natural father, Melissa hopes to reach out to others who are struggling, through Toddlers To Teens TV Show. She is passionate about helping others be their best self. She feels no one ought to be alone. "One needs to look after themselves, otherwise we are no good to anyone."

Special Gift

1 Page Advertorial in our virtual "Toddlers To Teens Parent Magazine" Please email melissa@toddlerstoteens.tv with the subject Free Advertorial/Janet Beckers

http://www.toddlerstoteens.tv

Janet Beckers

The Sweetness of Giving Dangerously

Michele DeKinder-Smith

A constant theme in my life is the importance of giving, and I'm at a time in my life where I want to Give Dangerously. In this context, I'm thinking of danger in terms of taking a risk, because I believe that without risk, there's far less reward. We can be safe and comfortable, or we can be bold and glorious.

I've always believed in giving, and giving a lot. The success of my first business, which broke a million in revenue a few years ago, was totally built on the concept of giving. At first, I gave outstanding service and informative research very fast and inexpensively (compared to my competition).

Later, I learned that my clients weren't buying fast or cheap, they were buying what I was unconsciously giving – myself. They came back again and again because I gave so much care to their businesses, to our relationships, and to helping them achieve their goals. I learned that sometimes what you think you're selling is not at all what your customer is actually buying.

Once I learned the lesson that my clients were actually buying my care, compassion, understanding, and attention, I stopped racing around trying to be the fastest and cheapest. I focused instead on giving as much as I could to each individual, and the business grew rich in deep, long-term trusting partnerships.

Along the way, I realized I loved giving so much, I wanted to help even more people, especially other women business owners. If there was anything I could do or say that would help another business owner on her journey, that was in turn a gift to me, just knowing I made a difference. Jane Out of the Box was born.

All births are beautiful and exciting, and also ripe with danger. Soon after launching Jane Out of the Box, I fell into the trap so many Janes do and I forgot what I learned the first time. I was racing around trying to build everything at once. I was giving and giving so much I grew tired. I had so much to learn and I began to confuse the gaps in my knowledge with gaps in myself, which in turn caused me to doubt whether I was even worthy of this big new dream. I focused on what I was doing wrong instead of what I was doing right; every day I struggled with the question, "Who am I to be doing this?"

But after a year of personal growth, I came to understand: If you want to give a lot, you must also be willing and able to receive a lot. Think about it! Imagine you are a big beautiful bucket of yummy giving-ness. You scoop out some for Sally, and Tim, and Crystal, and Sharon, and John. Your bucket of yummy giving is getting emptied out. If you're anything like me, you wait until all you have left is a tiny eyedropper and you have to tilt the bucket to squeeze out one tiny drop so you can give some more. And then you're empty. You have nothing left. Your giving is done.

The "obvious" answer – and one I have taught for a long time – is to practice self-care. With self-care strategies, you ladle for Sally and Tim, and then you go down to the river and get a fresh ladle there and put it into your own bucket. So as you're emptying, you're simultaneously working to fill yourself back up. As women, in particular, it's important to do this, because really, what we're doing with that trip to the hypothetical river, is giving to ourselves. It's critically important to do that because if YOU can't respect you, who will?

But now imagine this. If you want to Give Dangerously, risk it all, pour your whole heart into giving, what you really need to do is to let OTHER people ladle from the river too, and help you fill your bucket back up. Think how much FASTER you could be full! Consider how much EASIER not to have to make all those trips yourself!

Janet Beckers

Maybe it seems obvious to you, reading this, but it took me 43 years to get it, and only then reluctantly. All these years, I've helped and helped, but when anyone asked how they could help me in return, my standard response was to say, "Thank you, but I'm fine. Really." Until recently, when I was fortunate to be surrounded by people so determined to give to me that I had to force myself to let them. And it is from these loving friends and associates, the Givers as I'll call them, that I learned my biggest lesson about giving.

I realized over the past few months that it is the empty bucket that prevents us from giving all we can. The empty bucket causes us to play small, because it makes us both afraid of failing (we aren't worthy) and of succeeding (too much demand for the bucket). Trapped on both ends! That darned old empty bucket problem has gotten me every time in my life – until NOW. Now I know how I can always keep my bucket full – by being willing to receive from all the amazing people in my life. Knowing I don't ever have to run out of giving-ness has made me feel a little reckless. It's caused me to want to give dangerously! I'm even launching a foundation this year to help women business owners in a whole new way.

I'm vowing my commitment to give dangerously. Will you join me? Are you ready to take a risk, one that means allowing yourself to receive?

3 Tips To Stay Focused On Your Dreams

Get clear on what you have to offer.

Commit to growing your business by being of service to others.

Allow other people to give back to you, so you can keep on giving!

About The Author

Michele DeKinder-Smith is the founder and CEO of Linkage Research, Inc, a marketing research firm with Fortune 500 clients such as Starbucks, Frito Lay, Tropicana, Texas Instruments, Hoover Vacuums and Verizon Wireless. She parlayed this entrepreneurial knowledge and experience into founding Jane Out of the Box, a company that provides female entrepreneurs like YOU with powerful resources, such as educational blogs, teleclasses, newsletters, events, and books. Michele also owns

Team Women, Inc., a networking organization for women business owners with chapters nationwide. Michele is the author of See Jane Succeed: Five Types of Female Entrepreneurs Reveal What it Takes to Win in Business and in Life and co-author of See Jane Collaborate. Learn more about Michele and her companies by visiting www.JaneOutoftheBox.com and www.TeamWomenInc.com,

Special Gift

Take the complimentary Which Jane Are You? assessment to find out your business type! Visit www.janeoutofthebox.com.

http://www.janeoutofthebox.com

3 Simple Secrets to Stay Focused on Your Business So You Start Making BIG Money (AND Get Your Brilliance Out in the World in a BIG Way)

Michele PW (Pariza Wacek)

Last year I hit a big financial milestone in my business. Now, I'm not telling you this to brag. I'm telling you this because I want this for you, and I believe you can do it too. Look, I made every mistake in the book (and probably even a few that aren't in the book). I also probably started my business exactly the way you did -- as a solopreneur. In 1998 I started out as a freelancer copywriter, which basically meant I created a job for myself. The problem with that is because I was the one actually doing the work, the marketing part of my business was hit or miss (sound familiar?).

I created a horrible feast/famine cycle for myself and that was my life for years. It was 2005 that I finally decided I needed a different business model. The problem was I had no idea what it would look like or how to do it. Other writers were no help, they had the same business I had. So after a lot of struggling and flailing around, I finally got it together and started generating the success and income I had always dreamed of. What did I do? The first thing I did was start taking time to work ON my business rather than IN my business. Only then could I take a big picture view of what was going on and start making the necessary changes.

So how do you do that? Where do you start? Below are 3 tips to help you get focused and ready to shine!

1. Make sure you celebrate your past success

This one isn't easy for me to do either (much easier to make a list of all the things I want to get done). But if you don't celebrate what you DID accomplish, what would be the motivation for achieving your future goals? You need to give yourself a pat on the back. You deserve it! (And be honest, when was the last time you gave yourself any sort of credit?) Here's what I would suggest doing -- get a piece of paper and write down 50 things you accomplished in the past. Yes I said 50. And no I won't take "but I didn't accomplish 50 things" as an answer. You see, by setting an intention to come up with 50 means you're not going to stop at 3 and miss a bunch that you really need to congratulate yourself for. Next, celebrate! Buy yourself a nice cup of coffee, sit in a bathtub or call up a friend or associate and tell them what you accomplished. Let yourself feel good about what you accomplished -- you did good!

2. Write down your goals for the next 12 months

This is important -- especially the writing down part. If you don't write them down, the chances of you actually accomplishing them are pretty unlikely. In fact, it's pretty close to zero. According to a famous study of Harvard graduates, less than 5 percent of those who didn't write down their goals actually accomplished them. And don't rush this either. I'm not going to give you a number to hit, but take some time and actually think about what you want to accomplish in the next 12 months. And make them specific -- don't just say "make more money." Put a number in there -- how much money do you want to make. Even better, write down how you plan to

Janet Beckers

make more money -- launch a new product? Get X number of people into your coaching program?

3. Now break down your goals into steps

This is probably the biggest thing you can do to make sure you actually achieve your goals. The more specific you make your goals and the more you break them down into doable action steps, the easier it's going to be to follow through with them. So for instance, with the "make more money" goal, break it down into how you're going to make more money -- like launch a product or get your coaching program going. Get your calendar out and put those milestones in your calendar so you know what you're shooting for. Now the idea here isn't to make this a big, difficult task. Have fun with it. You're planning your business and you can turn it into anything you want it to be! This is exciting! Take time to enjoy the process. This is your life and your business -- you should be able to transform it into exactly what you want it to be.

3 Tips To Stay Focused On Your Dreams

Make sure you celebrate your past success.

Write down your goals for the next 12 months.

Now break down your goals into steps.

About The Author

Imagine: Your potential customers transforming into actual customers...all without you lifting a finger. Sound too good to be true? It's not...when you hire Michele PW (Michele Pariza Wacek) Your $Ka-Ching!$ Marketing Strategist. What Michele specializes in is writing copy and creating marketing campaigns that gets people to TAKE ACTION, whatever that action may be (signing up for your newsletter, buying a product, hiring you etc.). In fact, Michele has mastered psychological and hypnotic techniques designed to persuade your target market to become your customers. She also specializes in warm Web 2.0 traffic strategies that will bring a flood of hungry visitors to your Web site who want to buy exactly what you sell! Whether it's online or offline you need, Michele PW knows how to Rev Up Your Results!

Special Gift

Want to Transform Your Web Site Into a Cash Machine? Michele PW is offering a FREE Copywriting Rescue Kit! By implementing just a few of these steps, you WILL start seeing better results. If you'd like to learn more secrets and make more money through better copy, download my Copywriting Rescue Kit below, which includes: * A free 13-page white paper on how to get more leads, customers and sales through powerful copywriting tools and techniques. You'll learn my secrets on how I get fantastic results for my clients, like Lisa Sasevich, Ali Brown, Alex Mandossian, Brian Tracy and John Assaraf. * "5 Psychological Triggers to Turn Prospects Into Clients" mp3 audio download * "5 Secrets To Getting All The Business You Can Handle No Matter What the Economy is Doing" mp3 audio download. http://www.michelepw.com/freegift

http://www.michelepw.com

Janet Beckers

Self-Love - Would That Change Anything? Or Everything ...

Michelle Marie McGrath

Self-love – would that change anything? Or everything? Self-love. It's interesting to notice the different reactions that these words can bring up to the surface. Some common reactions are 'well isn't that selfish, me-me-me, a bit narcissistic.' We seem to be more comfortable with constantly putting others first, trying to juggle a myriad of family obligations and work responsibilities with barely a moment to ourselves as we race from one thing to the next. We wonder why we can't remember what our dreams were and don't even know what our passions are. Then we express dismay at the rising numbers of divorce, various cancers, heart disease, eating disorders, depression, numerous mental health issues and suicide. If you are down the road and en route to one of these problems, then what use will you be to anyone else?

Do you remember learning health and wellbeing life-skills when you were at school? I certainly do not. Self-love is not selfish. It's vital. It's self-responsibility. Accepting that YOU and you alone are responsible for your own happiness and fulfillment. No-one else can do that for you. No-one. Not your partner, not your parents, not your children and not your friends. It's up to you. Yet how often do we blame those significant others in our lives and project unrealistic expectations onto them, because we are not happy with the way our lives are unfolding. You can change this situation in an instant. Make a commitment to yourself right now, to take full responsibility for your own well-being and your own happiness. That decision is one of the most empowering you will ever make.

I made a commitment to myself several years ago to open myself up to 100% self-love. Little did I know the deeply buried horrors and treats that would reveal themselves to me, layer by layer by layer. Yet it was the wisest decision I ever made and the actions I have taken as a result of that, have changed the way I feel about myself and the world around me immeasurably. It's incredible and also wonderful about the impact that one small step can have and how our perception of our situation can change in a moment.

Is it time to stop playing the blame game and notice where you may be behaving like a victim? Everyone has challenges in their lives, but we can always decide how to react and respond. There is always a choice. This means not blaming everything on your parents, your upbringing, your children, your partner, your job, your colleagues, the weather, or whether or not the stars are aligned. Self-love is letting go of the victim mentality and attachment to 'the story'. Let's be honest, we've all got our stories and very strong emotional attachment to our interpretation of events in our lives, based on our personal filters and life experiences. Choose right now to let go of the justifications and excuses for why you may not always be making choices that fully honour and support your needs. Let go of your stories about the past. Allow yourself to live in this moment. This is where all your power resides.

Of course this can be challenging and takes practice, but just imagine how much energy and time you can free up. As Byron Katie asks "who would you be without your story?" A few years ago I started to use affirmations regularly. I would stick post-it notes in my wallet, on my bathroom mirror and also have one at my desk at work. Phrases such as "I am exactly where I am meant to be and accepting of all of me", "All of my power is in this moment", "Nothing to do, nothing to be, except me", "I am unique, I am one of kind, I allow magic to flow from my heart and mind." These served as reminders to change my flow of thoughts if I was feeling a bit depressed and sorry for myself. This then lead to creating the Self-love cards, which are part of the Sacred Self range.

Janet Beckers

I know that talk of the use of affirmations can seem as though it's oversimplifying, but it's just a reminder to change the direction of your thoughts and bring yourself into a more positive space. These are quick, easy reminders that can give you an immediate pick-me-up and change your energy in a moment. What could you do that would immediately make you feel better? Maybe you could create a lnourishing dinner for yourself or write down a list of all your positive qualities, in the way a friend would describe you. Another easy thing to do is when you are in the shower, imagine the water is full of pink light, washing over you and re-energising you with self-love. Ask yourself now 'what decision can I make today that would move me a step forward in a more empowering direction?

The purpose of this is not to be self-critical. It's about developing more self-awareness, so that you can learn to honour your feelings more and trust yourself. Get very accustomed to noticing how your body feels in response to your thoughts, words and actions. The more awareness you experience, the easier it will become to recognise which decisions are in your best interest. When faced with a decision that you are unsure about, stop for a moment.

Take a deep breath and just notice when you consider your decision, does it make you feel contracted or expanded? Just notice and allow this sensation to make your decision for you. Then you will become clearer and clearer and automatically move more towards what feels right for you and your happiness. Embrace your uniqueness and also acknowledge how much the same we all are.

We all want to be loved and accepted for who we are – that is a given. So do yourself a favour (and everyone around you) and make a commitment to the journey of loving and accepting yourself now. Exactly as you are right now. You deserve it. Treat yourself as though you were your own best friend. Make a decision today to demonstrate how you want to be treated – as someone who is loved and valued.

There is no-one on this planet like you. You are irreplaceable and you have your own unique gifts to share with the world. Believe it. Just imagine this – the more love you are able to feel for yourself, the more you will be able to share with others. Win/win.

3 Tips To Stay Focused On Your Dreams

Make a commitment to yourself to take full responsibility for your own happiness. That's your job – no-one can do it for you. Light a candle, grab a notebook and keep an open heart. This is your life we're talking about ... write down your commitment to yourself. Make it official.

Stop playing the blame game. Let go of your 'stories' about the past and choose to explore the possibilities that are available right in this moment. Make peace with the past.

When faced with a decision, ask yourself is this coming from a place of love or fear? Notice if your body feels expanded or contracted. You'll start to develop a stronger connection with yourself the more you practice this and you will feel clearer.

About The Author

Michelle is the creator of Sacred Self's self-love cards and aromatherapy wellbeing perfumes. After looking for love in all the wrong places, she decided to try a different approach. In 2003, she asked herself what she most needed and received the answer 'self-love'. She made a commitment to open herself up to 100% self-love. All sorts of challenging curve balls followed but fortunately, she retained a sense of humour. Hence the arrival of Sacred Self's self-love oil and what followed was a rollercoaster of colourful twists and turns. She began to learn what surrender meant and to see that everything comes back to self-love. After repeatedly experiencing rejection, it started to sink in. Nothing external could be held responsible for her happiness. Sacred Self Alchemical oils (currently 20 of what will be 33 in the range) provide pathways to self-love, through our most challenging aspects. The more we observe and embrace these parts, rather than deny or ignore them, the more inner peace we experience. Michelle is passionate about falling in love with all parts of herself and celebrating all she is - not just the nice bits. This lifelong journey is also about creating self-love products that gently remind others to do the same.

Janet Beckers

Special Gift

Email sacred@sacredself.com.au for your FREE ebook –

7 steps to self-love. For each purchase from the Sacred Self range, I will also send you a FREE sample of the latest Alchemical oil and a card from the box of Self-love cards. Offer limited to once per person for the first 100 people. Contact me via email to order with "The Power of 100" in the subject header.

http://www.sacredself.com.au   http://www.facebook.com/SacredSelf
http://www.twitter.com/sacredselftips

An Inspiring Story From Our Partner Opportunity International and The 1 Million Women Out Of Poverty Project

Zenaida's story (The Phillipines)

Before her first loan seven years ago, Zenaida Guray and her husband lived in a pig pen, with old boxes and sacks their only protection against the weather.

Her only son had left home and Zenaida and her husband were surviving on just Php.150 (A$3.75) a day. Their daily intake of food consisted of no more than a single meal of rice. Their only source of income came under threat after her husband had an accident at his carpentry job, so Zenaida applied to ASKI (Alalay Sa Kaunlaran Sa Gitnang Luzon, the local partner in the Phillipines) for a small loan. With a first loan of Php.5,000 (A$125), Zenaida laid the foundations to lift herself and her husband out of poverty.

Purchasing, raising and selling piglets, she soon added Php.1,550-2,250 (A$39-56) a month to the family's income. "Now I can say that I am really blessed. The blessings that I am receiving are far past my expectations ... the loan that they offer is really very helpful," says Zenaida.

Zenaida now owns four sows and thirteen piglets, allowing her the financial freedom to continually improve her family's quality of life. Last year, with the help of another small loan, Zenaida and her husband established a small fish farm, which has further increased their income.

Now on her fourteenth loan cycle with ASKI and living in a house of her own, Zenaida is saving to buy a small piece of land and build a boarding house.

In just seven years, Zenaida has progressed from struggling to survive in a pig pen to providing accommodation for other people.

You can help families just Zenaida's by donating at www.WonderfulWebWomen.com/recommends/opportunity

Janet Beckers

Art of Adventure/ Adventure of Art

Nerida Osborne

Growing up in a small coastal village on the east coast of Australia, where after-school activities revolved around the ocean or surrounding bush, the young explorer began to evolve. It was a safe place to go off exploring, generally with one of my 5 siblings, surfing, beach combing or fishing. There was no influence of fashion trends or keeping up with what anyone else did in their lives. It was a great freedom lifestyle.

To this day people tell me I have a very free spirit. I did well at school and moved away from home to attend university. I studied some art courses during my teacher training which was to become the turning point in my life. I completed my teacher training to find a glut of teachers in Australia so I set up a pottery studio in my home town and went to work on creating works selling at local markets. I've taught many students pottery.

I was fortunate to spend 7 weeks in Japan making pottery alongside 16 other international artists. Somehow I have always managed to travel to many Asian countries on my artists' income. I had always felt a little different, as though I don't fit in with the crowd. As I nurtured my children as a sole parent, I made sure I kept in touch with my creativity and learning, involving myself with many workshops as a participant as well as a tutor; studied business skills and a wide variety of computer skills. After all the years of learning I finally feel comfortable who I am; an artist and adventurer.

Daily focus

Discipline was always a struggle for me on a daily basis until a mentor gave me some great tips:-

- Everyday write out your goals. This doesn't mean read them out...it means write them!

- The clearer the goal, the more power it has.

- "Is what you are doing getting you closer to what you want?"

- What do I need to do to become the person I want to be?

- If you were the CEO of your company looking at your activities, would you be hired or fired? (This is the statement that keeps me aware of my actions.)

- Get in line, stay in line. (Don't jump from one idea to the next and jump back again.)

Keeping the vision

One of my dreams is to show others various art skills so that they can explore creativity. I am aiming towards several art centres where artists from all over the world can stay for a few weeks or months to create works in a new environment. One of the offshoots of this I hope will be to inspire others to get more vitality and peace in their lives; showing what a healthy lifestyle can bring. To keep my vision alive I have a book where I draw images, glue pictures, write my ideas, web links and any other relevant details. I also have the goal written. Each day as I write the goal on a separate piece of paper I visualize the end result. These are short and long term goals.

When I have feelings of doubt I take out a sheet of paper and write out a list of what I am grateful for or look around at my creations and remember that I have many years of experience and that I have plenty to offer. I am grateful for all the learning that I have done as well as many life experiences. I have to remember to be grateful for being true to my individuality and that it is O.K. to be an artist, to be spontaneous and to have fun. I am very cautious with whom I share my vision as it is too easy to have negative feedback from those who do not have the some beliefs or know my strengths. I prefer to only tell when the final stages are coming together unless I know I will have encouragement from the people I share the vision to.

Getting organised.

Being an artist, and a procrastinator I have finally learnt a way to being organized. I have observed when I work most efficiently. For me it is 6am to 9am; 2pmto 6pm and then 9pm to 1am. Of course with a child to get off to school the morning session is broken for an hour, as is the late afternoon session. Having discovered these most productive hours I use the other times to do chores, exercise, socialize, repairs etc.

To stay on task I do the following:

- Firstly I need to know the deadline.
- List all the steps that need to be done.
- Breakdown each step into smaller steps if need be.
- Estimate the time required to do each step.
- Make a timeline of the required activities.
- On a calendar/diary write in all tasks to be done, spreading them over a few days if necessary.

Daily.

- Do the most difficult job first. Leaving the easier tasks to last.
- Prioritize what has to be done.
- Exercise at least 20 min.
- Give thanks at the end of every day i.e; gratitude.

3 Tips To Stay Focused On Your Dreams

List at least 200 things you are grateful for.

Every morning write out your goals, (specific and measurable with a date).

Give thanks at the end of the day for all the tasks you have achieved, connections you have made, and gratefulness to be alive

About The Author

Nerida Osborne. Nerida is known for being fully involved with a life of adventure and creativity. Being a sole parent of 2 for the past 20 years has not curbed the enthusiasm for participating in many activities. She trained as a teacher then chose to become a full time ceramic artist. During the past 30 years she has discovered many ways of creating artworks, including photography, printmaking, batik, screen-printing, felting, weaving with fibres, as well as using many other materials. She has exhibited in many exhibitions in Australia and two in Japan. Nerida has a passion for imparting her knowledge and skills and this ensures results are achieved from participants in her workshops. Nerida also loves adventure, exploring new grounds, travel to other countries, caving, surf-board riding, scuba diving, snorkeling, beach walking, bushwalking, camping, finding peace in nature, looking for beauty in all things. She focuses on health and wellbeing, and enjoys good fresh food. She has guided groups to Bali, taking them off the tourist route. She is passionate about helping others discover the artist/adventurer within themselves and to find peace amongst the busyness of life.

Special Gift

A list of ideas to get you creating. Special offer. Mention Wonderful Web Women for a 10% discount on classes, including workshops.

http://www.artistadventures.com.au/gift.html

Janet Beckers

Millionaire Attitude

Pam Brossman

Millionaire Attitude – Pam Brossman CEO Social Media Woman *"Lifestyle is a choice that only YOU can choose. Make sure you choose wisely!"* I knew from a very young age that I was going to be successful. Some people are born with a millionaire attitude and for some people it comes from the desire for a better quality of life. Either way it does not matter, anyone can have the life of their dreams….you just have to want it, believe in it and take action to achieve it. The problem with society these days is most people see the glass half empty instead of seeing it half full. If they only knew that if they put in a little extra effort, that same glass would be overflowing in no time at all. Let me share my story so that you too can strive to have the lifestyle that you deserve and an overflowing glass that just keeps refilling for the rest of your life.

I was born in Canada to a Jamaican mother and an English father. When I was 8 years old my parents decided to move our family to New Zealand and I was very sad. On the morning that we were to leave for the airport, I went in search of my siblings playing down by the lake. I could not find them and sat down amongst the clovers crying because I was so sad to leave the only home I had ever known. As I sat and picked out the clovers in the clover patch, all of a sudden I stopped and looked…one, two, three……four, no it could not be so I counted again, one, two, three, yes there was definitely four leaves. I had found a real four leaf clover.

I was so excited I ran home to confirm it with my Mum and yes I was right. Something shifted inside of me that day. And although I believe people create their own luck, opportunities and lifestyle choices, and that lottery tickets are for lazy people, my belief in myself that I could achieve anything I wanted started with that four leaf clover. These days I believe I was born with that drive to succeed and I spend my life teaching other women to create their own lifestyle choices by taking their expertise and turning it into their own Lifestyle Business Model online.

So how does one turn their dream into a reality you may ask? Here are some tips to help you get started – the rest is up to you!

- Know what you want first - have a clear destination of where you want to go

- Have a reason why – the stronger the 'why' the faster and more determined you will be to reach the goal eg my why….'To give my son the lifestyle he deserves and to help women create more lifestyle choices'

- Create a plan – it is okay to take detours along the way but at least have a starting point and start on the journey to your destination

- Give yourself a deadline to reach that destination – you don't want it to take a lifetime to get there

- Reward yourself along the way – each stop along the way is a milestone on the road to your destination and needs to be acknowledged to keep you heading in the right direction

- When you hit a pothole, learn from your mistake, fix it and keep going

- Create a vision board or a digital vision board (on the computer) that you can look at every day to remind you and keep you passionate and driven

- Hang out with people who are where you want to be - Success leaves clues, and the best place to find those clues is hanging out, associating, learning from those who are already at your destination

- Fake it till you make it – some people disagree with this and believe it is not authentic – has nothing to do with authenticity it is about mindset.

It is about self belief that you can do it by living it already. 10 years ago I met my husband and before we had our son I told him the lifestyle I wanted. I even created

Janet Beckers

my own millionaire mindset workbook based on every area of my life (my free gift to you, don't forget to claim it, details at the end of my chapter). We were earning a good wage, but not the million dollar wage. But I had been taught to hang out with people that you want to become, and so that is what we did. Moved to a millionaire suburb, drove a BMW (older model) and started hanging out with millionaires.

These days we live in a 6 bedroom home overlooking the ocean, in the same millionaire suburb. We live a millionaire lifestyle and we are creating our very own million dollar business. You can do the same! Have a dream, truly believe you can achieve it, hang out with people who are already there and go and live your dream…..just go do it today! To Your Success Pam Brossman

3 Tips To Stay Focused On Your Dreams

Decide what you want to do - create your why

Look for those people who are already successful at your chosen dream lifestyle

Create a plan on how to start your own journey to that destination

About The Author

After 25 years in the Corporate Communications industry and the birth of her son Hunter, Pam decided the corporate life was no longer for her and went in search of a lifestyle change. Almost by accident she found herself in the world of internet marketing and fell in love with the ability to make money while she slept and still spend quality time with her son. Fast forward 6.5 years and she still loves her online cyber life. Just recently Pam joined forces with her marketing husband Steve Brossman to teach people the power of 'Digital Marketing' and 'Social media Marketing'. Pam has achieved more success through video than any other marketing medium online and is passionate about teaching entrepreneurs and small businesses how to connect with their audience, build a global brand and create a loyal customer following using the power of digital marketing. Pam is the CEO of socialmediawoman.com and recently launched an international online magazine called Social Media Woman. Her vision is to help women all around the world grow their business, their brand and effectively get their message, to their target market, using the power of video and digital marketing. Pam is also a contributing author to the books "Ms Millionaire" and "The Relationship Age" and is a highly sought after international speaker on the topic of video marketing.

Special Gift

Gift: Millionaire Mindset Workbook – Pam is a contributing Author to Ms Millionaire Book as well and would like to share this special gift with you to help you become your very own 'Ms Millionaire' if that is your dream.

http://socialmediawoman.com/msmillionairegift/msmillionaire/

http://www.socialmediawoman.com http://www.sheexperts.com

http://www.magneticdigitalmarketing.com

Janet Beckers

"When All Else Fails…"

Pat Lynch

For most of my life, I prayed for, and longed for, a direct revelation about what I was supposed to contribute in this lifetime. When it came, it was through a vision that happened as part of a process called "holodynamics." I felt blessed, and even though I had no real resources at the time, I was so inspired that I began in attract amazing people with the knowledge and ability to help move things forward. My vision was to give women a larger voice over a greater geographic area, to bring greater balance to the universe.

I started by creating a health program featuring a woman doctor who was syndicated nationally. I attracted a producer from a major broadcasting company and another who had produced programs for NPR. By some miracle, we attracted a short-term advertiser which paid for the initial overhead. My job was to attract terrestrial radio stations and audiences while simultaneously attracting national advertisers to continue the program. In 30 days, we went from zero to 35 radio affiliates nation-wide and had several national sponsors lined up. But, "oops," something happened – the U.S. Congress passed the 1996 Telecommunications Act on our 31st day – and it had the affect of killing our new program.

When I came to an apparent "end of the road," I had to ask myself (and God/The Universe) if it was time to quit – or I had to look for a new road to take me to my goal. I had one more similar dead-end before turning to the Web. Since that time, the road blocks have been lack of needed technology, lack of personnel to do the work, little financial backing – and life – my elderly mother came to live with us and then died 18 months later; my daughter who was distraught over my mother moving in, fell in love and went to live with her boyfriend and his family; and my husband asked for a divorce.

How has it turned out? By keeping our eyes open for what we needed, (and blessed with little capital), we learned how to make "strategic relationships" with people who had the technology we needed but need our ability to market and sell. Through this process, we developed a great media tool that not only helped us move our project forward, but which now helps thousands of people around the world move their projects forward.

Our media (WomensRadio.com, WomensCalendar.org, The WR Music Review, and the WR Music Channel) are the first and the best of their breed, serving thousands of wonderful women leaders. My personal life – my husband (decided to change rather than leave) is my partner and my daughter (who swore she would never do what I was doing) is now the President of our company. Life (God/The Universe) is inscrutable – you just can't really know where things are going to take you or how it will end.

And it's not the goal to "know." The goal is to fill your heart each day. And when all else failed, I would have a talk with God/The Universe, and it went something like this: "If you have something else in mind, or you have someone else you'd prefer to do this work, just let me know – and I'll head to the beaches. So, if something doesn't happen here soon, I'll take that as a sign, and pack for the beaches." Something always seemed to happen to get things back on track -- quickly.

I suppose it was my way to surrender and open for the next thing. After a while, I got more comfortable steering the course outside, from the guidance from within. Initial inspiration is a big help. There's no substitute for hard work and perseverance. But when all else fails, you have to know yourself, your own heart, and have a willingness to listen to what is needed in the moment – even to lay down your project and walk away with a certain knowledge that you will be just fine.

Janet Beckers

3 Tips To Stay Focused On Your Dreams

Never stop searching for your special path – something that compels your heart.

Diligence and perseverance are all they are cracked up to be!

Find your balance and your edge, and be willing to surrender and listen at every moment.

About The Author

In 1969 at the age of 25, Pat was the first woman to begin an advertising agency single-handedly in the South. By 1977, she had been listed twice in The World's Who's Who of Women and most recently in the International Who's Who and Strathmore's Who's Who. In 1996, she began WomensRadio to "give women a greater voice!" WomensRadio, a converging medium, had its beginning on the Web as a rich, content Website for women leaders (www.WomensRadio.com). In 2001, her company also began WomensCalendar (www.WomensCalendar.org). Today it is the largest databank of women's events in the world. In 2003, a stronger branding program was implemented with a site and logo redesign and the launch of the SpeakerSpot, a dynamic speaker referral program was launched. In 2005, the company launched AudioAcrobat®, a unique, easy, and inexpensive, Web-based, audio and video production, streaming and podcasting service. (www.AudioAcrobat.com). In 2009, the company launched an all-new, socially interactive WomensRadio site. In 2010, the WR Music Channel was launched, a free, 24/7, syndicated, all-women's, all music Web radio! Pat is a frequent speaker on the value of opening the media to women's voices. She can be contacted in at 888 658 4635x225 or by email: Pat@WomensRadio.com.

Special Gift

Pat's Gift to You: Pat is offering to the people who respond in the first 30 days, a free Webinar how to use media (both 'terrestrial' media and social media) to promote your products and services successfully, with an emphasis on useful, free or inexpensive online tools and strategies that can help you promote and manage the media you choose, more effectively. Of those who attend, one person will be chosen for a special 3-month, mentorship program.

http://www.WomensRadio.com http://www.WomensCalendar.org

Janet Beckers

Success Comes from Listening to Your Heart

Pat Marcello

In 2003, I was in the process of writing my 10th book, and I'm here to tell you that as great as it is to see your name on the cover of a hardback book, that doesn't mean you're a celebrity or a millionaire, even when your books sit in hundreds of libraries and book stores around the U. S. I will say that I received fairly decent advances for the books I wrote, which were all sold before I even started writing them, but... when it came time to see the royalty checks, they never arrived. At least, not for the first several years.

I had to pay back those advances and the way publishers work accounting, it would be a very long time before any checks came rolling in. So, I had to come up with a process to make the royalty payback happen much sooner, and that's when I stumbled onto Internet marketing. It seemed like a really great way to attract people who might be interested in my books, right? I figured it was my salvation. Well... As we know, doing business online can be quite lucrative, but it takes lots of determination, persistence and learning -- lots and lots of learning.

The very first thing I learned was just because you build it, doesn't mean they'll come. But I was like so many other folks who try to make money online. I thought I knew a whole LOT, stuff that I'd come by from other people and stuff I'd picked up on my own, but still, NOTHING was working. I made very little money online, and things weren't getting any better. I was at a crossroads. Either I figured it all out, or I gave up and walked away. After 2-1/2 years, I had very little to show for all of my efforts!

That year was also the year of The Secret. You remember that movie, right? It was so inspiring, and I just knew that if I stopped listening to other people, who really weren't making a lot online either, and started hearing what the Universe was trying to tell me -- things would work out. So, I had been following a young man online for about two years prior. He was fun and smart, and he'd been doing a series on interviews with big-name marketers, called "List Crusade," and the premise was that he would build a list of 1 million subscribers in six months. Sure I'd heard all the old axioms, "The money's in the list," and "You make $1 for every person on your list each month," but the importance of building a list just never sunk in.

I couldn't wait for those calls to begin each week, and was learning so much that I was interested in everything that young guy did from that time on. His name was Tellman Knudson. I thought it was interesting that his company was called "Overcome Everything," and I was determined to do just that. Right about that soul-searching time for me, something happened. Tellman was having a call that wasn't part of List Crusade. I didn't care; I stayed on and listened to every word. Near the end of that call, Tellman sold his personal coaching program, where you would call into a group coaching session and be able to ask Tellman any question you wished.

As he spoke about the opportunity to become a coaching client, it seemed as though he was speaking directly to me, as if nobody else was on the phone at all. And then, he gave the price -- $500 a month! I choked. I knew that on my meager writerly earnings, that was a huge commitment. Plus, my husband had just finished telling me, "You'll never make a dime online." That made me even more determined. Something inside me said, "Go get that credit card you just paid off. Do it! Don't think, just do it!" And I did. And I started with my first call that week. I figured that if I could just talk to Tellman, my problems would be solved and that I could afford at least a couple of months before I had to quit. But the story gets stranger...

On that very first coaching call, Tellman asked for volunteers for a new program he was starting called "The Traffic Apprentice Program," where you would learn one form of traffic really well and in exchange for the training, drive traffic for Overcome Everything while you learned. Seemed like a good deal to me to be able to work with Tellman one-on-one, right? So, I applied.

Janet Beckers

Nobody was more thrilled than me when Tellman's sister called me the next day and said I'd been accepted as an apprentice. Wow! I figured it was an incredible opportunity, but I had no idea how incredible it would be. Tellman found out I was a professional writer, straight away, and asked me to write articles for him. I became an employee, and... Well... the rest is history.

For the last almost 5 years I've been working with Tellman and his company and am now the Product Development Manager there, and have learned so much from Tellman that I have my own affiliate marketing business and SEO consulting gig on the side. And I feel blessed. The people in our company are some of the smartest, most fun, and honest, hard-working people I've ever known. They're like my family. NONE of it would have happened, if I hadn't done one thing -- listened to my heart and the Universe, and did what it told me I needed to do. Sometimes, you just have to go that way. When you feel something is important or will be important, you should take that leap of faith.

You'll be amazed, but more times than not, it will work for you. If you pass these opportunities by, you'll never know great they could have been for you IF you had only taken that leap of faith. Listen to your heart. Listen to the Universe. Tell it what you want, and then... take action to make it happen. Wishing doesn't help. Hard work and effort in the appropriate direction does. The Secret is truly great, and if you haven't seen it, you should. And yet, you can't just visualize and expect things to work. You have to DO, and then, you'll be amazed at how awesome the results can be.

3 Tips To Stay Focused On Your Dreams

When the Universe speaks... listen.

Search for people who are successful at what you want to do and follow them.

Take action in the direction you want to go to make things happen.

About The Author

Pat Marcello is a professional writer, turned SEO and Blogging ninja. She came online to sell her books, but got caught up in the excitement of Internet Marketing. Two years later, she became a coaching client of Tellman's, who was so impressed with her skills that he asked her to come onboard at Overcome Everything. Today, she is the Product Development Manager for OE. Through her & Tellman's SEO project SpiderLanguage.com she teaches the newest marketers about attaining high rankings with the search engines. Her superhero name is "The Optimzer." Look for her in a search engine listing near you.

Special Gift

Get 10 Secret SEO Strategies for Your Blog that Crush the Competition when you visit http://SpiderLanguage.com

http://SpiderLanguage.com

Four Essential Principles for Turning your Divine Dreams into Everyday Reality

Paula Tarrant

"Dreams come true. Without that possibility, nature would not incite us to have them." - **John Updike**

I like this quote from the writer, John Updike, because it reminds us that our dreams and aspirations are not random. Their existence is intentional. They are a reminder from the world of Spirit of all that we are capable of and all that we are entitled to.

But because our dreams exist in the Unseen World, it sometimes becomes difficult to maintain our hold on them, to keep them in focus. The vision becomes blurry and can easily fade from our awareness if we don't have a way to maintain a crystal clear picture of our deepest desires and keep our dreams alive in our waking lives. A common belief about staying focused on our dreams is that we can achieve them by continuing to take action and move in their direction. This is definitely better than not doing anything at all! But I want to submit for your consideration an alternate paradigm for Dream Fulfillment, and the 4 Essential Principles necessary for this paradigm to be successful.

A New Paradigm

The fact that you are reading this book says something about you. It says you are an action taker. You have an idea about who you are and, even more importantly, you have an idea about who you want to be. And you know that by taking some kind of action step you bring yourself closer to your goals and dreams. I want to honor you for what you are already doing. And I want to open you up to a bigger possibility. That bigger possibility is realized when you recognize that you are Spiritual and Physical. It's when you use Inner Processes that activate you Energy and connection with Spirit and blend them with the Outer Practices of taking action that you begin to accelerate the manifestation of your dreams into your reality.

This is the new paradigm of Dream Fulfillment. Partnering Universal Laws and Spiritual Principles with practical how-to's and resources allows you to tap into an energetic support system that will not only keep your dreams in focus, but will continually act as a compass for making sure you are on your path. If you are like many success minded people, you may even already have spiritual practices that are a part of your life. You may be using meditation, a gratitude practice, or affirmations. You may do visualization, use energy tapping, or do contemplative writing. All of these are powerful portals to your Inner Wisdom and can connect you with the Divine.

Inspired Action

So, if you have learned to be a great action taker, that's great. If you have learned to value your intuition and listen to the still voice within, that's great as well. Now you are going to learn to synergistically blend the two and shift from action to Inspired Action. And what is inspired Action? It's a direct path to your dreams without all of the detours and random side roads that slow you down and make your journey to fulfilling your dreams seem more challenging than it need be.

Inspired action is knowing that you are connecting with people and resources that have been specifically brought into your awareness to move you closer to your dreams. It's taking steps and engaging in work that is authentic to you and your purpose. It's making your choices intentionally, with confidence and clarity. Inspired Action creates momentum.

Partnership and Alignment

One of the benefits of daily spiritual practices is that you not only connect in with your Inner Wisdom, but you become aware of your emotional energy and what kind of energy vibration you are maintaining. I want you to begin to take the time each day to check in with yourself and begin to notice your emotional energy. Are you vibrating low level energy like discouragement, anger, insecurity, or unworthiness? Are you somewhere in the middle with worry, doubt, frustration or pessimism? Or are you vibrating in the high level energies of optimism, enthusiasm, empowerment , appreciation, love and joy?

Wherever you are, you can use your spiritual practice to assess where you are, and begin to move yourself up the emotional scale, and raise your energy vibration. At the same time, as you contemplate the actions you desire to engage in for the day, feel into them for any hesitancy, doubt or disbelief that you are sensing. As much as you can, begin to shift those disbeliefs to empowering beliefs.

You want to align your beliefs with your energy before you begin to take action. It is through this partnership that you will activate the energy that fuels inspired action. Align first. Take action second. Rinse and repeat. This is how you learn to take inspired action. And inspired action will turn your dreams into reality. Your goal is to live the life of your dreams. This is soul work. It takes time, so be patient and be gentle with yourself.

Realizing your dreams requires you to hold the intention and believe in the process over the long term.

4 Essential Principles

There are 4 essential principles for this new Dream Fulfillment Paradigm to be successful. Each one by itself can empower you to stay focused on your dreams and aspirations. Together, they are a powerful formula for manifestation.

1. **Connection to Spirit** Decide that you will be committed to nurturing your connection to the Divine, to your inner wisdom, and to the Universal laws and spiritual principles that govern our existence. Make connection a part of your daily

round. Choose a practice that brings the Sacred into your life in an everyday way that nourishes your Spirit and helps you to hear the still voice within.

2. **Preparation** As you are waiting for your dreams to become real, you have the gift of time for preparation. Use it to acquire the knowledge, skills and connections that will be a part of your dream-come-true-life. Discover your life's purpose and calling if you haven't already. Stay true to what is authentic for you. Do what it takes to "follow your dreams, for as you dream you shall become."

3. **Implementation** You have learned how to partner your Inner Spirit and Outer Self to create Inspired Action. It is said that the Universe loves speed! Be bold! When the opportunities that you have prepared for show up, take inspired action and move forward! You are creating in-the-flow forward momentum when you take inspired action. Be confident that the Divine guidance you are relying on and the preparations you have made are putting you in synchronistic connection with your dreams.

4. **Create a Supportive Environment** You are the heroine of your journey. And the heroine is not meant to make her journey alone, and unaided. There are teachers and mentors, companions and helpers who will encourage you and assist you in staying focused on your dreams and can be a beacon to light the way. Find a mentor who is a little further along the path than you who will inspire you.

As someone once said, ""So many of our dreams at first seem impossible, then they seem improbable, and then, when we summon the will, they soon become inevitable." Be committed and you will be amazed at what you can accomplish. Do what it takes, with bold, inspired action and you will get the results you desire. Your dreams will indeed become your reality.

3 Tips To Stay Focused On Your Dreams

1. Make a commitment to connect with your Inner Wisdom through your spiritual practice.

2. Activate and align your energy and beliefs daily to move you into Inspired Action.

3. Find a mentor who will support and inspire you.

Janet Beckers

About The Author

Paula Tarrant is a certified Spiritual Life Coach and Transformation Expert, writer, speaker, teacher and mentor to women in the midst of life and career transitions who want to know how to make the shift to making a living doing what they love. She helps women awaken their creativity, find their authentic path, and design their authentic work. She is known for her blend of spiritual, practical and creative principles that provide the framework for moving beyond self-doubt and sabotage, creating instead a connection to Spirit, a wholeness of heart, and alignment of purpose. A lifelong student of spiritual teachings and personal empowerment, Paula believes fiercely in the power within each of us to be brilliant, creative and amazing individuals. It's her desire to help others discover that power, and with it the confidence, sense of deep self-knowing and worth and "in-the-flow" forward momentum that empowers them to experience the beauty of a well lived life, that fully expresses their originality and authenticity. Paula offers private coaching and group coaching programs virtually via telephone and Skype with clients all over the world. She is a contributing author of "Law of Attraction In Action, Vol. 3", and is working on a new program called "The Heroine's Journey to Authenticity: Healing Your Heart and Discovering Your Place In The World".

Special Gift

If what you want is a thriving, authentic and empowered life doing work that allows you to make a positive difference in the world, then I invite you to taste for yourself the deliciousness of what Inspired Women Work does. Transition, and all of its changes, is the catalyst for transformation. Within that transformation lies the gift of what's true for you. Inspired Women Work can provide you with the guidance and support to discover your true calling, find more fulfillment, achieve more, and make contributions that matter. The first step: Get your free audio report "The 7 Keys to Gracefully Turn Transition Into Soul Satisfying Transformation". In it you'll learn the 7 elements necessary to gracefully make the shift from transition to soul satisfying transformation. It begins with where you are right now and shows you how the Alchemy of Spirit can connect you with your purpose and your life's vision from a soul perspective. http://inspiredwomenwork.com/free-resources/

http://www.InspiredWomenWork.com

Tough Questions Yield Big Results. What's your Big Goal?

Rebecca Squires

HAVE you ever been surprised by the memories that pop up into your head at the most random of times? Those memories that seem bizarre but you just can't let go of? In 2008, while hiking a South American mountain, a life-long dream I had forgotten returned to remind me it had not yet been fulfilled. What happened next tested me, rocked me, but ultimately shaped my future.

Like many young Australians I spent time living abroad and travelling Europe. After three eye-opening and adventurous years, I decided to return to Australia. On my way home, I spent almost three months backpacking through South America. As part of this amazing holiday, I hiked the majestic and well-trodden Inca Trail. On day two of this three- day climb, we passed over the highest point of the trek. It was here, in this spot known as Dead Woman's Pass, I had a realisation that less than one year later proved to save my life.

Janet Beckers

Have you ever been on the way to somewhere, or something, and then thought you're not really sure what you're going to do when you arrive?

Getting motion – or making a change – has never been something I shy away from. The saying 'Ready, Fire, Aim' has applied to many situations in my life. There can be many negative and positive effects to this method. An issue with this approach for me in the past was that sometimes I even forgot to 'Aim' as a final step. This created great motion through much of my teens and early twenties, but as I got older, just following an urge because it felt right often left me feeling lost.

So, here I was on my way to Dead Woman's Pass, climbing what felt like a 90-degree ascent toward a point resting 4200m above sea level. It was the middle of the day, the sun was blaring down, and this climb was beginning to take a toll on my mental state. While I was walking with a guided group, all of a sudden I found myself alone and short of breath. I knew I could physically make it, I just had to keep my mind busy. I began counting from 1 to 20 on continual cycles. It was all I could think to do to continue moving forward. Then, out of the blue, two life-altering questions popped into my thoughts: "Bec, what are you going home for? What do you really want to do when you get there?"

Ask yourself the tough questions

The reason I was going home was an easy one: I wanted to be much closer to my growing family, but the 'really want' part of my question took me off guard. At no point in my preparations to leave London did that question get a look-in. I'd thought about who I was looking forward to seeing, the foods I would again have loads of regular access to, and the new family members I would grow to know. But what would I do after the first few weeks, after that list had been satisfied? Whoa, until that moment, I had no idea what I longed for. I didn't recall anyone ever asking me what I really wanted, and I'd never asked myself. So, you can only imagine the power in that moment when the answer came in the form of a childhood dream.

When I was seven years old, I started playing netball. My mum had played it, my two elder sisters played it, and so I of course wanted in on the action. It was there on the grass courts of the local netball association that my big dream, that big goal that hit me during that struggle up Dead Woman's Pass, was born. I wanted to play in the Australian Netball League.

In the year 1999, I got close to reaching my ultimate goal. I made my first underage Queensland netball team, and was offered a scholarship with the Queensland Academy of Sport. Then I turned 20 and my focus moved away from sport and that ultimate goal and into a career writing about it. In 2005 I moved away from writing about sport to just focusing on career and travel. Sport goals, and more precisely netball goals, had dropped completely off the radar. Until that moment on the side of a huge mountain in South America, I had not realised how much playing elite level netball still meant to me.

Raise the bar for yourself

Having spent almost five years out of competitive sport, I knew that getting my hands on my goal wouldn't be easy. At the same time, I recognised this desire had come from a deep place within me, so was worth having a good go at. Then and there, struggling to keep one foot in front of the other on the side of a South American mountain, I made the decision to REALLY go for it. When I got home to Australia, I would do all that was in my power to make it happen. I knew there were hurdles, but I was willing to have a shot at overcoming whatever was thrown my way. Three months after touching down in Australia, the first roadblock appeared and I was tested.

At this point, I was overweight; feeling emotionally unsupported by family and friends; and without a physical place to call home. My thoughts were moving at one hundred miles an hour, consistently questioning what other people thought about me; suggesting that I was past my prime; that I'd never make the grade. I was riddled with self-doubt. As a result, I began feeling incredibly insecure and began suffering from severe anxiety. For a period there, I was experiencing up to eight panic attacks a day. They would hit me anywhere – in the car, at a shopping centre, and especially in a group of people. I was constantly frightened by my own thoughts, by what 'might happen'. My life at this point felt horrendously difficult.

Have you ever talked yourself out of going for what you want out of fear?

Despite my low state of mind, I remembered the promise I made to myself overseas; I sought help for the anxiety, and at the same time continued to make headway for myself on achieving my goal to play in the Australian Netball League.

As a believer in the Laws of Attraction, I knew that I needed to clearly ask for what I wanted, but that simply putting this goal out into the universe was not enough. I knew I had to take some steps into action. Prior to the onset of anxiety, I set about establishing relationships and was quickly asked to join a team. I had created a good routine for myself with fitness training and games, and outside of netball had established a small network of support, with the latter proving integral to my recovery once insecurity hit me hardest. At the height of this period of fear and panic, I was asked to join the Canberra Darters training squad – meaning I had overcome a massive hurdle and was one step closer to my ultimate goal.

Many times during this period I made attempts to sabotage this experience when fear of failure or fear of rejection surfaced. I deeply wanted to change my situation, to raise my confidence and self esteem levels, and to do so I drew on all my courage to face my fears. I wanted to do this through achieving a goal I had set. I knew deep down that by achieving this goal I would have renewed faith and belief in myself. So, I took a deep breath and focused on the next step. I got myself out of the house and continued training and playing. In April 2009, I was selected for the Canberra Darters team to play in the Australian Netball League.

The routine of netball training, selections and then the 2009 season, gave me focus outside of myself, and a chance to rebuild from the inside. During this period I threw myself into gathering the skills to transform quickly and gained an incredible passion to support others aiming to achieve their big goals too. I had gained confidence within myself, taught myself to dream big and then go for it. Most importantly, I overcame anxiety and panic to again find satisfaction and happiness in my life. In essence, in keeping on track with my efforts toward this big goal, I saved my own life.

While achieving my childhood dream, my next big passion materialized, and it appeared at ninety degrees to anything I expected. To help me achieve my goals and overcome anxiety I joined a 12-month mindset and personal development program that transformed my life. It was here under the teachings of Mr Mindset Millionaire, Paul Blackburn that I launched my own business supporting others to first put the big ideas out there and then to grab them with both hands.

Surround yourself with people who know you are worth it

What I learnt most about myself during the path to that BIG childhood goal, was that to get what I want, I actually have to allow myself the privilege of first going there in my mind. Once there in my mind, in my imagination, I had to feel what it was like to be that person. And then in reality, I had to surround myself with people willing to help me prove myself to myself by achieving that big goal. As American author and speaker John Maxwell says: "If we're growing, we're always going to be out of our comfort zone". To me, the period of intense anxiety I experienced was a symbol of how far out of my comfort zone I had leapt. When I started coaching other people to set and reach their own big goals, I felt those old fears of failure and rejection surface. Thankfully, that same work I do with my clients allowed me to utilize the tools to overcome these quickly and achieve that next goal.

3 Tips To Stay Focused On Your Dreams

1. Ask yourself the question: "What is the one thing I'd really love to have done in my life, but have just never gotten around to?" When you have the answer, next ask yourself: "When is now a good time to make it happen?" In reality, most dreams

from our youth are possible as an adult, you may just have to think a little outside the square and find someone who can support you without judgment. Through this process, you'll discover YOUR big goal.

2. Write down your goal with as much clarity as possible, being sure to include a date by which you'd like to achieve it, and any feelings you will experience as a result of achieving this goal.

3. Take one small step toward making your big goal happen, then watch your path toward it unfold. My first step was a phone call. What will yours be?

About The Author

Rebecca Squires is the Founder and Director of Rock Paper Scissors Consulting, and a specialist coach in the area of overcoming fears and achieving goals. Bec's natural curiosity for life has always guided her career. Her inquisitive nature led her to obtain a sought-after position as a newspaper journalist following a degree in Communications in 2002. After a three-year stint, Bec moved to London, where she worked in corporate communications for a global firm while traveling as much of Europe as she could on weekends and holidays. Returning to Australia in 2008, she took up a public relations position for a non-profit organisation working with children and young people, before finding her true passion in Coaching. Rebecca has also represented two states in netball and was part of the Canberra Darters team competing in the 2009 Australian Netball League. Rebecca draws on her professional skills in Communications to help people clearly articulate their own passion and potential – then reach it. She enjoys helping people and businesses create a strong sense of identity, and supporting them to make changes in their lives to embrace their uniqueness.

Special Gift

Want to know more about how to reach your big goal? Email info@rockpaperscissorsconsulting.com, with subject line "Goal Setting for Greater Success" for your FREE copy of the video 'Five Ways To Achieve More Than You Ever Thought Possible' and learn the #1 Secret to setting successful goals.

Janet Beckers

Or, if you're keen to make your big goal a big reality right now, let's work together.

The BIG Goal Package: One of the key things to having access to someone who will help you stay on track, ask you the big, tough questions and help you overcome those things that in the past have stopped you getting what you want. If you have a goal that you really want to get your hands on, take action now with this intensive coaching package.

- Full personality profile: Understand who you are and what has held you back in the past, then harness your personality to help you achieve what you want;

- The Starting Gun: A detailed assessment reviewing where you are now, and where you want to be;

- The Greater Success Goal Tool - your personalised accountability system; and

- Coaching session with Bec, to shift the roadblocks of your past and create your own action plan to achieve your goal quicker and more easily than you ever imagined.

The Big Goal Package is valued at $997, but this intensive package is yours through this book for $497. To register your interest in this package and claim your special offer log on to www.rockpaperscissorsconsulting.com/big- goal-package and use the password biggoalpackage.

http://www.rockpaperscissorsconsulting.com

Staying Motivated - Less is More!

Ruth Thirtle

Avoid Overwhelm and Get More Done. I am very clear in my vision to support and to inspire. That is why I do what I do and this drives me forward every single day. The way that this vision plays out does change as my business and ideas grow and focus. However, I trust that this chapter (and I am sure the rest of this book) inspires you and supports you in your own endeavours and the pursuit of your own vision.

There are 2 main themes that I will be discussing here – the first involves avoiding overwhelm in daily tasks and the other involves avoiding overwhelm and being focussed when networking. These are 2 of the main things that I work with my clients on that helps them to achieve great results quickly and easily.

Time and To Do Lists

I really hate to break it to you but time management really is a myth. Time is the one commodity that we all have the same amount of and there is nothing we can do to manage to get more. The trick is about managing yourself in relation to time rather than attempting to manage time itself. Having a manageable To Do List is one of the first tips to managing yourself in relation to time – so let's start there!!

Janet Beckers

As I trained as an NLP Master Practitioner one of the principles that I discovered is "Seven Plus or Minus Two Chunks". This principle is to do with how much information our brains can cope with at any one time. Psychologist George Miller discussed this principle going back to 1956 in relation to short term memory. Basically, our brains are bombarded with millions of bits of information every single second of every single day through all of our senses. If we actually tried to process all of this information, our heads would explode – we've all had days where we feel like that was going to happen I am sure!! So the amazingly clever Super Computer that is our human brain deletes, distorts and generalises the information that we receive into manageable chunks. And the Magic Number 7 (plus or minus 2 chunks) is the way that we are able to process the information that comes to us to really get results. So what does all of this have to do with motivation and avoiding overwhelm?

Let me ask you a question – how many things go on your To Do Lists? Is it closer to the "millions" or "magic number 7"? Many people I talk to and clients that I work with have incredibly long lists of tasks they must do.

We all have many things to do yet having a lengthy list often has the following effect.

1. At the end of the day you do not feel you have achieved anything as you have achieved such a small percentage of the things you felt you needed to do.

2. So many things are carried over that the list gets longer and longer as new tasks and appointments come in.

3. Looking at that list leads to a heavy feeling of overwhelm or even low self esteem as the thoughts of "I really haven't done much" creep in.

4. People sometimes will pick the easy tasks from the list just to be able to cross something off. Because they are the simple and easy things they don't automatically lead to results and the lack of motivation spirals.

5. Because the overwhelming and scary To Do List is so huge, many people will put off tackling and the dreaded P word (procrastination of course) rears it's ugly head.

6. We can then end up running around like headless chickens in order to get something, anything done – the results aren't there and the motivation goes through the floor.

So what's the alternative? The alternative is what I do and what I advise clients and friends to do – since I started, my motivation has been through the roof and I achieve so much more in any given day. Use the principle of "Magic 7" and have a To Do List of between 5 and 9 chunks on it (I usually advise starting with a maximum of 7 as urgent things do happen throughout the day).

While you are focussing on one task your brain can actually take in all of the information on the list so your unconscious can start figuring out other tasks for you while you are working on one. This is then the effect that your To Do List can have.

1. Of an evening plan the top 7 things that you will achieve the next day (or even the next morning).

2. Your unconscious can start working on some of the trickier tasks while you consciously are not working.

3. You can focus on one thing at a time, knowing that each thing is moving you towards your goal.

4. Each thing takes less time and effort due to the work your unconscious has already done.

5. As you cross things off your To Do List you get a great satisfaction at the percentage of work that you have done.

6. Overwhelm is avoided, productivity and motivation are high – and you are soon through that To Do List and ready to start on the next Magic 7 List.

Motivated – and achieving! This seems simple but I cannot tell you how much more productive, focussed and motivated I have been towards my vision since I cut down the amount of things I was trying to focus on at any one time. All I can say is – give it a go and see what happens for you!

Networking

The other area to consider is how to apply this magic 7 rule (I call is the Magic 7 for Focus and Motivation) to networking. I spend a lot of time helping people to get even better results from their investment in networking. In many cases, this is in helping people to develop their elevator pitches so as to get results. Consider how many people you heard at the last networking event you went to tell you what they did. And how many did you actually remember? If we are able to focus on 7 plus or minus 2 chunks of information it is probably fair to think that you will only remember the elevator pitch of between 5 and 9 people.

So how do you get people to remember you? To want to know more and refer you on to people, (not to buy from you there and then). The 2 best pieces of advice for that are:-

1. Be specific. Tell people who you really want to work with, don't tell them you can do anything for anyone.

2. Tell Stories. Spend a few seconds giving an example of the work you do and HOW MUCH BENEFIT your clients get from you.

Which of these would you be most likely to remember from me?

1. My name is Ruth Thirtle from Your Abundance Now and I am a small business coach and networking trainer. I can help any small business owner or sales person get better results in their business and from their networking…..

2. My name is Ruth Thirtle from Your Abundance Now and I help people get maximum returns for their investment in networking. Last week I helped a client get their message out in 20 seconds not 90 – and with more success…. Same amount of time, much greater impact.

I have spoken about these 2 things as I spend a lot of time working with clients in these areas. To coin an old, sometimes doubtful and in this case COMPLETELY TRUE phrase – less really is more!!!

3 Tips To Stay Focused On Your Dreams

Write a list of the Top 7 Things you want to achieve tomorrow. "Chunk" (get to a level of specificity) where those 7 things, once completed, would be a great day for you – then sleep on them before acting on them.

If you are working with a big To Do List now, get it out and go through it – what can you delegate, what can you reschedule, what is urgent, what is going to make the biggest impact on your business.

Think of 5 20-second stories of people that you have helped or satisfied customers that you have. Start implementing these stories when you are networking and people ask you "What do you do?"

About The Author

Ruth Thirtle is passionate about helping business people to achieve even greater levels of success. She is a specialist in inspiring and supporting business owners to rapidly improve their business results - particularly through improving their networking skills. Through one on one consultation, online training and regularly speaking at networking events, Ruth spreads her message of success and abundance with her company "Your Abundance Now".

Ruth has worked with the world's largest business referral organization and is involved in launching the UK's fastest growing networking business into Australia. She knows the power of maximizing word of mouth referrals and understands how this can greatly help small business.

Ruth has now launched her online Business Booster programme to allow business owners to work on their business rather than in it from the comfort of their own computer and at times that suit them. This allows people to think differently about their business, take action and achieve amazing results!

Special Gift

1. Business Booster Programme – Go at your own pace, work on not in your business from the comfort of your own office. Normally US$97 per month, exclusive link for readers here – just US$67 per month. Get immediate access now https://www.jigsawbox.com/signup/abundantyou/2564/2705

2. Networking Session – 60 minute Skype session to work one on one on your own networking challenges and opportunities. US$125 – more than 50% discount on normal one-on-one consultancy hourly rate. Email info@abundantyou.com to arrange your appointment.

http://www.abundantyou.com   http://www.ruththirtle.com

Finding Focus

Samantha Leith

Focus is a funny thing, easy for some and hard for others. It's a natural state some days and yet on other days, focus is the hardest thing in the world to hold on to. Why is this? Why can't focus be like bike riding, reading or swimming? Something that is there always, part of our natural make up and able to be called on at anytime.

Well the good news is that it is. The bad news is, that if what you are trying to focus on, is not high enough on your 'care factor chart' than it's going to be really hard to hold on to. That's the trouble with so many of us. We feel like failures because we haven't been able to focus, when the truth is, it was probably something we weren't meant to focus on at all, or at that time.

I used to sing professionally. There is nothing like it. The feeling of being completely alive when walking onto that stage or into a studio is incredibly hard to replicate. The only time I have come close to feeling that sense of completeness is when I'm hugging my daughter. Yet, I no longer sing. Why? I don't know anymore. I did have an arsenal of reasons stashed away in my mind to excuse me from that life, but I

The Power of 100

don't even know what they are anymore. What I do know is that when I find anything in my life that is 100% true to me, my goals, beliefs, desires, needs and my daughters then I can replicate that focus. If it's something that I just need to do, I find focus hard to find – but not impossible.

I was working full time in 1999, touring with my one woman show Samantha Leith – Made Up and well, having a great life. Then I had the opportunity to record an album, with pre-sales of a couple of thousand copies (something very hard to do). It was for a Romance Pack for a department store and a direct mail Christmas catalogue. People would get this gorgeous gift box with massage oil, bubble bath, champagne flutes and a CD of love songs recorded by me. What an opportunity!!!

Well, it was unless you think about the fact the song choice, recording, mixing, artwork, photos, production and distribution had to be done in 6 weeks (all while I was working). As I couldn't get a double, I needed to focus, and that is what I did. I chunked it down, and became a time management wiz. My day was divided into 30 min time slots. Everything from breakfast to getting my nails done for photos had to be listed. I recorded most nights till 3am, and would be up again and at work by 9am. Was I tired? A little, but the adrenalin from doing something you truly believe in is a miracle worker. It was also during Sydney's gorgeous spring weather, when my social life (at that stage) was normally pumping. Did I let that go?

Yes, I had to in order to stay focused. It's a choice. Distractions are so easily found, but you can choose to ignore them. It was all worth it. The pack was a hit and I survived. Could I have maintained that focus for a longer period of time? Probably a little bit longer, but not consistently. Burning the candle at 3 ends is not something I would recommend. You can do it for small chunks, and as long as you stay focused you will survive, and maybe even flourish.

On the flip side of that example is me being the wandering disaster, unable to keep focus on anything, let along the task at hand. A few years ago, a friend and I decided we would give the e-book business a go. He bought the program from a very successful couple and we started researching. Well, I did my usual starting thing of chunking down my time. I had to even more so, as I was now working full time and a single mum of a baby (I think she was about 16months old). This time though I couldn't focus. I tried every trick I had up my sleeve, and was just unable to do it. In the end my friend took over the project and went on to publish an ebook about dog training at home.

No wonder I couldn't focus. I'm not much of an animal person, and the thought of having a dog to train terrifies me. At that point I hadn't figured out that I could have focused, if I had changed what my thoughts were about the project. If I had made it about the end result of money in the bank that would have enabled me to afford a cleaner, or a holiday – anything, then I would have been able to focus. These days I am still working full time, am still a single mum and still surround myself with lots of projects – however I am more focused with each one. I have a big enough motivator with each to remain focused. I fall off the rail sometimes, but just like working on your goals, if you get off the path, you just jump back on when you can, or change the direction a little – and do this without feeling guilty. If the overall project, job, event etc is something you find hard to focus on – find something about it that really drives you and focus on that. For example, if you need to do a big OH & S project for work, and you have never wanted to read the Act just for funs sake, then you may need to make the focus something else. Will it get you a promotion, pay rise, recognition or even save a life at work? If you can find one of these, then the focus will be easier to find.

Embrace technology

Time management is a huge part of being able to focus, so make the most of the tools out there. I set aside time every week, to organise my time. Right down to an allocation for social media!!! I use an app that synchs with my ipad, iphone and desktop. When something changes they all change. When I need to start working on a particular thing an alarm with go off on my phone and there I go. If you're more of a written diary person, do that – but stick to it!!!!!

Surround yourself with a reason for focus

I'll go back to the OH & S example. If you think that's going to get you a pay rise, what will you do with your pay rise? If it's a holiday, put posters up at work, at home and in your diary. Set a date and make it a countdown.....24 pages and 96 days till Fiji. Visual aids are one of the most important when maintaining focus. Chunk it down and celebrate the completion of each chunk. This doesn't need to be huge, but it works for me.

I'm currently re-working my online shop www.SomeKindOfBliss.com to include corporate hampers. I know how many photos, phone calls, hours of web work, orders and profit etc I need to pay for my daughter and I to go to New York for Xmas and then Disneyland and Hawaii this year. Powerful motivator – you bet. For each step the celebration is booking another thing for the trip. Surround yourself with positive influences and influencers.

I cannot stress just how important this is. If you are in a situation where focus is hard to maintain and along comes a 'friend' who says something negative about the situation, project or goal etc, you will more than likely come off track. Believe me, I have. These days I am incredibly careful when it comes to sharing my goals, and I chose to not include those negative people in those parts of my life. We all have negative people in our lives, and some are family so it's hard to remove yourself. Don't try to, but don't share with them either. If they didn't support you before, chances are they wont this time.

On this crazy road call life, I would like to spend my time combing a couple of my greatest loves. Speaking from the stage to help people believe that they can achieve anything and by creating a friendly, educational and inspiring community with My Goal Friend.

I love to see you somewhere online or off and watch you as you Go For Goal'd.

3 Tips To Stay Focused On Your Dreams

Write out the thing you currently need to focus on. If it's a goal make sure you write it out in a SMART way (see www.MyGoalFriend.com if you are unsure about what this is).

Chunk it down into baby steps, and work out timing and a celebration for each.

Create a visual tool for this goal. I sometimes use Mind Movies, posters, a goal book, vision boards and I even write on my bathroom mirror.

About The Author

I'm Samantha Leith and throughout my life I have been both a perfect example of someone who can focus and a complete wandering disaster. I've had a varied working life, probably because I get bored easily and am currently working on 4 major projects, with 4 focus points. Getting to a healthy body weight (to save my

Janet Beckers

life) , working full time as the Financial Controller of a publishing company (to pay the mortgage and for living in Sydney), running an online shop (to pay my daughters private school fees and for holidays) and starting my baby www.MyGoalFriend.com (to change mine and other peoples lives). You see, I believe that everybody can achieve anything they put their mind to, if it is realistic and true to their soul. I would like to help people to do this by creating a safe online and offline environment for them to share their dreams, learn from others and get encouragement to Go For Goal'd. I would eventually like to take this on the road, fulfilling 2 of my passions - speaking from the stage and helping others.

Special Gift

I hope you have found this interesting, and maybe even learnt something. If you have and you'd like to learn a little more, please head over to my baby www.MyGoalFriend.com . If you leave your details you will get a copy of my 52 Tips to Go for Goal'd. You'll also get sent 1 tip each week in greater detail. My Goal Friend will be expanded during the year, to include interviews, a forum, individual blogs, focus groups and more, so keep an eye open. I'd also like to offer everyone who reads this a discount from www.SomeKindOfBliss.com . If you use the code WWW11 you will get 25% off any of the gorgeous Australian made Bath, Body and Home Frangrancing products we sell online (I'll even throw in a copy of my album just to say thank you).

www.SomeKindofBliss.com   www.MyGoalFriend.com

The Power of 100

Self-Imposed Glass Ceilings are the toughest – and the most important – to shatter!

Sandi Givens

The term glass ceiling is one readily recognized by many people as referring to the barrier(s) women may face as they progress towards more senior levels in organizations. But is it something that only affects women? And does it exclusively refer to roadblocks in our careers? www.Answers.com suggests the 'glass ceiling' is "an unacknowledged discriminatory barrier that prevents women and minorities from rising to positions of power or responsibility."

www.thefreedictionary.com says this term describes "a situation in which progress, especially promotion, appears to be possible, but restrictions or discrimination create a barrier that prevents it." And their Thesaurus suggests the synonyms of 'ceiling', 'roof' or 'cap', as in an upper limit on what is allowed. In truth, I believe a glass ceiling is any barrier that keeps anyone from progressing in their desired direction. And I sincerely believe the most resistant of these and the most important to breakthrough are those that reside in our minds and hearts. Our beliefs about our capabilities, how we value and esteem ourselves and how courageous we are in letting our own light shine can be significant blocks to our progress towards our goals and aspirations in life.

How do I know? Because my life has given me opportunities to show this to be true. At 15 years of age, my family migrated to Australia from the USA and I found myself at school surrounded by angry and hate-filled anti-American sentiment. At 22, I woke in my apartment alone unable to move my legs. When in my 30's I at last gave birth to my longed-for child, I had severe post natal depression, requiring a 4 month stay in hospital. And most recently, I have been diagnosed with a serious back condition and lost all my hair as a result of alopecia. Having said all this, I truly believe these challenges are no more significant than those faced by countless other human beings that walk the planet (and absolutely less traumatic than those faced by even more people).

We all have struggles – situations that force us to our knees – obstacles that seem insurmountable and overwhelming. For me the difference is in how we respond to these. We have more direct and effective control over ourselves than we typically have over other people, company processes, government legislation and forces of nature. It is up to us to take charge of our thoughts, beliefs and attitudes – especially during those times when it seems hardest to do so.

If you're ready to shatter some of your glass ceilings, here are 3 steps to get you started!

1. Put your beliefs under a microscope

Although formed for what were originally good reasons (to protect or guide us), as we progress through our lives, we can find that many of these no longer serve us. Do you believe you are unworthy of success? Not capable of advancement? Too old (or young, set in your ways, inexperienced, tired, unintelligent – insert any adjective here) to achieve your heart's desires? Growing up, I somehow developed a belief that 'rich people are snobs'. And, of course, I didn't want to be a 'snob'.

At the time I never realized it, but looking back, I can see ways in which I subtly but surely sabotaged my success in business, believing financial success would automatically turn me into someone I didn't want to be. Remember ... beliefs are not truths. If they were, we'd still think the human body would explode if we ran one mile in less than 4 minutes! Discover if there is any real evidence that supports your beliefs – and if not, discard them.

2. Define your unique value to the world

Others won't buy you until you do. What is it you offer? What skills, abilities and characteristics are your strengths and can add value to projects and tasks you undertake? Being self-employed since 1989 has forced me to realise that there is a huge difference between being 'boastful' and 'bragging' and simply letting people know what your skills are and how you can help them. In fact, as Marianne Williamson said in her book, A Return to Love … "… as we let our own light shine, we unconsciously give other people permission to do the same." Knowing yourself well and being able to articulate your uniqueness is a vital skill in advancing your career – and life – towards your desired destination. And, of course, this keeps you motivated, inspired and proactive in achieving your goals.

3. Focus on what you can influence

Too often, we can find ourselves spending time fretting and frustrated as we attempt to change things that are well beyond our control. Not only does this fail to produce any tangible, beneficial result, it leaves us feeling disempowered and exhausted. Our overall motivation drops as we feel increasingly less capable of achieving a positive difference in a situation that concerns us. When I received the distressing news of my back condition, expert opinion was that little if anything could be done to help me. Yet, I was in so much pain and my sleep was so disturbed, I felt absolutely desperate to do something that would help.

So one day, I took myself off to our local pool. One length (25 metres) was barely possible. I said I hated every minute in the pool. Thanks to a good friend who helped me reframe my experience of swimming (he suggested a mantra while I swam of 'I'm fit and healthy and getting better every day'), I soldiered on. Within a few months, I was swimming between 1 and 2 kilometres, the pain was more manageable … and I felt a whole lot better, both physically and emotionally. I was doing something I could control. And yes, I am still swimming 4 to 5 times a week to this day! To keep your spirits up and maintain your focus, choose to channel your energies on those things that are under your control and over which you can exert some influence. You will find that with time, experience and making strong connections with others in your network, your circle of influence expands – and you will gradually find an increasing number of areas in which you can make an impact.

Janet Beckers

There is no better time than right now to shatter the glass ceilings that have held you back – believe you can … and you will!

3 Tips To Stay Focused On Your Dreams

Put your Beliefs under a microscope – what evidence is there that supports your belief? And what about the evidence that contradicts it?

Define your unique value to the world – get clear on what your true skills and capabilities are – and develop the courage to tell others about these!

Focus on what you can influence – take control of what you can, work on things you can affect – and learn to let go of the rest.

About The Author

About The Author

Sandi Givens – Author, Speaker, Facilitator, MC & Coach. Sandi is a leading expert in Shattering the Glass Ceilings that limit success, with a focus on Women's Development, Teams & Leadership and attaining work/life balance. Certified Speaking Professional (one of only 92 as of March 2011) Speaker of the Year, Victoria (2004), Past President, Victoria (2005) - National Speakers Association of Australia, Patron – Australian Institute of Office Professionals (Victoria Division), Member of the Advisory Board – The Global Good Foundation.

Frequently cited as one of Australia's most authentic and engaging presenters, Sandi has the unique ability to connect with people, irrespective of their background, age or position at work. Teaching people to esteem themselves and each other, she is well-known for her light-hearted and down-to-earth approach to life. Moreover, Sandi is a huge advocate of living your life by choice, rather than by chance. For more details, free information and to preview Sandi as a coach or speaker for you and your team, visit http://www.sandigivens.com.au or phone +61 3 9844 4612.

Special Gift

Receive a complimentary copy of Sandi's popular e-Book: The 7 Biggest Blocks to having 100% Confidence 100% of the Time (and the Secrets to Overcoming them!) (RRP AUD$24.95) and join our on-line community by sending an email to request@sandigivens.com.au with the word "Confidence" in the subject line.

http://www.sandigivens.com.au   http://women-on-the-move.ning.com/

Janet Beckers

Treading Softly How to Keep Your Dreams Alive With Little Children Underfoot

Sarah Buchanan-Smith

Our dreams are delicate things, visions of a better life that need to be nurtured and fed but keeping them alive is not always easy. As a mother of 3 young children I saw my dreams begin to disappear as I lost myself in a sea of new responsibility. As they became fainter I knew I needed to act to keep my precious dreams alive. Here are the 3 key actions I took to keep myself motivated and inspired through some pretty tough times, simple actions that you can take yourself to keep focussed on your vision and move yourself forward.

First things First, Get your House in Order

Dreams can't flourish in a chaotic home. Chaos brings with it overwhelm and procrastination which will diminish even the most passionate vision.

Dreams need space, not reasons to give up before you've even started. Create an organised environment for yourself. Clear out your physical and emotional clutter and put yourself on a sparkling path to success. Clean your house from top to bottom, clear out all your junk and fix the bits that are broken, give everything you no longer use to charity. Be ruthless. Put a household chore plan together and stick to it, plan your meals on a week by week basis and shop online for your groceries, buy birthday presents in advance and have a treasure chest. I'm sure you're getting the picture; create yourself a home that is happy and well organised, one that you can dream in constructively without constantly being sidetracked by day to day responsibilities.

Know Where You Are Going

See Your Dream Realised

Once you have space to dream again you need to feed your vision, make it strong and compelling. The most powerful way to do this is to write about your dream in the finest of detail and experience your success now, even before you've achieved it. What does your life look like now you have realised your dream, what do you feel like? What are you doing? What have you learnt? How did you achieve your vision? Say your dream is to set up and run a profitable business from home using your baking skills, you might start like this...."It is February 2013 and I'm taking a short break from work this morning before I start replying to some emails. I'm working from home now, running a fantastic, profitable business teaching children how to cook with online cookery lessons....let me tell you a bit about how I got here and what I have learnt over the last 2 years....." Write as if you are telling someone all about your dream and how you have achieved it; go in to all the details. Let your mind go and realise your dream. Live it now and enjoy it.

Be The Change you Want To Be

No matter how much you organise yourself and visualise your success sometimes it can be very difficult to achieve your dreams if your inner talk is sabotaging all your efforts. Your personal story can sometimes stop your vision becoming anything more that pie-in-the sky if left unchecked. A great test to see if you are playing an unhelpful story in your head is to write a bio about yourself.

Write your story in a short paragraph, no more than 200 words, just like the ones you see in this book, it is fascinating to see what you say about yourself. A précis of what I said about myself a couple of years ago is something like this, " Highly educated, successful career woman gets married, has 3 children one straight after the other, leaves work, lives in the past and feels sorry for herself". And I couldn't work out why I wasn't getting anywhere with my dreams! Even though I wanted more than anything else in the world to set up a successful business from home I had a victim mindset and was making life at home a misery for myself. It wasn't until I realised I needed to change my story and get myself in line with a happily married mother of 3 running a successful business from home that I started to see results. Get congruent with your dream and give it the chance to flourish. Never ever give up.

So, there you are, 3 really simple steps you can take to keep your dreams alive. Get organised, see your future and make sure everything about you is in line with your dreams. It sounds easy but life often throws you curve balls. When it does make sure you are kind to yourself and take your time. Nurturing dreams is a gentle art and patience truly is a virtue. Tread softly and never, ever, give up. Here's to you, your family and your dreams.

3 Tips To Stay Focused On Your Dreams

1. Clear out all your physical and emotional clutter to create a clear environment for your dreams to flourish.

2. See your dreams realised today. Write down in detail exactly how your life will look when you are living your dream. Have a practice run.

3. Tell yourself the right story. Make sure your inner talk is in line with your dreams. Don't sabotage your vision with negative thinking.

About The Author

Sarah studied International Relations at University and moved in to a career as a financial analyst and Management Consultant in the City of London. Sarah married in 2002 and had 3 children within 4 years. Finding it difficult to find a balance between raising her children and her career she left work and has spent the last 3 years at home caring for her family. Sarah's dream is to set up a successful home based online business that will enable her to support her family financially. Sarah's ultimate dream is to take her experience and empower mothers all around the world to harness the incredible opportunities we have today and use their skills and passions to start their own profitable businesses from home.

Special Gift

Please visit Applebower Fitness www.applebowerfitness for fabulous tips on running and keeping fit and healthy as a Mum. Sign up for brilliant weekly emails and a free monthly e-zine packed with healtlhy tips and lifestyle advice.

http://www.applebowerfitness.com

3 Succulent Steps To Claim Your Goddess Status In Life And Business

Shannon Bush

I bet you would secretly love to be referred to as a Goddess. I used to think that a Goddess was a mythical, magical woman out of reach of the modern day average woman that I used to believe I was. I'm pleased to say I no longer believe Goddess status is out of reach and in fact use the term to describe myself and the amazing women I have the honour of working with

I actually call them Creative Goddesses, because that is exactly what they are. They are women just like you; mothers, wives, sisters, daughters, friends, artists, writers, designers, inventors, healers, coaches, spiritually focused, creative, business owners, solo-preneurs, entrepreneurs, mum-preneurs, passionate about and brilliant at what they do.

They are literally 'creating' rewarding, abundant, empowered lives and businesses they love that are expressions of their authentic purpose

In my eyes a Creative Goddess is "an empowered woman who is actively creating and living a rewarding, abundant life she loves as an expression of her brilliance and soul's purpose" These Creative Goddesses weren't always like this. They used to feel just like you might do right now. They used to struggle to attract and keep well paying clients they wanted to work with, didn't know how to share their brilliance with the world and didn't believe anyone wanted what they were offering They were experiencing something I like to call the anti-Goddess phenomenon. They didn't value themselves and their natural gifts as women, like intuition and creativity, or have any idea how to live from a place of authentic succulent abundance. They struggled, over and over, time and time again.

They were fearful; consciously and unconsciously hid themselves so no-one could find them; believing because they had no clients that what they were offering wasn't of value. Living an anti-Goddess life is about playing small, staying hidden, undervaluing yourself, ignoring your greatest natural gifts and living from a place of scarcity I know this story inside out and upside down and I know all the different versions it comes in because it is, or should I say was, my story. Fuelled by a compulsion to share my creative gifts with the world I gave up my well paying corporate career to live my dream helping women to connect with and leverage the immense potential that comes with creative expression.

I was full of ambition, full of the best intention, full of determination, full of possibility and then nothing happened. Absolutely nothing! I had a website, lots to offer, great experience and 'pieces of paper' and I desperately wanted to work with others, teaching them how to creatively value and empower themselves to create life and business success. In fact, I wanted to do exactly what I do today. But nothing happened. That was until I decided that it was time something changed! I took a step back from where I was and re-aligned myself with my reason for starting my business.

I founded Creative Possibility because I was tired of watching the women around me suffer and struggle with their lives and businesses, continually undervaluing themselves. The few clients I had were experiencing amazing results but there just weren't enough of them so I too struggled and let things like fear and overwhelm get hold of me. I'd become one of the women I wanted to help and knew I had to turn things around and re-claim my Goddess-ness. How did I do it?

I got back to basics and looked at all the things I had naturally done before I started my business, the things that had made me feel successful previously and made me who I was. I immersed myself in each of them with concentrated determination and as they say, the rest is history

Janet Beckers

So here are the three key steps I took to re-claim my Goddess-ness and get back on track to living my purpose, on purpose, and to being the Creative Goddess of my own life and business and guide for other creative women entrepreneurs wanting to do the same

Step 1 ~ Value yourself and live in the 'light'

Women are terrible at valuing themselves. Some of us are brilliant at it but that's not that common unfortunately; positive self value is not something that happens naturally for a lot of us. We undervalue ourselves to the point of sabotaging any action and effort we put into birthing and living our dreams. To re-claim your Goddess-ness you need to understand one essential thing ~ YOU are valuable and no-one can take that value away from you other than you   Hold yourself in high regard, with respect, self love; value just how worthy you are and things will change in your life and business for the better. With a new sense of value get out in the 'light' and show off what you've got! This doesn't mean being a show off. It means being visible and showing off who you are, the valuable, incredible Goddess the world is waiting for   Here's my favourite Value Affirmation to get you started; "I am valuable, I am valued, I am worthy, I am visible and the world needs me to share my brilliance"

Step 2 ~ Embrace your creative gifts

I want all women to know how important connecting with their creativity is. Before you say "I can't draw / paint / write" or "I'm not creative" stop and re-think your definition of creativity. I am not talking about artistic talent. When I refer to creativity I refer to your innate ability as a woman to create; to innovate; to share meaningful conversations with others; to inspire; to intuit; to express yourself with passion, heart and soul; to generate new ideas and 'birth' new projects. When we connect with our inner 'creative space' we are

- focused and more likely to use our time better

- clearer about things and less likely to feel overwhelmed or stressed

- able to switch off from the distractions and stress of every day life

- in a position to look at things from different perspectives to gain new insights, solutions and answers and

- more likely to bring our dreams into reality We give ourselves time to re-charge and renew on all levels which is essential, in my experience, to creating what we want and being a success on our terms. Get out there and embrace your Creative Goddess-ness and 'create'!

Step 3 ~ Live succulent abundance and gracious gratitude

Abundance and gratitude go hand in hand. One of the actions I encourage my clients to take and something I do every day is to take a few minutes to stop and reflect on how abundant I have been and the things I'm grateful for

Abundance is the riches of life, both material and non-material and is a measure of how well I value myself and how creative and expansive I have been. Sometimes it's measured by how much money I've made but mostly it's measured by how rich I feel. Ask yourself that question each day; "How rich do I feel?" and then in answering it include all the things that you are grateful for.

Focusing on abundance and gratitude helps us to focus on what we have, where we are headed and what we need to do to get there instead of what we don't have or have missed out on. They say that 'like attracts like' so I know what I'm choosing Wishing you every success Creative Goddess!

3 Tips To Stay Focused On Your Dreams

Value yourself and live in the light every day with the following affirmation "I am valuable, I am valued, I am worthy, I am visible and the world needs me to share my brilliance"

Re-define your definition of creativity, make a weekly Creative Goddess date with yourself to play and be creative, expressing yourself in any way that feels right for you and ooze you Creative Goddess-ness!

Start an Abundance Journal and take 5 minutes at the end of each day to ask yourself "How rich do I feel?" and fill your answer with all the things you are grateful for.

Janet Beckers

About The Author

Inspired by her own creative journey and a belief that all women are creative and deserve to know how their creativity can unlock their true value, Shannon Bush left the world of corporate health to turn her creative dreams into a reality as the Creative Possibility Coach   Many women struggle to make it living their creative dreams despite being brilliant at what they do. They are valuable but don't know just how valuable they really are and how to embrace their creativity and leverage it to create a successful, abundant life and business. A creativity and empowerment specialist, Shannon helps creative women entrepreneurs understand their real value, attract well paying clients, get paid what they are worth and infuse their creativity into their lives and businesses whilst living their life purpose, doing what they love Visit her website to see how you can work with Shannon and participate in the monthly Creative Goddess webinars   Shannon is a mindset breakthrough coach for creative women entrepreneurs, abundance, creativity and empowerment specialist, certified Money Breakthrough CoachTM, Transpersonal Art Therapist, Artist, Writer and Creative Goddess of her own life and business

Special Gift

Get started on your own journey to value with my e-workbook '3 Simple Steps to Uncover Your Real Value', valued at $97 and yours for free. Claim today at http://www.creativepossibilitycoach.com/www-gift-of-value.html

http://www.creativepossibilitycoach.com

'Create Your Own Champion GPS (Goal Planning System): How to Achieve Your Goals with Champion Habits ... that Stick!"

Shelley Taylor-Smith

It has always baffled me why some people achieve and others don't. It has baffled even more why people think that success is reserved for the lucky few. So when I retired from competing for Australia and switched swimsuit for business suit; I made a commitment to de-mystifying success and how to achieve your goals in a relatable and easy to implement way for my clients.

Fact: Only about 2 out of every hundred people know precisely what they desire from life and have a workable plan for attaining their goals. These are the people who are leaders. They have found success that has made life pay off on their terms. The strangest thing about these people is that they have the same amount of opportunities as those who have never achieved success. If you know exactly what you want and have absolute belief in your ability to get it, you can achieve success. If you are not sure what you want from your life start now! Start this very second and decide definitely what you want, how much of it you want and when you want to have it in your possession.

Follow this 4-step tried and proven formula to achieving your goals:

1. Establish Your Why Write out a clear statement of what you most desire. That thing that once you achieve it, in your opinion, would make you successful.

2. Make a Plan Formulate a personal strategy that will allow you to achieve your goal that you established in Step 1. This plan creates a step by step process that you will follow to achieve your goal including the amount of personal time committed to achieve that goal. Your plan should be based on the Critical Path to Success and the Cycle of Duplication

3. Establish Targets. Write down immediate, short term and long term goals that will be stepping stones to your ultimate goal.

4. Commit. Commit to memorising and repeating your reason for doing your business or career. Commit yourself to achieving your goals. Commit to your plan of action. Commit to having fun.

Goal Setting

1. Goal Setting - Establish Your "WHY"

Your success and attainment of your goals depend on your ability to creatively overcome every obstacle that comes between you and your dreams. Now is the time to establish why you want to build this business. Use your why as the motivation to carry you through any difficult times. Your reason why will also keep you motivated and keep you on track all the way to the finish line Close your eyes for a moment and visualise your dreams. What would you do if you had more free time? What would your ideal day be like? Do you dream of spending more time with your family? Driving around in a new car? Do you want greater freedom in your life? Do you want the ability to choose what you do when you want to do it?

Goal Setting Tips -> Want it! Make sure your goal is something you really want and something you can control. If you want your kids to be physicians, that is not your goal! -> Believe it! Have faith and confidence that you are capable of achieving your goal. Muhammad Ali never said, "One day I hope to be pretty good." He said, "I am the greatest!" -> Write it! This reinforces desire because it holds you accountable. It also helps you remember. Commit your goal to memory and repeat it often!

2. Goal Setting - Make a Plan

Look at previous successes and failures in any area of your life - know what worked and what did not. Duplicating your Winning Formula is your clear plan for success. You must follow this critical path of success. Your winning formula is the fuel that you moves your forward. But first you must determine how much time can you commit to your business? How many free hours do you have each week? How many of those hours are you willing to commit to building your business? Take out a calendar. Which days and hours are you going to work over the course of the month? Schedule time in your calendar for your business and commit to it!

3. Goal Setting - Establish Targets

Before we can show you how to build a business you need to choose your destination. Before starting your vacation, you need to know where you are going. Your business is the same way. You can't start your journey if you don't know where you are going. In Step 1 you should have written down your ultimate goal, the reason why you are starting/building your business. It is big step from where you are now to that ultimate goal. To help bridge that gap you need to define some immediate, short term and long term targets. These should be clearly defined and act as stepping stones to your ultimate goal. You should establish a 1 Year Goal & 90 Day Goal For example: It is _____ and I am making $_____ per month

Now review your goals. Be sure that your goals are realistic based on the time you have available and the time you are willing to commit to the business. If they aren't you need to either adjust the amount of time you are committing to you business or adjust your goals. At the beginning of each month you should decide on 4 business targets. These are your immediate targets. These targets could be the number of new customers/clients you want or number of sales per product/item. Whatever you choose your targets to be, there should be 4 things that will move you towards your 90 day goal. Write down 4 targets for the month that move you toward your 90 day goal.

4. Commit! Great!

So, now you have determined why you are doing this business, how much time you are willing to commit and you have a series of targets that are stepping stones to your ultimate goal. Now, you must commit to this. Take some time, preferable in the morning or before you go to bed and visualise your goals. As your business grows along with your personal development you may find that the reasons for doing your business change.

3 Tips To Stay Focused On Your Dreams

Goal Setting Tips

Want it! Make sure your goal is something you really want and something you can control. If you want your kids to be physicians, that is not your goal!

Believe it! Have faith and confidence that you are capable of achieving your goal. Muhammad Ali never said, "One day I hope to be pretty good." He said, "I am the greatest!"

Write it! This reinforces desire because it holds you accountable. It also helps you remember. Commit your goal to memory and repeat it often!

About The Author

SHELLEY TAYLOR-SMITH http://www.championmindset.com.au/ 7-time World Marathon Swimming Champion/2-time Australian of Year Finalist/Speaker/Trainer Motivation, Performance and Success expert Shelley Taylor-Smith is one of the World's most renown teachers, best-selling authors and presenters and she delivers it just as she is – honest, from the heart, down to earth, passionate and patriotic Her inspirational message is living with conviction in life, both personally and professionally and how to create our own Champion Mindset with focus, self-belief and attitude. Shelley Taylor-Smith is a 7-time Women's World Marathon Swimming Champion, but more important to both Shelley and her clientele, she's an ordinary Australian who achieved extraordinary results and now teaches how she did it and how you can to. Australia's No.1 Mental Toughness Coach; Shelley Taylor-Smith works with teams and individuals, corporations and small business owners; helping them transform their Champion potential into performance, demonstrating how harnessing the power of your mind and boosting your self-belief helps you achieve your goals. Discover your mental toughness to stay on top of your game despite the daily obstacles you face in your business and career thinking like a Champion; with her everyday life motto: "Get Up, Get Over It & Get On With It."

Special Gift

In need of motivation, inspiration, education or a kick in the pants? Subscribe at http://www.championmindset.com.au/inspire.htm and receive the fortnightly Champion Motivations ezine...full of tips and tools to boost your self confidence and energise for success! Bonuses include "Taylor-Made Solutions to Achieve Your Success Report" plus more...valued at $97.

http://www.championmindset.com.au

Life Begins Now

Sherri Mulconry

Starting a business or any new journey can be exciting and yet daunting at the same time. Staying motivated and on track can be hard especially when the normal day to day trials get in the way. Goals need to be set and decisions need to be made. Goals give you a clear focus and direction and enable you to reach your dreams. I read somewhere that goals are a commitment to focus your energy in a particular direction. Short term goals are stepping stones to your long term goals. Write Your Goals Down One of the things I do regularly to stay on track is to write my goals down. I then write out a few paragraphs describing my life in present tense as though the goals have already been reached. The key is to believe the changes have already taken place. I read this daily and feel the positive emotion inside my body and mind. Positive energy attracts positive things into your life!

One of the most important things I have learned along the way is that it is important to focus on what you WANT and NOT on what you DON'T want. You attract what you think about! When you believe that you can have what you want, your mind is open to the opportunities around you. You tend to take notice of things that may have passed you by in the past. When your conscious and subconscious minds regularly receive positive messages, your subconscious creates the situations and attracts the people that can help you accomplish your goals. I have found that one thing leads to another, one connection leads to another, one person leads to an opportunity and one opportunity leads to another opportunity. When good things fall into place it is easy to stay motivated and excited.

Habits Are Life-Shapers Obviously it takes action, commitment to goals and hard work to follow up on opportunities. When your goals become your priority you need to develop habits that move you toward your goals. Habits are life-shapers. I regularly assess if my current habits are taking me toward or moving me away from my current goals. Regular exercise, healthy eating, using positive self-talk, having family time and making time for relaxation allow me to stay energised, focussed and motivated.

I know stress is unavoidable but by identifying when I am feeling stressed I can actively take measures to bring my stress levels down. I regularly take a brisk walk, enjoy a bubble bath, watch favourite DVD's and chat with friends on the phone. When I am feeling really stressed I will book in for a massage, go for a walk along the beach or listen to relaxation CD's.

Practicing positive self talk is a really important habit to develop. A great technique to change negative self talk is to say to yourself the word STOP whenever you have a negative thought and replace it with a positive affirmation. It has been proven that people respond best to others who are enthusiastic, positive and happy. Positive people are more enjoyable to be around. I have learnt over the years, that the words you choose to use when you talk about yourself, not only influences other people's perception of you but also your own personal confidence.

An Attitude of Gratitude

Another strategy to stay motivated while striving for goals is to take time out and be thankful for what we already have. I try to focus on all the good things in my life. Good health, the love and support of my family, time spent with friends over a nice meal, wine or coffee, and the fresh air and sunshine are some of my favourite things. I find that when I appreciate the little rewards that each day brings and feel thankful, I generate more positive emotions and as a result attract more positive things into my life. As I said before, it is easier to stay motivated when good things are constantly happening.

Janet Beckers

Create the Vision

Every year I enjoy creating a vision board. It's fun to cut out pictures and inspiring, motivating words and quotes from magazines that represent the things and experiences that I want to create in my life. After arranging and posting them onto my board I hang it in my bedroom so I can see it every morning and every night. The collection of pictures motivates me to stay focused on my goals for the year. This makes it easy for me to visualise my goals in my mind no matter where I am.

Saying affirmations that relate to your goals is another great way of attracting these things to you. I'll never forget the Sunday I was driving along a road in my suburb after a week or two of reciting wealth attraction affirmations. I looked in the rear vision mirror to see a ten dollar note blowing around in the wind. It seemed to come out of nowhere and was frantically trying to catch my attention. I laughed as I stopped the car and got out and caught it. This was the Universe telling me that my affirmations were working. Although it was only ten dollars, I knew how important it was to feel thankful and happy that the Universe was working for me.

Change Your Thoughts

Of course, as a hypnotherapist, I find hypnotherapy to be the most effective way to stay motivated and focussed. Through hypnotherapy, people can let go of limiting beliefs and self-sabotaging behaviours. Positive and motivating thoughts replace the negative ones and give people the confidence they need to pursue their goals. To find out more about how you can change your thoughts and change your life visit www.lifemakeovers.com.au

3 Tips To Stay Focused On Your Dreams

Write Your Goals Down – Believe the changes have already taken place.

Habits are Life-Shapers – Are your habits moving you toward your goals?

Create the Vision – See the pictures clearly in your mind.

About The Author

Sherri Mulconry is the director of Life Makeovers. She has a passion for assisting others to gain confidence in themselves and reach their goals. Sherri runs programs that combine coaching, counselling and hypnotherapy for issues such as weight loss, stress, anxiety, interview skills, motivation and relationships. Life Makeovers also provides workplace seminars and success coaching and offers online and phone coaching. Sherri is a co-author of The Rest of Your Life.

Special Gift

To receive a copy of Life Makeovers "Making Time For Life" E-Book absolutely free, email enquiries@lifemakeovers.com.au and enter Time For Life in subject line

http://www.lifemakeovers.com.au

Feel Your Way To Success

Stephanie Kathan

When I first discovered for myself a little over 3 years ago, that my success in life depended on the thoughts I think.....My entire life changed. I began studying everything I could find on the topic of personal growth and I made it my intention to learn from the best teachers by surrounding myself with the finest minds in the world. What I also discovered is that there are a million people trying to make money teaching you what they think they know.

One of the best pieces of advice came from one of my mentors who told me "the most valuable thing you can have is discernment". So, that's what I asked for.....and what I found was my "inner guidance system".

We all have it, just like we all have lungs and other vital organs that keep us alive, we also have an inner guidance system to tell us if we are on track. You can't see it in an X-Ray, but trust me it's there. And you know it.....every time you feel good, or feel bad. When you feel good, you notice all the things going good. Those are the times when you hit all the green lights, you make your appointments with time to spare, You're having a great hair day and you feel good in your skin. And when you're feeling bad, you notice yourself stuck in traffic, late for your appointments, no cell service and you just discovered you have a run in your pantyhose.

When you set your inner guidance system before you take action, you are actually setting your vibrational tuner, and you attract thoughts similar to generate more of what you are feeling. You are attracting whether you take the time to do it deliberately or not. If you are not doing it deliberately .....you are attracting by default. This little exercise may seem like a time waster to some....and you can find those people still sitting in traffic, in the constant pursuit of feeling better because they didn't take the time to feel good first. All that is required is that you follow your feelings. It's why you buy anything you buy......because of how you felt when you came across the product, and how you think you will feel after having it.

When you begin to understand the system is in place to serve you, and you believe in its power, you'll discover freedom beyond your wildest imagination. Which is really what success is isn't it? Experiencing the freedom to have, do or be anything you want, and then experiencing the deliciousness of doing it and feeling the exhilaration of the experience! This process sounds amazingly simple and it is......which is exactly why it's called the "simple" truth, and why more people don't do it.

We as humans tend to want to complicate things, and if it's too easy, we feel there won't be any benefit. Nothing could be farther from the truth in this case! The ones who think it's not complicated enough are the ones who are complaining about everything and blaming everyone for their current state of affairs. This also clears up any of that crap. You are responsible for your own thoughts, and your own feelings. No one can do this work for you. No one can think your thoughts, and no one can feel your feelings......and no one is responsible for your happiness other than You. I have put this process to the test, and I can tell you it works every time without question.

Whatever circumstances you are experiencing at this moment, are nothing more than a temporary "indicator" of what your past thoughts, actions and words have been! That should have you jumping up and down with Joy! That means....that YOU have all the power to change whatever you are experiencing that is not pleasing to you, and you can do it by simply shifting your thoughts to something that feels better and holding onto it in your mind until you have generated the feelings and emotions to attach to it.

When you are picturing everything going wrong.....you are using your imagination, you are just using it in a way that does not serve you. So when you find yourself in a state of overwhelm....Don't Worry! It's just temporary and all the power to change it is in your hands....your mind...and in your control. That should have you feeling better already! When I first began this process, I knew that to get where I wanted to be in life I had to commit to myself to do whatever it took to get the results I wanted. Through years of research and self-discovery I found that all it took was for me to put my emotional well being ahead of everything else and all the pieces just seemed to fall into place.

I literally began running into the perfect people, at the perfect time who had the exact information or opportunity I needed to bring me closer to my goals. I began being presented with opportunities to do some very exciting projects, money began to show up through creative and unusual ways, and I began to realize how eager and excited I was to wake up and experience all the wonderful things that were in store for me.

The best part for me was seeing my children grow within themselves just by watching me live the example of what I am telling you now. My children began catching the "vibes" of my well-being which helped them to experience their own state of well-being....and it all happened because I was "selfish" enough to put my own well-being above all else and the result of that decision is that my children now know how to master their own thoughts and create their own state of well-being. My mentor told me long ago the best way for me to help the ones I love most in this world is to master my own mind, and deliberately create my own life.....and there have never been truer words spoken.

When you discover that you can determine how you feel on purpose, you are attracting more of the people you like to be around. People respond to your energy whether you know it or not. If you are a traveling stream of negative energy.....you are going to have many negative experiences to keep you there. The same is true for positive energy. The more positive you Feel, the more things you will experience that keeps you feeling that way. The power your emotions have is a mighty one. You have the ability to begin with absolutely nothing, and create a magnificent something...when you simply make the decision and accept nothing less than feeling good.

In Summary: * Everyone has an inner guidance system * Feeling good is the key to success * You have total power and control over the circumstances you experience when you take time to align with yourself and put your well-being first. * You can begin with nothing and create a magnificent something when you Feel your way to Success.

3 Tips To Stay Focused On Your Dreams

Before you go to bed at night, spend the last 30-45 minutes putting yourself in a total state of appreciation for everything in your life. It is everything you have experienced that has brought you to the fabulous person you are at this moment.

Make time to do what ever feels really good to you. Whether it is singing at the top of your lungs, walking on the beach, or taking a long bath. Whatever it is, make time for it. You deserve it.

Use your imagination to serve you Every chance you get. If you can see it in the eye of your mind....You CAN experience it in your life, if you believe you can.

About The Author

Stephanie Kathan is a living example of what is possible when you learn to master your mind. Through her own journey from homeless waitress to successful entrepreneur and Internet Radio Host, Stephanie creates ripples of awareness by sharing her own journey and the lessons life has taught her, as well as bringing you an intimate look into the lives of the successful through her Blog Talk Radio Show "The Journey". Stephanie travels between the West coast and East coast working together with some of the finest minds in the world, and is eager to share her journey with you.

Janet Beckers

Toughen Up Princess!

Sue Henry

Toughen Up Princess! I never thought in my career those words would be so significant, and I never dreamt that my mentor and good friend would use them on me. But that is exactly what happened 4 years into my business. Like most small business owners I was off to a flying start. I had a big dream – I want to live on my own island, a place where family and friends can escape to, relax and enjoy the community that is my family & friends. I was keen, I networked like crazy, I followed up on leads, I promoted myself and the business and I was getting excellent exposure and great results.

That was until I decided I would move into professional speaking. Ever since I was a child I have had the gift of the gab – put me in front of an audience of 1 or 1000 I'm going to shine! For me it was a natural progression in my consulting career. I enrolled in all the how-to seminars, read all the books, joined the right associations and took on a speaking coach and I was set ready to go. I booked myself to speak (for free) at over 50 events, groups and associations in the first six months to 'earn my stripes' and get my experience.

My first job went sensationally. The audience loved my presentation so much I got a standing ovation, I invited a speakers bureau to that talk and they gave me some excellent praise and feedback – they said I had what it takes! Yippee, my vision, goal setting, and action steps all working. It wasn't until my second presentation when my perfect world fell apart. The speaking coach I had engaged hated my presentation style and said my stories had no significance and I had a long way to go if I thought I'd make it as a speaker. Wow! It was like a punch in the stomach it literally took the wind out of me. I was so focused on his words that I spent the remainder of the day in tears, questioning my self-belief, my skills and my dream. What I failed to do that day was think about the 20 plus people that came up to me at the end of the presentation full of praise for my talk. I never took any notice of the 10 emails I received thanking me for my 'inspiring and fun' presentation. All I could do was think about the words of the speaking coach – he was after all an expert in his field!

Until my mentor called 'to see how the talk went' I was a mess. Through a lot of sobbing I finally got my story out of what had happened. I ran through the presentation and what I said, how the audience reacted and how I felt at the end. And I told her it was unlikely I would ever do another public speaking engagement. Then came those powerful words… Toughen up Princess! What… That stopped my crying instantly what did she just say? And she repeated it and followed up with this…

What in your belief system tells you that one person's opinion of that one presentation can determine your destiny to follow your dreams?

That one question changed my entire outlook on life, on business and on expert opinion. You see what I hadn't done was check his credentials, I'd never seen him speak and he didn't have a thriving speaking business.

I had also overlooked the most significant aspect – the audience loved me and my subject matter. I had a gift, a gift I almost put on the shelf because of one opinion. The next presentation was the most difficult in my career. It was the battle of self doubt, his words and my dream. I said to myself one minute before the presentation "toughen up princess" and on I went to give what was one of my best presentations to date. You see in the end it is only our dreams that can truly drive our desire to take action. We must respect them, ourselves and not let the opinions of one destroy your dreams. Keep them alive and remind yourself to toughen up princess!

3 Tips To Stay Focused On Your Dreams

Take time each day (1 -2 mins) to remind yourself of what your dream is and why it is important to you.

Janet Beckers

> Once per week look at your testimonials and customer feedback, these are the people that love you and what you have to offer - FOCUS on them!
>
> Toughen Up Princess!

About The Author

Sue Henry is networking expert and co-author (Network or Perish and Accelerate: How to accelerate your business, yourself & your networking skills) and Professional Sticky-beak who has worked in training, facilitation, sales, and marketing for the past 20+ years. She provides programs in sales, networking, customer service, team building, communication skills and much more. Sue has been engaged as a Sales Manager, National Marketing Manager, Training Manager, Sales Representative, Trainer, Project Manager and all round trouble shooter across a range of industries. Sue's unique approach coupled with her innate passion to see others succeed places her perfectly in the role of leading others to learn. She is gifted with being able to immediately assess what is required and is quick in her thinking to deliver that information in a relevant, timely and practical manner.

Special Gift

Receive a copy of "Seven Things You Must Know About Business to Succeed e-book valued at $47. Register your details at - http://www.professionalstickybeak.com for instant download.

http://www.suehenry.biz

http://www.professionalstickybeak.com

http://www.acceleratewomen.com

Promoting my Dream and Yours

Sue Murphy

How do I promote everybody else and keep them motivated all the time? It starts with me feeling motivated and inspired everyday. Is this easy? My suggestion to you is that it can be. It may not be initially, but once you make a conscious decision to have a positive mindset you're halfway there. If you take steps to consciously create this every day it will start to become a habit and eventually a lifestyle. There are some very particular ways I've done this in my life that I would like to share with you. It's essential to practice self care on a daily basis. Look after yourself! Adopt healthy living strategies.

I eat a healthy diet, limit alcohol, walk on the beach regularly, spend precious time enjoying my children and cherish everyday. I consciously look for the blessings in every day life and express gratitude on a daily basis.

The second strategy I've implemented to keep myself positive on my journey is being part of a Mastermind group. This is something I learned as part of Janet's program.

When I joined Wonderful Web Seminars, I was put into a Mastermind group which has been instrumental in getting me started in my business. Having seen first hand the power of this, I decided to create my own Mastermind group in my local area. We have over 17 quality business women who support, encourage and share knowledge with one another and nurture each other's goals and dreams in business and life. We all cannot wait to get to those meetings and since starting the group 6 months ago, we have all really powered forward in our businesses.

I highly encourage and urge you to join a Mastermind Group. If there's not one in your local area, create one or join one online. Surround yourself with like minded people and watch how this will start to change your life.

The third strategy I'd like to share with you is about living your life on purpose. Be purposeful in all you do and will realise how much of a difference you can make in your world. All the hard work in the world is meaningless, if it doesn't have a higher purpose than just making money. Discover what your values are and what your true purpose is here on this earth. I believe mine is to encourage, inspire and support others. That makes my heart sing and brings me so much joy.

Once you discover what your true purpose is you will bounce out of bed every day with the greatest enthusiasm. I love to shine and spread my joy to those around me. I can do this through my business and help others to shine as well. Acknowledge "what it is you do" that's amazing and start living purposefully. You will be amazed how much of a difference you will start to make in the lives of others.

You can shine and be amazing. Believe it, feel it and create it.

3 Tips To Stay Focused On Your Dreams

Practice healthy lifestyle habits. Eat a healthy diet and exercise regularly. Spend quality time with those you love and make a conscious decision everyday to acknowledge the blessings in your life.

Surround yourself with positive like-minded people. Join a mastermind group and draw from the support, encouragement and motivation you can gain from it. Also give as much support, encouragement and motivation as you can to these people, who will be your greatest assets in business and life. Limit your time with negative people who create discouragement and dysfunction in your life. Don't allow these people to have an affect on you and put good boundaries in place.

Be purposeful in all you do. Know your values and your true desires and incorporate them into all your everyday actions. Live your life on purpose, believing that you are making a difference in the lives of those around you. You can change your world.

About The Author

Sue Murphy is co-founder of Red Hot Events and Seminars. Her business partner Toni-Louise Forsyth and her conduct 'Purposeful Promotion' for experts they believe have integrity and are offering high value content at their events, workshops and seminars. They promote these experts by connecting them to their target market through live webinars, social media and their regular newsletter.

Special Gift

Subscribe over at our website http://www.redhoteventsandseminars.com and receive FREE bonus audios from some of our guest speakers. "How to Generate Free Publicity for Your Business" MP3 audio to download - Our interview with Sue Papadoulis of Home Biz Chicks "How to Flirt and Convert on Facebook" MP3 audio to download - Our interview with Kylie Bartlett - The Web Celeb "How to Make Passive Income selling Info Products Online" MP3 audio for you to download - Our interview with Daryl Grant of Our Internet Secrets

http://www.redhoteventsandseminars.com

Janet Beckers

Stay Focused and Keep Your Dream Alive

Susanne Ridolfi

I was so close to not submitting this article at all. Having registered my interest already in the middle of December, with plenty of time to write – life took over! I did get a 'reminder' early January and printed out the information for myself. Put it away and got on with life. Yesterday I had a big clearing out of papers in my office and what did I find? The information paper around the article and saw that the submission date is 7th February (today is the 6th!). A little inner voice in my head, immediately started to tell me things like - Well, I missed that one…. - No way will you get it ready in time…. - You are not an author anyway…(well, I am, actually and I have a few books out there from the past…) - What do you have to contribute amongst everyone else? - No time!!! Then I thought – 'Don't give in, don't give up!

This is exactly what you are about, Susanne – inspiring people to live their true potential and you love what you do! You ask people, especially women, to dare to dream big, take action and move towards that Dream of theirs. You love sharing with others and Janet asked you to do just that – share your daily actions and challenges'. So here we go – my contribution:

Love is The Force that moves you! I agree with Rhonda Byrne – 'It is the positive force of love that inspires you to move and gives you the desire to be, do, or have anything.' When I do things out of love and passion, it is really easy to stay focused to the task in hand and the result is successful. I do make my choices, as we all do, and when I choose to move and do things that are in alignment with my life purpose and listen to my inner voice, my intuition, things work out very well and it feels so right. I watch my son, who has great problems with focus and attention, and see him struggle to do and complete things he doesn't like doing. This happens very often around school work and it takes a long time to get the task done. On the other hand, when he occupies himself in an activity he has chosen, or someone else has directed him to do, that he likes and has interest in – his focus is fantastic!

He can stay on the same task for hours, without becoming distracted, without taking breaks and his face is 'lit up' throughout the whole process. He took part in a candle making workshop before Christmas. He loved every minute of it and stayed for over three hours making his own candles. It was a pleasure to see and be part of and the feedback on his creations, were amazing. So, my first suggestion is to listen within, follow your heart and move with love and passion in anything you choose to do. The road you choose to travel will be so much easier to follow. My Dream! My dream is to see people on this planet be well! I love seeing healthy, happy and joyful people, free from stress.

There is so much we can do to feel well and I'm passionate about having people climb up the ladder of wellness and feel better every day. Take the stresses out of your life, become aware of how you can deal better with those stresses and there will be a completely new sense of calmness within. Imagine waking up feeling rested, ready for the day ahead and with plenty of energy to do the things you want to do in your life.

Through an enhanced sense of calmness within, your communication with You, will improve. Communication within the family will be easier and you will most likely find it easier to listen to others and truly hear what they have to say. With improved communication, coming from a calm space, imagine what we can create worldwide – peace on this planet. Well that is a big Dream and why not dream Big! Goals! I'm a Goal achiever and have always been. As a gymnast I was taught to set goals and goals were often set for me. We had our competition date, we knew our performance goals and we set a plan of action, training goals to achieve this. My father was another great goal setter, so I have had some great teachers here. With a clear goal in mind, the road to get there will be so much easier travelled.

A clear 'WHY?' is important. Write down your goals and read them daily – long term goals and short term goals. Create a Dream Board with pictures that 'talks' to you. Listen to music that connects you with your Goals and with the emotions on how you will feel when you have achieved your goals. This is so important for me and a great way of keeping me focussed and remind me of Why? To help me keep my big vision alive, I attend self development seminars.

Every time I go back to a self development seminar, I get to look at who I am being in the moment and what I intend for my life. The seminar offers a wonderful, safe space where I can identify my life's purpose and the path for attaining it. This is a brilliant self-discovery process, where I'm given time to reflect, renew and reconnect. I'm looking forward to go again and remind myself to go with an 'open mind'! Daily Actions to stay on task. What works for me? - Well, take this morning as an example – realising how late I was with writing this article, I then took my daily time for me and went for a run with our lovely dog, Shrek. This I do on a daily basis – I create time for me in the morning, I do something that makes me feel good and centred, so I can get on with the chores in the house/family when I come back. My own choice is to be up before the rest of the family, go for a run, walk or swim on the beach – I love nature and feel good having moved physically.

Doing it first thing in the morning makes the day so much easier. It clears my mind and gives me an opportunity to remind me of my goals, work on my visualizations and get into the feelings and emotions connected to them. - When I come back home, I have my lemon/lime water to drink. Yes, I realise how important good hydration is for my body and mind, so plenty of water first thing in the morning to set myself up for the day. A nice fresh shower and I feel ready to go! What works for you? What works for me, doesn't necessarily work for you. You might want to sit down for a short meditation session, or practice some yoga instead. We are all individuals and what works for one person, doesn't necessarily work for others. You find out what works for you and is practically possible to create in your life. And remember, everything is possible!

I have found my days so much more focused and enjoyable, if I do create this space for me in the mornings. The busier day I have ahead, the more important it is for me – try it, please and work out what works for you!

Commitment List. One of my business mentors is Bob Proctor. He was the first person who taught me to write my 'action list' and do it last thing before closing down your activities for the day. This way you have it nice and clearly there in the morning, don't have to think about what to do, just get on with it and do it. Make this list a 'commitment list', please. Very different to a 'to do list'... 'Until one is committed there is hesitance, the chance to draw back, always ineffectiveness.' Bob Proctor also suggests you write only five things on your list and then decide in which priority you are going to take action upon these tasks. Start each day by looking at your list, evaluating your day and decide upon an affirmation that will be of benefit to the events and actions you have planned.

The first and most fundamental thing in achieving what you really want out of life is just by saying it – affirm it to yourself. Simple and yes, it works. It all starts with a thought. Repeat the affirmation throughout the day and take note on how they affect you. Complete the first task on your list and then move to the next. If you end up not completing the whole list that day, just shift the task to the top of the following day. This way you will always have acted on the most important issue that day.

I have found this a great way to help me stay focused! My Journal. I have a Journal I write in every evening. Last thing at night, I bring it out and write a few reflections from my day. I aim to stay on the positive aspect of what has occurred. This is about acknowledging me for my actions and results, small successes on the way towards the bigger goal. The more challenging the day has been, the more important for me. I write about business, family, anything that has come up during the day – challenges will creep up in all those areas and create little stresses for us to overcome.

Write yourself a minimum of three acknowledgments, please! You want to fall asleep feeling good and remembering the positive aspect of your day! I also write down things I am grateful for in my life. Here I aim to write a least three different things every day and make it not the same over and over again. A wonderful practice and it really makes me realise how many things I have in my life to be grateful for.

Janet Beckers

3 Tips To Stay Focused On Your Dreams

Take some time aside and go within, listen to your heart's desire and follow your inner voice – What is your Dream? What is your Why? Create your Dream Board! Set your Goals – long term and short term Goals! Write them down and read them every morning and night!

Go to the shop and buy yourself a nice Journal! This is where you will, on a daily basis, write down your acknowledgements and all the things you feel grateful for in life.

Remember to write your Commitment list - space for yourself in the morning, affirmation for the day and then get into Action! "Whatever you can do, or dream you can – begin it – boldness has genius, power and magic in it" (W.M. Murray – The Scottish Himalayan Expedition, 1951)

About The Author

Biography - Susanne Ridolfi   Susanne is Swedish and has been involved in body work and Shiatsu for over 30 years. In 1989, she moved to London and started to work at the British School of Shiatsu-Do, as a company director, co-principal and education director, as well as a Shiatsu-Do teacher, therapist, and team development trainer for the teaching and administration staff. Together with her husband, Ray, she set up a network of franchises throughout UK and travelled across Europe to teach and lecture in the areas of Shiatsu, health and wellbeing.   Susanne and her family, moved over to Australia in 2002. They spent six years in Sydney, on the Northern Beaches, running their Nikken Wellness business from their home and enjoying the lifestyle of living close to the beach. The Nikken Wellness business, which started up in 1996 over in UK, has grown to an international network with over 10,000 members worldwide - Europe, Israel, Australia and Russia being the biggest markets. In June, 2008, Susanne and family, moved up to the Gold Coast and now lives in Palm Beach, where she is continuing to expand the Nikken business from home.   In addition, Susanne is a certified CranioSacral therapist and author of several books:

- 'Shiatsu For Women' (co-author with Ray Ridolfi)
- 'Guide to Natural Therapies' (author of chapters on Shiatsu and Do-In)
- 'The New Life Library, Shiatsu '(author) and
- Shiatsu for Health and Well-Being' (author)

Susanne started her career as a physical education teacher and she has an active background, including being one of the top twenty Swedish gymnasts during her teenage years. She has also trained in dance, worked as a fitness instructor, and coached gymnastics teams. Her educational background also includes university studies in psychology and sociology.

Special Gift

Download your free report: 'The Importance of good Hydration and how to achieve it'. From http:// www.everybodyneedswater.com.au/hydrationreport

http://www.enikken.com.au/bodydynamics
http://www.everybodyneedswater.com.au

Janet Beckers

The Art of Change: A Passion To Make A Difference.

Suzie Cheel

"Be the change you want to see in the world"- Gandhi. My mission is to help others who want to make a difference in the world. And first I help them to realise and apply the Gandhi principle – to create real, lasting change, we must start with ourselves. Change can be inspiring, change can be empowering and change can create feelings of fear. Sometimes change is forced upon us by circumstances, at other times we make the choice to change. This sometimes can be a small shift or it can be a time of major re-invention. With change we generally experience different emotions. Through the many changes I have made in my life I have come to understand that in order to change our attitudes and behaviour about ourselves and the world we live in, we must fully experience the feelings generated by the process of change that we have embarked on. The feelings I have experienced in those circumstances include, in various measures, fear, pain, anguish, trust, joy and happiness. One of the things I have discovered over the years is that, for the most part, I love change and the journey of change allows me to continue to grow. It is empowering.

The Power of 100

A long time ago I wrote this: Sometimes our challenges can seem daunting. But there is so much to be gained in meeting our challenges head on. All we have to do is handle our emotions and trust the process. I believe more than ever that trust in ourselves and the process is crucial. And yet, sometimes in the trusting we can stumble. This is when those feelings of "I'm not good enough", "I should have…" "If only…" and "How could I have been so dumb?" come bubbling up and so often stop us in our tracks. The big mistake at that moment is to look outwards for rescue or solution, or some other, hopefully easier path. I know. I have done it. What I have learnt is that to really break through, we must take the tougher journey, inward.

I have found out, the hard way, there are no short cuts. But there are things we can do to make the journey more enjoyable, less of a chore, more of an exciting adventure. The breakthrough for me in all of that has been to learn two lessons in particular: to allow, not always try to control. To be grateful, always I now work much more from my heart than in my head. I am more trusting of my inner wisdom, no longer constantly looking for some other to be an expert for me, or some magic, silver bullet solution. My experience in this process of change actually reflects my work over years as an artist. With my art, the more I allowed the creative process to flow and the more I left myself open to the inspiration of the moment, the better the work. And I learned how to teach this to others. I used to teach a course to others who did not see themselves as "artistic" or "creative": the course was "Untap Your Creativity".

Now I have developed a coaching program to apply that methodology to different processes, including setting up or reviving a business, attracting abundance, or – and this is my new favourite – becoming a change warrior. I call this process, this methodology, The Art of Change. The Art of Change is not about working harder, although there is work involved. It's about working more intuitively, more trustingly, letting go of old fears and old "shoulds" that don't serve us or anyone else. The Art of Change is a liberating process and because it engages the whole person, not just our left brains, it enables us to create greater harmony and synchronicity between who are and what we do. It has inbuilt integrity. It leads to joy, not pain. Because the Art of Change embraces and engages our whole person, we are empowered to sustain our passion to make a difference, even when the going gets tough. There is work involved to sustain that passion, but I find the work enjoyable. It entails developing new habits, new practices. For me, these have included as daily practice: meditation, journal, gratitude, exercises, angel cards, planning my day, walking on the beach or by the river, yoga, doing what raises my vibes and makes me feel good, surrounding myself with like minded people who support my dreams, asking for help- something I am still mastering. Have 1 task (3 is ideal) that you do first thing that will bring your dream into reality and do these before you open your email, log on to Facebook or twitter!

Other practices: vision board, abundance journal, hobbies: I love to cook, reading and watching inspirational material, write out your ideal day and review it, review your week, celebrate what you have achieved, attend workshops, seminars if they will empower you, increase you networking skills etc be careful not to become a workshop warrior. Go on a retreat, add to you dream list in your dream journal- you might be surprised when you come to the end of the years how many of your dreams you can check off. Learn a new skill – this year I plan to learn to paddle a surf canoe I know this might seem an overwhelming list. Just choose one or two and develop a daily habit first, than add another. Remember to do what makes you feel good and listen to that still small voice inside that knows.

3 Tips To Stay Focused On Your Dreams

Meditate each day- start with 5 minutes and sit in stillness. To get you started here is a morning mediation video I made http://www.youtube.com/watch?v=A98cc-Ww1vA

Be Grateful: Start a gratitude journal, start by recording 5 things you are grateful for each day. I usually do this at night. Take time each day to stop and look around you and see the abundance that you already have.

Learn to ask and listen: Ask you small still voice inside for guidance, to help solve a problem, to move closer to realizing your dream and do not be afraid to ask you colleagues and friends for support.

About The Author

Suzie Cheel is a Law of Attraction Facilitator and Empowerment Coach, artist and author. She holds a Masters in Applied Science (Social Ecology). Suzie has been an early childhood teacher and has also trained teachers in that field. She is an award-winning artist and had her own textile clothing and design business – Suzie Cheel

Handpainted Originals – for fourteen years. Over twenty years ago she wrote and illustrated her own book, "Emergings, a meditation on the emotions of change". The book draws on her own experience of negotiating major life changes and her observations of others' emotional reactions in times of change. This has been published on Amazon.   Suzie's mission now is to guide and support people who have a desire to create change in the world but are held back by fear and self-doubt, people Suzie calls the "Change Warriors in Hiding". Drawing on her own experience of change, her teaching knowledge and many years' applied study of personal development, she is able to help people create their own stories of re-invention and to learn and apply a new and empowering process Suzie has dubbed The Art of Change.   Suzie lives on Australia's Gold Coast and, as she says, "online".   As an acknowledged expert in social media and social networking, Suzie also helps her clients tap into the power of social media, safely and effectively, and use this new online environment to share their own message way beyond their immediate offline circle.

Special Gift

Suzie's gift to you: An MP3 recording of Suzie reading her poem emergings:a meditation on the emotions of change and Learn How To Attract Abundance: 3 tools and an Abundance Journal at http://suziecheel.com/gift

The Change Warrior Project:
http://www.suziecheel.comhttp://www.suziecheel.tv
Suzie's Book: http://www.theemergingsbook.com
Follow Suzie on Twitter: @suziecheel
Join The Change Warrior Tribe at Facebook: http://www.suziecheel.com/facebook

Keeping it Simple

Suzie Williams

Be real, stay grounded, enjoy the moment.

My Life

I consider myself to be one of the lucky people who have found their passions in life, and even moreso that I am able to work with them rather than being tied to a 'normal' job. I have a variety of ways of working in the world and I am lucky to be able to say I thoroughly enjoy them all. I am a people person so relish my one on one therapy sessions with clients, as well as working with groups of students in classes all over the ACT (Australian Capital Territory). I love teaching, it totally energises me! It is such a privilege helping people explore their amazing potential! Through Dru yoga they feel a sense of inner calm, resilient energy and wellbeing. With the relaxing Massage and Reiki classes I teach, people become really excited to rediscover their innate ability to comfort and heal others with their touch. I am currently venturing into the internet world with several health related businesses and joint ventures, to extend my reach to people who can't come to me. I am a devoted Mum and have a delightful family of active sons - who keep me busy, happy and very grounded. So sometimes something has to go by the wayside and it is often tidying up my paperwork! (Working from home has its pluses and minuses!)

Keep it flexible

I won't lie and say I have a perfectly organised life and routine. Like most people, I sometimes find it tricky to stay on track with all the other demands on my time and energy. Though I do dream about being well organised and once we have finished renovating, I will become ruthless and declutter and keep more organised ... (that is the plan!) Despite the lack of order around me at the moment I do manage to get a lot done. I start my days by giving thanks for another day and planning my activities based on my bookings. The days may not always go as planned if things pop up unexpectedly, but I am very flexible and can usually adjust things as needed 'on the fly'. I enjoy the challenge and freedom of being in my own business – although I tend to resist and rebel against rigid routine and timeframes, the fact that I am my own boss gives me that extra flexibility!

Support Team

I am lucky to have a very supportive husband who helps me out in many little (and big) ways when I need him. He always listens to my dreams and plans and often has great ideas.

I feel it is important to get other people's perspective on some matters as you can be too close to your own dream project or "baby' and get a bit stuck or unable to see what is not working and why. Another person's point of view can often be just what you need to inspire you into a better, more creative or effective way of solving the problem. I often talk things over with my husband or close friends and peers. Whoever seems to be around is usually the right person at the right time and they know I love what I do, so they encourage me to go for it. I also claim my 'mama hugs' from my boys and my dog; they make me feel loved and connected to what is real.

Keeping energised!

To keep myself energised and focused I use breathing and Dru yoga. Some of the flowing movements create instant energy and I find the wonderfully simple deep yogic breath amazing. I do it on and off all day. Seeing as I am breathing anyway, why not make it count? So I utilise the 'in-between times' - when driving, preparing for clients, waiting for a class to start, or even doing the dishes or sitting at the computer. To focus on my breath refreshes my mind, recharges my body and brings instant calm and clarity to all of my being – physical, mental, emotional and spiritual. There is nothing quite as effective as a long, slow, deep breath in ... and ... out.

I also meditate and pray ... and then remain aware for the answers that may appear when I least expect them to. I also practise mindfulness when I am doing simple things like the dishes or cleaning. In addition, I visualise light entering into my crown and flowing all the way through my body, cleansing and clearing away any unnecessary thoughts, doubts, feelings and filling me with positive, uplifting and healing energy. This is subtle, but very powerful once you get in the habit. I also laugh a lot!

Gratitude and Appreciation

Often when we get busy, we lose our centre and connection with nature. I find it beneficial and fulfilling to consciously live with an "attitude of gratitude". It is easy to take things for granted. But there are so many things to be grateful for when observing all the everyday miracles around us. Life is full of little magic moments if you look for them. I love to see the sunshine, blue sky, and listen to the rain. Our family loves to watch the storm clouds blow across the valley and the amazing sunsets over the mountains. Every day I listen to the birds, admire the flowers, watch the wind in the trees and feel the breeze on my face. I love time with my family, smiling faces, hugs and kisses, belly laughs and my funny dog.

I notice people doing or saying kind things; it helps keep my faith in human nature. My Dad always taught me to look for the good in everyone I meet, and for the lesson in every situation. This puts a positive spin on all interactions. Even 'bad' situations become meaningful.

My dreams are many! Will you join me?

- To teach amazing Dru Yoga and Healing Retreats in beautiful locations around the world.

- To help our unsung heroes "the carers" of the world live less stressful, happier, healthier lives.

- To help the stressed out corporate world manage their stress and their lives through an incredible relaxation and communication joint venture program I am developing with a communications expert.

3 Tips To Stay Focused On Your Dreams

Seek help, advice and encouragement from trusted others.

Breathe: take a long, slow, deep breath in ... enjoy the satisfaction of a full breath and then exhale and enjoy the spaciousness inside. Feel the calmness flowing through you.

Practice Gratitude: look for the small things in every day that make your heart sing.

About The Author

- *Suzie works with carers and business professionals assisting them to relax, rebalance and reconnect with their real self using a powerful blend of Dru yoga, meditation, NLP, and natural therapies. These tools allow people to release stress and eliminate mental, physical and spiritual clutter so they function efficiently in their business and love living life again.*

- *After a long career in health and healing Suzie now focuses on teaching her passions of Dru Yoga, Meditation and Natural Therapies. Her regular yoga retreats are becoming a sanctuary of peace, relaxation, laughter and sharing with everyone who attends.*

- *Suzie is currently developing CD's, DVD's, programs and online resources for carers, the corporate world and other stressed out people who don't know how to relax. These easy to do techniques are designed to help everyone enjoy their lives with less stress, tension and pain – no pretzel yoga!*

Special Gift

http://www.essencehealingandyoga.com

Janet Beckers

Healthy, Wealthy & Wise

Tracey Thomson

Any small business owner knows that there are times when you're flying high as a kite, over flowing with joy, loving what you do and thrilled that you have taken the opportunity to create your dream and live your dream lifestyle. If you're not there yet, you're grateful for having the courage to get started and be on the path! However there are also days, weeks and sometimes months when things are not looking so great, it's challenging, the results may not be coming in the door as fast as you would like and yet cash is going out the door in the blink of an eye. It's 2011 and I haven't worked a "job" or earned a salary since 2007. Since my last job I searched high and low for what's next for me, and then when I realised what it was, I started creating it. A line of Australian made, certified organic skincare. A product range that is of the highest quality available, using pure ingredients, made here by an Australian company. Products that women love, that work and that they want to use. A range of skincare that is good for your health & well being, the environment and philanthropy.

That was my dream and now it's a reality. But I would have to say there have been many ups and downs along the way. So what keeps my vision alive and how do I stay focussed in the long term through the good and the bad? Firstly I researched the market for years both before I embarked on this piece of the journey and after I decided to create Integrity Cosmetics. As a female I was searching for high quality, pure and natural skincare for years and found that I really couldn't find what I was looking for. There was one European brand I came across, but otherwise everything else I found wasn't certified organic and that was my benchmark. I would walk into pharmacies and department stores, health food stores and beauty shops world wide and ask do you have any natural skincare products. I would be very nicely guided to a counter or a shelf to be told about a product which in fact contained petrochemicals sometimes including carcinogens and ingredients which are banned in Canada and the EU. When I have a tough day, I remind myself that I'm doing this for a reason and that the improving women's health, the environment and contributing to philanthropy on a greater level is worthwhile and something that has me stick it out on the tough days to follow through with my dream. Being flexible and listening to my intuition would have to be one of the greatest gifts that I am grateful for on a daily basis. Having a plan is essential, and you need to create a plan and follow your plan, but you also need to have the foresight to listen to your intuition and when it sends you in a different direction, sometimes that's the tap on the shoulder you need to start down a new path, building on what you've created thus far.

My original business coach Marcus Bird from Intrinsic Success was great at having me be grounded and listen to my intuition. In the early days way before Integrity Cosmetics was launched Marcus worked with me and had a talent for listening for what was simply a new shiny object (a good idea to distract me and take me off my path) versus taking something new on, or slightly changing direction because the universe had delivered what I was asking for, but in a form which looked different to what I was expecting. This is not always easy to distinguish, and sometimes we make mistakes, which are of course only lessons to learn. You can cultivate and develop your sense of intuition and tap into it on a regular basis to your advantage. How do you do this? The first requirement is being grounded, peaceful and relaxed. Yes, easily said, not so easily done when you're a business owner.

Ensure that you take sufficient time out for yourself on a regular basis. Working long hours can be required at times and you can also get into the habit of working long unconsciously, so be sure that you still take time out for you, to stay connected to who you are. Contemplation time is critical, as is time with nature. I meditate on a regular basis and do yoga, take walks in nature, or ride my bike, even if it's only for 20-30 minutes. It gets you out and about and shifts your energy. Exercise on some level is important as is a healthy diet. I always feel better about myself when my diet is healthy. Listening to my favourite music, dancing and spending time in the garden also ground me, even if it's only for 5-10 minutes. Longer sessions have an even better impact. Find what grounds you and make sure you find time to do these things even if only for a short time, on a regular basis. You will honour yourself by doing this.

3 Tips To Stay Focused On Your Dreams

1. Do your research. It gives you peace of mind and reassurance. You won't regret it.

2. Create your vision – write it down, share it with people in your life, have it be present for you at all times.

3. Be grounded by taking time out for you, cultivate your intuition and follow it.

About The Author

Tracey Thomson is CEO & Founder of Australian owned organic skincare brand Integrity Cosmetics, creating certified organic skincare that combines the most pure and natural ingredients. Leaving behind an impressive career in telecommunications Thomson craved a new challenge and in 2008 things started to take shape. While tackling health concerns in 2000, Thomson took stock of her life. At the forefront of this was to eliminate harmful chemicals from her daily life. Not only those she consumed, but what she put on her skin, in her hair and on her body. She became obsessed with ingredient lists! It was this staggering reality of her chemical-ridden life that inspired Thomson to create an organic skincare range. It's just one way in which Thomson saw that she could spread some goodness.

With a belief that surface beauty is just one piece of the wellness package, Thomson talks about beauty in a very different way. "The most beautiful people I know care for themselves, for others and for our environment. They radiate a sense of peace and happiness and for me this translates into real beauty. Good quality products feed wellness." says Thomson.

Special Gift

A discount of 10% when you use the discount code Webwomen2011 (not valid with any other special offer)

http://www.integritycosmetics.com.au

Janet Beckers

How to Start with the End in Mind

Tracy Repchuk

If you want a great way to stay motivated, inspired and focused on your dreams and visions, the key is to know them, and work backwards in your planning. After helping thousands of people go after their dreams using the internet as a medium, there is a common thread that can result in failure. Here's what I recommend that has been successful for me and my clients. Let me start with motivation. How did I stay motivated, or even get motivated. The answer to that was how I got started. I had a very concrete dream, and was willing to do whatever it took. My dream was to become a bestselling author by time I was 40. I was 59 days from that day and I announced that I would become a bestseller on the 58th day - the day before my birthday.

So I was now accountable for my word. That day I started writing, and I split my time, 7 days a week, for 58 days, between 8 hours of research and writing and testing, and 9 hours of marketing and planning. I did nothing else - but focused on the book. Now this was easy in one sense, in that absolutely nobody knew me so I didn't have a lot of people pulling me in different directions, and I had the support of my husband who did everything else with the family so that I could go that goal. But that's not to say though, there weren't obstacles along the way. So what kept me going past the obstacles?

The motivation was two-fold - a personal lifetime goal, and I announced it and now needed to make it a reality. But, that doesn't mean it was easy. Working 17 hours a day took extreme focus. Fear of failure started to creep in as I really had no idea what I was doing. But when my husband (my support system for home, office and kids) had to leave for a few weeks because his mum took ill and when he came back just 2 weeks before the launch, and his mum died - we had a big decision to make - reschedule the book launch, or go forward anyway. It was very hard to do - but I decided to keep the dream alive, I dug deep for the motivation I decided and I did whatever it took. The next thing is where all my efforts could have been for nothing. When I launched the book, and it became an instant success, I had nothing else beyond it. My 'end' was the book - but I quickly realized when I got asked what is your back end, that I had not planned far enough ahead. This is where luck played me a good hand because as I was examining other book launches to see what a back end should be, mine fell in my lap.

Tons of people started to call me and ask if I would coach them through the book (31 Days to Millionaire Marketing Miracles). I said sure. This is another point I want to highlight - I was not a coach, but I said Yes - because it was the natural path. What I did here was look for the best mentor I could find for teaching coaches, hired him, and started a practice. I made 6 figures in my first 5 months, and it completely changed everything for me. Because what happened after that - it was legends are made of. Now some people say about my speaking career, that I was lucky. However, this is where I want you to remember no matter where you are, or what you want, launch your dreams. Because me becoming a speaker wasn't random, as 5 months earlier at the very first internet marketing show I was at, after 4 days and 12 men later, I realized there wasn't one woman on that stage. So I launched a dream and said in 1 year I was going to be on that stage. I had no idea how - but I wanted to make sure woman started to appear on that stage. Which is a point I want you to remember here - and that is launch your dreams any time you want because even when you're not paying attention, they can happen. I wasn't a speaker, nobody knew me, I had no special skills - and yet not only did I appear on that very stage - the World Internet Summit - they paid me to be there. I had won new internet marketing success of the year and got flown all expenses paid to Singapore to appear on the world's largest stage and present for my first time in front of 3400 people. That launched me to rock star status around the world, as I started to get invited to show, after show, after show. Dreams do come true, even if you have no idea how.

3 Tips To Stay Focused On Your Dreams

Write down where you would like to be in one year.

Work backwards from that point - with a few key points on what you can do to help you get there.

Create a landing page, and start to build a list of people that know you, like you, trust from you, and when you're ready - buy from you. Bonus - If you can afford it, pick a mentor and get the proper guidance right away. If you can't afford it, follow that person specifically and model what they do. If there was one major successful action I did through my entire career, it would be I hired mentors for EVERY step so that I could get what I wanted fast.

About The Author

Tracy Repchuk who is the #1 Woman Speaker in the World for Internet Marketing, and bestselling author of '31 Days to Millionaire Marketing Miracles' shows you how to create a million dollar internet marketing foundation for every idea you have. Tracy is an award winning entrepreneur, writer, coach and international speaker and has just returned from her world tour where she empowers others with her internet marketing knowledge. She is often referred to as the "Robert Kyosaki" of internet marketing. Tracy has been an entrepreneur since the age of 18, and moved from Canada to the US in 2006 where she now operates an international empire of companies.

Special Gift

Free full ebook on how to start a stay at home business, complete with resources. http://www.InternetMarketingforStayatHomeMoms.com

http://www.MillionaireMarketingMiracles.com

A Song in my Heart

Trish Rock

For as long as I can remember I have always known there are great things waiting for me in this world. I feel as if I have something special to contribute to mankind and that one day I will be helping to change people's lives for the better. A lot of people. I have always followed my heart and acted on the way I feel about something rather than how others feel or what my mind or ego were saying. When I was younger it was relatively easy to do, although I did seem to get into trouble a lot! As I grew up and started my career in the Nail Industry, I knew this was where I was meant to be. I absolutely loved it from the beginning and excelled at it.

The skills were so easy for me to achieve and it never felt like hard work. I have achieved many successful Nail Salon businesses and accomplishments in this Industry with ease and excitement.

This is the feeling of living from your heart, your passion and your purpose. I am also very spiritual and have had many experiences with the world beyond, connecting with souls no longer in human form. I know for sure we are more than our body and mind and one experience in particular showed me true, unconditional love with no

http://wonderfulwebwomen.com |

Janet Beckers

judgement, concern or any thought really, just love. This is what keeps me going sometimes, when things get rough, knowing I am more than what is happening to me at that moment.

I have helped a lot of clients over my career with different things that were happening in their lives. I was happy to do so and the advice came easily, almost from out of thin air (but we know where it really came from, right!) In my 30's and early 40's I was not feeling settled anymore. I didn't feel aligned and at the same time really didn't know what it was I was searching for, what was missing in my life or what I needed to be truly happy again.

I think this is the age when it happens to a lot of us. We feel a bit lost? Of course I blamed it on partners, jobs and anything I could find to blame because I didn't know how to take responsibility for myself. One thing I was sure of was that I was not following my heart. I was doing what people expected me to do and I hated the feeling of that. I was unhappy, unfulfilled and lonely, even though there were people around me comstantly. At the end of 2009, I gave up my former life as a Nail Technician. I didn't feel my messages were being heard anymore and no one wanted my help.

The truth was that I just had the wrong audience. I had a bigger message to share and I had to find it. I now have a business where I help other Nail Technicians with their success. My big vision is to help as many Nail techs as possible to achieve success in their business and life. I truly want them to have a fantastic career in this Industry that we love and not have to go through some of the things I did.

I know I can help them to master the work/life balance that is vital and to show them how to listen to their heart, always. I am back to living from my heart, passion and purpose and the journey hasn't finished yet. It is not always an easy path we take ourselves on but anyone willing to take the harder road will know that after you have pushed through, the view is so much better and I believe if your vision is big enough, clear enough and for a purpose outside of yourself, you will find a way to make it work, no matter what it takes. I would encourage you to follow your heart.

Listen to the messages and see the opportunities. They are there every day you just have to be open to them. You will always be guided and if you can live in love and faith, anything is possible for you! I hope this has inspired you, whether in the Nail Industry or not, to go for your big dreams. The world is waiting for you! To your success Trish.

3 Tips To Stay Focused On Your Dreams

Find yourself a mentor, coach, great friend, mastermind buddy or accountability partner to help you. There will be days (lots of them) when you need someone to help get you through things.

Only associate with positive, like minded people! The others will bring you down and turn you away from your dreams!

This is important- you have to know the BIG WHY of what you are working toward. This will help get you through the tougher days.

About The Author

Hi, my name is Trish and I have been in the Nail Industry for over 28 years now. I started at the age of 17 and have loved it from the beginning. I have built many successful Nail Salons in this time and have also achieved numerous awards including Overall Champion, 1991, at the Australian Fingernail Championships in Sydney. I have been a judge, a trainer and have employed and inspired highly successful staff. I organised the first Nail Competition in Canberra which was a huge success. I have also worked as a Property Manager and was highly successful at that too, winning Property Manager of the Year for QLD with Raine and Horne by doubling their rent roll.

I have 2 beautiful children, Matthew and Jess, who are now grown up and I am blessed to have 2 gorgeous grandchildren. My daughter in law Kelly also has a career as a talented Nail Technician. I know firsthand what Nail Technicians need to do to run a successful business and keep happy clients. Many people over the years have asked me how I managed to fill my salons so quickly, no matter what town I was in or where it was I set the salon up. I am now dedicated to helping other Nail Technicians with their salon success, their career passion and life.

Janet Beckers

Special Gift

There is a FREE GIFT - An interview with Trish - at http://nailsalonsuccesscoach.com that you can access immediately! I also offer personal mentoring and if you would be interested in this I offer a FREE Get Acquainted session. Details here: http://www.nailsalonsuccesscoach.com

http://www.nailsalonsuccesscoach.com   http://www.acrylicnailsonline.com

Time to Step into the Real you

Wendy Moore

Do you love what you do? Are you leaping out of bed each morning to get the day started? Be honest. If money was no object, would you still be doing what you are doing? Makes you think about it, doesn't it?

So what are you waiting for? What has to change for you to step up and realise life is not a dress rehearsal. This is it. What are you doing with it? When the time comes, the reality is your business will not mourn you. Your house will not mourn you. Your car will not mourn you.

The people will. Those you've loved. Those you've touched. Those you've connected with. Those you've inspired, empowered, challenged, supported

Each of you brings a very special gift to this planet. It's up to you what you choose to do with it. You can make a difference, however small. You just need to believe you can.

So what's the secret to keeping yourself motivated?

Surround Yourself With Inspiring People.

Those people who are truly going for it. When you think about your circle of friends, if you stand head and shoulders above those around you, as the one that is clearly achieving, succeeding or making a difference, find new friends!

In order to keep stepping up, you need to surround yourself with people who will keep you honest to the true you. It is too easy to wallow in our comfort zone and avoid being challenged. It's called a comfort zone for a reason. Find people you can model, bounce ideas off, who'll play devil's advocate to get the best out of you and support you.

In order to grow, you need to be a little adventurous.

Try it – I dare you …

Watch Your Thoughts

If you think you can do it or you think you can't do it, you are absolutely right. And that leads to the result you will get. Stop and listen to the thoughts you are having. Is something not working? How are you thinking about it – positively or negatively? You get exactly what you expect. It is that simple.

Beware The Dream Stealers

They surround us and we need to be mindful of those trying to "help". You know exactly who I am referring to because we all have them. That one person who "looks out for you" but in truth, they live in fear of their own inadequacy or guilt about their own lack of action. They hold on to you tightly so you won't leave them behind. They mean well, they are not trying to hurt you, but they are not doing you any favours either. Politely let them go.

You can do it! Don't let anyone ever tell you otherwise.

Make Time For YOU Every Day

This is not negotiable. It took me a long time to learn this one, as I was a human "doing". Doing, doing, doing. Non-stop. It's exhausting! I now enjoy living like a human "being". If you are not looking after yourself and being kind to yourself, how can you expect it of others? Each morning take time out for you, to centre yourself before you launch into all that the day holds for you.

Find a quiet spot. Close your eyes. Visualise. Meditate. Breathe. Whatever works best for you. We get so caught up in doing "stuff" that we forget to pause and absorb all that is around us. Pause, often. Do it now …

Be Genuine

Act with integrity in all that you do. This one flows from your personal life right through to how you run your business. If you are not being congruent to who you are and what you stand for, it will show. What's more, people will see it.

Be confident in who you are and be yourself. Everyone else is taken! Follow these few simple steps and you'll quickly find staying motivated and inspired will become a whole lot easier. In fact, you'll be amazed at how many great ideas pop into your head when you take a little time to just BE.

I'd love to hear how you go. Feel free to drop me a line and say hello.

3 Tips To Stay Focused On Your Dreams

1. I will be kind to myself
2. I will be true to myself
3. I will do one thing just for me, every day

About The Author

Wendy Moore is a speaker, International Best Selling Author and Business Entrepreneur who is passionate about showing business owners and entrepreneurs how to attract clients and build a targeted responsive list in their business niche.

Wendy has over 15 years experience in the IT industry, having been a highly paid, Senior IT Project Manager managing $45M budgets before gut-wrenching stress demanded she reappraise her life and follow her true passion.

Janet Beckers

Wendy founded http://www.savvywebwomen.com and the Savvy List Building Blog www.WendyMoore.net and says, "It's all about learning and gaining from other's experiences. I'm passionate about showing business owners and entrepreneurs how to get in front of an audience that wants to buy what they are selling."

Special Gift

To grab your free gift valued at $127, plus loads of tips and strategies to add to your online toolkit, head to www.savvywebwomen.com.

Love Social Media? Connect with Wendy via:

Facebook – http://www.facebook.com/savvywebwomen

Twitter – http://www.twitter.com/wendy_moore

LinkedIn – http://au.linkedin.com/in/wendymoore

The Secret Weapon of "Blissipline" in Manifesting your Big Dream

Zoe Routh

There's really only one way to keep your dream alive: 'Bliss-ipline'. Here's the juice on 'blissipline' that will really float your boat. First, you need to know that there is a fundamental tension for achieving all goals that demands rigorous attention. This is: The tension between appreciation of current reality and looking forward to the future reality. I call this 'manifestational anticipation'. It means loving where you are, who you are, what you are doing right here right now (even it really sucks the big wang) and looking forward to what's next with delighted expectation. There are some key strategies to implement to master the first part of this equation. Because let's be frank, the only reason you want something new in your life is because you are not that excited about what's here right now.

Abraham calls it 'contrast'. Contrast is a good thing! it shows us where we can grow and what we would like to experience next. It's an irritating springboard. If it wasn't irritating we wouldn't change anything and we would still be wearing nappies. So here's the part where people get tripped up all the time (myself included). How do you create delight in current reality when at best it's irritating and at worst, a serious pain in the butt?

The key is cutting the energy that fuels focus on what you don't want. So quit complaining about that big old butt or that empty bank account or that phone that never rings. Start telling a new story about it all. Like how things are changing, like how that butt keeps you warm at night, like how an empty bank account makes room for so much more to come in. Appreciation and gratitude gives you another kick in the right direction. The much-Oprah-lauded gratitude journal keeps you firmly pointed downstream and the right manifestational anticipation zone.

Celebrating successes and lots of giant pats on the back also create a keen sense of acceptance and loving what is. Can you feel your vibe rising even as we talk about this stuff? Woohoo! But the real high-vibing strategy is 'blissipline'. This is a relentless practice of bliss in all things that will have you loving everything from dog pooh on your shoe to to tea stains on your favourite jumper to that blank bank account. Blissipline means that you focus on making all your activities fun and exciting. Everything you do, do from a place of relish and enjoyment. Even washing the bathroom. This is how I turned bathroom cleaning into a fun, bliss-filled event. First rumble of thoughts started with "I really need to get a housekeeper again, this is taking too much of my time, I am going to have to fight Rob again on this one..." Blah blah blah. Same old bad news story. WOOP WOOP! Bad vibe alert!

Here is the 'blissipline' intervention. If you can't change it now, make it fun now. So I cranked some house cleaning dance tunes and scrubbed the tub naked. I was giggling the whole time - who knew that tub scrubbing could be so titillating! Hee hee! Blissipline is the art and focus of managing how you feel, and setting the dial to 'awesome' every day. It takes practice and effort, especially if you are clearing up long-standing habitual woe-is-me stories. That's the 'discipline' aspect of blissipline. But isn't blissipline as a concept so much more delicious than 'discipline'? That's because the payoff is in the process, not the end result! With discipline you are doing something to get a result: exercise at gym to get hot body. It implies uncomfortable effort for feel-good result. Whereas blissipline is feel-good effort for feel-good results!   It cannot get any better than that!

3 Tips To Stay Focused On Your Dreams

Appreciate the patooties out of everything in your current reality. Go for it - find ways of appreciating your little toe, the neighbour's dog, the messy cupboard. It's all good.

Rehearse the fulfilment of your dream. See it, say it, hear it, feel it, do it, be it. Allow yourself to feel the full awesomeness of your dream come to reality.

Repeat and enjoy with a nice glass of red wine.

About The Author

Zoe Routh is a Magnetic Leadership coach, speaker, and author with over 20 years experience in leadership and personal development, maximising the potential of youth and adults through outdoor adventure. She has worked with thousands of individuals and groups and counts amongst her previous leadership roles Staff and Training Director of Outward Bound Australia, President of the Chamber of Women in Business, and Chair of the Outdoor Council of Australia. Zoe also develops and delivers leadership programs for the Australian Rural Leadership Foundation. Zoe works with amazing groups and individuals who are committed to personal growth for service to the global community. Zoe helps clients with big dreams, to get big results. In her various adventures Zoe has paddled 30 weeks by canoe in northwest Ontario, run 6 marathons, hiked hundreds of kilometers in Australia's outback, bellydanced at various festivals, lived through cancer, married a fair dinkum Aussie bloke, and wrestled a 6 meter crocodile. It's all true, except for the crocodile part.

Special Gift

Awesome results need awesome leadership. Awesome leadership begins with YOU. Get a compimentary membership to Magnetic Leaderchip Club with free law of attraction leadership tips at http://www.innercompass.com.au

http://www.innercompass.com.au

Janet Beckers

Photographer Acknowledgements

The publisher thanks the photographers and copyright owners of image used in this book. The publisher has made reasonable attempts to make contact and seek permission from the copyright owner, and any images reproduced within, without specific copyright attribution are done in good faith.

The Power of 100 publisher would like to confirm that authority has been granted to reproduce the supplied images of the following persons by the photographers listed beside the respective author's name.

Author	Photographer
Cath Resnick	Cathy Morrissey
Dana Hughes	Anthea Jones
Eve Grace-Kelly	Dianna Bonner
Judith Sherven	Manuela Marin
Kim Lambert	Cathy Morrissey
Kirsty Greenshields	Pieta and Nicole
Lisa Robbins	Alexandra Robbins
Louise Brogan	Ankya Klay
Michelle McGrath	Nicole Rigato
Pam Brossman	Tania Niwa
Ruth Thirtle	Paul Holland
Tracey Thomson	Paul Simpson
Trish Rock	Cathy Morrissey

Cover Artwork by Michael Petter

Born in Tasmania in 1962, Michael moved with his family to Queensland as a very young child. It was evident even during his youth that Michael had a strong connection to the environment and social justice. His Uni studies included Environmental Sciences and during these years he became extremely proficient with the computer and its many applications and programs. This led to his love of and his exploration of the Mandlebrot Set and the unique fractal images that he designs.

For over the past 20 years Michael Petter author, artist and environmental activist from Brisbane has worked to build participatory watershed organisations to protect the environment, build social cohesion and work for social justice. In 2003 he was awarded an Australian Land & Water Australia Community Fellowship "in recognition of a special personal contribution to community understanding about wiser ways of managing Australia's unique natural resources". He has been publically acknowledged many times since for his outstanding community involvement and his unique ability on the computer. At present working with http://www.SEQCatchments.com.au

To view more of Michael's unique Fractal Artwork visit his online gallery http://www.fractals.com.au

---

Do You Want To Lose Weight? Need a Solution That Really Works?

The Paleo Weight Loss Program is a revolutionary system for ultimate weight loss

- All natural diet and nutrition program that guarantees permanent weight loss
- Simple to follow system to help you reach your ideal weight easily
- Eat lots of delicious, tasty food and never get hungry or bored
- No measuring, counting calories, weighing, or steep portion controls
- Get support, encouragement and guidance from an online community

ARE YOU READY TO MAKE THE CHANGE?

Get your **FREE startup gift** go to

http://paleoweightlosscoach.com/ww-free-gift

Janet Beckers and Wonderful Web Women support Opportunity International and their 1 Million Women Project

About Opportunity International Australia

Opportunity International Australia exists to provide opportunities for people living in poverty to transform their lives. With over 35 years' experience in microfinance and support services, they enable the empowerment of individuals by using a business approach to solve poverty. Rather than a hand-out, they provide their clients with a loan as small as $100 to help grow their small business. This allows them to earn an income and afford food, water, shelter and an education for their children.

Here's how it works...

By helping a mother buy a sewing machine to start a tailoring business or a father to buy seeds to plant a vegetable garden, small loans enable people in poverty to earn an income and provide for their families. As each business grows, loans are paid back and lent out again. And with 97% of loans repaid, the cycle continues, year after year. Each successful business feeds a family, employs more people and eventually helps to empower a whole community.

Part of a global network, Opportunity's aim is to see people lifted out of poverty permanently.

To donate, please visit
http://www.wonderfulwebwomen.com/recommends/opportunity

About the 1 Million Women Project

In 2007, Opportunity International Australia established a team based in Delhi to manage and implement a significant poverty alleviation program for the women of India. In December 2009, the program passed the milestone of one million clients and the 1 Million Women Project was born.

The 1 Million Women Project is about taking the India program to the next one million women. It's people and businesses saying 'I believe in that' and joining together to make a difference. India accounts for the largest share of the world's poor, with more than 900 million people living on less than US$2 a day. Hundreds of millions of Indian people are trapped in an intergenerational cycle of poverty.

Women in particular are disenfranchised and are too often unable to access education and fair employment. Yet women remain the brightest hope for change in India. When women and girls earn an income, they reinvest 90% of it into their families, compared to only 30-40% for men. Investing in women is the most effective way to bring about change in poor communities.

To donate, please visit
http://www.wonderfulwebwomen.com/recommends/opportunity

Janet Beckers

About the Author

On the day that Janet Beckers launched the Internet community, Wonderful Web Women she had no list, no money and no track record. Within 8 weeks she had built a community of thousands of people world-wide, matched her previous 12 months income and won an award for best membership site. That was just the first 8 weeks.

Since then Janet has helped thousands of people world-wide to create success on-line, is a sought-after international speaker, best-selling author and mentor. She has achieved this without spending a cent on advertising. Instead she uses the power of relationships and communication to build an Internet business and teaches her many students how to quickly and easily create an internet business that makes you stand out in the crowd of millions of web sites. She shows you how to attract loyal and passionate customers that will grow your business for you.

Janet has a reputation for taking the mystery out of the Internet and focuses on creating an automated business that supports freedom of lifestyle. She runs her successful business from her home office with a team of staff spread throughout the world and different states of Australia. She has the freedom to be with her family and regularly travels overseas for pleasure and business and teaches her students how to do the same.

She was recently awarded Australian Marketer of The Year and is passionate about using her marketing skills to help people create businesses around their passions using the power of the Internet. She does this through online membership programs, group coaching, private mentoring and workshops in Australia and overseas.

You can join Janet and her international community at
http://www.WonderfulWebWomen.com

How You Can Distribute This Book Yourself

If you have been given this book as a gift or as a bonus with a product you bought – lucky you! You can use this book for yourself but you cannot give away copies yourself.

But there is a way....

All members of Wonderful Web Women – free, GOLD and VIP have the right to distribute the digital version of this book. This means (when you join) you can:

- add this book as a bonus to products you are selling

- grow your mailing list by giving this book away in return for contact details

- print it out and post it to your favourite customers

- email it to your customers as a way of rewarding their loyalty

To get the rights to distribute this book simply visit http://www.wonderfulwebwomen.com and join for free. As well as getting the rights to distribute this book, we also give you web pages, marketing material and instructions on how to make the most of this opportunity.

See you there.

Janet Beckers

www.ingramcontent.com/pod-product-compliance
Lightning Source LLC
Chambersburg PA
CBHW070602230426
43670CB00010B/1382